Lecture Notes in Computer Science 3057

Commenced Publication in 1973
Founding and Former Series Editors:
Gerhard Goos, Juris Hartmanis, and Jan van Leeuwen

Springer

Berlin
Heidelberg
New York
Hong Kong
London
Milan
Paris
Tokyo

Bharat Jayaraman (Ed.)

Practical Aspects of Declarative Languages

6th International Symposium, PADL 2004
Dallas, TX, USA, June 18-19, 2004
Proceedings

 Springer

Volume Editor

Bharat Jayaraman
University at Buffalo, The State University of New York
Department of Computer Science and Engineering
201 Bell Hall, Buffalo, NY 14260-2000, USA
E-mail: bharat@cse.buffalo.edu

Library of Congress Control Number: 2004107018

CR Subject Classification (1998): D.3, D.1, F.3, D.2

ISSN 0302-9743
ISBN 3-540-22253-7 Springer-Verlag Berlin Heidelberg New York

Springer-Verlag is a part of Springer Science+Business Media

springeronline.com

© Springer-Verlag Berlin Heidelberg 2004
Printed in Germany

Typesetting: Camera-ready by author, data conversion by PTP-Berlin, Protago-TeX-Production GmbH
Printed on acid-free paper   SPIN: 11014027   06/3142   5 4 3 2 1 0

Preface

The International Symposium on Practical Aspects of Declarative Languages (PADL) is a forum for researchers and practitioners to present original work emphasizing novel applications and implementation techniques for all forms of declarative concepts, especially those emerging from functional, logic, and constraint languages. Declarative languages have been studied since the inception of computer science, and continue to be a vibrant subject of investigation today due to their applicability in current application domains such as bioinformatics, network configuration, the Semantic Web, telecommunications software, etc.

The 6th PADL Symposium was held in Dallas, Texas on June 18–19, 2004, and was co-located with the Compulog-Americas Summer School on Computational Logic. From the submitted papers, the program committee selected 15 for presentation at the symposium based upon three written reviews for each paper, which were provided by the members of the program committee and additional referees.

Two invited talks were presented at the conference. The first was given by Paul Hudak (Yale University) on "An Algebraic Theory of Polymorphic Temporal Media." The second invited talk was given by Andrew Fall (Dowlland Technologies and Simon Fraser University) on "Supporting Decisions in Complex, Uncertain Domains with Declarative Languages."

Following the precedent set by the previous PADL symposium, the program committee this year again selected one paper to receive the 'Most Practical Paper' award. The paper judged as the best in the criteria of practicality, originality, and clarity was "Simplifying Dynamic Programming via Tabling," by Hai-Feng Guo, University of Nebraska at Omaha, and Gopal Gupta, University of Texas at Dallas. This paper presents an elegant declarative way of specifying dynamic programming problems in tabled logic programming systems.

The PADL symposium series is sponsored in part by the Association of Logic Programming and Compulog Americas, a network of research groups devoted to the promotion of computational logic in North and South America.

We thank the University at Buffalo and the University of Texas at Dallas for their support. We gratefully acknowledge the contributions of Shriram Krishnamurthy and Pete Hopkins, Brown University, for maintaining the PADL website which provided much needed assistance in the submission and review process. Finally, we thank the authors who submitted papers to PADL 2004 and all who participated in the conference.

April 2004   Bharat Jayaraman
                                                              Program Chair

Program Committee

Maurice Bruynooghe	KU Leuven, Belgium
Veronica Dahl	Simon Fraser University, Canada
Olivier Danvy	University of Aarhus, Denmark
Stefan Decker	USC Information Sciences Institute, USA
Matthew Flatt	University of Utah, USA
Julia Lawall	DIKU, Denmark
Gopal Gupta	Univ. of Texas at Dallas, USA (General Chair)
Michael Hanus	University of Kiel, Germany
John Hughes	Chalmers University, Sweden
Joxan Jaffar	National University of Singapore
Bharat Jayaraman	University at Buffalo, USA (Program Chair)
Michael Leuschel	University of Southampton, UK
Gopalan Nadathur	University of Minnesota, USA
Enrico Pontelli	New Mexico State University, USA
C.R. Ramakrishnan	University at Stony Brook, USA
Tim Sheard	Oregon Graduate Institute, USA
Vitor Santos Costa	University of Rio de Janiero, Brazil
Paul Tarau	University of North Texas, USA

Referees

Alma Barranco-Mendoza	Martin Henz
Bernd Braßel	Glendon Holst
Stefan Bressan	Frank Huch
Manuel Carro	Maarten Mariën
Luis Castro	Ilkka Niemela
Alvaro Cortés-Calabuig	Nikolay Pelov
Stephen J. Craig	Ricardo Rocha
Diana Cukierman	Mads Torgersen
Dan Elphick	Son Cao Tran
Anderson Faustino	Remko Tronçon
Antonio Mario Florido	Jan Wielemaker

Table of Contents

An Algebraic Theory
of Polymorphic Temporal Media

Paul Hudak

Department of Computer Science
Yale University
paul.hudak@yale.edu

Abstract. *Temporal media* is information that is directly consumed by a user, and that varies with time. Examples include music, digital sound files, computer animations, and video clips. In this paper we present a polymorphic data type that captures a broad range of temporal media. We study its syntactic, temporal, and semantic properties, leading to an algebraic theory of polymorphic temporal media that is valid for underlying media types that satisfy specific constraints. The key technical result is an axiomatic semantics for polymorphic temporal media that is shown to be both sound and complete.

1 Introduction

The advent of the personal computer has focussed attention on the *consumer*, the person who buys and makes use of the computer. Our interest is in the consumer as a person who *consumes information*. This information takes on many forms, but it is usually dynamic and time-varying, and ultimately is consumed mostly through our visual and aural senses. We use the term *temporal media* to refer to this time-varying information. We are interested in how to represent this information at an abstract level; how to manipulate these representations; how to assign a meaning, or interpretation, to them; and how to reason about such meanings.

To achieve these goals, we define a polymorphic representation of temporal media that allows combining media values in generic ways, independent of the underlying media type. We describe three types of operations on and properties of temporal media: (a) syntactic operations and properties, that depend only on the structural representation of the media, (b) temporal operations and properties, that additionally depend on time, and (c) semantic operations and properties, that depend on the meaning, or interpretation, of the media. The latter development leads to an axiomatic semantics for polymorphic temporal media that is both sound and complete.

Examples of temporal media include music, digital sound files, computer animations, and video clips. It also includes representations of some other concepts, such as dance [10] and a language for humanoid robot motion [5]. In this paper we use two running examples throughout: an abstract representation of *music* (analogous to our previous work on *Haskore* and *MDL*, DSLs for computer music

B. Jayaraman (Ed.): PADL 2004, LNCS 3057, pp. 1–15, 2004.
© Springer-Verlag Berlin Heidelberg 2004

[9,6,7,8]), and an abstract representation of *continuous animations* (analogous to our previous work on *Fran* and *FAL* [4,3,7]).

The key new ideas in the current work are the polymorphic nature of the media type, the exploration of syntactic and temporal properties of this media type that parallel those for lists, the casting of the semantics in a formal algebraic framework, the definition of a normal form for polymorphic temporal media, and a completeness result for the axiomatic semantics. The completeness result relies on a new axiom for swapping terms in a serial/parallel construction.

We present all of our results using Haskell [12] syntax that, in most cases, is executable. Haskell's type classes are particularly useful in specifying constraints, via implicit laws, that constituent types must obey. Proofs of most theorems have been omitted in this extended abstract.

2   Polymorphic Media

We represent temporal media by a polymorphic data type:

```
data Media a = Prim a
             | Media a :+: Media a
             | Media a :=: Media a
```

We refer to T in `Media T` as the *base media type*. Intuitively, for values `x :: T` and `m1, m2 :: Media T`, a value of type `Media T` is either a primitive value `Prim x`, a sequential composition `m1 :+: m2`, or a parallel composition `m1 :=: m2`. Although simple in structure, this data type is rich enough to capture quite a number of useful media types.

Example 1 (Music): Consider this definition of an abstract notion of a *musical note*:

```
data Note = Rest Dur | Note Pitch Dur
type Dur    = Real
type Pitch  = (NoteName, Octave)
type Octave = Int
data NoteName = Cf | C  | Cs | Df | D  | Ds | Ef | E  | Es | Ff | F
              | Fs | Gf | G  | Gs | Af | A  | As | Bf | B  | Bs
```

In other words, a `Note` is either a pitch paired with a duration, or a `Rest` that has a duration but no pitch. `Dur` is a measure of time (duration), which ideally would be a real number; in a practical implementation a suitable approximation such as `Float`, `Double`, or `Ratio Int` would be used. A `Pitch` is a pair consisting of a note name and an octave, where an octave is just an integer. The note name `Cf` is read as "C-flat" (normally written as C♭), `Cs` as "C-sharp" (normally written as C♯), and so on.[1] Then the type:

```
type Music = Media Note
```

---

[1] This representation corresponds well to that used in music theory, except that in music theory note names are called *pitch classes*.

is a temporal media for music. In particular, a value `Prim (Rest d)` is a rest of duration d, `Prim (Note p d)` is a note with pitch p played for duration d, `m1 :+: m2` is the music value m1 followed sequentially in time by m2, and `m1 :=: m2` is m1 played simultaneously with m2. This representation of music is a simplified version of that used in the Haskore computer music library [9,6], which has been used successfully in several computer music applications. As a simple example:

```
let dMinor  =  Note (D,3) 1 :=: Note (F,3) 1 :=: Note (A,3) 1
    gMajor  =  Note (G,3) 1 :=: Note (B,3) 1 :=: Note (D,4) 1
    cMajor  =  Note (C,3) 2 :=: Note (E,3) 2 :=: Note (G,3) 2
in dMinor :+: gMajor :+: cMajor
```

is a ii-V-I chord progression in C major.

Example 2 (Animation): Consider this definition of a base media type for *continuous animations*:

```
type Anim = (Dur, Time -> Picture)
type Dur  = Real
type Time = Real
data Picture = EmptyPic | Circle Radius Point
             | Square Length Point | Polygon [Point]
type Point = (Real, Real)
```

A `Picture` is either empty, a circle or square of a given size and located at a particular point, or a polygon having a specific set of vertices. An `Anim` value (d, f) is a continuous animation whose image at time $0 \leq t \leq d$ is the `Picture` value f t. Then the type:

```
type Animation = Media Anim
```

is a temporal media for continuous animations. This representation is a simplified version of that used in Fran [4,3] and FAL [7]. As a simple example:

```
let ball1 = (10, \t -> Circle t origin)
    ball2 = (10, \t -> Circle (10-t) origin
    box   = (20, \t -> Square 1 (t,t))
in (ball1 :+: ball2) :=: box
```

is a box sliding diagonally across the screen, together with a ball located at the origin that first grows for 10 seconds and then shrinks.

3   Syntactic Properties

Before studying semantic properties, we first define various operations on the *structure* (i.e. syntax) of polymorphic temporal media values, many of which are analogous to operations on lists (and thus we borrow similar names when the analogy is strong). We also explore various *laws* that these operators obey, laws that are also analogous to those for lists [2,7].

Map. For starters, it is easy to define a polymorphic *map* on temporal media, which we do by declaring `Media` to be an instance of the `Functor` class:

```
instance Functor Media where
  fmap f (Prim n)    = Prim (f n)
  fmap f (m1 :+: m2) = fmap f m1 :+: fmap f m2
  fmap f (m1 :=: m2) = fmap f m1 :=: fmap f m2
```

`fmap` shares many properties with `map` defined on lists, most notably the standard laws for the `Functor` class:

Theorem 1. For any finite `m :: Media T1` and functions `f, g :: T1 -> T2`:

```
fmap (f . g) = fmap f . fmap g
fmap id      = id
```

`fmap` allows us to define many useful operations on specific media types, thus obviating the need for a richer data type as used, for example, in our previous work on Haskore, MDL, Fran, and Fal. For example, tempo scaling and pitch transposition of music, and size scaling and position translation of animation.

Fold (i.e. catamorphism). A fold-like function can be defined for media values, and will play a critical role in our subsequent development of the semantics of temporal media:

```
foldM :: (a->b) -> (b->b->b) -> (b->b->b) -> Media a -> b
foldM f g h (Prim x) = f x
foldM f g h (m1 :+: m2) = foldM f g h m1 `g` foldM f g h m2
foldM f g h (m1 :=: m2) = foldM f g h m1 `h` foldM f g h m2
```

Theorem 2. For any `f :: T1 -> T2`:

```
foldM (Prim . f) (:+:) (:=:) = fmap f
foldM Prim (:+:) (:=:)       = id
```

More interestingly, we can also state a *fusion law* for `foldM`:

Theorem 3. (Fusion Law) For `f :: T1->T2`, `g, h :: T2->T2->T2`, `k :: T2->T3`, and `g', h' :: T1->T3`, if:

```
f' x = k (f x)
g' (k x) (k y) = k (g x y)
h' (k x) (k y) = k (h x y)
```

then: `k . foldM f g h = foldM f' g' h'`.

Example: In the discussion below a reverse function, and in Section 4 a duration function, are defined as catamorphisms. In addition, in Section 5 we define the standard interpretation, or semantics, of temporal media as a catamorphism.

Reverse. We would like to define a function `reverseM` that *reverses*, in time, any temporal media value. However, this will only be possible if the base media type is itself reversible, a constraint that we enforce using type classes:

```
class Reverse a where
  reverseM :: a -> a
instance Reverse a => Reverse (Media a) where
  reverseM (Prim a)    = Prim (reverseM a)
  reverseM (m1 :+: m2) = reverseM m2 :+: reverseM m1
  reverseM (m1 :=: m2) = reverseM m1 :=: reverseM m2
```

Note that `reverseM` can be defined more succinctly as a catamorphism:

```
instance Reverse a => Reverse (Media a) where
  reverseM = foldM (Prim . reverseM) (flip (:+:)) (:=:)
```

Analogous to a similar property on lists, we have:

Theorem 4. For all finite `m`, if the following law holds for `reverseM :: T -> T`, then it also holds for `reverseM :: Media T -> Media T`:

```
reverseM (reverseM m) = m
```

We take the constraint in this theorem to be a law for all valid instances of a base media type `T` in the class `Reverse`. It is straightforward to prove this theorem using structural induction. However, one can also carry out an inductionless proof by using the fusion law of Theorem 3.

Example 1 (Music): We declare `Note` to be an instance of class `Reverse`:

```
instance Reverse Note where
  reverseM = id
```

In other words, a single note is the same whether played backwards or forwards. The constraint in Theorem 4 is therefore trivially satisfied, and it thus holds for music media.[2]

Example 2 (Animation): We declare `Anim` to be an instance of `Reverse`:

```
instance Reverse Anim where
  reverseM (d, f) = (d, \t -> f (d-t))
```

Note that `reverseM (reverseM (d, f)) = (d, f)`, therefore the constraint in Theorem 4 is satisfied, and the theorem thus holds for continuous animations.

---

[2] The reverse of a musical passage is called its *retrograde*. Used sparingly by traditional composers (two notable examples being J.S. Bach's "Crab Canons" and Franz Joseph Haydn's Piano Sonata No. 26 in A Major (Menueto al Rovescio)), it is a standard construction in modern twelve-tone music.

4   Temporal Properties

As a data structure, the `Media` type is fairly straightforward. Complications arise, however, when *interpreting* temporal media. The starting point for such an interpretation is an understanding of temporal properties, the most basic of which is *duration*. Of particular concern is the meaning of the parallel composition `m1 :=: m2` when the durations of `m1` and `m2` are different. In this paper we simply disallow this situation: i.e. `m1` and `m2` must have the same duration in a "well-formed" `Media` value. This approach does not lack in generality, since other approaches can be expressed by padding the media values appropriately (for example with rests in music, or empty images in animation).

Duration. To compute the *duration* of a temporal media value we first need a way to compute the duration of the underlying media type, which we enforce as before using type classes:

```
class Temporal a where
  dur  :: a -> Dur
  none :: Dur -> a
instance Temporal a => Temporal (Media a) where
  dur = foldM dur (+) max
  none = Prim . none
```

The `none` method allows one to express the absence of media for a specified duration, as discussed earlier.

We take the constraint in the following lemma to be a law for any valid instance of a base media type `T` in the class `Temporal`:

Lemma 1. If the property `dur (none d) = d` holds for `dur :: T -> Dur`, then it also holds for `dur :: Media T -> Dur`.

Note that, for generality, the duration of a parallel composition is defined as the maximum of the durations of its arguments. However, as discussed earlier, we wish to restrict parallel coompositions to those whose two argument durations are the same. Thus we define:

Definition 1. A *well-formed* temporal media value `m :: Media T` is one that is finite, and for which each parallel composition `m1 :=: m2` has the property that `dur m1 = dur m2`.

Example 1 (Music): We declare `Note` to be `Temporal`:

```
instance Temporal Note where
  dur (Rest d)  = d
  dur (Note p d) = d
  none d        = Rest d
```

Example 2 (Animation): We declare `Anim` to be `Temporal`:

```
instance Temporal Anim where
  dur (d, f) = d
  none d     = (d, const EmptyPic)
```

Take and Drop. We now define two functions `takeM` and `dropM` that are analogous to Haskell's `take` and `drop` functions for lists. The difference is that instead of being parameterized by a number of elements, `takeM` and `dropM` are parameterized by *time*. As with other operators we have considered, this requires the ability to take and drop portions of the base media type, so once again we use type classes to structure the design. The expression `takeM d m` is a media value corresponding to the first `d` seconds of `m`. Similarly, `dropM d m` is all but the first `d` seconds. Both of these are very useful in practice.

```
class Take a where
   takeM :: Dur -> a -> a
   dropM :: Dur -> a -> a
instance (Take a, Temporal a) => Take (Media a) where
   takeM d m | d <= 0  = none 0
   takeM d (Prim x)    = Prim (takeM d x)
   takeM d (m1 :+: m2) = let d1 = dur m1
           in if d <= d1 then takeM d m1 else m1 :+: takeM (d-d1) m2
   takeM d (m1 :=: m2) = takeM d m1 :=: takeM d m2
   dropM ... = ... (details omitted) ...
```

Perhaps surprisingly, `takeM` and `dropM` share many properties analogous to their list counterparts, except that indexing is done in time, not in the number of elements:

Theorem 5. For all non-negative `d1`, `d2 :: Dur`, if the following laws hold for `takeM`, `dropM :: Dur -> T -> T`, then they also hold for `takeM`, `dropM :: Dur -> Media T -> Media T`:

```
takeM d1 . takeM d2 = takeM (min d1 d2)
dropM d1 . dropM d2 = dropM (d1+d2)
takeM d1 . dropM d2 = dropM d2 . takeM (d1+d2)
dropM d1 . takeM d2 = takeM (d2-d1) . dropM d1     -- if d2>=d1
```

There is one other theorem that we would *like* to hold, whose corresponding version for lists in fact does hold:

Theorem 6. For all finite well-formed `m :: Media a` and non-negative `d :: Dur <= dur m`, if the following law holds for `takeM`, `dropM :: Dur->T->T`, then it also holds for `takeM`, `dropM :: Dur -> Media T -> Media T`:

```
takeM d m :+: dropM d m = m
```

However, this theorem is false; in fact it does not hold for the base case:

```
takeM d (Prim x) :+: dropM d (Prim x)
=  Prim (takeM d x) :+: Prim (dropM d x)
/= Prim x
```

We cannot even state this as a constraint on the base media type, because it involves an interpretation of `(:+:)`. We will return to this issue in a later section.

Example 1 (Music): We declare `Note` to be an instance of `Take`:

```
instance Take Note where
  takeM d1 (Rest d2)   = Rest (min d1 d2)
  takeM d1 (Note p d2) = Note p (min d1 d2)
```

The constraints on Theorem 5 hold for this instance, and thus the theorem holds for Music values.

Example 2 (Animation): We declare Anim to be an instance of Take:

```
instance Take Anim where
  takeM d1 (d2, f) = (max 0 (min d1 d2), f)
```

The constraints on Theorem 5 hold for this instance, and thus the theorem holds for Animation values.

5   Semantic Properties

Temporal properties of polymorphic media go beyond structural properties, but do not go far enough. For example, intuitively speaking, we would expect these two media fragments:

    m1 :+: (m2 :+: m3)   (m1 :+: m2) :+: m3

to be equivalent; i.e. to deliver precisely the same information to the observer (for visual information they should *look* the same, for aural information they should *sound* the same, and so on).

In order to capture this notion of equivalence we must provide an *interpretation* of the media that properly captures its "meaning" (i.e. how it looks, how it sounds, and so on). And we would like to do this in a generic way. So once again we use type classes to constrain the design:

```
class Combine b where
  concatM :: b -> b -> b
  merge   :: b -> b -> b
  zero    :: Dur -> b
class Temporal a, Temporal b, Combine b => Meaning a b where
  meaning :: a -> b
instance Meaning a b => Meaning (Media a) b where
  meaning = foldM meaning concatM merge
```

Intuitively speaking, an instance Meaning T1 T2 means that T1 can be given meaning in terms of T2. More specifically, Media T1 can be given meaning in terms of T2, and expressed as a catamorphism, as long as we can give meaning to the base media type T1 in terms of T2.

As laws for the class Meaning, we require that:

```
meaning . none = zero
dur . meaning  = dur
```

Also, in anticipation of the axiomatic semantics that we develop in Section 7, we requre that the following laws be valid for any instance of Combine:

```
b1 'concatM' (b2 'concatM' b3) = (b1 'concatM' b2) 'concatM' b3
b1 'merge' (b2 'merge' b3) = (b1 'merge' b2) 'merge' b3
b1 'merge' b2              = b2 'merge' b1
zero 0 'concatM' b = b
b 'concatM' zero 0 = b
zero d1 'concatM' zero d2 = zero (d1+d2)
zero d 'merge' b          = b, if d = dur b
(b1 'concatM' b2) 'merge' (b3 'concatM' b4)
  = (b1 'merge' b3) 'concatM' (b2 'merge' b4),
      if  dur b1 = dur b3  and  dur b2 = dur b4
```

We then define a notion of equivalence:

Definition 2. m1, m2 :: Media T are *equivalent*, written m1 === m2, if and only if meaning m1 = meaning m2.

Example 1 (Music): We take the meaning of music to be a pair: the *duration* of the music, and a *sequence of events*, where each event marks the start-time, pitch, and duration of a single note:

```
data Event = Event Time Pitch Dur
type Time = Real
type Performance = (Dur, [Event])
```

Except for the outermost duration, the interpretation of Music as a Performance corresponds well to low-level music representations such as MIDI [1] and csound [14]. The presence of the outermost duration in a Performance allows us to distinguish rests of unequal length; for example, Prim (Rest d1) and Prim (Rest d2), where d1 /= d2. Without the durations, these phrases would both denote an empty sequence of events, and would be indistinguishable. More generally, this allows us to distinguish phrases that end with rests of unequal length, such as m :+: Prim (Rest d1) and m :+: Prim (Rest d2).

Three instance declarations complete our interpretation of music:

```
instance Combine Performance where
  concatM (d1, evs1) (d2, evs2) = (d1 + d2, evs1 ++ map shift evs2)
                    where shift (Event t p d) = Event (t+d1) p d
  merge (d1, evs1) (d2, evs2) = (d1 'max' d2, sort (evs1 ++ evs2))
  zero d = (d, [])
instance Temporal Performance where
  dur (d, _) = d
  none = zero
instance Meaning Note Performance where
  meaning (Rest d)   = (d, [])
  meaning (Note p d) = (d, [Event 0 p d])
```

Note that, although the arguments to (:=:) in well-formed temporal media have equal duration, we take the max of the durations of the two arguments for increased generality. Also, note that the event sequences in a merge are concatenated and then sorted. A more efficient ($O(n)$ instead of $O(n \log n)$) but less concise way to express this is to define a time-ordered merge function.

We can show that the two laws for class Meaning, as well as the eight for class Combine, hold for these instances, and thus they are valid.

Example 2 (Animation): We take the meaning of animation to be a pair: the *duration* of the animation, and a *sequence of images* sampled at some frame rate r:

```
type Rendering = (Dur, [Image])
picToImage   :: Picture -> Image
combineImage :: Image -> Image -> Image
emptyImage   :: Image
```

(Details of the Image operations are omitted.) This interpretation of animation is consistent with standard representations of videos/movies, whether digitized, on analog tape, or on film. Three instance declarations complete our interpretation of continuous animation:

```
instance Combine Rendering where
  concatM (d1,i1) (d2,i2) = (d1 + d2, i1 ++ i2)
  merge (d1,i1) (d2,i2) = (d1 'max' d2,zipWith' combineImage i1 i2)
  zero d = (d, take (truncate (d*r)) [EmptyPic ..]   )
instance Temporal Rendering where
  dur (d,_) = d
  none = zero
instance Meaning Animation Rendering where
  meaning (d,f) = (d, map (picToImage . f)
                        (take (truncate (d*r)) [0, 1/r ..]))
```

(zipWith' is just like Haskell's zipWith, except that it does not truncate the result to the shorter of its two arguments.)

Unfortunately, not all of the laws for classes Meaning and Combine hold for these instances. The problem stems from discretization. For example, suppose the frame rate r = 10. Then:

```
z1 = zero 1.06 = (1.06, take 10 [EmptyPic ..])
z2 = zero 2.12 = (2.12, take 21 [EmptyPic ..])
```

However, note that:

```
z1 'concatM' z1 = (2.12, take 20 [EmptyPic ..])
```

which is not the same as z2. So the Combine law does not hold. This problem can be remedied by requiring that all Anim durations be integral multiples of the frame rate r. We say that such animations are *integral*. With the additional assumption that the image operator combineImage is associative and commutative, it is then straightforward to show that all of the laws for classes Combine and Meaning hold, and thus the above are valid instances for integral animations.

Finally, returning to the motivating example in this section, we can show that:

```
m1 :+: (m2 :+: m3) === (m1 :+: m2) :+: m3
```

In other words, (:+:) is associative. Indeed, there are several other such equivalences, each of which contributes to an *axiomatic semantics* of polymorphic temporal media. We discuss this in detail in Section 7.

6   Algebraic Structure

An *algebraic structure* (or just *algebra*) <S,op1,op2,...> consists of a nonempty carrier set (or *sort*) S together with one or more n-ary operations op1, op2, ..., on that set [13]. We define an algebra of *well-formed temporal media over type* T as <Media T,:+:,:=:>. The Haskell algebraic data type definition for Media can be seen as the generator of the elements of this algebra, but with the additional constraint of well-formedness discussed in Section 4. We also define an *interpretation* as an algebra <I,concatM,merge> for some type I (for example, Performance in the case of music, and Rendering in the case of animation).

Theorem 7. The semantic function meaning is a *homomorphism* from <Media T,:+:,:=:,none> to <I,concatM,merge,zero>.

Theorem 8. (===) is a *congruence relation* on the algebra <Media,:+:,:=:>.

Definition 3. Let [[m]] denote the equivalence class (induced by (===)) that contains m. Let Media T/(===) denote the quotient set of such equivalence classes over base media type T, and let <Media T/(===),:+:,:=:> denote the quotient algebra, also called the *initial algebra*. The function g :: Media T -> Media T/(===) defined by g m = [[m]] is called the *natural homomorphism* from <Media T,:+:,:=:> to <Media T/(===),:+:,:=:> [13]. Also define h :: Media T/(===) -> I by h [[m]] = meaning m. Note that h is an isomorphism, since g is the natural homomorphism induced by (===).

Theorem 9. The diagram in Figure 1 commutes.

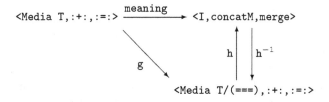

Fig. 1. The Structure of Interpretation

7 Axiomatic Semantics

In Section 5 we noted that (:=:) was associative. Indeed, we can treat this as one of the *axioms* in an *axiomatic semantics* for polymorphic temporal media. The full set of axioms is given in the following definition:

Definition 4. The axiomatic semantics A for well-formed polymorphic temporal media consists of the eight axioms shown in Figure 2, as well as the usual reflexive, symmetric, and transitive laws that arise from (===) being an equivalence relation, and the substitution laws that arise from (===) being a congruence relation. We write A ⊢ m1 = m2 iff m1 === m2 can be established from the axioms of A.

For any finite well-formed m, m1, m2 :: Media T, and non-negative d :: Dur:

1. (:+:) is associative: m1 :+: (m2 :+: m3) === (m1 :+: m2) :+: m3
2. (:=:) is associative: m1 :=: (m2 :=: m3) === (m1 :=: m2) :=: m3
3. (:=:) is commutative: m1 :=: m2 === m2 :=: m1
4. none 0 is a left (sequential) zero: none 0 :+: m === m
5. none 0 is a right (sequential) zero: m :+: none 0 === m
6. none d is a left (parallel) zero: none d :=: m === m, if d = dur m
7. none is additive: none d1 :+: none d2 === none (d1+d2)
8. serial/parallel swap:
   (m1 :+: m2) :=: (m3 :+: m4) === (m1 :=: m3) :+: (m2 :=: m4),
   if dur m1 = dur m3 and dur m2 = dur m4

Note that none d is also a right zero for (:=:), but is derivable from (3) and (6).

Fig. 2. The Axioms of A

7.1 Soundness

Theorem 10. (Soundness) The axiomatic semantics A is *sound*. That is, for all well-formed m1, m2 :: Media T:

$$A \vdash m1 = m2 \implies m1 === m2$$

As an example of a non-trivial theorem that can be proven from these axioms, recall Theorem 6 from Section 4, which we pointed out was false. By changing the equality in that theorem to one of equivalence as defined in this section, we can state a valid theorem as follows:

Theorem 11. For all finite x :: T and non-negative d :: Dur <= dur m, if takeM d (Prim x) :+: dropM d (Prim x) === Prim x then for all finite well-formed m :: Media T, takeM d m :+: dropM d m === m.

Example 1 (Music): Theorem 11, which holds for lists, does *not* hold for Music, since, for example, if m = Prim (Note p 2), then:

```
takeM 1 m :+: dropM 1 m = Prim (Note p 1) :+: Prim (Note p 1)
```

which is not equivalent to m = Prim (Note p 2).

Example 2 (Animation): Theorem 11 *does* hold for Animation, since, if d2>d1, then:

```
meaning (takeM d1 (Prim (d2,f)) :+: dropM d1 (Prim (d2,f)))
= meaning (Prim (d2,f))
```

A similar argument holds when d1>d2. Although Theorem 11 holds for animation, this is not necessarily a good thing, as we will see in the next section.

7.2   Completeness

Soundness of A tells us that if we can prove two media values are equivalent using the axioms, then in fact they are equivalent. We are also interested in the converse: if two media values are in fact equivalent, can we prove the equivalence using only the axioms? If so, the axiomatic semantics A is also *complete*.

Completeness results of any kind are usually much more difficult to establish than soundness results. The key to doing so in our case is the notion of a *normal form* for polymorphic temporal media values. Recall from the previous section the isomorphism between the algebras <P,concatM,merge> and <Media T/(===),:+:,:=:>. What we need to do first is identify a canonical representation of each equivalence class in Media T/(===):

Definition 5. A well-formed media term m :: Media T is in *normal form* iff it is of the form none d, where $d \geq 0$, or:

$$(\text{none } d_{11} \text{ :+: Prim } x_1 \text{ :+: none } d_{12}) \text{ :=:}$$
$$(\text{none } d_{21} \text{ :+: Prim } x_2 \text{ :+: none } d_{22}) \text{ :=:}$$
$$\cdots$$
$$(\text{none } d_{n1} \text{ :+: Prim } x_n \text{ :+: none } d_{n2}), n \geq 1,$$
$$\wedge \; \forall \; (1 \leq i \leq n), d_{i1} + d_{i2} + \text{dur } x_i = \text{dur } m,$$
$$\wedge \; \forall \; (1 \leq i < n), (d_{i1}, x_i, d_{i2}) \leq (d_{(i+1)1}, x_{(i+1)}, d_{(i+1)2})$$

We denote the set of media normal-forms over type T as MediaNF T.

Defining a normal form is not quite enough, however. We must show that (a) each normal form is unique: i.e. it is not equivalent to any other, and (b) any media value can be transformed into an equivalent normal form using only the axioms of A. We will treat (a) as an assumption, and return later to study situations where this is not true. For (b), we prove the following lemma:

Lemma 2. The function normalize in Figure 3 converts any m : Media T into a media normal-form using only the axioms of A.

Theorem 12. (Completeness) The axiomatic semantics A is *complete*, that is: for all m1, m2 :: Media T:

$$\text{m1} === \text{m2} \; \Rightarrow \; A \vdash \text{m1} = \text{m2}$$

```
normalize :: (Ord (Media a), Temporal a) => Media a -> Media a
normalize m = sortM (norm (dur m) 0 m)

norm :: (Ord (Media a), Temporal a) => Dur -> Dur -> Media a -> Media a
norm d t m | isNone m = m
norm d t (Prim x)    = none t :+: Prim x :+: none (d-t-dur x)
norm d t (m1 :+: m2) = norm d t m1 :=: norm d (t+dur m1) m2
norm d t (m1 :=: m2) = norm d t m1 :=: norm d t m2
```

Fig. 3. Normalization Function

iff the normal forms in `MediaNF T` are *unique*, i.e. for all `nf1,nf2 :: MediaNF T`:

$$\text{nf1} \neq \text{nf2} \quad \Rightarrow \quad \neg(\text{nf1} === \text{nf2})$$

Theorem 12 is important not only because it establishes completeness, but also because it points out the special nature of the normal forms. That is, there can be no other choice of the normal forms – they are uniquely tied to completeness.

Example 1 (Music): The normal forms for `Music`, i.e. `MusicNF Note`, are unique. In fact, the domain is isomorphic to `Performance`. To see this, we can define a bijection between the two domains as follows:

1. The music normal form `none d` corresponds to the interpretation
   `meaning (none d) = zero d`.
2. The non-trivial normal form, call it `m`, written in Definition 5, corresponds to the performance `meaning m =`
   `(dur m, [(d11,p1,d12),(d21,p2,d22),...,(dn1,pn,dn2)],dur m)`.
   This correspondence is invertible because each `di3` is computable from the other durations; i.e. `di3 = dur m - di1 - di2`.

Example 2 (Animation): The normal forms of the `Animation` media type are *not* unique. There are several reasons for this. First, there may be pairs of primitive images that are equivalent, such as a circle of radius zero and a square of length zero, or a square and a polygon that mimics a square. Second, there may be pairs of animations that are equivalent because of the effect of occlusion. For example, a large box completely occluding a small circle is equivalent to a large box completely occluding any other image. It is possible to include additional axioms to cover these special cases, in which case the resulting axiomatic semantics may be complete, but the proof will not be automatic and cannot rely exclusively on the uniqueness of the normal forms.

8   Related Work

There has been a lot of work on embedding semantic descriptions *in* multimedia (XML, UML, the Semantic Web, etc.), but not on formalizing the semantics *of* concrete media. There are also many authoring tools and scripting languages for designing multimedia applications. The one closest to a programming language is SMIL [15], which can be seen as treating multimedia in a polymorphic way. Our own work on Haskore and MDL [9,6,7,8] is of course related, but specialized to music. Graham Hutton shows how fold and unfold can be used to describe denotational and operational semantics, respectively [11], and thus our use of fold to describe the semantics of temporal media is an instance of his framework.

Acknowledgement. The NSF provided partial support for this research under grant number CCR9900957.

References

1. International MIDI Association. Midi 1.0 detailed specification: Document version 4.1.1, February 1990.
2. Richard S. Bird. *Introduction to Functional Programming using Haskell (second edition)*. Prentice Hall, London, 1998.
3. Conal Elliott. Modeling interactive 3D and multimedia animation with an embedded language. In *Proceedings of the first conference on Domain-Specific Languages*, pages 285–296. USENIX, October 1997.
4. Conal Elliott and Paul Hudak. Functional reactive animation. In *International Conference on Functional Programming*, pages 263–273, June 1997.
5. Liwen Huang and Paul Hudak. Dance: A language for humanoid robot motion. Technical Report YALEU/DCS/RR-1253, Yale University, Department of Computer Science, July 2003.
6. Paul Hudak. Haskore music tutorial. In *Second International School on Advanced Functional Programming*, pages 38–68. Springer Verlag, LNCS 1129, August 1996.
7. Paul Hudak. *The Haskell School of Expression – Learning Functional Programming through Multimedia*. Cambridge University Press, New York, 2000.
8. Paul Hudak. *Describing and Interpreting Music in Haskell*, chapter 4. Palgrave, 2003. *The Fun of Programming*, edited by Jeremy Gibbons and Oege de Moor.
9. Paul Hudak, Tom Makucevich, Syam Gadde, and Bo Whong. Haskore music notation – an algebra of music. *Journal of Functional Programming*, 6(3):465–483, May 1996.
10. Ann Hutchinson. *Labanotation*. Routledge Theatre Arts Books, New York, 1991.
11. Graham Hutton. Fold and unfold for program semantics. In *International Conference on Functional Programming*. ACM Press, 1998.
12. Simon Peyton Jones, editor. *Haskell 98 Language and Libraries – The Revised Report*. Cambridge University Press, Cambridge, England, 2003.
13. J.P. Tremblay and R. Manohar. *Discrete Mathematical Structures with Applications to Computer Science*. McGraw-Hill, New York, 1975.
14. B. Vercoe. Csound: A manual for the audio processing system and supporting programs. Technical report, MIT Media Lab, 1986.
15. World Wide Web Consortium (W3C). Synchronized Multimedia Integration Language (SMIL), 2003. http://www.w3.org/AudioVideo.

Supporting Decisions in Complex, Uncertain Domains with Declarative Languages

Andrew Fall

Gowlland Technologies Ltd., Victoria, B.C., Canada, and
School of Resource and Environmental Management,
Simon Fraser University

Abstract. Domains with high levels of complexity and uncertainty pose significant challenges for decision-makers. Complex systems have too many linkages and feedbacks among system elements to easily apply analytical methods, and yet are too structured for statistical methods. Uncertainty, in terms of lacking information on system conditions and inter-relationships as well as inherent stochasticity, makes it difficult to predict outcomes from changes to system dynamics. In such situations, simulation models are key tools to integrate knowledge and to help improve understanding of systems responses in order to guide decisions.

Landscape management is a domain with high levels of both complexity and uncertainty (Holling 1978). Often broad spatial and temporal scales are considered (e.g. thousands to millions of hectares over decades to centuries) at relatively fine resolution (Baker 1989). These scales encompass complex spatio-temporal feedbacks between configuration of land cover information and processes of landscape change (e.g. growth, disturbance, harvesting, land-use practices). In addition, high uncertainty in terms of current spatial information (e.g. the age of forest stands across the landscape is seldom known with precision) and knowledge of all the key processes combine with inherent variability of natural disturbance regimes (etc. wind, fires, insects). Yet, landscape managers must make decisions on land-use practices, questions regarding sustainable resource utilization, endangered species recovery, and responses to natural disturbance (Selin 1995). Spatio-temporal projection models can integrate current best knowledge of a landscape system to help shed light on likely outcomes of various management choices (Sklar and Costanza 1991).

How can models of complex systems be integrated into the decision-making process?

Tenet #1: The model must be made to fit the decision process, not vice versa.

To develop models and then propose their use for improving management is putting the cart before the horse. To help decision-makers, models must be built to address their concerns as closely as possible, using information from local data sources and topic experts (Fall et al. 2001). If the latter is not accomplished, then model acceptance by local experts, and indirectly by decision-makers, is at risk (Selin 1995). In addition, the model-building cycle must be consistent with decision-making

B. Jayaraman (Ed.): PADL 2004, LNCS 3057, pp. 16–22, 2004.

timeframes. The timeframe of the decision process sets the bounds on the time allotted for model construction and application. Since the people who learn the most about a system from a complex model are those closest to the analysis (Schuler and Namioka 1992), a collaborative analysis framework (Gray 1989) provides an effective approach to embed model building within the decision process (Figure 1).

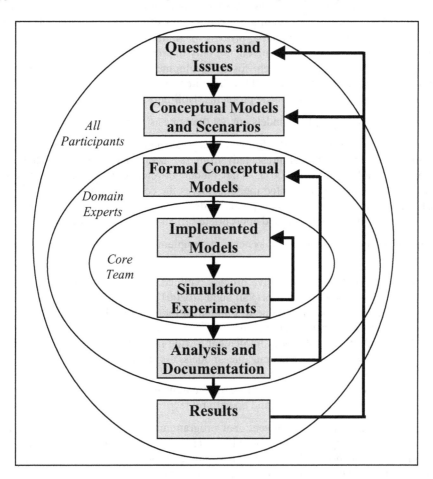

Fig. 1. Our nested, iterative model development process (Fall et al 2001). Groups participate in all circles that surround them. All participants (stakeholders, decision-makers, domain experts, core team members) set objectives, select scenarios, develop conceptual models, and discuss model results. Domain experts and the core team develop and verify the formal models. The core modelling team is responsible for organizing workshops and communication, gathering required information, implementing models, ensuring equivalence to formal conceptual models, running simulations, analyzing outputs and documentation.

One key aspect of collaborative modelling is to include appropriate people at the right time in the process. Decision-makers are usually extremely busy, and so should only be included to ensure the appropriate issues are being addressed, and when presenting final results. Topic experts and data managers are critical to ensure that the best information is used and to help design formal conceptual models, as well as to assess intermediate outputs and to improve implemented models. The core team is responsible to implement and verify models, run and analyze simulations, and document and communicate results. We have found a collaborative approach to be essential to the ultimate success of a project in terms of results actually being applied to inform decisions. A collaborative process maximizes the shared learning that can take place between all people involved, not only improving common understanding of systems dynamics, but also to help foster development of common vision for more appropriate management (Kyng 1991). The iterative process supports an adaptive management approach to landscape problems (Holling 1978).

Tenet #2: Formal conceptual models are not the same as implemented models.

It is important to distinguish the formal conceptual model that will be discussed and documented (i.e. the model presented) from the actual model implemented in a computer (Fall and Fall 2001). The model developer must ensure, through verification, that the implemented model captures the conceptual model, but it is still just one realization of the conceptual model. The collaborative process focuses attention on constructing clear and appropriate formal conceptual models.

How must models of complex systems be implemented to support collaborative analysis?

In order to support the collaborative process outlined, tools for implementing models must possess a range of objectives (Fall and Fall 2001):
1. Efficiency: the time frame to implement models must be consistent with the timeframe for decision-making.
2. Flexibility: capability to implement a wide range of models is key to ensure that appropriate, customizable models are built for a specific decision process.
3. Transparency: models must be transparent to ensure that assumptions and behaviours are explicit, and open to review.

These attributes imply that conventional programming languages are inappropriate tools for model implementation in this context because, although highly flexible, model implementation and modification can take too long, and resulting models are opaque (Derry 1998). If assumptions are not clear, models in complex systems cannot be fully scrutinized and may be discarded as "black boxes". Hidden assumptions increase the risk that behaviour due to model artefacts will be attributed to the system under study. Conversely, the use of existing models is also problematic, since they are inflexible and also tend to be opaque (even though this approach seems more most efficient).

Tenet #3: Model development tools should be domain-specific.

Domain-specific tools and languages provide a balance between these objectives (Barber 1992). Constraining to a certain domain of inquiry can provide guidance to help implement models relatively efficiently, while retaining flexibility to adapt models to novel circumstances. As an example, STELLA (Costanza et al. 1998) is a tool to build models that can be cast in terms of stocks and flows (Forrester 1961).

Tenet #4: Model development languages should be declarative.

Declarative languages can provide a level of transparency required for complex models that cannot be matched by procedural languages. Although model development tools themselves may be implemented using a procedural language (as are many declarative programming languages), the tool itself should provide a platform for declarative specification of model dynamics. However, while maintaining functional and logical purity of a domain-specific language is a laudable objective, it shouldn't diminish the primary goal of supporting a particular application. Hence the functionality required to support complex decisions should drive system development, while structural elegance should be an objective, not a constraint.

SELES (Spatially Explicit Landscape Event Simulator) is a tool for building and running models of landscape dynamics (Fall and Fall 2001). It aims to support construction of models in the domain of landscape ecology and management (Turner 1989), and has at its core a declarative language for specifying spatio-temporal dynamics. While the details of the SELES modelling language are not relevant to this discussion, some key attributes and assumptions are worth highlighting.

1. Landscape dynamics arise as a result of interaction between *agents of landscape change* and *landscape state*. Landscape state consists of raster grids of one or more spatial attributes (e.g. stand age, species, elevation) as well as global variables. Agents of change interact directly with the state (i.e. behaviour modified by and/or modifying landscape state), but only indirectly with each other through changes to the landscape state. This allows complex problems to be decomposed into semi-independent modular units.

2. Models are discrete in time and space. Spatial scale is defined by the extent of landscape grids used in a particular model and by the resolution (size) of individual cells (e.g. a 1,000,000 ha landscape with 1 ha cells). Temporal scale is defined by the time horizon of a particular simulation run and the size of the smallest time increment. Note that while spatial grain is uniform (i.e. all cells are the same size), temporal grain may vary (e.g. there may be 1-year intervals between fire events, but fires may spread on a 1-day step). These scales, along with the set of spatial and non-spatial variables define the complete spatio-temporal state space of a model.

3. There are two general types of "agents of change". *Landscape events* capture discrete events that occur on the landscape, and possibly spread across it (e.g. species succession, harvesting, wildfire, seed dispersal). *Landscape agents* capture individual entities that have identities and can move across the landscape. These archetypes provide two general algorithms for navigating through a spatio-temporal state space, and to make changes to the landscape state at appropriate places and times in order to produce the desired landscape dynamics. Landscape events and agents specify *what* effect processes have on the state, while the SELES engine takes care of *how* these agents of change run their course.

4. Landscape events and agents are specified using a declarative language that separates model behaviour from state changes caused by the model. Model behaviour is declared by assigning values to a set of *properties*. For landscape events, properties define, among other things, how often an event recurs, in which cells it may initiate, rate of spread, and cells to which the event may spread (Figure 2). For landscape agents, properties define how many agents to initiate, in which cells agents may be initiated, movement rules, mortality and reproduction. State changes are associated with properties, to be processed in appropriate *spatio-temporal contexts* (i.e. dynamic locations and times in the state space). The declarative nature of the language supports easy comparison, modification, reuse and communication of models, allows rapid model prototyping, and provides a structured framework to guide model development.

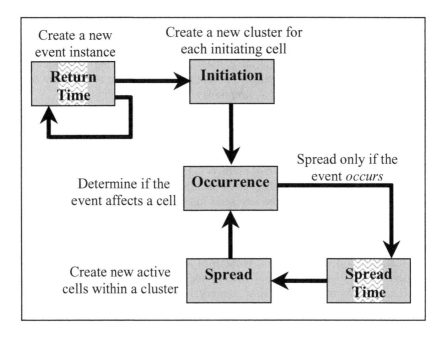

Fig. 2. Landscape events provide a general structure to model spatial processes (Fall and Fall 2001). Using the event properties, modellers control the return of the event, the cells in which the event initiates, whether the event affects the cells in which it starts, and for spreading events, the rate of spreading and to where a cell may spread. The zigzag pattern indicates time intervals occurring between separate instances of an event, and during spread within the same event instance.

SELES models can incorporate aspects of cellular automata (Itami 1994), percolation models (Turner 1989), discrete-event simulation, individual-based models (Lorek and Sonnenschein 1999) and spatio-temporal Markov chains. Models have been built for a broad range of processes, landscape types and pattern analyses. Projects have been conducted across Canada (e.g. Delong et al. 2004; Fall et al. 2004), as well as in the USA, Russia (Burnett et al. 2003), Scotland, Germany, and Brazil. Applications have ranged from land-use planning, natural disturbance modelling, endangered species risk assessments, and sustainable forest management exploration. The following briefly describes some relevant projects in which we have applied collaborative modelling in British Columbia (B.C.), Canada.

1. North Coast Land and Resource Management Plan (LRMP): The North Coast LRMP area is approximately 1 million hectares on north coastal B.C. A government land-use planning process set up a multi-stakeholder table to attempt to reach agreement on land-use zoning (protected areas, intensive management, general management, etc). This area has complex geography (e.g. coastal plains, islands, glaciated mountains), rich biodiversity values such as Grizzly Bear (*Ursus horribilis*) and Marbled Murrelet (Brachyramphus marmoratus), and valuable resources (forestry, mining, tourism). To support this process, we built a spatial landscape model to help identify tradeoffs between economic activity (primarily harvesting and road building) and ecological risk. Spatial scale: 1 million hectares at 1 hectare/cell. Temporal scale: decadal for 400 years. Model results have been used to help quantitatively bound the social tradeoffs between value emphasis across this landscape.

2. Provincial Mountain Pine Beetle Epidemic: An unprecedented outbreak of mountain pine beetle (MPB; *Dendroctonus ponderosae* Hopk.) is currently underway in the central interior of B.C., covering several million hectares at present. There is high uncertainty as to the precise pattern and effect this outbreak will follow, but forest managers and community leaders require information on the likely trends to help allocate resources and plan mitigative measures. Combining time series information of outbreak history with information scaled up from stand-level MPB modelling by the Canadian Forest Service (Safranyik et al. 1999), we constructed a provincial scale model to project likely outbreak patterns under a range of management options. Spatial scale: 900 thousand square kilometres at 16 hectares/cell. Temporal scale: annual for 20 years. Results are being used to help inform provincial strategies and responses.

3. Spotted Owl Recovery: Spotted Owls (*Strix occidentalis caurina*) are an endangered species, confined in B.C. to a few remaining pairs in the southwest mainland. A recovery team has been formed to make recommendations to help improve the prospects for this species. To support this team, we have been building a multi-faceted suite of models. The fist component consists of a combined forest management and habitat dynamics model that can be used to assess policy options, timber supply impacts and habitat supply impacts, and to output a time series of projected landscape states. These states provide input to pattern analysis models designed to assess structural connectivity of owl habitat. These in turn provide input to a spatial population model. The results of the various components will help formulate recommendations, informed by tradeoffs between risk to owl extirpation and costs to timber supply. Spatial scale: several million hectares at 1 hectare/cell. Temporal scale: annual for 1-2 centuries.

References

Baker WL. 1989. A review of models of landscape change. Landscape Ecology 2: 111-133.

Barber J. 1992. The need for application-specific software tools. Computer Design 31: 116.

Burnett C, A Fall, E Tomppo, and R Kalliola. 2003. Monitoring Current Status of and Trends in Boreal Forest Land-use in Russian Karelia. Conservation Ecology 7(2):8 [online] URL: http://www.consecol.org/vol7/iss2/art8.

Costanza R, D Duplisea, and U Kautsky. 1998. Ecological modelling and economic systems with STELLA. Ecological Modelling 110: 1-4.

Delong SC, A Fall, and GD Sutherland. 2004. Estimating the Impacts of Harvest Distribution on Road Building and Snag Abundance. Canadian Journal of Forest Research 34(2):323-331.

Derry JF. 1998. Modelling ecological interaction despite object-oriented modularity. Ecological Modelling 107: 145-158.

Fall A, D Daust, and D Morgan. 2001. A Framework and Software Tool to Support Collaborative Landscape Analysis: Fitting Square Pegs into Square Holes. Transactions in GIS 5(1): 67-86. Special issue of selected papers from the 4th International Conference on Integrating Geographic Information Systems and Environmental Modeling, Banff, Alberta, 2000.

Fall A and J Fall. 2001. A Domain-Specific Language for Models of Landscape Dynamics. Ecological Modelling 141(1-3): 1-18.

Fall A, M-J Fortin, DD Kneeshaw, SH Yamasaki, C Messier, L Bouthillier, and C Smyth. 2004. Consequences of Various Landscape-scale Ecosystem Management Strategies and Fire Cycles on Age-class Structure and Annual Harvest Target. Canadian Journal of Forest Research 34(2):310-322.

Forrester JW. 1961. Industrial Dynamics. MIT Press, Cambridge, MA.

Gray B. 1989. Collaborating: Finding Common Ground for Multi-party Problems. San Francisco, Jossey Bass.

Holling CS. 1978. Adaptive Environmental Assessment and Management. Chichester, John Wiley and Sons.

Itami R. 1994. Simulating spatial dynamics: Cellular automata theory. Landscape and Urban Planning 30: 27-47.

Kyng M. 1991. Designing for cooperation: cooperating in design. Special Issue: Collaborative Computing, Communications of the ACM, 34(12): 65-73.

Lorek H and M Sonnenschein. 1999. Modelling and simulation software to support individual-based ecological modelling. Ecological Modelling 225: 199-216.

Safranyik L, H Barclay, A Thomson, and WG Riel. 1999. A population dynamics model for the mountain pine beetle, *Dendroctonus ponderosae* Hopk. (Coleoptera: Scolytidae). Natural Resources Canada, Pacific Forestry Centre, Information Report BC-X-386. 35 pp.

Schuler D and A Namioka A (eds). 1992. Participatory Design. Hillsdale, N J, Lawrence Erlbaum Associates.

Selin S and D Chavez. 1995 Developing a collaborative model for environmental planning and modelling. Environmental Management 19(2): 189-195.

Sklar FH and R Costanza. 1991. The development of dynamic spatial models for landscape ecology: A review and prognosis. In: Turner, M.G., Gardner, R.H. (Eds.), Quantitative Methods in Landscape Ecology. Springer-Verlag, New York. pp. 239-288.

Turner MG. 1989. Landscape ecology: the effect of pattern on process. Annual Review of Ecological Systems 20: 171-197.

A Typeful Approach to Object-Oriented Programming with Multiple Inheritance*

Chiyan Chen, Rui Shi, and Hongwei Xi

Computer Science Department

Boston University

{chiyan,shearer,hwxi}@cs.bu.edu

Abstract. The wide practice of objected oriented programming (OOP) in current software practice is evident. Despite extensive studies on typing programming objects, it is still undeniably a challenging research task to design a type system that can satisfactorily account for a variety of features (e.g., binary methods and multiple inheritance) in OOP. In this paper, we present a typeful approach to implementing objects that makes use of a recently introduced notion of guarded datatypes. In particular, we demonstrate how the feature of multiple inheritance can be supported with this approach, presenting a simple and general account for multiple inheritance in a typeful manner.

1   Introduction

The popularity of object-oriented programming (OOP) in current software practice is evident. While this popularity may result in part from the tendency of programmers to chase after the latest "fads" in programing languages, there is undeniably some real substance in the growing use of OOP. For instance, the inheritance mechanism in OOP offers a highly effective approach to facilitating code reuse. There are in general two common forms of inheritance in OOP: single inheritance and multiple inheritance. In object-oriented languages such as Smalltalk and Java, only single inheritance is allowed, that is, a (sub)class can inherit from at most one (super)class. On the other hand, in object-oriented languages such as C++ and Eiffel, multiple inheritance, which allows a (sub)class to inherit from more than one (super)classes, is supported. We have previously outlined an approach to implementing objects through the use of guarded recursive datatypes [XCC03]. While it addresses many difficult issues in OOP (e.g., parametric polymorphism, binary methods, the self type, etc.) in a simple and natural manner, it is unclear, *a priori* whether this approach is able to cope with multiple inheritance. In this paper, we are to make some significant adjustment to this approach so that the issue of multiple inheritance can also be properly dealt with in a typeful manner, and we believe that such a typeful treatment of multiple inheritance is entirely novel in the literature.

---

* Partially supported by NSF grants no. CCR-0224244 and no. CCR-0229480

B. Jayaraman (Ed.): PADL 2004, LNCS 3057, pp. 23–38, 2004.

We take a view of objects in the spirit of Smalltalk [GR83,Liu96]; we suggest to conceptualize an object as a little intelligent being capable of performing actions according to the messages it receives; we suggest not to think of an object as a record of fields and methods in this paper. More concretely, we are to implement an object as a function that interprets messages received by the object. We first present a brief outline of this idea. Let MSG be a guarded recursive datatype constructor that takes a type τ to form a message type $MSG(\tau)$. We require that MSG be extensible (like the exception type in ML). Intuitively, an object is expected to return a value of type τ after receiving a message of type $MSG(\tau)$. Therefore, we assign an object the following type OBJ:

$$OBJ = \forall \alpha. MSG(\alpha) \to \alpha$$

Suppose that we have declared through some syntax that $MSGgetfst$, $MSGgetsnd$, $MSGsetfst$ and $MSGsetsnd$ are message constructors of the following types,

$$
\begin{array}{llll}
MSGgetfst & : & MSG(int) & \qquad MSGsetfst \quad : \quad int \to MSG(\mathbf{1}) \\
MSGgetsnd & : & MSG(int) & \qquad MSGsetsnd \quad : \quad int \to MSG(\mathbf{1})
\end{array}
$$

where $\mathbf{1}$ stands for the unit type.[1] We can now implement integer pairs as follows in a message-passing style:

```
fun newIntPair x y = let
  val xref = ref x and yref = ref y
  fun dispatch msg =
    case msg of
      | MSGgetfst => !xref
      | MSGgetsnd => !yref
      | MSGsetfst x' => (xref := x')
      | MSGsetsnd y' => (yref := y')
      | _ => raise UnknownMessage
in dispatch end
withtype int -> int -> OBJ
```

The above program is written in the syntax of ATS, a functional programming language we are developing that is equipped with a type system rooted in the framework *Applied Type System* [Xi03,Xi04]. The syntax should be easily accessible for those who are familiar with the syntax of Standard ML [MTHM97]. The withtype clause in the program is a type annotation that assigns the type $int \to int \to OBJ$ to the defined function $newIntPair$.[2] Given integers x and y, we can form an integer pair object $anIntPair$ by calling $newIntPair(x)(y)$; we can then send the message $MSGgetfst$ to the object to obtain its first component:

---

[1] Note that it is solely for illustration purpose that we use the prefix MSG in the name of each message constructor.

[2] The reason for $newIntPair$ being well-typed can be found in our work on guarded recursive datatypes [XCC03].

$anIntPair(MSGgetfst)$; we can also reset its first component to x' by sending the message $MSGsetfst(x')$ to the object: $anIntPair(MSGsetfst(x'))$; operations on the second component of the object can be performed similarly. Note that an exception is raised at run-time if the object $anIntPair$ cannot interpret a message sent to it.

Obviously, there exist some serious problems with the above approach to implementing objects. Since every object is currently assigned the type OBJ, we cannot use types to differentiate objects. For instance, suppose that $MSGfoo$ is some declared message constructor of the type $MSG(1)$; then $anIntPair(MSGfoo)$ is well-typed, but its execution leads to an uncaught exception $UnknownMessage$ at run-time. This is clearly undesirable: $anIntPair(MSGfoo)$ should have been rejected at compile-time as an ill-typed expression. We address this problem by providing the type constructor MSG with additional parameter. Given a type τ and a class C, $MSG(C, \tau)$ is now a type; the intuition is that a message of the type $MSG(C, \tau)$ should only be sent to objects in the class C, to which we assign the type $OBJ(C)$ defined as follows:

$$OBJ(C) = \forall \alpha.MSG(C, \alpha) \to \alpha$$

First and foremost, we emphasize that a class is *not* a type; it is really a tag used to differentiate messages and objects. For instance, we may declare a class ip and associate it with the following message constructors of the given types:

$MSGgetfst$	:	$MSG(ip, int)$	$MSGgetsnd$	:	$MSG(ip, int)$
$MSGsetfst$	:	$int \to MSG(ip, 1)$	$MSGsetsnd$	:	$int \to MSG(ip, 1)$

The type $int \to int \to OBJ(ip)$ can now be assigned to the function $newIntPair$; then $anIntPair$ has the type $OBJ(ip)$, and therefore $anIntPair(MSGfoo)$ becomes ill-typed if $MSGfoo$ has a type $MSG(C, 1)$ for some class C that is different from ip.

We refer the reader to [XCC03,Xi02] for further details on this typeful approach to OOP (with single inheritance). The treatment of multiple inheritance in this paper bears a great deal of similarity to the treatment of single inheritance in [XCC03,Xi02], though there are also some substantial differences involved.

In order to handle multiple inheritance, we are to treat a path from a (super)class to a (sub)class as a first-class value, and we use $PTH(C_1, C_2)$ as the type for paths from the (super)class C_1 to the (sub)class C_2. The message type constructor MSG is to take three parameters C_0, C and τ to form a type $MSG(C_0, C, \tau)$; an object tagged by C is expected to return a value of type τ after receiving a message of type $MSG(C_0, C, \tau)$, where C_0 indicates the original class in which the message constructor that constructs this message is declared. With this view, the type $OBJ(C)$ for objects tagged by C can now be defined as follows:

$$OBJ(C) = \forall c_0 : cls.\forall \alpha : type.PTH(c_0, C) \to MSG(c_0, C, \alpha) \to \alpha$$

where cls is the sort for class tags.

In the rest of the paper, we are to describe an implementation of programming objects based on the above idea that supports (a form of) multiple inheritance. The primary contribution of the paper lies in a simple and general account for multiple inheritance in a typeful setting, which we claim to be entirely novel. We emphasize that the approach to implementing multiple inheritance as is presented in this paper is intended to serve as a reference for more realistic implementations in future and thus should not be judged in terms of efficiency.

2   Implementing Multiple Inheritance

In this section, we describe a typeful approach to implementing objects that supports multiple inheritance. The presented code is written in the concrete syntax of ATS, which is rather close to the syntax of SML [MTHM97]. We think that the most effective strategy to understand this implementation is to first understand the various types involved in it. Therefore, our description of this implementation is largely guided by these types.

2.1   Run-Time Class Tags

As mentioned previously, there is a sort *cls* for class tags. Let us assume that we have class tags *obj* (for object class), *eq* (for equality class), *ip* (for integer pair class), *cip* (for colored integer pair class), etc. Let us further assume that *cip* is an immediate subclass of *ip*, which is an immediate subclass of both *obj* and *eq*. The following diagram illustrates this class structure:

The class tags here should really be called compile-time or static class tags as they only exist in the type system (of ATS) and are not available at run-time. To address the need for accessing class tags at run-time, we declare a (guarded) datatype *CLS* as follows:

```
datatype ClS (cls) =
   | CLSobj (obj) | CLSeq (eq) | CLSip (ip) | CLScip (cip) | ...
```

Intuitively, for each static class tag C, $CLS(C)$ is a singleton type that contains a value $\underline{C}$ corresponding to C. The above declaration simple means that for C to be *obj*, *eq*, *ip*, *cip*, $\underline{C}$ are *CLSobj*, *CLSeq*, *CLSip*, *CLScip*, respectively. We use ... in the declaration of *CLS* to indicate that *CLS* is extensible (like the exception type *exn* in SML).

2.2 Paths

We need to treat paths from (super)classes to (sub)classes as first-class values. For this need, we declare a (guarded) datatype PTH as follows, which takes two (static) class tags C_1 and C_2 to form a type $PTH(C_1, C_2)$.

```
datatype PTH (cls, cls) =
  | {c:cls} PTHend (c, c) of CLS (c)
  | {c1:cls,c2:cls,c3:cls}
      PTHcons (c1, c3) of (ClS (c1), PTH (c2, c3))
```

The syntax indicates that there are two value constructors $PTHend$ and $PTHcons$ associated with PTH, which are given the following types:

$$PTHend \quad : \quad \forall c : cls. CLS(c) \rightarrow PTH(c, c)$$
$$PTHcons \quad : \quad \forall c_1 : cls. \forall c_2 : cls. \forall c_3 : cls. (CLS(c_1), PTH(c_2, c_3)) \rightarrow PTH(c_1, c_3)$$

Given $\underline{C}_1, \ldots, \underline{C}_n$ for $n \geq 1$, we write $[\underline{C}_1, \ldots, \underline{C}_n]$ for $PTHcons(\underline{C}_1, [\underline{C}_2, \ldots, \underline{C}_n])$ if $n \geq 2$, or for $PTHend[\underline{C}_n]$ if $n = 1$. As an example, $[CLSobj, CLSip, CLScip]$, which stands for $PTHcons(CLSobj, PTHcons(CLSip, PTHend(CLScip)))$, is a path from class obj to cip.

Clearly, one may also form a value like $[CLScip, CLSip, CLSobj]$, which does not correspond to any legal path. It is possible to declare the datatype constructor PTH in a more involved manner so that only values representing legal paths can be formed. However, such a declaration would significantly complicate the presentation of the paper and is thus not pursued here. In the following presentation, we simply assume that only values representing legal paths are ever to be formed. It will soon be clear that the main use of a path is to direct method lookup when an object tries to interpret a received message. In practice, we anticipate that a overwhelming majority of paths in a program can be automatically constructed by a compiler. However, the construction of a path may need certain interaction from a programmer when there is some ambiguity involved, i.e., when there are more than one paths from a given (super)class to a (sub)class.

2.3 Regular Objects and Temporary Objects

We are to encounter two forms of objects: regular objects (or just objects) and temporary objects. Given a static class tag C, $OBJ(C)$ is the type for regular objects in class C. In the concrete syntax of ATS, OBJ is defined as follows,

```
typedef OBJ (c:cls) =
  {c0:cls,a:type} PTH (c0,c) -> MSG(c0,c,a) -> a
```

which means that $OBJ(C)$ is just a shorthand for the following type:

$$\forall c_0 : cls. \forall \alpha : type. PTH(c_0, C) \rightarrow MSG(c_0, C, \alpha) \rightarrow \alpha$$

Therefore, a regular object o in class C takes a path from C_0 to C for some class tag C_0 and a message of type $MSG(C_0, C, \tau)$ for some type τ, and is then expected to return a value of type τ.

There is another form of objects that are only constructed during run-time, and we use the name *temporary objects* for them. Given a static class tag C, we use $OBJ_0(C)$ as the type for temporary objects in class C, where OBJ_0 is defined as follows,

```
typedef OBJ0 (c:cls) = {c0:cls,a:type} MSG(c0,c,a) -> a
```

i.e., $OBJ_0(C)$ stands for the type $\forall c_0 : cls.\forall \alpha : type.MSG(c_0, C, \alpha) \to \alpha$. Given a temporary object o in class C, it takes a message of type $MSG(C_0, C, \tau)$ for some static class tag C_0 and type τ, and then is expected to return a value of type τ. A temporary object always does method lookup in a fixed manner, and one may think that a path is already built into a temporary object in some special manner. However, we emphasize that a temporary object is in general *not* constructed by applying a regular object to a given path.

2.4   Wrapper Functions

The notion of wrapper functions naturally occurs in the process of implementing a mechanism to support inheritance. A wrapper function (or just a wrapper, for short) for a class C is assigned the type $WRP(C)$, where WRP is defined as follows,

```
typedef WRP(c:cls) = OBJ(c) -> OBJ0(c)
```

i.e., $WRP(C)$ stands for the type $OBJ(C) \to OBJ_0(C)$ for each static class tag C. Therefore, a wrapper is a function that turns a regular object in class C into a temporary object in class C. The typical scenario in which a wrapper function is called can be described as follows: Given a regular object o, a path pth and a message msg, let us apply o to pth and msg; if the object o could not interpret the message msg directly, a wrapper function wrp is to be constructed according to the path pth and then be applied to the object o to form a temporary object o', to which the message msg is then subsequently passed.

2.5   Super Functions

As in the case of single inheritance [XCC03], the notion of super functions also plays a key role in implementing multiple inheritance. For each class C, there is a super function associated with C. In the following presentation, we use *SUPERobj*, *SUPEReq*, *SUPERip* and *SUPERcip* to name the super functions associated with the classes *obj*, *eq*, *ip* and *cip*, respectively. Given a static class tag C_0, the super function associated with C_0 is assigned the type $SUPER(C_0)$, which is a shorthand for the following type:

$$\forall c : cls.PTH(C_0, c) \to WRP(c) \to WRP(c)$$

```
fun SUPERobj pth wrp obj =
  let
      fun dispatch msg =
        case msg of
          | MSGcopy => obj
          | _ => wrp obj msg
      withtype {c0:cls,c:cls,a:type} MSG (c0,c,a) -> a
  in
      dispatch (* a temporary object *)
  end
withtype {c:cls} PTH (obj,c) -> WRP(c) -> WRP (c)

fun SUPEReq pth wrp obj =
  let
      fun dispatch msg =
        case msg of
          | MSGeq (obj') => not (obj pth (MSGneq (obj')))
          | MSGneq (obj') => not (obj pth (MSGeq (obj')))
          | _ => wrp obj msg
    in
      dispatch (* a temporary object *)
    end
withtype {c:cls} PTH (eq,c) -> WRP(c) -> WRP (c)

fun SUPERip pth wrp obj =
  let
      fun dispatch msg =
        case msg of
          | MSGswap =>
              let
                  val fst = obj pth MSGgetfst
                  and snd = obj pth MSGgetsnd
              in
                  (obj pth (MSGsetfst snd); obj pth (MSGsetsnd fst))
              end

          | MSGeq (other) =>
            if !xref = other [CLSip] (MSGgetfst) then
              if !yref = other [CLScip] (MSGgetsnd) then true
              else false
            else false

          | _ => wrp obj msg
  in
      dispatch (* a temporary object *)
  end
withtype {c:cls} PTH (ip,c) -> WRP(c) -> WRP (c)

fun SUPERcip pth wrp obj = wrp obj
withtype {c:cls} PTH (cip,c) -> WRP(c) -> WRP (c)
```

Fig. 1. The definition of some super functions

In Figure 1, the super functions *SUPERobj, SUPEReq, SUPERip* and *SUPERcip* are implemented, where the involved message constructors are of the following types:

$$
\begin{aligned}
MSGcopy &: \quad \forall c : cls.MSG(obj, c, OBJ(c)) \\
MSGeq &: \quad \forall c : cls.OBJ(c) \to MSG(eq, c, bool) \\
MSGneq &: \quad \forall c : cls.OBJ(c) \to MSG(neq, c, bool) \\
MSGgetfst &: \quad \forall c : cls.MSG(ip, c, int) \\
MSGgetsnd &: \quad \forall c : cls.MSG(ip, c, int) \\
MSGsetfst &: \quad \forall c : cls.int \to MSG(ip, c, 1) \\
MSGsetsnd &: \quad \forall c : cls.int \to MSG(ip, c, 1) \\
MSGswap &: \quad \forall c : cls.MSG(ip, c, 1)
\end{aligned}
$$

We have previously already explained the meaning of these message constructors except for *MSGneq* and *MSGswap*; sending $MSGneq(o')$ to an object o means to compare whether o and o' are not equal (according to some specific interpretation of the message $MSGneq(o)$ by o'); sending *MSGswap* to an (integer pair) object o is to swap the first and the second components in o.

The use of super functions in implementing inheritance is somewhat subtle, and we present below a rather informal explanation on this point. Let $super_C$ be the super function associated with some class C. Suppose o is an object of type $OBJ(C_1)$ for some class tag C_1, m a message of type $MSG(C_0, C_1, \tau)$ for some class tag C_0 and type τ, and p a path from C_0 to C_1 of the form $p_a {+\!\!+} [C] {+\!\!+} p_b$, i.e., p_a is a prefix of p, p_b is a suffix of p and C is on the path p. Then the call $o(p)(m)$ is essentially evaluated as follows: A method in o for interpreting m is invoked if it is implemented; Otherwise, the process to look for a method to interpret m is first done along the path p_b; now suppose this process of method lookup fails to find a proper method to interpret m; at this point, the super function $super_C$ associated with the class C is called on the path p and some wrapper function w (determined by the path p_a) to return another wrapper function, which is then applied to o to form a temporary object to interpret the message m; if the temporary object cannot interpret m, then w is applied to o to form yet another temporary object to interpret m. The picture is to become more clear later once we introduce an example.

2.6   Chaining Super Functions Together

Let *super* be the function that takes a run-time class tag $\underline{C}$ to return the super function associated with C. Therefore, *super* can be assigned the following type:

$$\forall c : cls.CLS(c) \to SUPER(C)$$

The function *path2wrapper* is implemented in Figure 2, which turns a path into a wrapper.

Let $pth = [\underline{C}_1, \dots, \underline{C}_n]$ be a path from (super)class C_1 to (sub)class C_n, and $pth_i = [\underline{C}_i, \dots, \underline{C}_n]$ for $i = 1, \dots, n$, and $wrp_1 = super(\underline{C}_1)(pth_1)(nullWrapper)$ and $wrp_{i+1} = super(\underline{C}_{i+1})(pth_{i+1})(wrp_i)$ for $1 \le i < n$. Then $path2wrapper(pth)$

```
fun nullWrapper (obj) = lam msg => raise UnknownMessage
withtype {c:cls} OBJ (c) -> OBJO (c)

fun path2wrapper pth = let
  fun aux pth wrp =
    case pth of
      | PTHend (c) => super c pth wrp
      | PTHcons (c, pth') => aux pth' (super c pth wrp)
  withtype {c0:cls,c:cls} PTH (c0, c) -> WRP (c) -> WRP (c)
in aux pth nullWrapper end
withtype {c0:cls,c:cls} PTH (c0, c) -> WRP (c)
```

Fig. 2. A function for chaining super functions together

returns the wrapper function wrp_n. For instance, we have

$$path2wrapper\ [CLSobj, CLSip, CLScip] =$$
$$SUPERcip\ [CLScip]$$
$$(SUPERip\ [CLSip, CLScip]$$
$$(SUPERobj\ [CLSobj, CLSip, CLScip]\ nullWrapper))$$

2.7   Constructing Objects

We now present a function *newIntPair* in Figure 3, which takes two integers to create an integer pair object.

```
fun newIntPair x y = let
  val xref = ref x and yref = ref y
  fun dispatch pth msg =
    case msg of
      | MSGgetfst => !xref
      | MSGgetsnd => !yref
      | MSGsetfst x' => (xref := x')
      | MSGsetsnd y' => (yref := y')
      | MSGcopy => newIntPair (!xref) (!yref)
      | _ => path2wrapper pth dispatch msg
in dispatch end
withtype int -> int -> OBJ (ip)
```

Fig. 3. A function for constructing integer pair objects

Given two integer pair objects o_1 and o_2, we now explain how method lookup is handled after o_1 receives the message $MSGneq(o_2)$. Formally, we need to evaluate $o_1\ [CLSeq, CLSip]\ (MSGneq(o_2))$ as the message constructor originates with the class *eq*. By inspecting the body of the function *newIntPair*, we see the need for evaluating the following expression

$$path2wrapper\ [CLSeq, CLSip]\ (o_1)\ (MSGneq(o_2))$$

as there is no code directly implemented for interpreting the message $MSGneq(o_2)$. Let us assume:

$$wrp_1 = SUPEReq\ [CLSeq, CLSip]\ nullWrapper$$
$$wrp_2 = SUPERip\ [CLSip]\ wrp_1$$

and we have $path2wrapper\ [CLSeq, CLSip] = wrp_2$. So we are to evaluate the expression $wrp_2\ o_1\ (MSGneq(o_2))$. By inspecting the body of the function *SUPERip*, we need to evaluate the following expression,

$$wrp_1\ o_1\ (MSGneq(o_2))$$

and by inspecting the body of the function *SUPEReq*, we then need to evaluate the following expression:

$$not(o_1\ [CLSeq, CLSip]\ (MSGeq(o_2)))$$

There is no code in the body of *newIntPair* for handling the $MSGeq(o_2)$ directly; instead, the message is finally to be handled by some relevant code in the body of *SUPERip*.

2.8   Syntactic Support for OOP

We now outline some syntax specially designed to facilitate object-oriented programming in ATS. We use the following syntax:

```
class obj {
  superclass: /* none */
  message MSGcopy (OBJ (myclass))
  method MSGcopy = myself
} // end of class obj
```

to introduce a class tag *obj* and a message constructor *MSGcopy* of the type $\forall c : cls.MSG(obj, c, OBJ(c))$. Please note the special use of *myclass* and *myself*: the former is a class tag and the latter is an object of the type $OBJ(myclass)$ that is supposed to receive the message. In general, a line as follows:

$$message\ MSGfoo\ (\tau)\ of\ (\tau_1, \ldots, \tau_n)$$

in the declaration of some class C introduces a message constructor *MSGfoo* of the type $\forall myclass : cls.(\tau_1, \ldots, \tau_n) \rightarrow MSG(C, myclass, \tau)$.

The super function associated with the class tag *obj*, which we refer to as *SUPERobj*, is also introduced automatically through the above syntax: the line

```
class ip {
  superclass: obj, eq // ip is a subclass of both obj and eq

  message MSGgetfst (int)
  message MSGsetfst (unit) of int
  message MSGgetsnd (int)
  message MSGsetsnd (unit) of int
  message MSGswap (unit)

  method MSGswap: unit =
    let
        val x = myself @ MSGgetfst and y = myself @ MSGgetsnd
    in
        myself @ (MSGsetfst y); myself @ (MSGsetsnd x)
    end

  method MSGeq (other): bool =
    if myself @ MSGgetfst = other @ MSGgetfst then
      if myself @ MSGgetsnd = other @ MSGgetsnd then else false
    else false

} // end: class ip

// newIntPair: int -> int -> OBJ (ip)

object newIntPair (x: int) (y: int): ip = {

  val xref = ref x and yref = ref y

  method MSGgetfst = !xref
  method MSGsetfst (x') = (xref := x)
  method MSGgetsnd = !yref
  method MSGsetfst (y') = (yref := y)
  method MSGcopy = newIntPair (!xref) (!yref)

} // end: object newIntPair
```

Fig. 4. Some code written in the special syntax for OOP

method MSGcopy = myself translates into the clause *MSGcopy ⇒ obj* in the definition of *SUPERobj* in Figure 1

The code in Figure 4 declares a class *ip* and some message constructors associated with the class *ip*, and then implements a function *newIntPair* for creating objects in the class *ip*. We write *obj @ msg* to mean sending the message *msg* to the object *obj*, which translates into *obj* (*pth*) (*msg*) for some path *pth* to be constructed by the compiler.[3] It should be straightforward to relate the code in Figure 4 to the code for the super function *SUPERip* in Figure 1 and the code for the function *newIntPair* in Figure 3.

---

[3] We plan to require the programmer to provide adequate information if there is ambiguity in constructing such a path.

2.9   Parametric Polymorphism

There is an immediate need for classes that parametrize over types. For instance, we may want to generalize the monomorphic function *newIntPair* to a polymorphic function *newPair* that can take values x and y of any types to create an object representing the pair whose first and second components are x and y, respectively. To do this, we first introduce a constant *pair* that takes two types τ_1 and τ_2 to form a class tag $pair(\tau_1, \tau_2)$, and then introduce a constructor *CLSpair* assigned the given type:

$$CLSpair \quad : \quad \forall \alpha : type. \forall \beta : type. CLS(pair(\alpha, \beta))$$

and then assume the message constructors *MSGgetfst*, *MSGsetfst*, *MSGgetsnd*, *MSGsetsnd* are given the following types:

$$
\begin{aligned}
MSGgetfst \quad &: \quad \forall \alpha : type. \forall \beta : type. \forall c : cls. MSG(pair(\alpha, \beta), c, \alpha) \\
MSGsetfst \quad &: \quad \forall \alpha : type. \forall \beta : type. \forall c : cls. \alpha \to MSG(pair(\alpha, \beta), c, \mathbf{1}) \\
MSGgetsnd \quad &: \quad \forall \alpha : type. \forall \beta : type. \forall c : cls. MSG(pair(\alpha, \beta), c, \beta) \\
MSGsetsnd \quad &: \quad \forall \alpha : type. \forall \beta : type. \forall c : cls. \beta \to MSG(pair(\alpha, \beta), c, \mathbf{1})
\end{aligned}
$$

All of this is handled by the following syntax:

```
class pair (a:type, b:type) = {
  superclass: obj

  message MSGgetfst (a)
  message MSGsetfst (unit) of a
  message MSGgetfst (b)
  message MSGsetfst (unit) of b
}
```

A function *newPair* for creating pair objects can then be properly implemented, which is assigned the type $\forall \alpha : type. \forall \beta : type. \alpha \to \beta \to OBJ(pair(\alpha, \beta))$:

```
object newPair{a:type, b:type} (x: a) (y: b): pair (a, b) = {
  ...
}
```

3   Facilitating Code Sharing

There is a great deal of code redundancy in the libraries of functional languages such as SML and Objective Caml as there is little code sharing across difference data structures. For instance, functions such as *map, foldLeft, foldRight* are defined repeatedly for lists and arrays. This issue is already studied in the context of generic programming [Hin00] and polytypic programming [JJ97], but the proposed solutions are not applicable to data structures that are given abstract types.

We now use a (contrived) example to outline an approach that can effectively address the issue of code sharing across difference data structures even when the data structures are given abstract types. Suppose that we declare a parameterized class *IsList* as follows:

```
class IsList (elt:type, lst:type) {
  superclass: ...
  message nil (lst)
  message cons ((elt, lst) -> lst)
  message uncons (lst -> (elt, lst))
  message isEmpty (lst -> bool)

  message foreach ((elt -> unit, lst) -> unit)
  method foreach = ...
    /* can be defined in terms of isEmpty and uncons */
  ...
}
```

Intuitively, an object of type $OBJ(IsList(\tau_1, \tau_2))$ can be thought of as a term that proves a value of type τ_2 can be treated as a list in which each element is of type τ_1. Now let us construct an object *intIsList1* of type $OBJ(IsList(unit, int))$ as follows:

```
object intIsList1: IsList (unit, int) = {
  method nil = 0
  method isEmpty (n) = (n == 0)
  method cons (_, n) = n + 1
  method uncons (n) =
    if n > 0 then ((), n - 1) else raise EmptyList
}
```

Then *intIsList1* @ *foreach* returns a function of type $(unit \rightarrow unit, int)$; applying this function to f and n means executing $f()$ for n times, where f is assumed to be a function of type $unit \rightarrow unit$ and n a natural number. Now let us construct another object *intIsList2* of type $OBJ(IsList(int, int))$ as follows:

```
object intIsList2: IsList (int, int) = {
  method nil = 0
  method isEmpty (n) = (n == 0)
  method cons (_, n) = n + 1
  method uncons (n) =
    if n > 0 then (n, n - 1) else raise EmptyList
}
```

Then *intIsList2* @ *foreach* returns a function of type $(int \rightarrow unit, int)$; applying this function to f and n means executing $f(n), f(n - 1), \ldots, f(1)$, where f is assumed to be a function of type $int \rightarrow unit$ and n a natural number. Now let us construct another object *arrayIsList* as follows,

```
object arrayIsList{elt:type} (A: array(elt)): IsList (elt,int) = {
  method nil = 0
  method isEmpty (n) = (n == 0)
  method cons (x, n) = (update (A, n, x); n + 1)
  method uncons (n) = (sub (A, n - 1), n - 1)
}
```

where *sub* and *update* are the usual subscripting and updating functions on arrays. Let A be an array of type $array(\tau)$. Then $arrayIsList(A)$ @ *foreach* returns a function of type $(\tau \to unit, int)$; applying this function to f and n means executing $f(v_{n-1}), f(v_{n-2}), \ldots, f(v_0)$, where we assume that f is a function of type $\tau \to unit$, n is a natural number less than or equal to the size of A, and $v_0, \ldots, v_{n-1}$ are the values stored in A, from cell 0 to cell $n - 1$.

Though this is an oversimplified example, the point made is clear: The code for *foreach* in the class *IsList* is reused repeatedly. Actually, the code for all the functions implemented in the class *IsList* in terms of *nil*, *isEmpty*, *cons*, and *uncons* can be reused repeatedly. Note that it is difficult to make this approach to code sharing available in OOP languages such as Java as it requires some essential use of parametric polymorphism. On the other hand, the approach bears a great deal of resemblance to the notion of type classes in Haskell [HHJW96, P+99]. However, the kind of inheritance mechanism supported by type classes is rather limited when compared to our approach. One may argue that what we have achieved here can also be achieved by using functors in SML. This, however, is not the case. First, functors are not first-class values and thus are not available at run-time. But more importantly, functors simply do not support code inheritance, a vital component in OOP. For the sake of space limitation, we could not show the use of inheritance in the above example, but the need for inheritance in practice is ubiquitous in practice. Please see some on-line examples [SX04].

4   Related Work and Conclusion

Multiple inheritance is supported in many object-oriented programming languages such as Eiffel and C++. In Eiffel, a straightforward approach is taken to resolve method dispatching conflicts that may occur due to multiple inheritance: If a class has multiple superclasses, each method in the class must determine statically at compile-time from which superclass it should inherit code. This approach, though simple, makes multiple inheritance in Eiffel rather limited. For instance, it cannot accommodate a scenario in which a method needs to be inherited from different superclasses according to where the method is actually called. When compared to Eiffel, C++ offers a more flexible approach to resolving method dispatching conflicts as the programmer can supply explicit annotation at method invocation sites to indicate how such conflicts should be resolved. However, it is still required in C++ that method dispatching conflicts be resolve statically at compile-time. With paths being first-class values, our approach to multiple inheritance can actually address the need for resolving method dispatching conflicts at run-time.

In some early studies on multiple inheritance in a typed setting [Wan89, Car88], the essential idea is to model inheritance relation by a subtyping relation on record types and multiple inheritance then corresponds to the situation where one record extends multiple records. However, this idea is unable to address the crucial issue of dynamic method dispatching, which is indispensable if abstract methods are to be supported. In [CP96], an approach to encoding objects is presented that supports both dynamic method dispatching and a restricted form of multiple inheritance (like that in Eiffel). This rather involved approach is based on higher-order intersection types and its interaction with other type features such as recursive types and parametric polymorphism remains unclear.

In the literature, most of existing approaches to typed OOP take the view of *objects as records*. They are often centered around the type system $F^\omega_\leq$ or its variants and use structural subtyping to support inheritance [BCP99,Bru02]. On the other hand, the realistic object-oriented programming languages that we know all rely on nominal subtyping. In this paper, we have developed a typeful approach to OOP that supports a form of multiple inheritance. This approach, which is based on the notion of guarded recursive datatypes [XCC03], does not use structural subtyping to model inheritance and is largely in line with the current practice of OOP.

References

[BCP99]   Kim B. Bruce, Luca Cardelli, and Benjamin Pierce. Comparing Object Encodings. *Information and Computation*, 155:108–133, 1999.

[Bru02]   Kim B. Bruce. *Foundations of Object-Oriented Languages*. The MIT Press, Cambridge, MA, 2002. xx+384 pp.

[Car88]   Luca Cardelli. A semantics of multiple inheritance. *Information and Computation*, 76(2–3):138–164, February–March 1988.

[CP96]   Adriana B. Compagnoni and Benjamin C. Pierce. Higher-Order Intersection Types and Multiple Inheritance. *Mathematical Structures in Computer Science*, 6(5):469–501, 1996.

[GR83]   A. Goldenberg and D. Robson. *Smalltalk-80: The Language and Its Implementation*. Addison Wesley, 1983.

[HHJW96]   Cordelia V. Hall, Kevin Hammond, Simon L. Peyton Jones, and Philip L. Wadler. Type Classes in Haskell. *ACM Transactions on Programming Languages and Systems*, 18(2):109–138, March 1996.

[Hin00]   Ralf Hinze. A New Approach to Generic Functional Programming. In *Proceedings of 27th Annual ACM SIGPLAN Symposium on Principles of Programming Languages (POPL '00)*, pages 119–132. Boston, 2000.

[JJ97]   P Jansson and J. Jeuring. PolyP - Polytypic programming language extension. In *Proceedings of 24th ACM Symposium on Principles of Programming Languages (POPL '97)*, pages 470–482. Paris, France, 1997.

[Liu96]   Chamond Liu. *Smalltalk, Objects, and Design*. Manning Publications Co., Greenwich, CT 06830, 1996. ISBN 1-884777-27-9 (hc). x+289 pp.

[MTHM97]   Robin Milner, Mads Tofte, Robert W. Harper, and D. MacQueen. *The Definition of Standard ML (Revised)*.   MIT Press, Cambridge, Massachusetts, 1997. ISBN 0-262-63181-4.

[P⁺ 99]   Simon Peyton Jones et al. Haskell 98 – A non-strict, purely functional language. Available at
`http://www.haskell.org/onlinereport/`, February 1999.

[SX04]   Rui Shi and Hongwei Xi. Some Examples of Structuring Libraries with Parametrized Classes, February 2004. Available at:
`http://www.cs.bu.edu/~hwxi/ATS/lib`.

[Wan89]   Mitchell Wand. Type Inference for Record Concatenation and Multiple Inheritance. In *Proceedings of Fourth IEEE Symposium on Logic in Computer Science*, pages 92–97. Pacific Grove, California, 1989.

[XCC03]   Hongwei Xi, Chiyan Chen, and Gang Chen. Guarded Recursive Datatype Constructors. In *Proceedings of the 30th ACM SIGPLAN Symposium on Principles of Programming Languages*, pages 224–235. New Orleans, January 2003.

[Xi02]   Hongwei Xi. Unifying Object-Oriented Programming with Typed Functional Programming. In *Proceedings of ASIAN Symposium on Partial Evaluation and Semantics-Based Program Manipulation (ASIA-PEPM '02)*, pages 117–125. Aizu-Wakamatsu, Japan, September 2002.

[Xi03]   Hongwei Xi. Applied Type System, July 2003. Available at:
`http://www.cs.bu.edu/~hwxi/ATS`.

[Xi04]   Hongwei Xi. Applied Type System (extended abstract). In *post-workshop Proceedings of TYPES 2003*. Springer-Verlag LNCS, February 2004. (to appear).

Compositional Model-Views with Generic Graphical User Interfaces

Peter Achten, Marko van Eekelen, and Rinus Plasmeijer

Department of Software Technology, University of Nijmegen,
Toernooiveld 1, 6525 ED Nijmegen, The Netherlands
Telephone: +31 24 365 2644, Fax: +31 24 365 2525,
{peter88,marko,rinus}@cs.kun.nl

Abstract. Creating GUI programs is hard even for prototyping purposes. Using the model-view paradigm makes it somewhat simpler since the model-view paradigm dictates that the model contains no GUI programming, as this is done by the views. Still, a lot of GUI programming is needed to implement the views.

We present a new method for constructing GUI applications that fits well in the model-view paradigm. Novel in our approach is that the views also contain no actual GUI programming. Instead, views are constructed in a fully compositional way by defining a model of the view. We use a technique developed earlier to generate the GUI part. We show how the method supports flexibility, compositionality and incremental change by introducing abstract components in the view models.

Keywords: Graphical User Interfaces, Generic and Functional Programming.

1 Introduction

The design of high quality user interfaces is an iterative process that has a great demand for rapid prototyping and flexible incremental change of versions of the UI under construction [14]. In practice, writing effective Graphical User Interfaces (GUI) with programming toolkits for even small programs (500 lines of code) is a complicated task. This is caused by two major obstacles:

A. The programmer needs to be skilled in the API of the used library and the tools that help him in his task (such as resource editors).
B. GUI programs tend to tie up the logic of the application with the realization of its user interface.

In this paper we show how contemporary functional language techniques using generic programming and strong type system features (existential types and rank-2 polymorphism) can be employed to obtain a programming toolkit that eliminates these obstacles. Even though the used techniques are advanced, the resulting API of this toolkit is concise, and the method-of-use is not hard, as will be demonstrated in this paper.

B. Jayaraman (Ed.): PADL 2004, LNCS 3057, pp. 39–55, 2004.

The system described in this paper fits well in the well-known *model-view* paradigm [12], introduced by Trygve Reenskaug in the language Smalltalk (the paradigm was then named the *model-view-controller* paradigm). In our approach the data type plays the *model* role, and the *views* are derived automatically from the generic decomposition of values of that type. The *controller* role is dealt with by both the automatically derived communication infrastructure and the views (as they need to handle user actions).

In our method we will eliminate obstacle **A** by using *Graphical Editor Components* [3]. A GEC_m is an interactive editor (the *view*) to edit values of arbitrary data type m (the *model*) in a type-safe way. Using generic programming techniques, the view is automatically derived from the type m of the model. Hence, the programmer does not need to know about GUIs. One might gather that this is also sufficient to eliminate obstacle **B**, but this is not the case. The obstacle is still present in two ways:

B.1. The type of the model not only represents the data that is used by the application logic, but at the same time it represents the information that is needed to automatically generate the intended view. In this sense, the view is not well separated from the model.

B.2. A different editor can only be specified by defining a different type. Consequently, changing views incrementally implies changing types which in its turn implies further changes reducing flexibility.

In this paper, **B.1** is dealt with by imposing a strict separation of concerns of the model. Instead of one model, the programmer defines a *data model and a view model* and their relation in the form of two conversion functions. Then, the *GEC* system can be used to derive the intended GUI from the view model. **B.2** is dealt with by introducing *abstract* views (*AGEC*s) that can be used as components of the view model. Due to the power of abstraction *AGEC*s are fully compositional.

The resulting system encourages an incremental methodology of programming GUIs. For rapid prototyping purposes, one starts with identical types for the data model and view model and the trivial *identity* transformation functions. Then, one can start to change views incrementally by changing instances of abstract component views in the view model.

The language that we have used is Clean, but it should be noted that the approach is applicable to other functional languages (with other I/O libraries) that support the above mentioned features as well, for instance Generic Haskell [9]. In principle, this can be done with any I/O library but using the Haskell Object I/O library [2,5] will minimize the effort of porting the system.

This paper is organized as follows. In Sect. 2 we recapitulate the concept of a *GEC*. Using these *GEC*s as basic building blocks, we show in Sect. 3 how we eliminate obstacles **B.1** and **B.2**, giving us the intended system. We present related work in Sect. 4 and conclude and point to future work in Sect. 5.

2   The Concept of a Graphical Editor Component

In [3] we introduced the concept of a Graphical Editor Component, a GEC_t. A GEC_t is an editor for values of type t. It is provided with an initial value of type t and it is guaranteed that an application user can only use the editor to create values of type t. At all times, a GEC_t contains a value of type t.

A GEC_t is generated with a *generic* function [10,4]. A generic function is a meta description on the structure of types. For any concrete type t, the compiler is able to automatically derive an instance function of this meta description for the given type. Currently, we support all Clean types, with exception of function and abstract types. The power of a generic scheme is that we obtain an editor for free for any data type. This makes the approach particularly suited for *rapid prototyping*.

Before explaining *GEC*s in more detail, we need to point out that Clean uses an explicit environment passing style [1] for I/O programming. This style is supported by the uniqueness type system [6] of Clean. Because *GEC*s are integrated with Clean Object I/O, the I/O functions that are presented in this paper are state transition functions on the program state (PSt st). The program state represents the external world of an interactive program, tailored for GUI operations. In this paper the identifier env is a value of this type. In the Haskell variant of Object I/O, a state monad is used instead. The uniqueness type system of Clean ensures single threaded use of the environment. Uniqueness type attributes that actually appear in the type signatures are not shown in this paper, in order to simplify the presentation.

2.1   Creating GEC_ts

A GEC_t is a graphical editor component to edit values of type t. These editors are *created* with the generic function gGEC. This function takes a *definition* (GECDef t env) of a GEC_t and *creates* the GEC_t object in the environment. It returns an *interface* (GECInterface t env) to that GEC_t object. It is a (PSt ps) transition function because gGEC modifies the environment.

```
generic gGEC t :: GECFunction t (PSt ps)

:: GECFunction t env :== (GECDef t env) → env →
(GECInterface t env,env)
```

A GEC_t is defined by GECDef t env which consists of two elements. The first is a value of type t which will be the initial value of the editor. The second is a call-back function of type t → env → env. The editor must know what parts of the program are interested in changes of the current value that are done by the user. This information is provided by its 'context' in the form of this call-back function. The editor uses this function when the user has changed the current value of the editor.

```
:: GECDef              t env :== (t, CallBackFunction t env)
:: CallBackFunction t env :== t → env → env
```

The GECInterface t env is a record that contains all *methods* that the 'context' can use to handle the newly created GEC_t.

```
:: GECInterface t env = { gecGetValue :: env → (t,env)
                        , gecSetValue :: t → env → env }
```

The method gecGetValue can be used to obtain the currently stored value of type t from the GEC_t component. The method gecSetValue can be used to set a new value in the corresponding GEC_t. GECInterface contains several other useful methods for a program that are not shown above. These are methods to open and close the created GEC_t and to show or hide its appearance.

The appearance of a standard GEC_t is illustrated by the following example. Assume that the programmer has defined the type Tree a as shown below and consider the following application of gGEC:

```
::  Tree a = Node (Tree a) a (Tree a) | Leaf
```

```
gGEC (Node Leaf 1 Leaf, const id) env
```

This creates a $GEC_{\text{Tree Int}}$ which displays the indicated initial value (see Fig. 1). The application user can manipulate this value in any desired order thus producing new values of type Tree Int. Each time a new value is created, the call-back function is applied automatically. The call-back function of this first example (const id) has no effect. The shape and lay-out of the tree being displayed adjusts itself automatically. Default values are generated by the editor when needed.

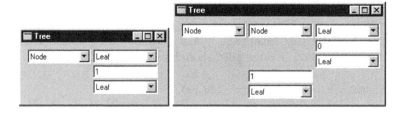

Fig. 1. The initial Graphical Editor Component for a tree of integers (Left) and a changed one (Right: with the pull-down menu the upper Leaf is changed into a Node).

2.2   Self-Adjusting Graphical Editor Components

In [3] a number of examples are given to show how graphical editor components can be combined relying on the call-back mechanism and method invocation. In this paper we only use one particular form of combination, namely that of an editor that *itself* reacts to edit operations by the user. In this way, an editor can be *self-correcting*: any property on edit values of type a that is expressable by means of a function f :: a → a can be considered to be an invariant on the editor. As an example, we can construct a *sorted-list* editor by applying the sort function to all edited values.

Self-adjusting editors can be created with the concise function selfGEC:

```
selfGEC :: (a → a) a (PSt ps) → (PSt ps) | gGEC{|a|}
selfGEC f va env = new_env
where
    (thisGEC,new_env) = gGEC (f va, λnva. thisGEC.gecSetValue (f nva)) env
```

The function selfGEC, when applied to a function f :: a → a and value va :: a, creates a GEC_a with initial value (f va). The call-back function of this GEC_a is quite remarkable. At each change of value the editor re-applies f to the new value of type a and sets it as the actual new value of *itself*. Notice that, due to the explicit environment passing style, it is trivial in Clean to connect GEC_a to itself. In Haskell's monadic I/O one needs to tie the knot with fixIO.

2.3   Customizing Graphical Editor Components

The generic definition of gGEC enables the system to derive a GEC_t for arbitrary values of type t. Occasionally one needs to deviate from the standard GEC_t because it does not suit the requirements of the particular application. In [3] we show that this can be done by defining special instances for the types that need to be customized. This has been demonstrated for the ubiquitous *counter* example. In Fig. 2 the self-correcting code (updCntr) and model type (Counter) is given. The default $GEC_{Counter}$ (shown at the bottom in Fig. 2) is a mirror image of the generic representation of the Counter model. It works as intended, and we get it for free. Unfortunately, its view is a counterexample of a good-looking counter.

```
updCntr :: Counter → Counter
updCntr (n,Up)   = (n+1,Neutral)
updCntr (n,Down) = (n-1,Neutral)
updCntr any      = any

:: Counter :== (Int,UpDown)
:: UpDown  = Up | Down | Neutral
```

Fig. 2. Two $GEC_{Counter}$s created by selfGEC updCntr (0,Neutral). The standard one (bottom) and a customized one (top).

The changes that are required to obtain the customized editor are to define new generic instances for (,) (hide the constructor and place its arguments next to each other) and UpDown (display ⬍ instead of ⬍Neutral▾).

Although in a slightly artificial way, this example demonstrates the obstacles **B.1** and **B.2** that we intend to remove. The increment/decrement behaviour that is captured with the `UpDown` type also fixes the derived GUI. The only ways to change the GUI are to use another type for this behaviour or to customize the editor for that type, as shown above.

3   Compositional Graphical Editor Components

Using the generic `gGEC` function, we automatically get an editor for any data type we invent. This is great for rapid prototyping. However, the appearance of the editor that we get for free in this way, might not resemble what we have in mind. We have explained in Sect. 2.3 that an editor can be customized for a specific type by defining a specialized instantiation of the generic function `gGEC` for that type. For certain basic types e.g. representing buttons and the like, this is exactly what we want. We also want to be able to create new editors from existing ones in a compositional way. Editors are automatically generated given a concrete type and a value of that type. The only way we can change this is by defining specialized editors for certain types. We need to invent a new way to realize abstraction and composition based on this specialization mechanism. In the following sections we show step by step how this can be accomplished.

First, we show in Sect. 3.1 how a program can be split such that a clear separation can be made between editor dependent and editor independent code. This makes it possible to choose any editor just by making changes to the editor dependent code, while we never have to make any changes to the editor independent code. Next, in Sect. 3.2 we show how to construct self-contained editors that take care of their own update and conversion behaviour. Finally, in Sect. 3.3 we turn these self-contained editors into *abstract reusable* editors, thus encapsulating all information about their implementation and behaviour. However, *abstract* types seem to be at odds with generic programming. We show in Sect. 3.3 how we have managed to solve this problem.

Although the solution requires high-level functional and generic language constructs, it should be emphasized that editors remain very straightforward to use. In this section we construct a running example to illustrate the technique. The code fragment (**1**) below shows the *data model*. Code fragments appear as framed pieces of `code`. The data model is a record of type `MyDataModel`. The intention is that whenever the user edits one of the fields `value1` or `value2`, then these new values are summed and displayed in field `sum`. This behaviour is defined by `updDataModel`. We want to emphasize that the types and code are 'carved in stone': they do not change in the rest of this paper.

```
:: MyDataModel                                               (1)
    = {value1 :: Int, value2 :: Int , sum :: Int}

initDataModel (v1,v2)
    = {value1 = v1, value2 = v2, sum = v1 + v2}

updDataModel :: MyDataModel → MyDataModel
updDataModel rec = { rec & sum = rec.value1 + rec.value2 }
```

The 'functional record update' notation $\{r \ \& \ f_0 = v_0 \ , \ldots, \ f_n = v_n\}$ creates a new record value in which all fields have the same value as in r except the updated fields $f_0 \ldots f_n$.

3.1 Separation of Concerns by Separating Types

First of all, we want to accomplish a good separation of concerns. Ideally, it should be possible to concentrate on the functionality of the program without worrying about the actual shape of the editors. If one is not happy with the standard editor, it should be possible to construct the appropriate editor later without being forced to modify code that is not shape-related.

Using the function selfGEC we can immediately get a $GEC_{\text{MyDataModel}}$ for free for testing purposes. Below we show what the $GEC_{\text{MyDataModel}}$ GUI looks like when created by the function standardEditor. Each time the application user changes a value with the editor, the function updDataModel is applied and a new sum is calculated and displayed.

```
standardEditor
    = selfGEC updDataModel
            (initDataModel (0,0))
```

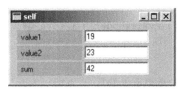

Now suppose that we do not like the look of this standard editor very much, and want a different one. This is myEditor shown below in code fragment (2). Again, this code is 'carved in stone'. We want to reuse the counters of the previous section for editing the two value fields. As the sum is calculated given these two values, we do not want the sum value to be editable at all.

```
myEditor to from                                        (2)
    = selfGEC (to o updDataModel o from)
            (to (initDataModel (0,0)))
```

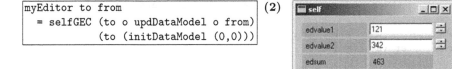

Since editors are created fully automatically just by looking at the type, the only way to obtain the desired editor is by using suitable data types. For the counters we use the Counter type. We assume that we have a specialized basic editor for the type `Display a`: this editor shows any value of type `a`, but the value cannot be changed in the editor. We combine these types in a new type to obtain the desired editor.

As we said before, we do not want to change the code fragments (**1**) and (**2**). For this reason we make a clear distinction between the *model* of the *data* (`MyDataModel`) and the *model* of the *view* used to generate the editor we want (`MyViewModel`). Conversion functions between these two models need to be defined (`toMyViewModel` and `fromMyViewModel`).

This strict separation of concerns removes obstacle **B.1**: the data model has nothing to do with the means of visualization; this is done by the view model.

We can now easily express in the function `myEditor` how the *view* and *model* are connected. To glue them together we just need two conversion functions `to` and `from` the editor domain. We convert the initial value `initDataModel` to the view domain and create an editor. After a change being made with the editor we convert the new values back to the data model domain, apply the algorithm `updDataModel`, and convert the result back to the view domain such that it can be displayed and edited again.

Consequently, we obtain a running editor by applying:

$$\boxed{\texttt{myEditor toMyViewModel fromMyViewModel}} \qquad (3)$$

The editor we get is completely determined by the type of `MyViewModel` and the definition of the conversion functions. If we want another editor, we only have to change this type and/or these conversion functions, all other code remains the same.

```
:: MyViewModel = { edvalue1 :: Counter        // an updown counter
                 , edvalue2 :: Counter        // an updown counter
                 , edsum    :: Display Int }  // non-editable integer value

toMyViewModel :: MyDataModel → MyViewModel
toMyViewModel rec     = { edvalue1 = toCounter rec.value1
                        , edvalue2 = toCounter rec.value2
                        , edsum    = toDisplay rec.sum }

fromMyViewModel :: MyViewModel → MyDataModel
fromMyViewModel edrec = { value1    = fromCounter (edrec.edvalue1)
                        , value2    = fromCounter (edrec.edvalue2)
                        , sum       = fromDisplay edrec.edsum }

toCounter    n    = (n,Neutral)
fromCounter (n,_) = n

:: Display a = Display a

toDisplay    x              = Display x
fromDisplay (Display x) = x
```

In this way we have created a separate layer on top of the *unchanged* existing program. Unfortunately, we did not really reach the desired compositional behaviour. By choosing another data type one does obtain another editor for free that *looks* the way we want, but one does not automatically get the desired self-contained *behaviour* with it. For instance, we have used the type `Counter` in the definition of `MyViewModel`. The generated editor displays a counter, but it does not take care of the updates of the counter. This is clearly not what we want. We have to invent a type from which self-contained editors can be generated.

3.2 Defining Self-Contained Editors

If we want to reuse an existing editor, it is not enough to reuse its type. We also want to reuse its functionality: each editor should take care of its own update. For this purpose we need a type in which we can store the functionality of an editor. If want to create a view v on a domain model d, we need to be able to replace a standard editor for type d by a self-contained editor for some isomorphic type v. Furthermore, since we generally also have to perform conversions between these types, we like to store them as well, such that each editor can take care of its own conversions. Finally, it is generally useful to take into account the old value of v when converting from d since editors may have an internal state.

Therefore we define a new type, `ViewGEC d v`, in which we can store the update and conversion functions, and we define a specialized version of our generic editor gGEC for this type (gGEC{|ViewGEC|}). The definitions are given below. Notice that in gGEC{|ViewGEC|} two additional parameters appear: gGECd and gGECv. This is caused by the fact that generic functions in Clean are kind-indexed functions. As `ViewGEC d v` is of kind $\star \rightarrow \star \rightarrow \star$, the generic function has two additional parameters, one for type d and one for type v.

The `ViewGEC` editor does the following. The value of type d is stored in the `ViewGEC` record, but a d-editor (gGECd) for it is not created. Taking the old value of v into account, the d-value is converted to a v-value using the conversion function `d_oldv_to_v :: d → (Maybe v) → v`. For this v-value we do generate a generic v-editor (gGECv) to store and edit the v-value.

Whenever the application user creates a new v-value with this editor, the call-back function of the v-editor is called (`viewCallback`) and the `update_v :: v → v` function is applied. This is similar to applying `selfGEC update_v` to the corresponding new value of type v. The resulting new v-value is shown in the v-editor again, and it is converted back to an d-value as well, using the function `v_to_d :: v → d`. This new d-value is then stored in the `ViewGEC` record in the `d_val` field, and the call-back function for the `ViewGEC` editor is called (`viewGECCallback`). The new d-value can be inspected in the program as if a new d-value was created with a standard generic d-editor.

```
:: ViewGEC d v = { d_val       :: d
                 , d_oldv_to_v :: d → (Maybe v) → v
                 , update_v    :: v → v
                 , v_to_d      :: v → d }

mkViewGEC :: d (d → v) (v → v) (v → d) → ViewGEC d v
```

```
mkViewGEC d fdv fvv fvd = { d_val        = d
                         , d_oldv_to_v  = fdvv
                         , update_v     = fvv
                         , v_to_d       = fvd }
where
    fdvv d Nothing  = fdv d
    fdvv _ (Just v) = v

gGEC{|ViewGEC|} gGECd gGECv (viewGEC, viewGECCallback) env
    = ({ gecSetValue = viewSetValue vInterface
       , gecGetValue = viewGetValue vInterface },new_env)
where
    (vInterface,new_env) = gGECv (viewGEC.d_oldv_to_v viewGEC.d_val Nothing
                                 ,viewCallback vInterface
                                 ) env

    viewCallback vInterface new_v env
        = viewGECCallback {viewGEC & d_val = new_d} new_env
    where
        new_upd_v = viewGEC.update_v new_v
        new_env   = vInterface.gecSetValue new_upd_v env
        new_d     = viewGEC.v_to_d new_upd_v

    viewSetValue vInterface new_viewGEC env
      = vInterface.gecSetValue new_v new_env
    where
        newb             = new_viewGEC.d_oldv_to_v new_viewGEC.d_val (Just old_v)
        (old_v,new_env) = vInterface.gecGetValue env

    viewGetValue vInterface env
        = ({viewGEC & d_val = viewGEC.v_to_d current_v},new_env)
    where
        (current_v,new_env) = vInterface.gecGetValue env
```

The concrete behaviour of the generated ViewGEC editor now not only depends on the type, but also on the concrete information stored in a value of type ViewGEC. Now it becomes very easy to define self-contained reusable editors, such as a counter editor, shown below. The corresponding editor takes care of the conversions and the update. The displayGEC does a trivial update (identity) and also takes care of the required conversions.

```
counterGEC :: Int → ViewGEC Int Counter
counterGEC i = mkViewGEC i toCounter updCntr fromCounter

displayGEC :: a → ViewGEC a (Display a)
displayGEC x = mkViewGEC x toDisplay id fromDisplay
```

Making use of these new self-contained editors we can repair and even simplify our previous editor definition. To replace it, we only have to provide a new definition of MyViewModel and of the conversion functions toMyViewModel and fromMyViewModel. All other definitions remain the same.

```
:: MyViewModel  = { edvalue1 :: ViewGEC Int Counter
                  , edvalue2 :: ViewGEC Int Counter
                  , edsum    :: ViewGEC Int (Display Int) }

toMyViewModel :: MyDataModel → MyViewModel
toMyViewModel rec = { edvalue1 = counterGEC rec.value1
```

```
                       , edvalue2 = counterGEC rec.value2
                       , edsum    = displayGEC rec.sum }

fromMyViewModel :: MyViewModel → MyDataModel
fromMyViewModel edrec = { value1 = edrec.edvalue1.d_val
                        , value2 = edrec.edvalue2.d_val
                        , sum    = edrec.edsum.d_val }
```

In the definition of `toMyViewModel` we can now simply choose any suited self-contained editor. Each editor handles the needed conversions and updates itself automatically. To obtain the value we are interested in, we just have to address the `d_val` field.

The example shows that we have obtained the compositional behaviour that we wanted to have. One problem remains. If we would replace a self-contained editor by another in `toMyViewModel`, all other code remains the same. However, we do have to change the type of `MyViewModel`. In this type it is completely visible what kind of editor has been used. The abstraction would be complete if we also manage to create an abstract data type for our self-contained editors.

3.3   Abstract Self-Contained Editors

The concrete value of type `ViewGEC d v` is used by the generic mechanism to generate the desired self-contained editors. The `ViewGEC d v` type depends on the type of the editor v that is being used. Put in other words, the type still reveals information about the implementation of editor v. This is undesirable for two reasons: one can not exchange views without changing types, and the type of composite views reflects their composite structure. For these reasons, we want a type that *abstracts* from the concrete editor type v.

However, if we manage to hide these types, how can the generic mechanism generate the editor for it? The compiler can only generate an editor for a given concrete type, not for an abstract type of which the content is unknown. The solution is as follows. When the abstraction is being made, we *do* know the contents and its type. Hence, we can store the *generic editor function* (of type `GECFunction`, see Sect.2.1) in the abstract data structure itself where the abstraction is being made. The stored editor function can be applied later when we really need to construct the editor. Therefore, we define an abstract data structure (`AGEC d`) in which we store the `ViewGEC d v` and its corresponding generic `gGEC` function for v. Technically this requires a type system that supports existentially quantified types as well as rank-2 polymorphism.

```
:: AGEC d = ∃.v: AGEC (ViewGEC d v)
                     (∀.ps: GECFunction (ViewGEC d v) (PSt ps))

mkAGEC :: (ViewGEC d v) → AGEC d | gGEC{|*|} v
mkAGEC viewGEC = AGEC viewGEC (gGEC{|* → * → *|} undef gGEC{|*|})

gGEC{|AGEC|} = ...   // similar to gGEC{|ViewGEC|}, but apply function stored in AGEC
```

The function mkAGEC creates the desired AGEC given a viewGEC. Looking at the type of AGEC, the generic system can deduce that the editor to store has to be a generic editor for type ViewGEC d v. To generate this editor, the generic system by default requires an editor for type d and type v as well. *We* know that in this particular case we do not use the d-editor at all. We can tell this to the generic system by making use of the fact that generic functions in Clean are kind indexed. The system allows us, if we wish, to explicitly specify the editors for type d (undef) and type v (gGEC{|*|}) to be used by the editor for ViewGEC (gGEC{|* → * → *|}). In this case we know that we do not need an editor for type d (hence the undef), and use the standard generic editor for type v. The overloading context restriction in the type of mkAGEC (| gGEC{|*|} v) states that for making an AGEC d out of a ViewGEC d v only an editor for type v is required.

We also have to define a specialized version of gGEC for the AGEC type. The corresponding generated editor applies the stored editor to the stored ViewGEC.

The types and kind indexed generic programming features we have used here may look complicated, but for the programmer an abstract editor is easy to make. To use a self-contained editor of type v as editor for type d, a ViewGEC d v has to be defined. Note that the editor for type v is automatically derived for the programmer by the generic system! The function mkAGEC stores them both into an AGEC. The functions counterAGEC and displayAGEC show how easy AGEC's can be made. One might be surprised that the overloading context for displayAGEC still requires a d-editor (| gGEC{|*|} d). This is caused by the fact that in this particular case type d is used in the definition of type Display.

```
counterAGEC :: Int → AGEC Int
counterAGEC i = mkAGEC (counterGEC i)

displayAGEC :: d → AGEC d | gGEC{|*|} d
displayAGEC x = mkAGEC (displayGEC x)
```

We choose to export AGEC d as a Clean abstract data type. This implies that code that uses such an abstract value can not apply record selection to access the d value. For this purpose we provide the following obvious projection functions to retrieve the d-value from an AGEC d (^^) and to store a new d-value in an existing AGEC d (the infix operator ^=).

```
(^^) :: (AGEC d) → d                      // Read current value
(^^) (AGEC viewGEC gGEC) = viewGEC.d_val

(^=) infixl :: (AGEC d) d → (AGEC d)      // Set new value
(^=) (AGEC viewGEC gGEC) nval = AGEC {viewGEC & d_val=nval} gGEC
```

The inclusion of the abstract type AGEC d together with its instance of gGEC, and the access functions provides the additional strength to the toolkit that is needed to successfully eliminate obstacle **B.2**.

We can now refine the three definitions of our running example for the last time and 'carve it in stone' as well in code fragment (**4**). All other code fragments remain unchanged. The complete code is formed by the code fragments **(1)**...**(4)** (with a few auxiliary functions).

```
:: MyViewModel        = { edvalue1 :: AGEC Int              (4)
                       , edvalue2 :: AGEC Int
                       , edsum    :: AGEC Int }

toMyViewModel :: MyDataModel → MyViewModel
toMyViewModel rec      = { edvalue1 = counterAGEC rec.value1
                         , edvalue2 = counterAGEC rec.value2
                         , edsum    = displayAGEC rec.sum }

fromMyViewModel :: MyViewModel → MyDataModel
fromMyViewModel edrec = { value1 = ^^ edrec.edvalue1
                        , value2 = ^^ edrec.edvalue2
                        , sum    = ^^ edrec.edsum }
```

The advantage we have obtained now is that, if we want to pick another editor, we only have to tell which one to pick in the definition of `toMyViewModel`. The types used in `MyViewModel` all remain the same (`AGEC Int`), no matter which editor is chosen. Also the definition of `fromMyViewModel` remains unaffected. It is instructive to compare the final definition with the one at the end of Sect. 3.2.

3.4   Abstract Editors Are Compositional

In order to show the compositional nature of abstract editors, we first turn the running example into an abstract editor, say `sumAGEC :: AGEC Int`. In disguise, it can be used *itself* as an `Int`-editor. Following the scheme introduced above, this is done as follows:

```
sumAGEC :: Int → AGEC Int                       // see counterAGEC (3.3)
sumAGEC i = mkAGEC (sumGEC i)
where sumGEC :: Int → ViewGEC Int MyViewModel  // see counterGEC (3.2)
      sumGEC i = mkViewGEC i to upd from
      where to   = toMyViewModel o toMyData
            from = fromMyData    o fromMyViewModel
            upd  = toMyViewModel o updDataModel o fromMyViewData

            toMyData   i = initData (0,i)
            fromMyData d = d.sum
```

Now `sumAGEC`, `counterAGEC`, and `displayAGEC` are interchangeable components. If we want to experiment with variants of the running example, we simply pick the instance of our choice in the `toMyViewModel` function. This is displayed in Fig. 3.

We are setting up a library of abstract components. One of these library functions `idAGEC` (which takes a value of any type and promotes it to an abstract

Alternative definition of toMyViewModel: **Corresponding GUI:**

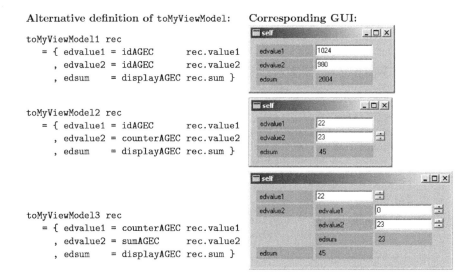

```
toMyViewModel1 rec
   = { edvalue1 = idAGEC        rec.value1
     , edvalue2 = idAGEC        rec.value2
     , edsum    = displayAGEC rec.sum }


toMyViewModel2 rec
   = { edvalue1 = idAGEC        rec.value1
     , edvalue2 = counterAGEC rec.value2
     , edsum    = displayAGEC rec.sum }


toMyViewModel3 rec
   = { edvalue1 = counterAGEC rec.value1
     , edvalue2 = sumAGEC      rec.value2
     , edsum    = displayAGEC rec.sum }
```

Fig. 3. *Plug-and-play* your favourite abstract editors to experiment with the running example. The only code that changes is the function **toMyViewModel**.

editor component for that type) is used in the example above. With this library it will be possible to rapidly create GUIs in a declarative style. This can be very useful e.g. for prototyping, education, tracing and debugging purposes.

4   Related Work

Our model-view approach has several interesting features that are not present in the standard approach [12]. Firstly, because views are derived automatically, a programmer in our system does not need to explicitly 'register' nor program views. Instead, the view is *specified* by the programmer by means of the types that are used in the model. This specification, which is defined in terms of data types only, is used by the generic system to derive the actual GUI. Secondly, views can be customized via overruling instance declarations of arbitrary types. Finally, the most distinguishing feature of our model-view approach is the nature of both the model and the views. The generic framework dissects the offered type of the model into the set of generic types, each of which is mapped to an interactive model-view unit. Put in other words, our approach can truly be called model-view *all the way*.

Frameworks for the model-view paradigm in a functional language use a similar value-based approach (Claessen *et al* [8]), or an event-based version [11]. In both cases, the programmer needs to explicitly handle view registration and manipulation. In our framework, the information-flow follows the structure that is derived by the generic decomposition of the model value. This suggests that we could have based our abstract GUI definitions on a stream-based solution such as FUDGETS [7]. However, stream based approaches are known to impose a much too rigid coupling between the stream based communication and the GUI structure resulting in a severe loss of flexibility and maintainability. For this reason, we have chosen to use a system with a call-back mechanism as the interface of its GUI components.

Martijn Schrage [13] also employs generic programming techniques to produce views in the *Proxima* PhD-project. It is specifically geared towards the design and development of a generic presentation-oriented XML-editor. Wolfram Kahl has developed a first version of editor combinators [17]. With editor combinators text-based structure editors can be defined and composed in a way which is similar to parser combinators.

We know of no other declarative work for describing general purpose GUIs that achieves a similar abstraction level with such a complete separation of model and view.

5   Conclusions and Future Work

We have introduced a technique for programming GUIs with the following properties:

- The programmer can *separate* application logic from view logic by defining a separate data model and view model.
- Using abstract *GEC*s (in which a complete model-view is encapsulated) the programmer can *incrementally* change the view model without modifying its type.
- The programmer can use a library of *abstract GEC*s to construct GUIs by *composition* without knowing anything about standard GUI libraries.
- The *ease of programming* with abstract GECs makes it very suited for use in education, tracing, debugging and rapid prototyping.

The Clean language that we have used in this project is a *functional* language with strong support for types, including *existential* types and *rank-2 polymorphism*. We rely essentially on *generic programming* with *kind indexed* types. The GUI part is implemented op top of the Object I/O library of Clean. The system could also have been realized in Generic Haskell using the Haskell Object I/O library.

Currently, function types are excluded from the system. We plan to include arbitrary function values by reusing the *Esther* system [15] which relies on Clean's support for *dynamics* [16]. Furthermore, we will investigate the expressive power of our graphical editor components by setting up a library for abstract GECs and by performing case studies, experimenting with multiple views and multiple models.

Acknowledgements. We like to thank Pieter Koopman and Arjen van Weelden for their valuable comments.

References

1. P. Achten and R. Plasmeijer. Interactive Functional Objects in Clean. In Clack, Hammond, and Davie, editors, *The 9th International Workshop on the Implementation of Functional Languages, IFL 1997, Selected Papers*, volume 1467 of *LNCS*, pages 304–321. St.Andrews, UK, Springer, 1998.
2. Achten, Peter and Peyton Jones, Simon. Porting the Clean Object I/O Library to Haskell. In M. Mohnen and P. Koopman, editors, *The 12th International Workshop on the Implementation of Functional Languages, IFL 2000, Selected Papers*, volume 2011 of *LNCS*, pages 194–213. Aachen, Germany, Springer, 2001.
3. Achten, Peter, van Eekelen, Marko and Plasmeijer, Rinus. Generical Graphical User Interfaces. In Greg Michaelson and Phil Trinder, editors, *Selected Papers of the 15th Int. Workshop on the Implementation of Functional Languages, IFL03*, LNCS. Edinburgh, UK, Springer, 2003. To appear.
4. A. Alimarine and R. Plasmeijer. A Generic Programming Extension for Clean. In T. Arts and M. Mohnen, editors, *The 13th International workshop on the Implementation of Functional Languages, IFL'01, Selected Papers*, volume 2312 of *LNCS*, pages 168–186. Älvsjö, Sweden, Springer, Sept. 2002.
5. Angelov, Krasimir Andreev. ObjectIO for Haskell. Description and Sources at www.haskell.org/ObjectIO/, Applications at /free.top.bg/ka2_mail/, 2003.
6. E. Barendsen and S. Smetsers. *Handbook of Graph Grammars and Computing by Graph Transformation*, chapter 2, Graph Rewriting Aspects of Functional Programming, pages 63–102. World Scientific, 1999.
7. M. Carlsson and T. Hallgren. FUDGETS - a graphical user interface in a lazy functional language. In *Proceedings of the ACM Conference on Functional Programming and Computer Architecture, FPCA '93*, Kopenhagen, Denmark, 1993.
8. K. Claessen, T. Vullinghs, and E. Meijer. Structuring Graphical Paradigms in TkGofer. In *Proceedings of the 1997 ACM SIGPLAN International Conference on Functional Programming (ICFP '97)*, volume 32(8), pages 251–262, Amsterdam, The Netherlands, 9-11 June 1997. ACM Press.
9. D. Clarke and A. Löh. Generic Haskell, Specifically. In J. Gibbons and J. Jeuring, editors, *Generic Programming. Proceedings of the IFIP TC2 Working Conference on Generic Programming*, pages 21–48, Schloss Dagstuhl, July 2003. Kluwer Academic Publishers. ISBN 1-4020-7374-7.
10. Hinze, Ralf. A new approach to generic functional programming. In *The 27th Annual ACM SIGPLAN-SIGACT Symposium on Principles of Programming Languages*, pages 119–132. Boston, Massachusetts, January 2000.
11. W. Karlsen, Einar and S. Westmeier. Using Concurrent Haskell to Develop Views over an Active Repository. In *Implementation of Functional Languages, Selected Papers*, volume 1467 of *LNCS*, pages 285–303, St.Andrews, Scotland, 1997. Springer.
12. G. Krasner and S. Pope. A cookbook for using the Model-View-Controller user interface paradigm in Smalltalk-80. *Journal of Object-Oriented Programming*, 1(3):26–49, August 1988.
13. Schrage M. *Proxima, a presentation-oriented XML editor*. PhD thesis, University of Utrecht. To appear in 2004.
14. B. Shneiderman. *Designing the User Interface: strategies for effective human-computer interaction*. Addison Wesley, 2nd edition, 1992.

15. A. van Weelden and R. Plasmeijer. A functional shell that dynamically combines compiled code. In P. Trinder and G. Michaelson, editors, *Selected Papers Proceedings of the 15th International Workshop on Implementation of Functional Languages, IFL'03*. Heriot Watt University, Edinburgh, Sept. 2003. To appear.
16. M. Vervoort and R. Plasmeijer. Lazy dynamic input/output in the lazy functional language Clean. In R. Peña and T. Arts, editors, *The 14th International Workshop on the Implementation of Functional Languages, IFL'02, Selected Papers*, volume 2670 of *LNCS*, pages 101–117. Springer, Sept. 2003.
17. Wolfram Kahl, Oliver Braun, Jan Scheffczyk. Editor Combinators - A First Account. Technical Report Nr. 2000-01, Fakultät für Informatik, Universität der Bundeswehr München, 2000.

An Implementation of Session Types

Matthias Neubauer and Peter Thiemann*

Universität Freiburg
Georges-Köhler-Allee 079
D-79110 Freiburg, Germany

Abstract. A session type is an abstraction of a set of sequences of heterogeneous values sent and received over a communication channel. Session types can be used for specifying stream-based Internet protocols. Typically, session types are attached to communication-based program calculi, which renders them theoretical tools which are not readily usable in practice. To transfer session types into practice, we propose an embedding of a core calculus with session types into the functional programming language Haskell. The embedding preserves typing. A case study (a client for SMTP, the Simple Mail Transfer Protocol) demonstrates the feasibility of our approach.

Keywords: Functional programming, types, domain specific languages

1 Introduction

Much foundational work on calculi for concurrency is devoted to studying synchronous, one-shot communications, for example, CCS [20], the π calculus [21], the chemical abstract machine [5], the join calculus [9], and the M-calculus [32]. However, in particular in distributed systems, the cost of one-shot communications can be too high because a new connection must be established for each message and synchronous operation may be too restrictive. Hence, calculi and programming languages have been developed that are either based on asynchronous communication [14] or that incorporate channel-based communication primitives [12,25,29]. Once a channel has been created, many distinct messages may be communicated through it. Channels are often homogeneous, that is, all messages must have the same type.

Session types [10] have emerged as an expressive typing discipline for *heterogeneous*, bidirectional communication channels. In such a channel, each message may have a different type with the possible sequences of messages determined by the channel's session type. Such a type discipline subsumes typings for datagram communication as well as for homogeneous channels. Session types have been used to describe stream-based Internet protocols such as POP3 [10,11].

A regular language on atomic communication actions describes the sequence of messages on each channel. The channel type specifies this language with a fixpoint expression. Each operation peels off the outermost action from the channel

---

* {neubauer,thiemann}@informatik.uni-freiburg.de

B. Jayaraman (Ed.): PADL 2004, LNCS 3057, pp. 56–70, 2004.

$l \in$ Label
Definitions
$d ::= x = \mathtt{Op}(\tilde{x}) \mid \mathtt{rec}\ x(\tilde{x}) = e$
$\quad \mid\ \mathtt{Send}\ l(x) \mid \mathtt{Close}\ ()$
Expressions
$e ::= \mathtt{Halt} \mid \mathtt{Let}\ d\ \mathtt{in}\ e \mid \mathtt{If}\ x\ \mathtt{then}\ e\ \mathtt{else}\ e \mid x\ (\tilde{x})$
$\quad \mid\ \mathtt{Receive}\ [g]$
$g ::= l(x) \to e \mid g, g$

Types
$\tau ::= b \mid \tilde{\tau}, \gamma \to 0$
Type Environments
$\Gamma ::= \emptyset \mid \Gamma(x : \tau)$
Session types
$\gamma ::= \emptyset \mid \varepsilon \mid [\eta] \mid \beta \mid \mu\beta.\gamma$
$\eta ::= \ell(b) : \gamma \mid \eta, \eta$
$\ell ::= l \mid \bar{l}$

Fig. 1. Syntax

type so that each operation changes the channel's type. For that reason, channels should not be duplicated but rather be treated linearly by the type system.

The resulting type system is amenable to type inference using techniques developed for recursive types. Session types are compatible with polymorphic type inference [15]. However, thus far no mainstream programming language supports session types, so it is hard to take advantage of them in practice.

The present work demonstrates how to embed session types into a functional programming language with a sufficiently powerful type system. (Extended) Haskell fits this bill, but other languages with constrained type systems would be suitable, too [33]. In particular, type classes with functional dependencies [16] are required to model the progression of the current state of the channel and functions with polymorphic parameters are required to model client and server side of a communication with one specification [23].

The main contribution of the present work is an encoding of session types in terms of type classes with functional dependencies. A key technical problem is the encoding of fixpoint (μ) expressions that occur in the description of the regular language mentioned above. We define a typed translation from a calculus with session types into Haskell and prove its soundness. Finally, we demonstrate the practicability of our approach with a case study, a typed client for the Simple Mail Transfer Protocol (SMTP) [30].

The paper is structured as follows. Section 2 defines a small calculus for asynchronous communication with session types. Section 3 specifies the basic ideas for translating the calculus to Haskell and Section 4 gives a detailed overview of the translation. Section 5 contains excerpts from our type-safe implementation of an SMTP client. Section 6 briefly discusses related work on domain modeling with types and Section 7 concludes. Due to lack of space, we have to assume that the reader is reasonably fluent in Haskell [13].

2   Calculus with Session Types

Figure 1 presents the syntax of a calculus with session types. For simplicity, the calculus only considers **one** end of **one** communication channel. The restriction to one end avoids the necessity and semantic complication of adopting an expression for concurrent execution in the syntax. It is adequate for the present purpose because the interest is in type checking the code for one peer (client or server), not it checking the consistency of a whole system of processes. The

$$\Gamma, \emptyset \vdash \texttt{Halt}$$

$$\frac{\Gamma, \gamma \vdash d \Rightarrow \Gamma', \gamma' \qquad \Gamma', \gamma' \vdash e}{\Gamma, \gamma \vdash \texttt{Let } d \texttt{ in } e} \qquad \frac{\Gamma(x) : b \qquad \Gamma, \gamma \vdash e_1 \qquad \Gamma, \gamma \vdash e_2}{\Gamma, \gamma \vdash \texttt{If } x \texttt{ then } e_1 \texttt{ else } e_2}$$

$$\frac{\Gamma(x) = \tilde{\tau}, \gamma \to 0 \qquad \Gamma(\tilde{z}) = \tilde{\tau}}{\Gamma, \gamma \vdash x \, \tilde{z}} \qquad \frac{\gamma = \overline{[l_i(b_i) : \gamma_i]_{i=1}^n} \qquad \Gamma(x_i : b_i), \gamma_i \vdash e_i}{\Gamma, \gamma \vdash \texttt{Receive } [l_i(x_i) \to e_i]}$$

Fig. 2. Typing rules for expressions

restriction to one communication channel transforms session types to communication effects [1], makes a linear treatment of the channel enforcable by syntactic means, and simplifies the translation in Section 4.

The calculus deals with three kinds of data, first-order base type values, functions, and labels. Labels have a status similar to labels in record and variant types, they occur in channel types and they can be sent and received via channels: each message is a base value tagged with a label.

The expressions of the calculus come in a sequentialized style reminiscent of continuation-passing style. More precisely, an expression e is a sequence of (let-) definitions which ends in either a $\texttt{Halt}$ instruction, a conditional, a function call, or a receive instruction that branches on the received label. All arguments are restricted to variables. The notation $\tilde{x}$ stands for the sequence $x_1, \ldots, x_n$ where n derives from the context.

A definition d is either the application of a primitive operation, the definition of a recursive function, the send operation, and the close operation for closing the communication channel.

A type is either a base type or a function type. Due to the sequential style, functions do not return values. Instead they must take a continuation argument. The function type also includes an effect specification. It defines the latent communication that will take place when the function is applied [1].

A session type is either empty (the channel is closed), the empty word (the channel is depleted but not yet closed), a label-tagged alternative of different session types (the value may be sent $l(b)$ or received $\overline{l(b)}$), or a type variable which is used in constructing a recursive type with the μ operator. The μ operator constructs a fixpoint, e.g., $\mu\beta.\gamma \approx \gamma[\beta \mapsto \mu\beta.\gamma]$. All uses of μ are *expansive*, that is, there can be no subterms of the form $\mu\beta_1 \ldots \mu\beta_n.\beta_1$.

The type system relies on two judgments, $\Gamma, \gamma \vdash e$, to check the consistency of an expression and prescribe its communication effect γ, and $\Gamma, \gamma \vdash d \Rightarrow \Gamma', \gamma'$ to model the effect of a definition and its transformation of the environment.

Figure 2 contains the rules for expressions. $\texttt{Halt}$ requires that the channel is closed. The let expression types the body after transforming the environment according to the definition. The conditional passes the environment unchanged to both branches. Applying a function requires that the function consumes the remaining effect. Receiving a tagged value eliminates a labeled alternative in the session type. The branches are typed with the remaining session type.

Figure 3 contains the typing rules for definitions. A primitive operation has base type arguments and result. It does not depend on the session type. Function formation is independent of the current session type, too. The body of the

$$\frac{\Gamma(x_i) = b}{\Gamma, \gamma \vdash x = \mathtt{Op}(x_1, \ldots, x_n) \Rightarrow \Gamma(x : b), \gamma} \qquad \frac{\Gamma(f : \tilde{\tau}, \gamma \to 0)(\tilde{x} : \tilde{\tau}), \gamma \vdash e}{\Gamma, \gamma' \vdash \mathtt{rec}\ f(\tilde{x}) = e \Rightarrow \Gamma(f : \tilde{\tau}, \gamma \to 0), \gamma'}$$

$$\frac{\Gamma(x_j) = b_j \qquad \gamma = [l_i(b_i) : \gamma_i]_{i=1}^{n}}{\Gamma, \gamma \vdash \mathtt{Send}\ l_j(x_j) \Rightarrow \Gamma, \gamma_j} \ 1 \le j \le n \qquad \Gamma, \varepsilon \vdash \mathtt{Close}\ () \Rightarrow \Gamma, \emptyset$$

Fig. 3. Typing rules for definitions

function must be checked with the session type prescribed by the call site of the function. Sending of a labeled value selects a part of the session type for the rest of the expression. Closing the communication channel requires that there are no exchanges left. The rule sets the remaining exchanges to the empty set.

The present paper does not define a semantics for the language. Suitable semantics (for extended languages) may be found in work of Gay et al [11].

3   Basic Framework

The mapping from the calculus with session types to Haskell rests on a few overloaded functions. Each message has its own specific type and it comes with functions to parse and unparse a message, as specific with the type class Command[1].

```
class Command command where
  parseCommand   :: ReadS command
  unparseCommand :: command -> ShowS
```

The underlying datatype is a function that maps the session type, a string, and a file handle to an IO action. The string contains the input and output is generated via the handle in the IO monad. Hence, the datatype is the composition of three reader monads and the IO monad.[2]

```
data Session st a = Session { unSession :: st -> String -> Handle -> IO a }
```

The attentive reader may wonder if this design of the session monad is the only possible. Consider the following two alternatives:

− Suppose that output is generated via some writer monad. Since the IO monad is still required because of IO actions that must be performed between the communication actions, the resulting type would look like IO (a, Output). Unfortunately, a value in the IO monad does not return anything before all actions specified by the value have been completed [27]. That is, any output generated through the Output component in the middle of a transaction would only appear at the very end of that transaction. Too late for an interactive response!

---

[1] ReadS and ShowS are predefined Haskell types for parsing and unparsing data.

[2] The obvious definitions to make Session st into a monad are omitted.

– Suppose that input is obtained directly via the IO monad, for example, by having the parsers call getChar :: IO Char directly. Unfortunately, as we will see, the parsers must be able to proceed speculatively and hence unget characters. While this option seems viable, it would have required the construction of an imperative parsing library based on getChar and unGetChar. We have not pursued this further due to lack of time.

The **send** operation takes the message to send (identified by its type) and a continuation to construct an action for the current session type. Executing **send** first sends the message, advances the session type as indicated by the typing rule, and then invokes the continuation on the new session type. The declaration of the operation (a type class) makes clear that the new type depends on the old type and the message by using a functional dependency.

```
class SEND st message nextst | st message -> nextst where
  send    :: message -> Session nextst () -> Session st ()
```

The **receive** operation takes a message continuation. It attempts to parse the message from the input, advances the session type, and invokes the continuation on the message and the new session type.

```
receive :: (RECEIVE st cont) => cont -> Session st ()
receive g = Session (\ st inp h -> case receive' g st inp h of
                                Just action -> action
                                Nothing     -> fail "unparsable")
```

When **receive** is applied directly to a message, cont has the form message -> Session nextst () but this is not always the case: an alternative of different messages is also possible in which case the type is an alternative of the different continuations. An auxiliary function attempts to parse the expected message and returns either the continuation or nothing.

```
class RECEIVE st cont | st -> cont where
  receive' :: cont -> st -> String -> Handle -> (Maybe (IO ()))
```

The io operation serves to embed IO operations between the **send** and **receive** operations.

```
io :: IO a -> Session st a
io action = Session (\_ _ _ -> action)
```

Finally, the operation close closes the communication channel. It is only applicable if the session type is EPS (the translation of ε).

```
close :: Session NULL () -> Session EPS ()
close cont = Session (\_ _ _ -> unSession cont NULL [])
```

$$\begin{array}{lll}
[\![\emptyset]\!] & = \text{NULL} & [\![\ell(b):\gamma]\!] = [\![\ell(b):\gamma]\!] & [\![\bar{l}(x):\gamma]\!] = \texttt{recv}\ [\![l(x)]\!]\ [\![\gamma]\!] \\
[\![\varepsilon]\!] & = \text{EPS} & [\![g_1,g_2]\!] \quad = \text{ALT}\ [\![g_1]\!]\ [\![g_2]\!] & [\![l(x):\gamma]\!] = \texttt{send}\ [\![l(x)]\!]\ [\![\gamma]\!]
\end{array}$$

$$\mathcal{T}[\![\beta]\!]\tilde{\beta} = \beta \qquad \mathcal{T}[\![\mu\beta.\gamma]\!]\tilde{\beta} = \text{REC}\ (\text{G}\ \texttt{send}\ \texttt{recv}\ \tilde{\beta})$$

$$\text{where}\quad \texttt{data G send recv}\ \tilde{\beta}\ \beta = \text{G}(\mathcal{T}[\![\gamma]\!]\tilde{\beta}\beta)$$

$$\text{and}\quad \texttt{send, recv :: * -> * -> *}$$

$$\mathcal{V}[\![\beta]\!] = \beta \qquad \mathcal{V}[\![\mu\beta.\gamma]\!] = \texttt{let}\ \beta = \text{REC}\ (\text{G}\ (\mathcal{V}[\![\gamma]\!]))\ \texttt{in}\ \beta$$

Fig. 4. Translation of Types and Values

4   Translation

To make the information in a session type available to the Haskell type checker, all parts must be translated accordingly. Each labeled message is lifted to a separate type where the base types correspond to Haskell base types. Each constructor of a session type is mapped to a type constructor:

```
data NULL         = NULL        -- the closed session
data EPS          = EPS         -- the empty session
data SEND_MSG m r = SEND_MSG m r  -- send message m, then session r
data RECV_MSG m r = RECV_MSG m r  -- receive message m, then session r
data ALT l r      = ALT l r     -- alternative session: either l or r
```

4.1   Translation of Session Types

The translation concerns types and values. It does not directly refer to SEND_MSG and RECV_MSG, instead it is parameterized over the send and receive operations, send and recv. This parameterization enables flipping the session type. Flipping is required to switch the point of view from one end of the channel to the other. In a session type it corresponds to exchanging all occurrences of $\bar{l}$ and l.

Hence, all types are parameterized over send and recv of kind * -> * -> * and all values are parameterized by *polymorphic functions* send and recv of type forall x y . send x y and forall x y . recv x y, respectively.

Figure 4 contains the definition of the translation. The $\mathcal{V}$ function defines the special cases for the value translation, $\mathcal{T}$ the cases for the type translation. The main difficulty is the treatment of the recursion operator. There are two problems due to restrictions on Haskell's type system. First, each use of recursion requires an explicit datatype definition. Fortunately, there is a generic encoding using a datatype that subsumes many recursively defined datatypes [19]:

```
data REC f = REC (f (REC f))
```

In this datatype, f is a constructor function of kind * -> *. Technically, REC constructs the fixpoint of this function f, up to lifting.

Second, instantiation of f is restricted to type constructor terms to keep the type system decidable. The ideal translation would be

$$\mathcal{T}[\![\mu\beta.\gamma]\!] = \text{REC}(\lambda\beta.\mathcal{T}[\![\gamma]\!])$$
$$\mathcal{T}[\![\beta]\!] \ = \beta$$

where $\lambda\beta\dots$ is a lambda expression at the type level. However, such lambda expressions are not admissible in Haskell types and $(\lambda\beta.\mathcal{T}[\![\gamma]\!])$ cannot always be η-reduced to a pure constructor term: as an example consider that $\mu\beta.[l_1 : \beta, l_2 : \varepsilon]$ would translate to $\mathtt{REC}(\lambda\beta.\mathtt{ALT}(\mathtt{send}\ [\![l_1]\!]\ \beta)(\mathtt{send}\ [\![l_2]\!]\ \mathtt{EPS}))$. Hence, the translation of types needs to introduce a new parameterized datatype for each occurrence of $\mu\beta.\gamma$ in a session type. Furthermore, since datatype definitions cannot be nested, the translation needs to keep track of the pending type variables (corresponding to occurrences of $\mu\beta$'s in the context) and parameterize the new type over all these variables.

The corresponding part of the translation on the value level requires the introduction of a recursive definition, too. Technically, the two translations should be merged to fix the association of each $\mu\beta.\gamma$ to its corresponding datatype G. We keep them separate for readability.

For the remaining cases, $\mathcal{V}[\![]\!]$ and $\mathcal{T}[\![]\!]$ are equal to $[\![]\!]$. In the type translation, the parameters $\tilde{\beta}$ are always passed unchanged to the recursive calls.

Lemma 1. *Let Γ contain the types for the data constructors listed above and γ be a closed, expansive session type.*

$$\Gamma \vdash_{haskell} \mathcal{V}[\![\gamma]\!] : \mathcal{T}[\![\gamma]\!]$$

The variables **send** and **receive** are provided as polymorphic parameters:

```
\ (send :: (forall x y . x -> y -> send x y))
  (recv :: (forall x y . x -> y -> recv x y)) -> V[γ]
```

Similarly, the type translation refers to type variables **send** and **recv** so that the full type of the value produced by the translation is

```
forall send recv.
  (forall x y . x -> y -> send x y) ->
  (forall x y . x -> y -> recv x y) -> T[γ]
```

Additionally, the translation might restrict the instantiation of **send** and **recv** so that the supplied operations are always opposites. A further two-parameter type class would be required to specify this relation.

4.2   Connecting Session Types with Messages

The specification of the connection between the message to send or receive and the actual session type requires three ingredients. First, atomic messages must be matched with their specification. Second, when the specification prescribes an alternative (with the **ALT** operator), the matching must be properly dispatched to the alternatives. Third, recursion must be unwound whenever matching encounters the **REC** operator. The first part is straightforward, the second and third require careful consideration.

Atomic Messages. If the session type prescribes that an atomic message of type m be send, then the actual message type must be m and the type of the remaining session is the stripped session type. Similarly, if the session type prescribes that a message of type m be received then there must be a continuation that expects a message of that type and continues in the stripped session state.

```
instance Command m => SEND (SEND_MSG m b) m b where
  send mess cont =
    Session (\ st inp h -> do hPutStr h (unparseCommand mess "")
                             unSession cont (send_next st) inp h)

instance Command m => RECEIVE (RECV_MSG m x) (m -> Session x ()) where
  receive' g st inp h =
    case parseCommand inp of
      ((e, inp'):_) -> Just (unSession (g e) (recv_next st) inp' h)
      []            -> Nothing
```

The functions send_next and recv_next are just projections on the last argument of SEND_MSG and RECV_MSG:

```
send_next (SEND_MSG m s) = s
recv_next (RECV_MSG m s) = s
```

Alternatives. When the current operation is a receive operation and the protocol prescribes an alternative of different messages, then the implementation attempts to parse the input according to the alternatives and selects the first successful parse. This trial is encoded in the **receive'** function (and is the main reason for keeping **receive** and **receive'** separate). It also serves as an example where the first argument of the **receive** operator is **not** a function.

```
instance (RECEIVE spec1 m1, RECEIVE spec2 m2) =>
        RECEIVE (ALT spec1 spec2) (ALT m1 m2) where
  receive' (ALT g1 g2) (ALT spec1 spec2) inp =
    case receive' g1 spec1 inp of
        Just action -> Just action
        Nothing     -> receive' g2 spec2 inp
```

When the current operation is a send operation and the protocol prescribes an alternative, then the automatic matching of the protocol specification against the message type would be fairly complicated [22]. For that reason, the alternatives must be explicitly selected prior to a send operation. Two primitive selector functions are provided for that task[3]:

```
left  :: Session l x -> Session (ALT l r) x
right :: Session r x -> Session (ALT l r) x

left  (Session g) = Session (\(ALT l r) inp -> g l inp)
right (Session g) = Session (\(ALT l r) inp -> g r inp)
```

---

[3] They also require a type class for unwinding recursion.

This design has another positive effect: subtyping of the session type for send operations! If a protocol states that a certain message must be received, then the implementor must make sure that the message is understood. Hence, the matching for the RECEIVE class must be complete. From the sender's perspective, a protocol often states that a selection of messages may be sent at a certain point. So the sender's implementation may choose to omit some of the alternatives. The above arrangement makes this possible: a sender may choose just to send the left alternative and leave the other unspecified.

Recursion. Matching against the recursion operator requires unwinding. Its implementation requires two steps. Due to the definition of REC, unwinding boils down to selecting the argument of REC. The second step derives from the observation that the body of each REC constructor has type G $\tilde{\beta}$, which was introduced by the translation. Now, G $\tilde{\beta}$ needs to be expanded to its definition so that matching can proceed. To achieve this expansion uniformly requires (yet) another type class, say, RECBODY:

```
class RECBODY t c | t -> c where recbody :: t -> c
```

with instances provided for each of the G $\tilde{\beta}$. If the definition is

$$\texttt{data G send recv } \tilde{\beta} = \texttt{G}(\mathcal{T}[\![\gamma]\!]\tilde{\beta})$$

then recbody is the selector function of type G send recv $\tilde{\beta} \to \mathcal{T}[\![\gamma]\!]\tilde{\beta}$:

```
instance RECBODY (G send recv β̃) T[γ]β̃ where
  recbody (G x) = x
```

Hence, unwinding boils down to two selection operations. In this case, there is no conceptual difference between the send and receive operations.

```
instance (RECEIVE t c, RECBODY (f (REC f)) t) => RECEIVE (REC f) c where
  receive' g = Session (\ (REC fRECf) inp ->
                          unSession (receive' g) (recbody fRECf) inp)
instance (SEND t x y, RECBODY (f (REC f)) t) => SEND (REC f) x y where
  send mess cont = Session (\ (REC fRECf) inp ->
                             unSession (send mess cont) (recbody fRECf) inp)
```

4.3   Translation of Expressions

The translation of expressions is given by the table in Figure 5. It assumes that primitive operations (may) have side effects. When sending a message, the translation requires information about the current session type. This information is needed to inject the **send** operation into the corresponding "slot" in the translated session type. The formulation of this injection (the last two lines) is nondeterministic: it has to search for the matching label in the tree of alternatives. However, the result is deterministic because each sending label appears exactly once in the session type. It can be shown that a typed expression in the session calculus is mapped to a typed Haskell program.

Lemma 2. *Suppose that* $\emptyset, \gamma \vdash e$. *Then* $\Gamma \vdash_{haskell} [\![e]\!] :$ Session $(\mathcal{T}[\![\gamma]\!])$ (), *where* Γ *is as in Lemma 1.*

$$\llbracket \texttt{Halt} \rrbracket = \texttt{return } ()$$
$$\llbracket \texttt{If } x \texttt{ then } e_1 \texttt{ else } e_2 \rrbracket = \texttt{if } x \texttt{ then } \llbracket e_1 \rrbracket \texttt{ else } \llbracket e_2 \rrbracket$$
$$\llbracket x \ \tilde{z} \rrbracket = x \ \tilde{z}$$
$$\llbracket \texttt{Receive } [g] \rrbracket = \texttt{receive } [g]$$
$$\llbracket g, g \rrbracket = (\texttt{ALT } (\llbracket g \rrbracket) \ (\llbracket g \rrbracket))$$
$$\llbracket l(x) \to e \rrbracket = (\lambda l(x) \to e)$$
$$\llbracket \texttt{Let } x = \texttt{Op}(x_1, \ldots, x_n) \texttt{ in } e \rrbracket = \texttt{io}(\texttt{Op}(x_1, \ldots, x_n)) \texttt{ >>= } (\lambda x \to \llbracket e \rrbracket)$$
$$\llbracket \texttt{Let rec } f(\tilde{x}) = e \texttt{ in } e' \rrbracket = \texttt{let } f(\tilde{x}) = \llbracket e \rrbracket \texttt{ in } \llbracket e' \rrbracket$$
$$\llbracket \texttt{Let Send } l^\gamma(x) \texttt{ in } e' \rrbracket = \llbracket \gamma \downarrow l \rrbracket (\texttt{send } (\llbracket l \rrbracket \ x) \ \llbracket e' \rrbracket)$$
$$\llbracket \texttt{Let Close } () \texttt{ in } e' \rrbracket = \texttt{close } (\llbracket e' \rrbracket)$$
$$\llbracket l(x) \to \gamma' \downarrow l \rrbracket = \texttt{id}$$
$$\llbracket \eta_1, \eta_2 \downarrow l \rrbracket = \texttt{left} \circ \llbracket \eta_1 \downarrow l \rrbracket \cup \texttt{right} \circ \llbracket \eta_2 \downarrow l \rrbracket$$

Fig. 5. Translation of Expressions

5   Case Study: A Simple SMTP Client

An excerpt of a real world application, our type-safe implementation of the *Simple Mail Transfer Protocol* (SMTP) [30], demonstrates the practicability of our Haskell encoding of session types. Our implementation expects an email as input and tries to deliver it to a specific SMTP server. It is automatically derived from the protocol specification in terms of a session type.

5.1   A Simplified SMTP Session Type

A session type corresponding to full SMTP is quite unreadable. Hence, we only consider a fragment of SMTP relevant to our application. The type is given from the client's point of view, flipping all decorations results in the server's type.

$$\gamma_C = [\,\overline{220} : \mu\beta_0.[\,\texttt{EHLO} : [\,\overline{250} : \mu\beta_1.[\,\texttt{MAIL} : [\,\overline{250} : [\,\texttt{RCPT} : \mu\beta_2.[\,\overline{250} : [\,\texttt{DATA} : [\,\overline{3yz} : (\texttt{LINES}, [\,\overline{250} : \beta_1,$$
$$\ldots]),$$
$$\texttt{RCPT} : \beta_2,$$
$$\ldots],$$
$$\ldots],$$
$$\ldots],$$
$$\ldots],$$
$$\texttt{QUIT} : \emptyset,$$
$$\ldots],$$
$$\overline{5yz} : \beta_0],$$
$$\ldots],$$
$$\ldots]$$

After receiving a greeting from the SMTP server (a $\overline{222}$ reply), the client initiates a mail session sending EHLO to perform several, consecutive email transactions with the server. A mail transactions starts with a MAIL command, followed by at least one RCPT command telling the server the recipients of the mail, by a DATA command announcing the mail content, and by the actual content (LINES). The client terminates the session issuing a QUIT command. The server usually acknowledges successful commands by sending a $\overline{250}$ reply. In the full

protocol, different kinds of error replies can return after client commands, the
server understands several administrative commands anytime during a session,
and the client may always quit the session.

5.2   Haskell Encoding of the SMTP Session Type

To implement the session specification in Haskell, we first translate the SMTP
commands and replies to Haskell data types.

```
-- SMTP commands
data EHLO = EHLO Domain
instance Command EHLO where ...

cEHLO = EHLO undefined                      -- for the protocol specification

-- SMTP replies
data Reply220 = Reply220 Domain [String]
instance Command Reply220 where ...

r220 = Reply220 undefined undefined    -- for the protocol specification
```

The above declarations show the encoding of the first two messages occurring
during an SMTP session, the 220 reply holding the Internet domain and additional information about the mail server, and the EHLO command, holding the Internet domain of the client. The Domain datatype represents either IP addresses
or domain names. To make commands and replies amenable both to parsing and
to printing, we make them instances of the Command type class introduced in
Section 3. The remaining SMTP commands are implemented analogously.

The translation of the previously specified SMTP session type arises from
applying the translation specified in Section 4.

```
smtpSpec
  (send:: (forall x y . x -> y -> s x y))
  (recv:: (forall x y . x -> y -> r x y)) =
  recv p220
    (let a0 = REC (Ga0
                  (send cEHLO
                  (ALT
                    (recv p250
                    (let a1 = REC (Ga1
                                  (ALT
                                  (send cMAIL
                                  (recv p250
                                  (send cRCPT
                                  (let a2 = REC (Ga2
                                              (recv p250
                                              (ALT
                                              (send cDATA
                                              (recv p354
                                              (send cMESG
                                              (recv p250 a1))))
                                              (send cRCPT a2))))
                                  in a2))))
                                  (send cQUIT NULL)))
                    in a1))
                    (recv p5yz a0)))))
        in a0)
```

For each occurrence of a $\mu\beta.\gamma$ in the session type, the translation introduces additional parameterized datatypes as explained in Section 4. Here, we only show the datatype declaration corresponding to β_0 and its instance declaration of the RECBODY type class.

```
data Ga0 send recv a0 =
  Ga0 (send EHLO
       (ALT (recv Reply2 (REC (Ga1 send recv a0))) (recv Reply5 a0)))

instance RECBODY
   (Ga0 send recv a0)
   (send EHLO (ALT (recv Reply2 (REC (Ga1 send recv a0))) (recv Reply5 a0)))
   where
   recbody (Ga0 x) = x
```

5.3   The SMTP Client

With the specification of SMTP sessions in place, we now encode the main function of an email client, sendMessage. The functions adhere to our SMTP session specification which is statically guaranteed by the Haskell type system.

```
sendMessage :: Client -> Server ->
               ReversePath -> [ForwardPath] -> [String] -> IO ()
sendMessage client server sender rcpts message =
  withSocketsDo $ do
  h    <- connectTo (showDomain (name server)) (Service "smtp")
  str <- hGetContents h
  let recv220  = receive (\ (Reply220 server_domain text_220) -> sendEHLO)
      sendEHLO = send (EHLO (cname client)) recvEHLO
      recvEHLO = receive (ALT (\ (Reply2 y z text_250) -> sendMail)
                              (\ (Reply5 y z text_5yz) -> sendEHLO))
      sendMail = left (send (MAIL sender []) (recv250 (sendRCPT rcpts)))
      recv250    cont      = receive (\ (Reply2 y z text_250) -> cont)
      sendRCPT  (rcpt:rcpts) = send (RCPT rcpt []) (recvRCPT rcpts)
      recvRCPT  rcpts        = recv250 (sendRCPT' rcpts)
      sendRCPT' []          = left sendDATA
      sendRCPT' (rcpt:rcpts) = right (send (RCPT rcpt []) (recvRCPT rcpts))
      sendDATA = send DATA recv354
      recv354  = receive (\ (Reply3 y z text_354) -> sendMESG)
      sendMESG = send (LINES message) (recv250 sendQUIT)
      sendQUIT = right (send QUIT finish)
   runSession h recv220 (smtpSpec SEND_MSG RECV_MSG) str
   hClose h
```

The sendMessagefunction takes five arguments: client and server arguments hold information about the parties involved, sender and rcpts encode the email addresses of the sender and the recipients of the message, and message holds the message body itself.

After opening a socket connection to the SMTP server and after getting a handle to the socket to read from it lazily using hGetContents, we first specify the different interaction steps of the client-server communication using send and receive. The first step, recv220, receives the greeting message and transfers the control to the next step, sendEHLO. The sendEHLO step simply sends out the initial command introducing the client to the server. Its continuation, recvHELLO, shows how to handle a choice of two possibly incoming messages: instead of a function, we apply an ALT value holding two alternative handlers branching to two different continuations to receive. The functions recvRCPT and sendRCPT' are recursive functions handling the transmission of a list of recipients. They show how to send a message of two possible alternatives. To continue with the first alternative, we wrap `left` around the continuation `sendDATA`, otherwise, we apply `right` to the second alternative continuation. `Close` in the continuation to the `QUIT` command terminates the session.

The function `runSession` starts the client/server interaction taking `recv220` as entry point, `smtpSpec` as SMTP specification, and the socket both as input stream and output stream.

6   Related Work

The introduction already mentioned some related work on concurrency and session types. A particular system close to session types is Armstrong's UBF [2]. Also relevant to the present work are other applications of domain modeling using type systems.

There are a number of applications, ranging from general techniques to modeling DTD's [22,18]. Also work on modeling type-safe casting [34], the encoding of type equality predicates [7,3], and the representation of type-indexed values [35] is relevant.

A foundational work by Rhiger [31] considers typed encodings of the simply typed lambda calculus in Haskell and clarifies the necessary prerequisites for such an encoding to be sound and complete. An example encoding is developed by Danvy and others [8]. Later work by Chen and Xi [6] extends their approach to a meta-programming setting.

Another application area is modeling external concepts like relational schemes in databases for obtaining a type-safe query language [17], wrapping accesses to COM components [26], and integrating access to Java library [4].

None of the listed works specifies an encoding of recursion as we do in our translation neither do they exploit polymorphism as in our guarantee that client and server specifications match up.

7   Conclusion

A calculus with session types can be embedded into the programming language Haskell in a type-safe way. We give a detailed account of the translation and prove its type safety. Our case study demonstrates that the embedding is practical and exhibits the benefits of declarative programming. The resulting program is straightforward to read and understand.

It would be interesting to further investigate alternative designs for the `Session` monad. In particular, pushing the idea character-based parsing to the extreme appears to lead to a pure implementation on the basis of stream transformers. This implementation would completely decouple the processing of the protocol from the underlying IO actions.

References

1. Torben Amtoft, Flemming Nielson, and Hanne Riis Nielson. *Type and Effect Systems: Behaviours for Concurrency.* Imperial College Press, 1999.
2. Joe Armstrong. Getting erlang to talk to the outside world. In *Proceedings of the 2002 ACM SIGPLAN workshop on Erlang*, pages 64–72. ACM Press, 2002.
3. Arthur I. Baars and S. Doaitse Swierstra. Typing dynamic typing. In Peyton-Jones [24], pages 157–166.
4. Nick Benton and Andrew Kennedy. Interlanguage working without tears: Blending SML with Java. In Peter Lee, editor, *Proc. International Conference on Functional Programming 1999*, pages 126–137, Paris, France, September 1999. ACM Press, New York.
5. Gérard Berry and Gérard Boudol. The chemical abstract machine. *Theoretical Computer Science*, 96, 1992.
6. Chiyan Chen and Hongwei Xi. Meta-programming through typeful code representation. In Olin Shivers, editor, *Proc. International Conference on Functional Programming 2003*, pages 275–286, Uppsala, Sweden, August 2003. ACM Press, New York.
7. James Cheney and Ralf Hinze. A lightweight implementation of generics and dynamics. In *Proceedings of the ACM SIGPLAN workshop on Haskell*, pages 90–104. ACM Press, 2002.
8. Olivier Danvy, Morten Rhiger, and Kristoffer Rose. Normalization by evaluation with typed abstract syntax. *Journal of Functional Programming*, 11(6):673–680, 2001.
9. Cédric Fournet and Georges Gonthier. The reflexive CHAM and the join-calculus. In POPL 1996 [28], pages 372–385.
10. Simon Gay and Malcolm Hole. Types and subtypes for client-server interactions. In Doaitse Swierstra, editor, *Proceedings of the 1999 European Symposium on Programming*, number 1576 in Lecture Notes in Computer Science, pages 74–90, Amsterdam, The Netherlands, April 1999. Springer-Verlag.
11. Simon Gay, Vasco Vasconcelos, and Antonio Ravara. Session types for inter-process communication. Technical Report TR-2003-133, Department of Computing Science, University of Glasgow, 2003.
12. Alessandro Giacalone, Prateek Mishra, and Sanjiva Prasad. FACILE: A symmetric integration of concurrent and functional programming. In J. Díaz and F. Orejas, editors, *TAPSOFT '89*, number 351,352 in Lecture Notes in Computer Science, pages II, 184–209, Barcelona, Spain, March 1989. Springer-Verlag.
13. Haskell 98, a non-strict, purely functional language. http://www.haskell.org/definition, December 1998.
14. Kohei Honda and Mario Tokoro. An object calculus for asynchronous communication. In Pierre America, editor, *5th European Conference on Object-Oriented Programming (ECOOP '91)*, number 512 in Lecture Notes in Computer Science, pages 133–147, Geneva, Switzerland, July 1991. Springer-Verlag.
15. Kohei Honda, Vasco Thudichum Vasconcelos, and Makoto Kubo. Language primitives and type discipline for structured communication-based programming. In Chris Hankin, editor, *Proc. 7th European Symposium on Programming*, number 1381 in Lecture Notes in Computer Science, pages 122–138, Lisbon, Portugal, April 1998. Springer-Verlag.
16. Mark P. Jones. Type classes with functional dependencies. In Gert Smolka, editor, *Proc. 9th European Symposium on Programming*, number 1782 in Lecture Notes in Computer Science, pages 230–244, Berlin, Germany, March 2000. Springer-Verlag.

17. Daan Leijen and Erik Meijer. Domain-specific embedded compilers. In *2nd Conference on Domain-Specific Languages*, Austin, Texas, USA, October 1999. USENIX. `http://usenix.org/events/dsl99/index.html`.

18. Conor McBride. Faking it—simulating dependent types in Haskell. `http://www.dur.ac.uk/~dcs1ctm/faking.ps`, 2001.

19. Erik Meijer and Graham Hutton. Bananas in space: Extending fold and unfold to exponential types. In Simon Peyton Jones, editor, *Proc. Functional Programming Languages and Computer Architecture 1995*, pages 324–333, La Jolla, CA, June 1995. ACM Press, New York.

20. Robin Milner. *Communication and Concurrency*. Prentice Hall, Englewood Cliffs, NJ, 1989.

21. Robin Milner, Joachim Parrow, and David Walker. A calculus of mobile processes, Part I + II. *Information and Control*, 100(1):1–77, 1992.

22. Matthias Neubauer, Peter Thiemann, Martin Gasbichler, and Michael Sperber. A functional notation for functional dependencies. In Ralf Hinze, editor, *Proceedings of the 2001 Haskell Workshop*, 2001. to appear.

23. Martin Odersky and Konstantin Läufer. Putting type annotations to work. In POPL 1996 [28], pages 54–67.

24. Simon Peyton-Jones, editor. *International Conference on Functional Programming*, Pittsburgh, PA, USA, October 2002. ACM Press, New York.

25. Simon Peyton Jones, Andrew Gordon, and Sigbjørn Finne. Concurrent Haskell. In POPL 1996 [28], pages 295–308.

26. Simon Peyton Jones, Erik Meijer, and Daan Leijen. Scripting COM components in Haskell. In *Proc. International Conference of Software Reuse*, 1998.

27. Simon L. Peyton Jones. Tackling the awkward squad: Monadic input/output, concurrency, exceptions, and foreign-language calls in Haskell. In Tony Hoare, Manfred Broy, and Ralf Steinbruggen, editors, *Engineering Theories of Software Construction*, pages 47–96. IOS Press, 2001.

28. *Proceedings of the 1996 ACM SIGPLAN Symposium on Principles of Programming Languages*, St. Petersburg, FL, USA, January 1996. ACM Press.

29. John H. Reppy. *Concurrent Programming in ML*. Cambridge University Press, 1999.

30. Simple mail transfer protocol. `http://www.faqs.org/rfcs/rfc2821.html`, April 2001.

31. Morten Rhiger. A foundation for embedded languages. *ACM Transactions on Programming Languages and Systems*, 25(3):291–315, 2003.

32. Alan Schmitt and Jean-Bernard Stefani. The m-calculus: a higher-order distributed process calculus. In *Proceedings of the 30th ACM SIGPLAN-SIGACT symposium on Principles of programming languages*, pages 50–61. ACM Press, 2003.

33. Peter J. Stuckey and Martin Sulzmann. A theory of overloading. In Peyton-Jones [24], pages 167–178.

34. Stephanie Weirich. Type-safe cast: Functional pearl. In Philip Wadler, editor, *Proc. International Conference on Functional Programming 2000*, pages 58–67, Montreal, Canada, September 2000. ACM Press, New York.

35. Zhe Yang. Encoding types in ML-like languages. In Paul Hudak, editor, *Proc. International Conference on Functional Programming 1998*, pages 289–300, Baltimore, USA, September 1998. ACM Press, New York.

UUXML: A Type-Preserving
XML Schema–Haskell Data Binding

Frank Atanassow, Dave Clarke*, and Johan Jeuring

Institute of Information & Computing Sciences
Utrecht University
The Netherlands
{franka,dave,johanj}@cs.uu.nl

Abstract. An XML data binding is a translation of XML documents into values of some programming language. This paper discusses a type-preserving XML–Haskell data binding that handles documents typed by the W3C XML Schema standard. Our translation is based on a formal semantics of Schema, and has been proved sound with respect to the semantics. We also show a program in Generic Haskell that constructs parsers specialized to a particular Schema type.

1   Introduction

XML [23] is the core technology of modern data exchange. An XML document is essentially a tree-based data structure, usually, but not necessarily, structured according to a type declaration such as a schema. A number of alternative methods of processing XML documents are available:

- **XML API's**. A conventional API such as SAX or the W3C's DOM can be used, together with a programming language such as Java or VBScript, to access the components of a document after it has been parsed.
- **XML programming languages**. A specialized programming language such as W3C's XSLT [24], XDuce [12], Yatl [5], XMλ [17,20], SXSLT [14], XStatic [8] etc. can be used to transform XML documents.
- **XML data bindings**. XML values can be 'embedded' in an existing programming language by finding a suitable mapping between XML types and types of the programming language [18].

Using a specialized programming language or a data binding has significant advantages over the SAX or DOM approach. For example, parsing comes for free and can be optimized for a specific schema. Also, it is easier to implement, test and maintain software in the target language. A data binding has the further advantages that existing programming language technology can be leveraged, and that a programmer need account for XML idiosyncracies (though this may be a disadvantage for some applications). Programming languages for which XML data bindings have been developed include Java [16] and Python, as well

---

* Now at: CWI, Amsterdam, Netherlands, dave@cwi.nl

B. Jayaraman (Ed.): PADL 2004, LNCS 3057, pp. 71–85, 2004.

as declarative programming languages such as Prolog [6] and Haskell [22,29]. Using Haskell as the target for an XML data binding offers the advantages of a typed higher-order programming language with a powerful type system.

Since W3C released XML, thousands of XML tools have been developed, including editors, databases, converters, parsers, validators, search engines, encryptors and compressors [7,9,10]. Many XML applications depend on a schema; we call such tools *schema-aware XML tools* [29]. Examples are a validator, which checks that an XML document exhibits the type structure described by a schema, and an XML editor that suggests admissible elements or attributes at the cursor position. Similarly, the performance of search algorithms and compressors improves when the structure of the document is known in advance. Another feature shared by such programs is that they do essentially the same thing for different schemas. In this sense these tools are very similar to generic algorithms such as the equality function, and the map, fold and zip functions. We claim that many XML tools are generic programs, or would benefit from being viewed as such.

In this paper we present UUXML, a translation of XML documents into Haskell, and more specifically a translation tailored to permit writing programs in Generic Haskell [11], a superset of Haskell that allows to define such generic programs. The documents conform to the type system described in the W3C XML Schema [26,27,28] standard, and the translation preserves typing in a sense we formalize by a type soundness theorem. More details of the translation and a proof of the soundness result are available in a technical report [1].

This paper is organised as follows. Section 2 describes a tool for translating an XML Schema to a set of Haskell data types. Section 3 describes a parser, implemented as a Generic Haskell program, for parsing an XML document into a Haskell value. Section 4 summarizes and discusses related and future work.

2   From Schema to Haskell

XML was introduced with a type formalism called Document Type Declarations (DTDs). Though XML has achieved widespread popularity, DTDs themselves have been deemed too restrictive in practice, and this has motivated the development of alternative type systems for XML documents. The two most popular systems are the RELAX NG standard promulgated by OASIS [19], and the W3C's own XML Schema Recommendation [26,27,28]. Both systems include a set of primitive datatypes such as numbers and dates, a way of combining and naming them, and ways of specifying context-sensitive constraints on documents.

We focus on XML Schema (or simply "Schema" for short—we use lowercase "schema" to refer to the actual type definitions themselves). To write Haskell programs over documents conforming to schemas we require a translation of schemas to Haskell analogous to the HaXml translation of DTDs to Haskell.

We begin this section with a very brief overview of Schema syntax which highlights some of the differences between Schema and DTDs. Next, we give a more formal description of the syntax with an informal sketch of its semantics. With this in hand, we describe a translation of schemas to Haskell data types, and of schema-conforming documents to Haskell values.

Our translation and the syntax used here are based closely on the Schema formal semantics of Brown *et al.*, called the Model Schema Language (MSL) [4]; that treatment also forms the basis of the W3C's own, more ambitious but as yet unfinished, formal semantics [25]. We do not treat all features of Schema, but only the subset covered by MSL (except wildcards). This subset, however, arguably forms a representative subset and suffices for many Schema applications.

2.1   An Overview of XML Schema

A schema describes a set of type declarations which may not only constrain the form of, but also affect the processing of, XML documents (values). Typically, an XML document is supplied along with a Schema file to a Schema processor, which parses and type-checks the document according to the declarations. This process is called *validation* and the result is a Schema value.

Syntax. Schemas are written in XML. For instance, the following declarations define an element and a compound type for storing bibliographical information:

```
<element name="doc" type="document"/>
<complexType name="document">
  <sequence>
    <element ref="author" minOccurs="0" maxOccurs="unbounded"/>
    <element ref="title"/>
    <element ref="year" minOccurs="0"/>
  </sequence>
</complexType>
```

This declares an element doc whose content is of type document, and a type document which consists of a sequence of zero or more author elements, followed by a mandatory title element and then an optional year element. (We omit the declarations for author, *etc.*) A document which validates against doc is:

```
<doc>
  <author>James Joyce</author>
  <title>Ulysses</title>
  <year>1922</year>
</doc>
```

While they may have their advantages in large-scale applications, for our purposes XML and Schema syntax are rather too long-winded and irregular. We use an alternative syntax close to that of MSL [4], which is more orthogonal and suited to formal manipulation. In our syntax, the declarations above are written:

def doc[*document*];   **def** *document* = author*, title, year? ;

and the example document above is written:

doc[author["James Joyce"],title["Ulysses"],year["1922"]]

Differences with DTDs. Schemas are more expressive than DTDs in several ways. The main differences we treat here are summarized below.

1. Schema defines more primitive types, organized into a subtype hierarchy.
2. Schema allows the declaration of user-defined types, which may be used multiple times in the contents of elements.
3. Schema's notion of mixed content is more general than that of DTDs.
4. Schema includes a notion of "interleaving" like SGML's & operator. This allows specifying that a set of elements (or attributes) must appear, but may appear in any order.
5. Schema has a more general notation for repetitions.
6. Schema includes two notions of subtype derivation.

We will treat these points more fully below, but first let us give a very brief overview of the Schema type system.

Overview. A document is typed by a *(model) group*; we also refer to a model group as a *type*. An overview of the syntax of groups is given by the grammar g.

$g ::=$	**group**
ϵ	empty sequence
$\mid g \, , \, g$	sequence
$\mid \emptyset$	empty choice
$\mid g \mid g$	choice
$\mid g \, \& \, g$	interleaving
$\mid g\{m,n\}$	repetition
$\mid \mathbf{mix}(g)$	mixed content
$\mid x$	component name

$m ::= \langle \text{natural} \rangle$	**minimum**

$x ::=$	
$\mid @a$	attribute name
$\mid e$	element name
$\mid t$	type name
$\mid \mathbf{anyType}$	
$\mid \mathbf{anyElem}$	
$\mid \mathbf{anySimpleType}$	
$\mid p$	primitive

$n ::=$	**maximum**
m	bounded
$\mid \infty$	unbounded

This grammar is only a rough approximation of the actual syntax of Schema types. For example, in an actual schema, all attribute names appearing in an element's content must precede the subelements.

The sequence and choice forms are familiar from DTDs and regular expressions. Forms $@a$, e and t are variables referencing, respectively, attributes, elements and types in the schema. We consider the remaining features in turn.

Primitives. Schema defines some familiar primitives types such as *string*, *boolean* and *integer*, but also more exotic ones (which we do not treat here) such as *date*, *language* and *duration*. In most programming languages, the syntax of primitive constants such as string and integer literals is distinct, but in Schema they are rather distinguished by their types. For example, the data "35" may be validated against either *string* or *integer*, producing respectively distinct Schema values "35" ∈ *string* and 35 ∈ *integer*. Thus, validation against a schema produces an "internal" value which depends on the schema involved.

The primitive types are organized into a hierarchy, via restriction subtyping (see below), rooted at **anySimpleType**.

User-defined types. An example of a user-defined type (or "group"), *document*, was given above. DTDs allow the definition of new elements and attributes, but the only mechanism for defining a new type (something which can be referenced in the content of several elements and/or attributes) is the so-called parameter entities, which behave more like macros than a semantic feature.

Mixed content. Mixed content allows interspersing elements with text. More precisely, a document d matches $\mathbf{mix}(g)$ if $unmix(d)$ matches g, where $unmix(d)$ is obtained from d by deleting all character text at the top level. An example of mixed content is an XHTML paragraph element with emphasized phrases; in MSL its content would be declared as $\mathbf{mix}(\mathsf{em}^*)$. The opposite of 'mixed content' is 'element-only content.'

DTDs support a similar, but subtly different, notion of mixed content, specified by a declaration such as:

```
< !ELEMENT text ( #PCDATA | em )* >
```

This allows `em` elements to be interspersed with character data when appearing as the children of `text` (but not as descendants of children). Groups involving `#PCDATA` can only appear in two forms, either by itself, or in a repeated disjunction involving only element names:

```
( #PCDATA | e₁ | e₂ | ⋯ eₙ )* .
```

To see how Schema's notion of mixed content differs from DTDs', observe that a reasonable translation of the DTD content type above is $[\,\mathsf{String} :+: [\![\mathsf{em}]\!]_G\,]$ where $[\![\mathsf{em}]\!]_G$ is the translation of `em`. This might lead one to think that we can translate a schema type such as $\mathbf{mix}(g)$ similarly as $[\,\mathsf{String} :+: [\![g]\!]_G\,]$. However, this translation would not respect the semantics of MSL for at least two reasons. First, it is too generous, because it allows repeated occurrences, yet:

$$\texttt{"hello"}, \mathsf{e}[], \texttt{"world"} \in \mathbf{mix}(\mathsf{e}) \quad \text{but} \quad \texttt{"hello"}, \mathsf{e}[], \mathsf{e}[], \texttt{"world"} \notin \mathbf{mix}(\mathsf{e}) \,.$$

Second, it cannot account for more complex types such as $\mathbf{mix}(\mathsf{e_1}, \mathsf{e_2})$. A document matching the latter type consists of two elements $\mathsf{e_1}$ and $\mathsf{e_2}$, possibly interspersed with text, but the elements *must occur in the given order*. This might be useful, for example, if one wants to intersperse a program grammar given as a type

$$\mathbf{def}\; module = \mathsf{header}, \mathsf{imports}, \mathsf{fixityDecl}^*, \mathsf{valueDecl}^* \,;$$

with comments: $\mathbf{mix}(module)$. An analogous model group is not expressible in the DTD formalism.

Interleaving. Interleaving is rendered in our syntax by the operator &, which behaves like the operator , but allows values of its arguments to appear in either order, *i.e.*, & is commutative. This example schema describes email messages.

$$\mathbf{def}\; email = (\mathsf{subject}\; \& \; \mathsf{from}\; \& \; \mathsf{to})\, , \mathsf{body}\,;$$

Although interleaving does not really increase the expressiveness of Schema over DTDs, they are a welcome convenience. Interleavings can be expanded to a choice of sequences, but these rapidly become unwieldy. For example, $[\![a \ \& \ b]\!] = a, b \mid b, a$ but $[\![a \ \& \ b \ \& \ c]\!] = a, (b, c \mid c, b) \mid b, (a, c \mid c, a) \mid c, (a, b \mid b, a)$. (Note that $[\![a \ \& \ b \ \& \ c]\!] \neq [\![a \ \& \ [\![b \ \& \ c]\!]]\!]$!)

Repetition. In DTDs, one can express repetition of elements using the standard operators for regular patterns: *, $+$ and ?. Schema has a more general notation: if g is a type, then $g\{m, n\}$ validates against a sequence of between m and n occurrences of documents validating against g, where m is a natural and n is a natural or ∞. Again, this does not really make Schema more expressive than DTDs, since we can expand repetitions in terms of sequence and choice, but the expansions are generally much larger than their unexpanded forms.

Derivation. XML Schema also supports two kinds of *derivation* (which we some-times also call *refinement*) by which new types can be obtained from old. The first kind, called *extension*, is quite similar to the notion of inheritance in object-oriented languages. The second kind, called *restriction*, is an 'additive' sort of subtyping, roughly dual to extension, which is multiplicative in character. As an example of extension, we declare a type *publication* obtained from *document* by adding fields at the end:

$$\textbf{def} \ publication \ \textbf{extends} \ document = \mathsf{journal} \mid \mathsf{publisher};$$

A *publication* is a *document* followed by either a journal or publisher field.

Extension is slightly complicated by the fact that attributes are extended 'out of order'. For example, if types t_1 and t_2 are defined:

$$\textbf{def} \ t_1 = @a_1, \mathsf{e}_1; \quad \textbf{def} \ t_2 \ \textbf{extends} \ t_1 = @a_2, \mathsf{e}_2; \qquad (1)$$

then the content of t_2 is $(@a_1 \ \& \ @a_2), \mathsf{e}_1, \mathsf{e}_2$.

To illustrate restriction, we declare a type *article* obtained from *publication* by fixing some of the variability. If an *article* is always from a journal, we write:

$$\textbf{def} \ article \ \textbf{restricts} \ publication = \mathsf{author}^*, \mathsf{title}, \mathsf{year}, \mathsf{journal};$$

So a value of type *article* always ends with a journal, never a publisher, and the year is now mandatory. Note that, when we derive by extension we only mention the new fields, but when we derive by restriction we must mention all the old fields which are to be retained.

In both cases, when a type t' is derived from a type t, values of type t' may be used anywhere a value of type t is called for. For example, the document:

$$\mathsf{author}[\,\text{"Patrik Jansson"}\,], \ \mathsf{author}[\,\text{"Johan Jeuring"}\,],$$
$$\mathsf{title}[\,\text{"Polytypic Unification"}\,], \ \mathsf{year}[\,\text{"1998"}\,], \ \mathsf{journal}[\,\text{"JFP"}\,]$$

validates not only against *article* but also against both *publication* and *document*.

Every type that is not explicitly declared as an extension of another is treated implicitly as restricting a distinguished type called **anyType**, which can be regarded as the union of all types. Additionally, there is a distinguished type **anyElem** which restricts **anyType**, and from which all elements are derived.

2.2   An Overview of the Translation

The objective of the translation is to be able to write Haskell programs on data corresponding to schema-conforming documents. At minimum, we expect the translation to satisfy a type-soundness result which ensures that, if a document validates against a particular schema type, then the translated value is typeable in Haskell by the translated type.

Theorem 1. *Let $[\![-]\!]_G$ and $[\![-]\!]_V^{g,u}$ be respectively the type and value translations generated by a schema. Then, for all documents d, groups g and mixities u, if d validates against g in mixity context u, then $[\![d]\!]_V^{g,u} :: [\![g]\!]_G\ [\![u]\!]_{mix}$.*

Let us outline the difficulties posed by features of Schema. As a starting point, consider how we might translate regular patterns into Haskell.

$$[\![\epsilon]\!]_G = () \qquad\qquad [\![\emptyset]\!]_G = \mathsf{Void}$$
$$[\![g_1\,,\,g_2]\!]_G = ([\![g_1]\!]_G, [\![g_2]\!]_G) \qquad [\![g_1 \mid g_2]\!]_G = \mathsf{Either}\ [\![g_1]\!]_G [\![g_2]\!]_G$$
$$[\![g^*]\!]_G = [\,[\![g_1]\!]_G\,] \qquad\qquad [\![g^+]\!]_G = ([\![g]\!]_G, [\![g^*]\!]_G)$$
$$[\![g?]\!]_G = \mathsf{Maybe}\ [\![g]\!]_G$$

This is the sort of translation employed by HaXml [29], and indeed we follow the same tack. In contrast, WASH [22] takes a decidedly different approach, encoding the state automaton corresponding to a regular pattern at the type level, and makes extensive use of type classes to express the transition relation.

As an example for the reader to refer back to, we present (part of) the translation of the *document* type:

```
data T_document u = T_document
  (Seq Empty (Seq (Rep LE_E_author ZI)
             (Seq LE_E_title (Rep LE_E_year (ZS ZZ))))) u) .
```

Here the leading T_ indicates that this declaration refers to the type *document*, rather than an element (or attribute) of the same name, which would be indicated by a prefix E_ (A_, respectively). We explain the remaining features in turn.

Primitives. Primitives are translated to the corresponding Haskell types, wrapped by a constructor. For example (the argument u relates to mixed content, discussed below):

```
data T_string u  =  T_string String .
```

User-defined types. Types are translated along the lines of HaXml, using products to model sequences and sums to model choices.

```
data Empty u    =  Empty
data Seq g1 g2 u =  Seq (g1 u) (g2 u)
data None u  {- no constructors -}
data Or g1 g2 u  =  Or1 (g1 u) | Or2 (g2 u) .
```

The translation takes each group to a Haskell type of kind $\star \to \star$:

$$[\![\epsilon]\!]_G = \mathsf{Empty} \qquad\qquad [\![g_1 \,,\, g_2]\!]_G = \mathsf{Seq}\ [\![g_1]\!]_G\ [\![g_2]\!]_G$$
$$[\![\emptyset]\!]_G = \mathsf{None} \qquad\qquad [\![g_1 \mid g_2]\!]_G = \mathsf{Or}\ [\![g_1]\!]_G\ [\![g_2]\!]_G \,.$$

Mixed content. The reason each group g is translated to a first-order type $t :: \star \to \star$ rather than a ground type is that the argument, which we call the 'mixity', indicates whether a document occurs in a mixed or element-only context.[1] Accordingly, u is restricted to be either String or (). For example, $e[t]$ translates as $\mathsf{Elem}\ [\![e]\!]_G\ [\![t]\!]_G$ () when it occurs in element-only content, and $\mathsf{Elem}\ [\![e]\!]_G\ [\![t]\!]_G\ \mathsf{String}$ when it occurs in mixed content. The definition of Elem:

$$\textbf{data Elem e g u} = \textit{Elem}\ \mathsf{u}\ (\mathsf{g}\ ())$$

stores with each element a value of type u corresponding to the text which immediately precedes a document item in a mixed context. (The type argument e is a so-called 'phantom type' [15], serving only to distinguish elements with the same content g but different names.) Any trailing text in a mixed context is stored in the second argument of the *Mix* data constructor.

$$\textbf{data Mix g u} = \textit{Mix}\ (\mathsf{g}\ \mathsf{String})\ \mathsf{String}$$

For example, the document

$$\texttt{"one"},\ e_1[],\ \texttt{"two"},\ e_2[],\ \texttt{"three"} \in \mathbf{mix}(e_1\,,\ e_2)$$

is translated as

$$\textit{Mix}\ (\textit{Seq}\ (\textit{Elem}\ \texttt{"one"}\ (\textit{Empty}\ ())))\ (\textit{Elem}\ \texttt{"two"}\ (\textit{Empty}\ ()))))\ \texttt{"three"}$$

Each of the group operators is defined to translate to a type operator which propagates mixity down to its children, for example:

$$\textbf{data Seq g1 g2 u} = \textit{Seq}\ (\mathsf{g1\ u})\ (\mathsf{g2\ u})\,.$$

There are three exceptions to this 'inheritance'. First, $\mathbf{mix}(g)$ ignores the context's mixity and always passes down a String type. Second, $e[g]$ ignores the context's mixity and always passes down a () type, because mixity is not inherited across element boundaries. Finally, primitive content p always ignores its context's mixity because it is atomic.

Interleaving. Interleaving is modeled in essentially the same way as sequencing, except with a different abstract datatype.

$$\textbf{data Inter g1 g2 u} = \textit{Inter}\ (\mathsf{g1\ u})\ (\mathsf{g2\ u})$$

An unfortunate consequence of this is that we lose the ordering of the document values. For example, suppose we have a schema which describes a conference

---

[1] We use the convention u for mixity because m is used for bounds minima.

schedule where it is known that exactly three speakers of different types will appear. A part of such a schema may look like:

def schedule[speaker & invitedSpeaker & keynoteSpeaker] ; .

A schema processor must know the order in which speakers appeared, but since we do not record the permutation we cannot recover the document ordering. More commonly, since attribute groups are modeled as interleavings of attributes, this means in particular that schema processors using our translation cannot know the order in which attributes are specified in an XML document.

Repetition.   Repetitions $g\{m, n\}$ are   modeled   using   a   datatype $Rep \; [\![g]\!]_G \; [\![m, n]\!]_B$ u and a set of datatypes modeling bounds:

$$[\![0, 0]\!]_B = \mathsf{ZZ} \qquad\qquad\qquad [\![0, m + 1]\!]_B = \mathsf{ZS} \; [\![0, m]\!]_B$$
$$[\![0, \infty]\!]_B = \mathsf{ZI} \qquad\qquad [\![m + 1, n + 1]\!]_B = \mathsf{SS} \; [\![m, n]\!]_B$$

defined by:

$$
\begin{array}{lcl}
\textbf{data } \mathsf{Rep\; g\; b\; u} & = & Rep \; (\mathsf{b\; g\; u}) \\
\textbf{data } \mathsf{ZZ\; g\; u} & = & ZZ \\
\textbf{data } \mathsf{ZI\; g\; u} & = & ZI \; [\mathsf{g\; u}] \\
\textbf{data } \mathsf{ZS\; b\; g\; u} & = & ZS \; (\mathsf{Maybe\; (g\; u)}) \; (\mathsf{Rep\; g\; b\; u}) \\
\textbf{data } \mathsf{SS\; b\; g\; u} & = & SS \; (\mathsf{g\; u}) \; (\mathsf{Rep\; g\; b\; u}) \; .
\end{array}
$$

The names of datatypes modeling bounds are meant to suggest the familiar unary encoding of naturals, 'Z' for zero and 'S' for successor, while 'I' stands for 'infinity'. Some sample translations are:

$$[\![e\{2, 4\}]\!]_G = Rep \; [\![e]\!]_G \; (SS \; (SS \; (ZS \; (ZS \; ZZ))))$$
$$[\![e\{0, \infty\}]\!]_G = Rep \; [\![e]\!]_G \; ZI$$
$$[\![e\{2, \infty\}]\!]_G = Rep \; [\![e]\!]_G \; (SS \; (SS \; ZI)) \; .$$

Derivation. Derivation poses one of the greatest challenges for the translation, since Haskell has no native notion of subtyping, though type classes are a comparable feature. We avoid type classes here, though, because one objective of our data representation is to support writing schema-aware programs in Generic Haskell. Such programs operate by recursing over the structure of a type, so encoding the subtyping relation in a non-structural manner such as *via* the type class relation would be counterproductive.

The type **anyType** behaves as the *union* of all types, which suggests an implementation in terms of Haskell datatypes: encode **anyType** as a datatype with one constructor for each type that directly restricts it, the direct subtypes, and one for values that are 'exactly' of type **anyType**.

In the case of our bibliographical example, we have:

data T_anyType u   = *T_anyType*
data LE_T_anyType u = *EQ_T_anyType* (T_anyType u)
                         | *LE_T_anySimpleType* (LE_T_anySimpleType u)
                         | *LE_T_anyElem* (LE_T_anyElem u)
                         | *LE_T_document* (LE_T_document u) .

The alternatives *LE_* indicate the direct subtypes while the *EQ_* alternative is 'exactly' **anyType**. The *document* type and its subtypes are translated similarly:

data LE_T_document u   = *EQ_T_document* (T_document u)
                             | *LE_T_publication* (LE_T_publication u)
data LE_T_publication u = *EQ_T_publication* (T_publication u)
                             | *LE_T_article* (LE_T_article u)
data LE_T_article u   = *EQ_T_article* (T_article u) .

When we *use* a Schema type in Haskell, we can choose to use either the 'exact' version, say T_document, or the version which also includes all its subtypes, say LE_T_document. Since Schema allows using a subtype of *t* anywhere *t* is expected, we translate all variables as references to an LE_ type. This explains why, for example, T_document refers to LE_E_author rather than E_author in its body.

What about extension? To handle the 'out-of-order' behavior of extension on attributes we define a function *split* which splits a type into a (longest) leading attribute group (ϵ if there is none) and the remainder. For example, if t_1 and t_2 are defined as in (1) then $split(t_1) = (@a_1, e_1)$ and, if t_2' is the 'extended part' of t_2, then $split(t_2') = (@a_2, e_2)$. We then define the translation of t_2 to be:

$$fst(split(t_1)) \text{ \& } fst(split(t_2')), \ (snd(split(t_1)) \ , \ snd(split(t_2'))) \ .$$

In fact, to accomodate extension, every type is translated this way. Hence T_document above begins with 'Seq Empty ...', since it has no attributes, and the translation of *publication*:

data T_publication u = *T_publication*
  (Seq (Inter Empty Empty)
     (Seq (Seq (Rep LE_E_author ZI) (Seq LE_E_title (Rep LE_E_year (ZS ZZ))))
        (Or LE_E_journal LE_E_publisher)) u)

begins with 'Seq (Inter Empty Empty) ...', which is the concatenation of the attributes of *document* (namely none) with the attributes of *publication* (again none). So attributes are accumulated at the beginning of the type declaration.

In contrast, the translation of *article*, which derives from *publication via* restriction, corresponds more directly with its declaration as written in the schema.

    data T_article u = *T_article*
       (Seq Empty (Seq (Rep LE_E_author ZI)
                    (Seq LE_E_title (Seq LE_E_year LE_E_journal)))) u)

This is because, unlike with extensions where the user only specifies the new fields, the body of a restricted type is essentially repeated as a whole.

3   From XML Documents to Haskell Data

In this section we describe an implementation of the translation outlined in the previous section as a generic parser for XML documents, written in Generic Haskell. To abstract away from details of XML concrete syntax, rather than parse strings, we use a universal data representation *Document* which presents a document as a tree (or rather a forest):

type Doc   =   [DocItem]
data DocItem   =   *DText* String | *DAttr* String Doc | *DElem* String Doc

We use standard techniques [13] to define a set of monadic parsing combinators operating over Doc. P a is the type of parsers that parse a value of type a. We omit the definitions here because they are straightfoward generalizations of string parsers. The type of generic parsers is the kind-indexed type $\mathsf{GParse}\{\!\{\kappa\}\!\}$ t and $gParse\{\!\{\mathsf{t}\}\!\}$ denotes a parser which tries to read a document into a value of type t. We now describe its behavior on the various components of Schema.

$$\begin{aligned}
\textbf{type } \mathsf{GParse}\{\!\{*\}\!\} \text{ t} \quad &= \quad \mathsf{P} \text{ t} \\
gParse\{\!\{\mathsf{t} :: \kappa\}\!\} \quad &:: \quad \mathsf{GParse}\{\!\{\kappa\}\!\} \text{ t} \\
gParse\{\!\{\mathsf{String}\}\!\} \quad &= \quad pMixed \\
gParse\{\!\{\mathsf{Unit}\}\!\} \quad &= \quad pElementOnly
\end{aligned}$$

The first two cases handle mixities: *pMixed* optionally matches *DText* chunk(s), while parser *pElementOnly* always succeeds without consuming input. Note that no schema type actually translates to Unit or String (by themselves), but these cases are used indirectly by the other cases.

$$\begin{aligned}
gParse\{\!\{\mathsf{Empty\ u}\}\!\} \quad &= \quad return\ Empty \\
gParse\{\!\{\mathsf{Seq\ g1\ g2\ u}\}\!\} \quad &= \quad \textbf{do } doc1 \leftarrow gParse\{\!\{\mathsf{g1\ u}\}\!\} \\
&\qquad\quad\ doc2 \leftarrow gParse\{\!\{\mathsf{g2\ u}\}\!\} \\
&\qquad\quad\ return\ (Seq\ doc1\ doc2) \\
gParse\{\!\{\mathsf{None\ u}\}\!\} \quad &= \quad mzero \\
gParse\{\!\{\mathsf{Or\ g1\ g2\ u}\}\!\} \quad &= \quad fmap\ Or1\ gParse\{\!\{\mathsf{g1\ u}\}\!\} \\
&<\!|\!> \quad fmap\ Or2\ gParse\{\!\{\mathsf{g2\ u}\}\!\}
\end{aligned}$$

Sequences and choices map closely onto the corresponding monad operators. $p <\!|\!> q$ tries parser p on the input first, and if p fails attempts again with q, and *mzero* is the identity element for $<\!|\!>$.

$$\begin{aligned}
gParse\{\!\{\mathsf{Rep\ g\ b\ u}\}\!\} \quad &= \quad fmap\ Rep\ gParse\{\!\{\mathsf{b\ g\ u}\}\!\} \\
gParse\{\!\{\mathsf{ZZ\ g\ u}\}\!\} \quad &= \quad return\ ZZ \\
gParse\{\!\{\mathsf{ZI\ g\ u}\}\!\} \quad &= \quad fmap\ ZI\ \$\ many\ gParse\{\!\{\mathsf{g\ u}\}\!\} \\
gParse\{\!\{\mathsf{ZS\ g\ b\ u}\}\!\} \quad &= \quad \textbf{do } x \leftarrow option\ gParse\{\!\{\mathsf{g\ u}\}\!\} \\
&\qquad\quad\ y \leftarrow gParse\{\!\{\mathsf{b\ g\ u}\}\!\} \\
&\qquad\quad\ return\ (ZS\ x\ (Rep\ y)) \\
gParse\{\!\{\mathsf{SS\ g\ b\ u}\}\!\} \quad &= \quad \textbf{do } x \leftarrow gParse\{\!\{\mathsf{g\ u}\}\!\} \\
&\qquad\quad\ y \leftarrow gParse\{\!\{\mathsf{b\ g\ u}\}\!\} \\
&\qquad\quad\ return\ (SS\ x\ (Rep\ y))
\end{aligned}$$

Repetitions are handled using the familiar combinators *many p* and *option p*, which parse, resp., a sequence of documents matching *p* and an optional *p*.

$$gParse\{|\mathsf{T\_string}|\} \quad = \quad fmap \ T\_string \ pText$$
$$gParse\{|\mathsf{T\_integer}|\} \quad = \quad fmap \ T\_integer \ pReadableText$$

String primitives are handled by a parser *pText*, which matches any *DText* chunk(s). Function *pReadableText* parses integers (also doubles and booleans— here omitted) using the standard Haskell *read* function, since we defined our alternative schema syntax to use Haskell syntax for the primitives.

$$gParse\{|\mathsf{Elem} \ e \ g \ u|\} \quad = \quad \mathbf{do} \ mixity \leftarrow gParse\{|u|\}$$
$$\mathbf{let} \ p = gParse\{|g|\} \ pElementOnly$$
$$elemt \ gName\{|e|\} \ (fmap \ (Elem \ mixity) \ p)$$

An element is parsed by first using the mixity parser corresponding to u to read any preceding mixity content, then by using the parser function *elemt* to read in the actual element. *elemt s p* checks for a document item *DElem s d*, where the parser *p* is used to (recursively) parse the subdocument *d*. We always pass in *gParse*{|g|} *pElementOnly* for *p* because mixed content is 'canceled' when we descend down to the children of an element. Parsing of attributes is similar.

This code uses an auxiliary type-indexed function *gName*{|e|} to acquire the name of an element; it has only one interesting case:

$$gName\{|\mathsf{Con} \ c \ a|\} = drop \ 5 \ (conName \ c)$$

This case makes use of the special Generic Haskell syntax Con *c a*, which binds *c* to a record containing syntactic information about a datatype. The right-hand side just returns the name of the constructor, minus the first five characters (say, LE_T_), thus giving the attribute or element name as a string.

$$gParse\{|\mathsf{Mix} \ g \ u|\} \quad = \quad \mathbf{do} \ doc \leftarrow gParse\{|g|\} \ pMixed$$
$$mixity \leftarrow pMixed$$
$$return \ (Mix \ doc \ mixity)$$

When descending through a Mix type constructor, we perform the opposite of the procedure for elements above: we ignore the mixity parser corresponding to u and substitute *pMixed* instead. *pMixed* is then called again to pick up the trailing mixity content.

Most of the code handling interleaving is part of another auxiliary function, *gInter*{|t|}, which has kind-indexed type:

$$\mathbf{type} \ \mathsf{GInter}\{|\star|\} \quad = \quad \forall a \ . \ \mathsf{PermP} \ (t \rightarrow a) \rightarrow \mathsf{PermP} \ a \ .$$

Interleaving is handled using these permutation phrase combinators [3]:

$$(<\|>) \qquad :: \quad \forall a \ b \ . \ \mathsf{PermP} \ (a \rightarrow b) \rightarrow \mathsf{P} \ a \rightarrow \mathsf{PermP} \ b$$
$$(<|?>) \qquad :: \quad \forall a \ b \ . \ \mathsf{PermP} \ (a \rightarrow b) \rightarrow (a, \mathsf{P} \ a) \rightarrow \mathsf{PermP} \ b$$
$$mapPerms \quad :: \quad \forall a \ b \ . \ (a \rightarrow b) \rightarrow \mathsf{PermP} \ a \rightarrow \mathsf{PermP} \ b$$
$$permute \qquad :: \quad \forall a \ . \ \mathsf{PermP} \ a \rightarrow \mathsf{P} \ a$$
$$newperm \qquad :: \quad \forall a \ b \ . \ (a \rightarrow b) \rightarrow \mathsf{PermP} \ (a \rightarrow b) \ .$$

Briefly, a permutation parser $q :: \mathsf{PermP}$ a reads a sequence of (possibly optional) documents in any order, returning a semantic value a. Permutation parsers are created using *newperm* and chained together using $<\|>$ and $<|?>$ (if optional). *mapPerms* is the standard map function for the PermP type. *permute* q converts a permutation parser q into a normal parser.

$$gParse\{\!|\mathsf{Inter\ g1\ g2\ u}|\!\} = permute\ \$\ (gInter\{\!|\mathsf{g2\ u}|\!\} . gInter\{\!|\mathsf{g1\ u}|\!\})\ (newperm\ Inter)$$

To see how the above code works, observe that:

$$
\begin{aligned}
&f1 = gInter\{\!|\mathsf{g1\ u}|\!\} && :: && \forall \mathsf{g1\ u\ b}\,.\,\mathsf{PermP\ (g1\ u \to b) \to PermP\ b} \\
&f2 = gInter\{\!|\mathsf{g2\ u}|\!\} && :: && \forall \mathsf{g2\ u\ c}\,.\,\mathsf{PermP\ (g2\ u \to c) \to PermP\ c} && \text{-- hence} \\
&f2\,.\,f1 && :: && \forall \mathsf{g1\ g2\ u\ c}\,.\,\mathsf{PermP\ (g1\ u \to g2\ u \to c) \to PermP\ c}\,.
\end{aligned}
$$

Note that if c is instantiated to $\mathsf{Inter\ g1\ g2\ u}$, then the function type appearing in the domain becomes the type of the data constructor *Inter*, so we need only apply it to *newperm Inter* to get a permutation parser of the right type.

$$(f1\,.\,f2)\ (newperm\ Inter) :: \forall \mathsf{g1\ g2\ u}\,.\,\mathsf{PermP\ (Inter\ g1\ g2\ u)}$$

Many cases of function *gInter* need not be defined because the syntax of interleavings in Schema is so restricted.

$$
\begin{aligned}
&gInter\{\!|\mathsf{t} :: \kappa|\!\} && :: && \mathsf{GInter}\{\!|\kappa|\!\}\ \mathsf{t} \\
&gInter\{\!|\mathsf{Con\ c\ a}|\!\} && = && (<\!\|\!>\ fmap\ Con\ gParse\{\!|\mathsf{a}|\!\}) \\
&gInter\{\!|\mathsf{Inter\ g1\ g2\ u}|\!\} && = && gInter\{\!|\mathsf{g1\ u}|\!\}\,.\,gInter\{\!|\mathsf{g2\ u}|\!\} \\
& && && .\,mapPerms\ (\lambda f\ x\ y \to f\ (Inter\ x\ y)) \\
&gInter\{\!|\mathsf{Rep\ g\ (ZS\ ZZ)\ u}|\!\} && = && (<\!|?\!>\ (Rep\ gDefault\{\!|\mathsf{(ZS\ ZZ)\ g\ u}|\!\} \\
& && && ,\,fmap\ Rep\ gParse\{\!|\mathsf{(ZS\ ZZ)\ g\ u}|\!\}))
\end{aligned}
$$

In the Con case, we see that an atomic type (an element or attribute name) produces a permutation parser transformer of the form $(<\!\|\!>\ q)$. The Inter case composes such parsers, so more generally we obtain parser transformers of the form $(<\!\|\!>\ q_1 <\!\|\!>\ q_2 <\!\|\!>\ q_3 <\!|\!> ...)$. The Rep case is only ever called when g is atomic and the bounds are of the form $\mathsf{ZS\ ZZ}$: this corresponds to a Schema type like $\mathsf{e}\{0,1\}$, that is, an optional element (or attribute).[2]

4 Conclusions

XML Schema has several features not available natively in Haskell, including mixed content, two forms of subtyping and a generalized form of repetition. Nevertheless, we have shown that these features can be accomodated by Haskell's datatype mechanism alone. The existence of a simple formal semantics

---

[2] The GH compiler does not accept the syntax $gInter\{\!|\mathsf{Rep\ g\ (ZS\ ZZ)\ u}|\!\}$. We define this case using $gInter\{\!|\mathsf{Rep\ g\ b\ u}|\!\}$, where b is used consistently instead of $\mathsf{ZS\ ZZ}$, but the function is only ever called when $\mathsf{b = ZS\ ZZ}$.

for Schema such as MSL's was a great help to both the design and implementation of our work, and essential for the proof of type soundness.

Though the translation is cumbersome for Haskell programs which process documents of a single schema, for schema-aware programs such as the parser of Section 3 this defect is not so noticeable because Generic Haskell programs usually do not need to pattern-match deeply into values of a datatype. In a companion paper [2] we show how to use Generic Haskell to automatically infer type isomorphisms to effectively customize our translation and make writing non-schema-aware XML software far simpler.

Besides its verbosity, there are some downsides to the translation. Although the handling of subtyping is straightforward and relatively usable, it does not take advantage of the 1-unambiguity constraint on Schema groups to factor out common prefixes. This has a negative impact on the efficiency of generic applications such as our parser. Another issue is the use of unary encoding in repetition bounds, though this could be addressed by using a larger radix. Finally, schema types, which obey equational laws, are always translated as abstract datatypes, which satisfy analagous laws only up to isomorphism; this lack of coherence means that users must know some operational details of our translator. Our work on isomorphism inference can help address this problem.

We have so far developed a prototype implementation of the translation and checked its correctness with a few simple examples and some slightly larger ones, such as the generic parser presented here and a generic pretty-printer. Future work may involve extending the translation to cover more Schema features such as facets and wildcards, adopting the semantics described in more recent work [21], which more accurately models Schema's named typing, and exploiting the 1-unambiguity constraint to obtain a more economical translation.

References

1. Frank Atanassow, Dave Clarke, and Johan Jeuring. Scripting XML with Generic Haskell. Technical Report UU-CS-2003, Utrecht University, 2003.
2. Frank Atanassow and Johan Jeuring. Inferring type isomorphisms generically. To appear in Proc. MPC '04.
3. A.I. Baars, A. Löh, and S.D. Swierstra. Parsing permutation phrases. In R. Hinze, editor, *Proceedings of the 2001 ACM SIGPLAN Haskell Workshop*, pages 171–182. Elsevier, 2001.
4. Allen Brown, Matthew Fuchs, Jonathan Robie, and Philip Wadler. MSL: A model for W3C XML Schema. In *Proc. WWW10*, May 2001.
5. Sophie Cluet and Jérôme Siméon. YATL: a functional and declarative language for XML, 2000.
6. Jorge Coelho and Mário Florido. Type-based XML processing in logic programming. In *PADL 2003*, pages 273–285, 2003.
7. Peter Flynn. *Understanding SGML and XML Tools*. Kluwer Academic Publishers, 1998.
8. Vladimir Gapeyev and Benjamin C. Pierce. Regular object types. In *European Conference on Object-oriented Programming (ECOOP 2003)*, 2003.
9. Lars M. Garshol. Free XML tools and software. Available from http://www.garshol.priv.no/download/xmltools/.

10. Google. Web Directory on XML tools. http://www.google.com/.
11. Ralf Hinze and Johan Jeuring. Generic Haskell: practice and theory, 2003. To appear.
12. Haruo Hosoya and Benjamin C. Pierce. XDuce: A typed XML processing language. In *Third International Workshop on the Web and Databases (WebDB), volume 1997 of Lecture Notes in Computer Science*, pages 226–244, 2000.
13. Graham Hutton and Erik Meijer. Monadic parser combinators. *Journal of Functional Programming*, 8(4):437–444, 1996.
14. Oleg Kiselyov and Shriram Krishnamurti. SXSLT: manipulation language for XML. In *PADL 2003*, pages 226–272, 2003.
15. Daan Leijen and Erik Meijer. Domain specific embedded compilers. In *Second USENIX Conference on Domain Specific Languages (DSL'99)*, pages 109–122, Austin, Texas, October 1999. USENIX Association. Also appeared in ACM SIG-PLAN Notices 35, 1, (Jan. 2000).
16. Brett McLaughlin. *Java & XML data binding*. O'Reilly, 2003.
17. Erik Meijer and Mark Shields. XMLambda: A functional language for constructing and manipulating XML documents. Available from http://www.cse.ogi.edu/~mbs/, 1999.
18. Eldon Metz and Allen Brookes. XML data binding. *Dr. Dobb's Journal*, pages 26–36, March 2003.
19. OASIS. RELAX NG. http://www.relaxng.org, 2001.
20. Mark Shields and Erik Meijer. Type-indexed rows. In *The 28th Annual ACM SIGPLAN - SIGACT Symposium on Principles of Programming Languages*, pages 261–275, 2001. Also available from http://www.cse.ogi.edu/~mbs/.
21. Jérôme Siméon and Philip Wadler. The essence of XML. In *Proc. POPL 2003*, 2003.
22. Peter Thiemann. A typed representation for HTML and XML documents in Haskell. *Journal of Functional Programming*, 12(4&5):435–468, July 2002.
23. W3C. XML 1.0. http://www.w3.org/XML/, 1998.
24. W3C. XSL Transformations 1.0. http://www.w3.org/TR/xslt, 1999.
25. W3C. XML Schema: Formal description. http://www.w3.org/TR/xmlschema-formal, 2001.
26. W3C. XML Schema part 0: Primer. http://www.w3.org/TR/xmlschema-0, 2001.
27. W3C. XML Schema part 1: Structures. http://www.w3.org/TR/xmlschema-1, 2001.
28. W3C. XML Schema part 2: Datatypes. http://www.w3.org/TR/xmlschema-2, 2001.
29. Malcolm Wallace and Colin Runciman. Haskell and XML: Generic combinators or type-based translation? In *International Conference on Functional Programming*, pages 148–159, 1999.

Improved Compilation of Prolog to C Using Moded Types and Determinism Information[*]

J. Morales[1], Manuel Carro[1], and Manuel Hermenegildo[1,2]

[1] C.S. School, Technical U. of Madrid,
jfran@clip.dia.fi.upm.es and {mcarro,herme}@fi.upm.es
[2] Depts. of Comp. Sci. and Elec. and Comp. Eng., U. of New Mexico (UNM)
herme@unm.edu

Abstract. We describe the current status of and provide performance results for a prototype compiler of Prolog to C, ciaocc. ciaocc is novel in that it is designed to accept different kinds of high-level information, typically obtained via an automatic analysis of the initial Prolog program and expressed in a standardized language of assertions. This information is used to optimize the resulting C code, which is then processed by an off-the-shelf C compiler. The basic translation process essentially mimics the unfolding of a bytecode emulator with respect to the particular bytecode corresponding to the Prolog program. This is facilitated by a flexible design of the instructions and their lower-level components. This approach allows reusing a sizable amount of the machinery of the bytecode emulator: predicates already written in C, data definitions, memory management routines and areas, etc., as well as mixing emulated bytecode with native code in a relatively straightforward way. We report on the performance of programs compiled by the current version of the system, both with and without analysis information.

Keywords: Prolog, C, optimizing compilation, global analysis.

1 Introduction

Several techniques for implementing Prolog have been devised since the original interpreter developed by Colmerauer and Roussel [1], many of them aimed at achieving more speed. An excellent survey of a significant part of this work can be found in [2]. The following is a rough classification of implementation techniques for Prolog (which is, in fact, extensible to many other languages):

- Interpreters (such as C-Prolog [3] and others), where a slight preprocessing or translation might be done before program execution, but the bulk of the work is done at runtime by the interpreter.

[*] This work is partially supported by Spanish MCYT Project TIC 2002-0055 *CUBICO*, and EU Projects IST-2001-34717 *Amos* and IST-2001-38059 *ASAP*, and by the Prince of Asturias Chair in Information Science and Technology at the University of New Mexico. J. Morales is also supported by an MCYT fellowship co-financed by the European Social Fund.

B. Jayaraman (Ed.): PADL 2004, LNCS 3057, pp. 86–103, 2004.

- Compilers to *bytecode* and their interpreters (often called emulators), where the compiler produces relatively low level code in a special-purpose language. Most current emulators for Prolog are based on the Warren Abstract Machine (WAM) [4,5], but other proposals exist [6,7].
- Compilers to a lower-level language, often ("native") machine code, which require little or no additional support to be executed. One solution is for the compiler to generate machine code directly. Examples of this are Aquarius [8], versions of SICStus Prolog [9] for some architectures, BIM-Prolog [10], and Gnu Prolog [11]. Another alternative is to generate code in a (lower-level) language, such as, e.g., C-- [12] or C, for which compilers are readily available; the latter is the approach taken by `wamcc` [13].

Each solution has its advantages and disadvantages:

Executable performance vs. executable size and compilation speed: Compilation to lower-level code can achieve faster programs by eliminating interpretation overhead and performing lower-level optimizations. This difference gets larger as more sophisticated forms of code analysis are performed as part of the compilation process. Interpreters in turn have potentially smaller load/compilation times and are often a good solution due to their simplicity when speed is not a priority. Emulators occupy an intermediate point in complexity and cost. Highly optimized emulators [9,14,15,16,17] offer very good performance and reduced program size which may be a crucial issue for very large programs and symbolic data sets.

Portability: Interpreters offer portability since executing the same Prolog code in different architectures boils down (in principle) to recompiling the interpreter. Emulators usually retain the portability of interpreters, by recompiling the emulator (bytecode is usually architecture-independent), unless they are written in machine code.[1] Compilers to native code require architecture-dependent back-ends which typically make porting and maintaining them a non-trivial task. Developing these back-ends can be simplified by using an intermediate RTL-level code [11], although different translations of this code are needed for different architectures.

Opportunities for optimizations: Code optimization can be applied at the Prolog level [18,19], to WAM code [20], to lower-level code [21], and/or to native code [8,22]. At a higher level it is typically possible to perform more global and structural optimizations, which are then implicitly carried over onto lower levels. Lower-level optimizations can be introduced as the native code level is approached; performing these low-level optimizations is one of the motivations for compiling to machine code. However, recent performance evaluations show that well-tuned emulators can beat, at least in some cases, Prolog compilers which generate machine code directly but which do not perform extensive optimization [11]. Translating to a low-level language such as C is interesting because it makes portability easier, as C compilers exist for most architectures and C

---

[1] This is the case for the Quintus emulator, although it is coded in a generic RTL language ("PROGOL") to simplify ports.

is low-level enough as to express a large class of optimizations which cannot be captured solely by means of Prolog-to-Prolog transformations.

Given all the considerations above, it is safe to say that different approaches are useful in different situations and perhaps even for different parts of the same program. The emulator approach can be very useful during development, and in any case for non-performance bound portions of large symbolic data sets and programs. On the other hand, in order to generate the highest performance code it seems appropriate to perform optimizations at all levels and to eventually translate to machine code. The selection of a language such as C as an intermediate target can offer a good compromise between opportunity for optimization, portability for native code, and interoperability in multi-language applications.

In `ciaocc` we have taken precisely such an approach: we implemented a compilation from Prolog to native code via an intermediate translation to C which optionally uses high-level information to generate optimized C code. Our starting point is the standard version of Ciao Prolog [17], essentially an emulator-based system of competitive performance. Its abstract machine is an evolution of the &-Prolog abstract machine [23], itself a separate branch from early versions (0.5–0.7) of the SICStus Prolog abstract machine.

`ciaocc` adopts the same scheme for memory areas, data tagging, etc. as the original emulator. This facilitates mixing emulated and native code (as done also by SICStus) and has also the important practical advantage that many complex and already existing fragments of C code present in the components of the emulator (builtins, low-level file and stream management, memory management and garbage collection routines, etc.) can be reused by the new compiler. This is important because our intention is not to develop a prototype but a full compiler that can be put into everyday use and developing all those parts again would be unrealistic.

A practical advantage is the availability of high-quality C compilers for most architectures. `ciaocc` differs from other systems which compile Prolog to C in that that the translation includes a scheme to optionally optimize the code using higher-level information available at compile-time regarding determinacy, types, instantiation modes, etc. of the source program.

Maintainability and portability lead us also not to adopt other approaches such as compiling to C--. The goal of C-- is to achieve portable high performance without relinquishing control over low-level details, which is of course very desirable. However, the associated tools do not seem to be presently mature enough as to be used for a compiler in production status within the near future, and not even to be used as base for a research prototype in their present stage. Future portability will also depend on the existence of back-ends for a range of architectures. We, however, are quite confident that the backend which now generates C code could be adapted to generate C-- (or other low-level languages) without too many problems.

The high-level information, which is assumed expressed by means of the powerful and well-defined assertion language of [24], is inferred by automatic global analysis tools. In our system we take advantage of the availability of relatively mature tools for this purpose within the Ciao environment, and, in particular the preprocessor, CiaoPP [25]. Alternatively, such assertions can also be simply provided by the programmer.

Our approach is thus different from, for example, wamcc, which also generated C, but which did not use extensive analysis information and used low-level tricks which in practice tied it to a particular C compiler, gcc. Aquarius [8] and Parma [22] used analysis information at several compilation stages, but they generated directly machine code, and it has proved difficult to port and maintain them. Notwithstanding, they were landmark contributions that proved the power of using global information in a Prolog compiler.

A drawback of putting more burden on the compiler is that compile times and compiler complexity grow, specially in the global analysis phase. While this can turn out to be a problem in extreme cases, incremental analysis in combination with a suitable module system [26] can result in very reasonable analysis times in practice.[2] Moreover, global analysis is not mandatory in ciaocc and can be reserved for the phase of generating the final, "production" executable. We expect that, as the system matures, ciaocc itself (now in a prototype stage) will not be slower than a Prolog-to-bytecode compiler.

2   The Basic Compilation Scheme

The compilation process starts with a preprocessing phase which normalizes clauses (i.e., aliasing and structure unification is removed from the head), and expands disjunctions, negations and if-then-else constructs. It also unfolds calls to is/2 when possible into calls to simpler arithmetic predicates, replaces the cut by calls to the lower-level predicates metachoice/1 (which stores in its argument the address of the current choicepoint) and metacut/1 (which performs a cut to the choicepoint whose address is passed in its argument), and performs a simple, local analysis which gathers information about the type and freeness state of variables.[3] Having this analysis in the compiler (in addition to the analyses performed by the preprocessor) improves the code even if no external information is available. The compiler then translates this normalized version of Prolog to WAM-based instructions (at this point the same ones used by the Ciao emulator), and then it splits these WAM instructions into an intermediate low level code and performs the final translation to C.

Typing WAM Instructions: WAM instructions dealing with data are handled internally using an enriched representation which encodes the possible instantiation state of their arguments.

---

[2] See [25] and its references for reports on analysis times of CiaoPP.

[3] In general, the types used throughout the paper are *instantiation types*, i.e., they have mode information built in (see [24] for a more complete discussion of this issue). *Freeness of variables* distinguishes between free variables and the *top* type, "term", which includes any term.

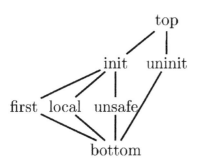

Fig. 1. Lattice of WAM types.

This allows using original type information, and also generating and propagating lower-level information regarding the type (i.e., from the point of view of the tags of the abstract machine) and instantiation/initialization state of the variables (which is not seen at a higher level). Unification instructions are represented as $\langle TypeX, X \rangle = \langle TypeY, Y \rangle$, where $TypeX$ and $TypeY$ refer to the classification of WAM-level types (see Figure 1), and X and Y refer to variables, which may be later stored as WAM X or Y registers or directly passed on as C function arguments. *init* and *uninit* correspond to initialized (i.e., free) and uninitialized variable cells. *First*, *local*, and *unsafe* classify the status of the variables according to where they appear in a clause.

Table 1 summarizes the aforementioned representation for some selected cases. The registers taken as arguments are the temporary registers $x(I)$, the stack variables $y(I)$, and the register for structure arguments $n(I)$. The last one can be seen as the second argument, implicit in the *unify_* WAM instructions. A number of other temporal registers are available, and used, for example, to hold intermediate results from expression evaluation. *_constant, *_nil, *_list and *_structure instructions are represented similarly. Only $x(\cdot)$ variables are created in an uninitialized state, and they are initialized on demand (in particular, when calling another predicate which may overwrite the registers and in the points where garbage collection can start). This representation is more uniform than the traditional WAM instructions, and as more information is known about the variables, the associated (low level) types can be refined and more specific code generated. Using a richer lattice and initial information (Section 3), a more descriptive intermediate code can be generated and used in the back-end.

Table 1. Representation of some WAM unification instructions with types.

put_variable(I,J)	$\langle$uninit,I$\rangle = \langle$uninit,J$\rangle$
put_value(I,J)	$\langle$init,I$\rangle = \langle$uninit,J$\rangle$
get_variable(I,J)	$\langle$uninit,I$\rangle = \langle$init,J$\rangle$
get_value(I,J)	$\langle$init,I$\rangle = \langle$init,J$\rangle$
unify_variable(I[, J])	if (initialized(J)) then $\langle$uninit,I$\rangle = \langle$init,J$\rangle$ else $\langle$uninit,I$\rangle = \langle$uninit,J$\rangle$
unify_value(I[, J])	if (initialized(J)) then $\langle$init,I$\rangle = \langle$init,J$\rangle$ else $\langle$init,I$\rangle = \langle$uninit,J$\rangle$

Table 2. Control and data instructions.

Choice, stack and heap management instructions	
no_choice	Mark that there is no alternative
push_choice(Arity)	Create a choicepoint
recover_choice(Arity)	Restore the state stored in a choicepoint
last_choice(Arity)	Restore state and discard latest choice point
complete_choice(Arity)	Complete the choice point
cut_choice(Chp)	Cut to a given choice point
push_frame	Allocate a frame on top of the stack
complete_frame(FrameSize)	Complete the stack frame
modify_frame(NewSize)	Change the size of the frame
pop_frame	Deallocate the last frame
recover_frame	Recover after returning from a call
ensure_heap(Amount, Arity)	Ensure that enough heap is allocated.
Unification	
load(X, Type)	Load X with a term
trail_if_conditional(A)	Trail if A is a conditional variable
bind(TypeX, X, TypeY, Y)	Bind X and Y
read(Type, X)	Begin read of the structure arguments of X
deref(X, Y)	Dereference X into Y
move(X, Y)	Copy X to Y
globalize_if_unsafe(X, Y)	Copy (safely) X to stack variable Y
globalize_to_arg(X, Y)	Copy (safely) X to structure argument Y
jump(Label)	Jump to *Label*
cjump(Cond, Label)	Jump to *Label* if *Cond* is true
not(Cond)	Negate the *Cond* condition
test(Type, X)	True if X matches *Type*
equal(X, Y)	True if X and Y are equal
Indexing	
switch_on_type(X, Var, Str, List, Cons)	Jump to the label that matches the type of X
switch_on_functor(X, Table, Else)	
switch_on_cons(X, Table, Else)	

Generation of the Intermediate Low Level Language: WAM-like control and data instructions (Table 2) are then split into simpler ones (Table 3) (of a level similar to that of the BAM [27]) which are more suitable for optimizations, and which simplify the final code generation. The *Type* argument in the unification instructions reflects the type of the their arguments: for example, in the instruction *bind*, *Type* is used to specify if the arguments contain a variable or not. For the unification of structures, write and read modes are avoided by using a two-stream scheme [2] which is implicit in the unification instructions in Table 1 and later translated into the required series of assignments and jump instructions (*jump*, *cjump*) in Table 2. The WAM instructions *switch_on_term*, *switch_on_cons* and *switch_on_functor* are also included, although the C back-end does not exploit them fully at the moment, resorting to a linear search in some cases. A more efficient indexing mechanism will be implemented in the near future.

Builtins return an exit state which is used to decide whether to backtrack or not. Determinism information, if available, is passed on through this stage and used when compiling with optimizations (see Section 3).

```
    while (code != NULL)
        code = ((Continuation (*)(State *))code)(state);
```

`Continuation foo(State *state) {`	`Continuation foo_cont(State *state) {`
`...`	`...`
`  state->cont = &foo_cont;`	`  return state->cont;`
`  return &bar;`	`}`
`}`	

Fig. 2. The C execution loop and blocks scheme.

Compilation to C: The final C code conceptually corresponds to an unfolding of the emulator loop with respect to the particular sequence(s) of WAM instructions corresponding to the Prolog program. Each basic block of bytecode (i.e., each sequence beginning in a label and ending in an instruction involving a possibly non-local jump) is translated to a separate C function, which receives (a pointer to) the state of the abstract machine as input argument, and returns a pointer to the continuation. This approach, chosen on purpose, does not build functions which are too large for the C compiler to handle. For example, the code corresponding to a head unification is a basic block, since it is guaranteed that the labels corresponding to the two-stream algorithm will have local scope. A failure during unification is implemented by (conditionally) jumping to a special label, *fail*, which actually implements an exit protocol similar to that generated by the general C translation. Figure 2 shows schematic versions of the execution loop and templates of the functions that code blocks are compiled into.

This scheme does not require machine-dependent options of the C compiler or extensions to ANSI C. One of the goals of our system –to study the impact of optimizations based on high-level information on the program– can be achieved with the proposed compilation scheme, and, as mentioned before, we give portability and code cleanliness a high priority. The option of producing more efficient but non-portable code can always be added at a later stage.

An Example — the `fact/2` *Predicate:* We will illustrate briefly the different compilation stages using the well-known factorial program (Figure 3). We have chosen it due to its simplicity, even if the performance gain is not very high in this case. The normalized code is shown in Figure 4, and the WAM code corresponding to the recursive clause is listed in the leftmost column of Table 3, while the internal representation of this code appears in the middle column of the same table. Variables are annotated using information which can be deduced from local clause inspection.

This WAM-like representation is translated to the low-level code as shown in Figure 5 (ignore, for the moment, the framed instructions; they will be discussed in Section 3). This code is what is finally translated to C.

For reference, executing `fact(100, N)` 20000 times took 0.65 seconds running emulated bytecode, and 0.63 seconds running the code compiled to C (a speedup of 1.03). This did not use external information, used the emulator data structures to store Prolog terms, and performed runtime checks to verify that the arguments are of the right type, even when this is not strictly necessary. Since the loop in Figure 2 is a bit more costly (by a few assembler instructions) than the WAM emulator loop, the speedup brought about by the C translation alone is, in many cases, not as relevant as one may think at first.

```
fact(0, 1).              fact(A, B) :-    fact(A, B) :-
fact(X, Y) :-                0 = A,           A > 0,
    X > 0,                   1 = B.           builtin__sub1_1(A, C),
    X0 is X - 1,                              fact(C, D),
    fact(X0, Y0),                             builtin__times_2(A, D, B).
    Y is X * Y0.
```

Fig. 3. Factorial, initial code.   **Fig. 4.** Factorial, after normalizing.

Table 3. WAM code and internal representation without and with external types information. Underlined instruction changed due to additional information.

WAM code	Without Types/Modes	With Types/Modes
put_constant(0,2)	$0 = \langle \text{uninit},\text{x}(2)\rangle$	$0 = \langle \text{uninit},\text{x}(2)\rangle$
builtin_2(37,0,2)	$\langle \text{init},\text{x}(0)\rangle > \langle \text{int}(0),\text{x}(2)\rangle$	$\langle \text{int},\text{x}(0)\rangle > \langle \text{int}(0),\text{x}(2)\rangle$
allocate	builtin__push_frame	builtin__push_frame
get_y_variable(0,1)	$\langle \text{uninit},\text{y}(0)\rangle = \langle \text{init},\text{x}(1)\rangle$	$\langle \text{uninit},\text{y}(0)\rangle = \langle \text{var},\text{x}(1)\rangle$
get_y_variable(2,0)	$\langle \text{uninit},\text{y}(2)\rangle = \langle \text{init},\text{x}(0)\rangle$	$\langle \text{uninit},\text{y}(2)\rangle = \langle \text{int},\text{x}(0)\rangle$
init([1])	$\langle \text{uninit},\text{y}(1)\rangle = \langle \text{uninit},\text{y}(1)\rangle$	$\langle \text{uninit},\text{y}(1)\rangle = \langle \text{uninit},\text{y}(1)\rangle$
true(3)	builtin__complete_frame(3)	builtin__complete_frame(3)
function_1(2,0,0)	builtin__sub1_1(	builtin__sub1_1(
	$\langle \text{init},\text{x}(0)\rangle, \langle \text{uninit},\text{x}(0)\rangle)$	$\langle \text{int},\text{x}(0)\rangle, \langle \text{uninit},\text{x}(0)\rangle)$
put_y_value(1,1)	$\langle \text{init},\text{y}(1)\rangle = \langle \text{uninit},\text{x}(1)\rangle$	$\langle \text{var},\text{y}(1)\rangle = \langle \text{uninit},\text{x}(1)\rangle$
call(fac/2,3)	builtin__modify_frame(3)	builtin__modify_frame(3)
	fact($\langle \text{init},\text{x}(0)\rangle, \langle \text{init},\text{x}(1)\rangle$)	fact($\langle \text{init},\text{x}(0)\rangle, \langle \text{var},\text{x}(1)\rangle$)
put_y_value(2,0)	$\langle \text{init},\text{y}(2)\rangle = \langle \text{uninit},\text{x}(0)\rangle$	$\langle \text{int},\text{y}(2)\rangle = \langle \text{uninit},\text{x}(0)\rangle$
put_y_value(2,1)	$\langle \text{init},\text{y}(1)\rangle = \langle \text{uninit},\text{x}(1)\rangle$	$\langle \text{number},\text{y}(1)\rangle = \langle \text{uninit},\text{x}(1)\rangle$
function_2(9,0,0,1)	builtin__times_2($\langle \text{init},\text{x}(0)\rangle,$	builtin__times_2($\langle \text{int},\text{x}(0)\rangle,$
	$\langle \text{init},\text{x}(1)\rangle,\langle \text{uninit},\text{x}(0)\rangle)$	$\langle \text{number},\text{x}(1)\rangle, \langle \text{uninit},\text{x}(0)\rangle)$
get_y_value(0,0)	$\langle \text{init},\text{y}(0)\rangle = \langle \text{init},\text{x}(0)\rangle$	$\langle \text{var},\text{y}(0)\rangle = \langle \text{init},\text{x}(0)\rangle$
deallocate	builtin__pop_frame	builtin__pop_frame
execute(true/0)	builtin__proceed	builtin__proceed

3   Improving Code Generation

In order to improve the generated code using global information, the compiler can take into account types, modes, determinism and non-failure properties [25] coded as assertions [24] — a few such assertions can be seen in the example which appears later in this section. Automatization of the compilation process is

```
fact(x(0), x(1)) :-                    last_choice(2)
    push_choice(2)                     load(x(2),int(0))
    ensure_heap(callpad,2)             >(x(0),x(2))
    deref(x(0),x(0))                   push_frame
    cjump(not(test(var,x(0))),V3)      move(x(1),y(0))
    load(temp2,int(0))                 move(x(0),y(2))
    bind(var,x(0),nonvar,temp2)        init(y(1))
    jump(V4)                           complete_frame(3)
  V3:                                  builtin__sub1(x(0), x(0))
    cjump(not(test(int(0),x(0))),fail) move(y(1),x(1))
  V4:                                  modify_frame(3)
    deref(x(1),x(1))                   fact(x(0), x(1))
    cjump(not(test(var,x(1))),V5)      recover_frame
    load(temp2,int(1))                 move(y(2),x(0))
    bind(var,x(1),nonvar,temp2)        move(y(1),x(1))
    jump(V6)                           builtin__times(x(0), x(1), x(0))
  V5:                                  deref(y(0),temp)
    cjump(not(test(int(1),x(1))),fail) deref(x(0),x(0))
  V6:                                  =(temp,x(0))
    complete_choice(2)                 pop_frame
;
```

Fig. 5. Low level code for the `fact/2` example (see also Section 3).

achieved by using the CiaoPP analysis tool in connection with ciaocc. CiaoPP implements several powerful analysis (for modes, types, and determinacy, besides other relevant properties) which are able to generate (or check) these assertions. The program information that CiaoPP is currently able to infer automatically is actually enough for our purposes (with the single exception stated in Section 4).

The generation of low-level code using additional type information makes use of a lattice of moded types obtained by extending the *init* element in the lattice in Figure 1 with the type domain in Figure 6. `str(N/A)` corresponds to (and expands to) each of the structures whose name and arity are known at compile time. This information enriches the *Type* parameter of the low-level code. Information about the determinacy / number of solutions of each call is carried over into this stage and used to optimize the C code.

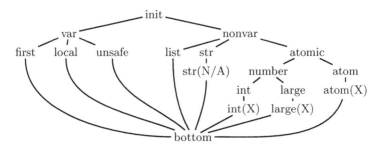

Fig. 6. Extended *init* subdomain.

In general, information about types and determinism makes it possible to avoid some runtime tests. The standard WAM compilation also performs some optimizations (e.g., classification of variables and indexing on the first argument), but they are based on a per-clause (per-predicate, in the case of indexing) analysis, and in general it does not propagate the deduced information (e.g. from arithmetic builtins). A number of further optimizations can be done by using type, mode, and determinism information:

Unify Instructions: Calls to the general *unify* builtin are replaced by the more specialized *bind* instruction if one or both arguments are known to store variables. When arguments are known to be constants, a simple comparison instruction is emitted instead.

Two-Stream Unification: Unifying a register with a structure/constant requires some tests to determine the unification mode (read or write). An additional test is required to compare the register value with the structure/constant. These tests can often be removed at compile-time if enough information is known about the variable.

Indexing: Index trees are generated by selecting literals (mostly builtins and unifications), which give type/mode information, to construct a decision tree on the types of the first argument.[4] When type information is available, the search can be optimized by removing some of the tests in the nodes.

Avoiding Unnecessary Variable Safety Tests: Another optimization performed in the low level code using type information is the replacement of globalizing instructions for unsafe variables by explicit dereferences. When the type of a variable is nonvar, its globalization is equivalent to a dereference, which is faster.

Uninitialized Output Arguments: When possible, letting the called predicate fill in the contents of output arguments in pre-established registers avoids allocation, initialization, and binding of free variables, which is slower.

Selecting Optimized Predicate Versions: Calls to predicates can also be optimized in the presence of type information. Specialized predicate versions (in the sense of low level optimizations) can be generated and selected using call patterns deduced from the type information. The current implementation does not generate specialized versions of user predicates, since this can already be done extensively by CiaoPP [18]. However it does optimize calls to internal *builtin* predicates written in C (such as, e.g., arithmetic builtins), which results in relevant speedups in many cases.

Determinism: These optimizations are based on two types of analysis. The first one uses information regarding the number of solutions for a predicate call to deduce, for each such call, if there is a known and fixed fail continuation. Then, instructions to manage choicepoints are inserted. The resulting code is then re-analyzed to remove these instructions when possible or to replace them by simpler ones (e.g., to restore a choice point state without untrailing, if it is known at compile time that the execution will not trail any value since the choice point

---

[4] This is the WAM definition, which can of course be extended to other arguments.

was created). The latter can take advantage of additional information regarding register, heap, and trail usage of each predicate.[5] In addition, the C back-end can generate different argument passing schemes based on determinism information: predicates with zero or one solution can be translated to a function returning a boolean, and predicates with exactly one solution to a function returning void. This requires a somewhat different translation to C (which we do not have space to describe in full) and which takes into account this possibility by bypassing the emulator loop, in several senses similarly to what is presented in [28].

An Example — the fact/2 *Predicate with program information:* Let us assume that it has been inferred that fact/2 (Figure 3) is always called with its first argument instantiated to an integer and with a free variable in its second argument. This information is written in the assertion language for example as:[6]

```
:- true pred fact(X, Y) :  int * var => int * int.
```

which reflects the types and modes of the calls and successes of the predicate. That information is also propagated through the normalized predicate producing the annotated program shown in Figure 7, where program-point information is also shown.

```
fact(A, B) :-                  fact(A, B) :-
    true(int(A)),                  true(int(A)),
    0 = A,                         A > 0,
    true(var(B)),                  true(int(A)), true(var(C)),
    1 = B.                         builtin__sub1_1(A, C),
                                   true(any(C)), true(var(D)),
                                   fact(C, D),
                                   true(int(A)), true(int(D)),
                                   true(var(B)),
                                   builtin__times_2(A, D, B).
```

Fig. 7. Annotated factorial (using type information).

The WAM code generated for this example is shown in the rightmost column of Table 3. Underlined instructions were made more specific due to improved information — but note that the representation is homogeneous with respect to the "no information" case. The impact of type information in the generation of low-level code can be seen in Figure 5. Instructions inside the dashed boxes are

---

[5] This is currently known only for internal predicates written in C, and which are available by default in the system, but the scheme is general and can be extended to Prolog predicates.

[6] The true prefix implies that this information is to be *trusted and used*, rather than to be *checked* by the compiler. Indeed, we require the stated properties to be correct, and ciaocc does not check them: this is a task delegated to CiaoPP. Wrong *true* assertions can, therefore, lead to incorrect compilation. However, the assertions generated by CiaoPP are guaranteed correct by the analysis process.

removed when type information is available, and the (arithmetic) builtins enclosed in rectangles are replaced by calls to specialized versions which work with integers and which do not perform type/mode testing. The optimized `fact/2` program took 0.54 seconds with the same call as in Section 3: a 20% speedup with respect to the bytecode version and a 16% speedup over the compilation to C without type information.

Table 4. Bytecode emulation vs. unoptimized, optimized (types), and optimized (types and determinism) compilation to C. *Arithmetic – Geometric* means are shown.

Program	Bytecode (Std. Ciao)	Non opt. C	Opt1. C	Opt2. C
queens11 (1)	691	391 (1.76)	208 (3.32)	166 (4.16)
crypt (1000)	1525	976 (1.56)	598 (2.55)	597 (2.55)
primes (10000)	896	697 (1.28)	403 (2.22)	402 (2.22)
tak (1000)	9836	5625 (1.74)	5285 (1.86)	771 (12.75)
deriv (10000)	125	83 (1.50)	82 (1.52)	72 (1.74)
poly (100)	439	251 (1.74)	199 (2.20)	177 (2.48)
qsort (10000)	521	319 (1.63)	378 (1.37)	259 (2.01)
exp (10)	494	508 (0.97)	469 (1.05)	459 (1.07)
fib (1000)	263	245 (1.07)	234 (1.12)	250 (1.05)
knights (1)	621	441 (1.46)	390 (1.59)	356 (1.74)
Average Speedup		(1.46 – 1.43)	(1.88 – 1.77)	(3.18 – 2.34)

4   Performance Measurements

We have evaluated the performance of a set of benchmarks executed by emulated bytecode, translation to C, and by other programming systems. The benchmarks, while representing interesting cases, are not real-life programs, and some of them have been executed up to 10.000 times in order to obtain reasonable and stable execution times. Since parts of the compiler are still in an experimental state, we have not been able to use larger benchmarks yet. All the measurements have been performed on a Pentium 4 Xeon @ 2.0GHz with 1Gb of RAM, running Linux with a 2.4 kernel and using `gcc` 3.2 as C compiler. A short description of the benchmarks follows:

crypt: Cryptoarithmetic puzzle involving multiplication.

primes: Sieve of Erathostenes (with N = 98).

tak: Takeuchi function with arguments `tak(18, 12, 6, X)`.

deriv: Symbolic derivation of polynomials.

poly: Symbolically raise `1+x+y+z` to the 10th power.

qsort: QuickSort of a list of 50 elements.

exp: 13^{7111} using both a linear- and a logarithmic-time algorithm.

fib: F_{1000} using a simply recursive predicate.

knight: Chess knight tour in a 5×5 board.

A summary of the results appears in Table 4. The figures between parentheses in the first column is the number of repetitions of each benchmark. The second column contains the execution times of programs run by the Ciao bytecode emulator. The third column corresponds to programs compiled to C without compile-time information. The fourth and fifth columns correspond, respectively, to the execution times when compiling to C with type and type+determinism information. The numbers between parentheses are the speedups relative to the bytecode version. All times are in milliseconds. Arithmetic and geometric means are also shown in order to diminish the influence of exceptional cases.

Table 5. Speed of other Prolog systems and Mercury

Program	GProlog	WAMCC	SICStus	SWI	Yap	Mercury	$\frac{\text{Opt2. C}}{\text{Mercury}}$
queens11 (1)	809	378	572	5869	362	106	1.57
crypt (1000)	1258	966	1517	8740	1252	160	3.73
primes (10000)	1102	730	797	7259	1233	336	1.20
tak (1000)	11955	7362	6869	74750	8135	482	1.60
deriv (10000)	108	126	121	339	100	72	1.00
poly (100)	440	448	420	1999	424	84	2.11
qsort (10000)	618	522	523	2619	354	129	2.01
exp (10)	—	—	415	—	340	—	—
fib (1000)	—	—	285	—	454	—	—
knights (1)	911	545	631	2800	596	135	2.63
						Average	1.98 – 1.82

Table 5 shows the execution times for the same benchmarks in five well-known Prolog compilers: GNU Prolog 1.2.16, wamcc 2.23, SICStus 3.8.6, SWI-Prolog 5.2.7, and Yap 4.5.0. The aim is not really to compare directly with them, because a different underlying technology and external information is being used, but rather to establish that our baseline, the speed of the bytecode system (Ciao), is similar and quite close, in particular, to that of SICStus. In principle, comparable optimizations could be made in these systems. The cells marked with "—" correspond to cases where the benchmark could not be executed (in GNU Prolog, wamcc, and SWI, due to lack of multi-precision arithmetic).

We also include the performance results for Mercury [29] (version 0.11.0). Strictly speaking the Mercury compiler is not a Prolog compiler: the source language is substantially different from Prolog. But Mercury has enough similarities to be relevant and its performance represents an upper reference line, given that the language was restricted in several ways to allow the compiler, which generates C code with different degrees of "purity", to achieve very high performance by using extensive optimizations. Also, the language design requires the necessary information to perform these optimizations to be included by the programmer as part of the source. Instead, the approach that we use in Ciao is to infer automatically the information and not restricting the language.

Going back to Table 4, while some performance gains are obtained in the *naive* translation to C, these are not very significant, and there is even one program which shows a slowdown. We have tracked this down to be due to a combination of several factors:

- The simple compilation scheme generates clean, portable, "trick-free" C (some compiler dependent extensions would speed up the programs). The execution profile is very near to what the emulator would do.
- As noted in Section 2, the C compiler makes the fetch/switch loop of the emulator a bit cheaper than the C execution loop. We have identified this as a cause of the poor speedup of programs where recursive calls dominate the execution (e.g., factorial). We want, of course, to improve this point in the future.
- The increment in size of the program (to be discussed later — see Table 6) may also cause more cache misses. We also want to investigate this point in more detail.

As expected, the performance obtained when using compile-time information is much better. The best speedups are obtained in benchmarks using arithmetic builtins, for which the compiler can use optimized versions where several checks have been removed. In some of these cases the functions which implement arithmetic operations are simple enough as to be inlined by the C compiler — an added benefit which comes for free from compiling to an intermediate language (C, in this case) and using tools designed for it. This is, for example, the case of queens, in which it is known that all the numbers involved are integers. Besides the information deduced by the analyzer, hand-written annotations stating that the integers involved fit into a machine word, and thus there is no need for infinite precision arithmetic, have been manually added.[7]

Determinism information often (but not always) improves the execution. The Takeuchi function (tak) is an extreme case, where savings in choicepoint generation affect execution time. While the performance obtained is still almost a factor of 2 from that of Mercury, the results are encouraging since we are dealing with a more complex source language (which preserves full unification, logical variables, cuts, call/1, database, etc.), we are using a portable approach (compilation to standard C), and we have not yet applied all possible optimizations.

A relevant point is to what extent a sophisticated analysis tool is useful in practical situations. The degree of optimization chosen can increase the time spent in the compilation, and this might preclude its everyday use. We have measured (informally) the speed of our tools in comparison with the standard Ciao Prolog compiler (which generates bytecode), and found that the compilation to C takes about three times more than the compilation to bytecode. A considerable amount of time is used in I/O, which is being performed directly from Prolog, and which can be optimized if necessary. Due to a well-developed machinery (which can notwithstanding be improved in a future by, e.g, compiling CiaoPP itself to C), the global analysis necessary for examples is really

---

[7] This is the only piece of information used in our benchmarks that cannot be currently determined by CiaoPP. It should be noted, though, that the absence of this annotation would only make the final executable less optimized, but never incorrect.

Table 6. Compared size of object files (bytecode vs. C) including *Arithmetic - Geometric* means.

Program	Bytecode	Non opt. C	Opt1. C	Opt2. C
queens11	7167	36096 (5.03)	29428 (4.10)	42824 (5.97)
crypt	12205	186700 (15.30)	107384 (8.80)	161256 (13.21)
primes	6428	50628 (7.87)	19336 (3.00)	31208 (4.85)
tak	5445	18928 (3.47)	18700 (3.43)	25476 (4.67)
deriv	9606	46900 (4.88)	46644 (4.85)	97888 (10.19)
poly	13541	163236 (12.05)	112704 (8.32)	344604 (25.44)
qsort	6982	90796 (13.00)	67060 (9.60)	76560 (10.96)
exp	6463	28668 (4.43)	28284 (4.37)	25560 (3.95)
fib	5281	15004 (2.84)	14824 (2.80)	18016 (3.41)
knights	7811	39496 (5.05)	39016 (4.99)	39260 (5.03)
Average Increase		(7.39 – 6.32)	(5.43 – 4.94)	(8.77 – 7.14)

fast and never exceeded twice the time of the compilation to C. Thus we think that the use of global analysis to obtain the information we need for ciaocc is a practical option already in its current state.

Table 6 compares object size (in bytes) of the bytecode and the different schemes of compilation to C and using the same compiler options in all cases. While modern computers usually have a large amount of memory, and program size hardly matters for a single application, users stress computers more and more by having several applications running simultaneously. On the other hand, program size does impact their startup time, important for small, often-used commands. Besides, size is still very important when addressing small devices with limited resources.

As mentioned in Section 1, due to the different granularity of instructions, larger object files and executables are expected when compiling to C. The ratio depends heavily on the program and the optimizations applied. Size increase with respect to the bytecode can be as large as 15× when translating to C without optimizations, and the average case sits around a 7-fold increase. This increment is partially due to repeated code in the indexing mechanism, which we plan to improve in the future.[8] Note that, as our framework can mix bytecode and native code, it is possible to use both in order to achieve more speed in critical parts, and to save program space otherwise. Heuristics and translation schemes like those described in [30] can hence be applied (and implemented as a source to source transformation).

The size of the object code produced by wamcc is roughly comparable to that generated by ciaocc, although wamcc produces smaller intermediate object code files. However the final executable / process size depends also on which libraries are linked statically and/or dynamically. The Mercury system is somewhat incomparable in this regard: it certainly produces relatively small component files but then relatively large final executables (over 1.5 MByte).

---

[8] In all cases, the size of the bytecode emulator / runtime support (around 300Kb) has to be added, although not all the functionality it provides is always needed.

Size, in general, decreases when using type information, as many runtime type tests are removed, the average size being around five times the bytecode size. Adding determinism information increases the code size because of the additional inlining performed by the C compiler and the more complex parameter passing code. Inlining was left to the C compiler; experiments show that more aggressive inlining does not necessarily result in better speedups.

It is interesting to note that some optimizations used in the compilation to C would not give comparable results when applied directly to a bytecode emulator. For example, a version of the bytecode emulator hand-coded to work with small integers (which can be boxed into a tagged word) performed worse than that obtained doing the same with compilation to C. That suggests that when the overhead of calling builtins is reduced, as is the case in the compilation to C, some optimizations which only produce minor improvements for emulated systems acquire greater importance.

5   Conclusions and Future Work

We have reported on the scheme and performance of `ciaocc`, a Prolog-to-C compiler which uses type analysis and determinacy information to improve code generation by removing type and mode checks and by making calls to specialized versions of some builtins. We have also provided performance results. `ciaocc` is still in a prototype stage, but it already shows promising results.

The compilation uses internally a simplified and more homogeneous representation for WAM code, which is then translated to a lower-level intermediate code, using the type and determinacy information inferred by CiaoPP. This code is finally translated into C by the compiler back-end. The intermediate code makes the final translation step easier and will facilitate developing new back-ends for other target languages.

We have found that optimizing a WAM bytecode emulator is more difficult and results in lower speedups, due to the larger granularity of the bytecode instructions. The same result has been reported elsewhere [2], although some recent work tries to improve WAM code by means of local analysis [20].

We expect to also be able to use the information inferred by CiaoPP (e.g., determinacy) to improve clause selection and to generate a better indexing scheme at the C level by using hashing on constants, instead of the linear search used currently. We also want to study which other optimizations can be added to the generation of C code without breaking its portability, and how the intermediate representation can be used to generate code for other back-ends (for example, GCC RTL, CIL, Java bytecode, etc.).

References

1. Colmerauer, A.: The Birth of Prolog. In: Second History of Programming Languages Conference. ACM SIGPLAN Notices (1993) 37–52

2. Van Roy, P.: 1983-1993: The Wonder Years of Sequential Prolog Implementation. Journal of Logic Programming **19/20** (1994) 385–441
3. Pereira, F.: C-Prolog User's Manual, Version 1.5, University of Edinburgh. (1987)
4. Warren, D.: An Abstract Prolog Instruction Set. Technical Report 309, Artificial Intelligence Center, SRI International, 333 Ravenswood Ave, Menlo Park CA 94025 (1983)
5. Ait-Kaci, H.: Warren's Abstract Machine, A Tutorial Reconstruction. MIT Press (1991)
6. Taylor, A.: High-Performance Prolog Implementation. PhD thesis, Basser Department of Computer Science, Unversity of Sidney (1991)
7. Krall, A., Berger, T.: The VAM_{AI} - an abstract machine for incremental global dataflow analysis of Prolog. In de la Banda, M.G., Janssens, G., Stuckey, P., eds.: ICLP'95 Post-Conference Workshop on Abstract Interpretation of Logic Languages, Tokyo, Science University of Tokyo (1995) 80–91
8. Van Roy, P., Despain, A.: High-Performace Logic Programming with the Aquarius Prolog Compiler. IEEE Computer Magazine (1992) 54–68
9. Swedish Institute for Computer Science PO Box 1263, S-164 28 Kista, Sweden: SICStus Prolog 3.8 User's Manual. 3.8 edn. (1999) Available from `http://www.sics.se/sicstus/`.
10. Mariën, A.: Improving the Compilation of Prolog in the Framework of the Warren Abstract Machine. PhD thesis, Katholieke Universiteit Leuven (1993)
11. Diaz, D., Codognet, P.: Design and Implementation of the GNU Prolog System. Journal of Functional and Logic Programming **2001** (2001)
12. Jones, S.L.P., Ramsey, N., Reig, F.: C--: A Portable Assembly Language that Supports Garbage Collection. In Nadathur, G., ed.: International Conference on Principles and Practice of Declarative Programming. Number 1702 in Lecture Notes in Computer Science, Springer Verlag (1999) 1–28
13. Codognet, P., Diaz, D.: WAMCC: Compiling Prolog to C. In Sterling, L., ed.: International Conference on Logic Programming, MIT PRess (1995) 317–331
14. Quintus Computer Systems Inc. Mountain View CA 94041: Quintus Prolog User's Guide and Reference Manual—Version 6. (1986)
15. Santos-Costa, V., Damas, L., Reis, R., Azevedo, R.: The Yap Prolog User's Manual. (2000) Available from `http://www.ncc.up.pt/~vsc/Yap`.
16. Demoen, B., Nguyen, P.L.: So Many WAM Variations, So Little Time. In: Computational Logic 2000, Springer Verlag (2000) 1240–1254
17. Bueno, F., Cabeza, D., Carro, M., Hermenegildo, M., López-García, P., Puebla, G.: The Ciao Prolog System. Reference Manual (v1.8). The Ciao System Documentation Series–TR CLIP4/2002.1, School of Computer Science, Technical University of Madrid (UPM) (2002) System and on-line version of the manual available at `http://clip.dia.fi.upm.es/Software/Ciao/`.
18. Puebla, G., Hermenegildo, M.: Abstract Specialization and its Applications. In: ACM Partial Evaluation and Semantics based Program Manipulation (PEPM'03), ACM Press (2003) 29–43 Invited talk.
19. Winsborough, W.: Multiple Specialization using Minimal-Function Graph Semantics. Journal of Logic Programming **13** (1992) 259–290
20. Ferreira, M., Damas, L.: Multiple Specialization of WAM Code. In: Practical Aspects of Declarative Languages. Number 1551 in LNCS, Springer (1999)
21. Mills, J.: A high-performance low risc machine for logic programming. Journal of Logic Programming (6) (1989) 179–212
22. Taylor, A.: LIPS on a MIPS: Results from a prolog compiler for a RISC. In: 1990 International Conference on Logic Programming, MIT Press (1990) 174–189

23. Hermenegildo, M., Greene, K.: The &-Prolog System: Exploiting Independent And-Parallelism. New Generation Computing **9** (1991) 233–257
24. Puebla, G., Bueno, F., Hermenegildo, M.: An Assertion Language for Constraint Logic Programs. In Deransart, P., Hermenegildo, M., Maluszynski, J., eds.: Analysis and Visualization Tools for Constraint Programming. Number 1870 in LNCS. Springer-Verlag (2000) 23–61
25. Hermenegildo, M., Puebla, G., Bueno, F., López-García, P.: Program Development Using Abstract Interpretation (and The Ciao System Preprocessor). In: 10th International Static Analysis Symposium (SAS'03). Number 2694 in LNCS, Springer-Verlag (2003) 127–152
26. Cabeza, D., Hermenegildo, M.: A New Module System for Prolog. In: International Conference on Computational Logic, CL2000. Number 1861 in LNAI, Springer-Verlag (2000) 131–148
27. Van Roy, P.: Can Logic Programming Execute as Fast as Imperative Programming? PhD thesis, Univ. of California Berkeley (1990) Report No. UCB/CSD 90/600.
28. Henderson, F., Somogyi, Z.: Compiling Mercury to High-Level C Code. In Nigel Horspool, R., ed.: Proceedings of Compiler Construction 2002. Volume 2304 of LNCS., Springer-Verlag (2002) 197–212
29. Somogyi, Z., Henderson, F., Conway, T.: The execution algorithm of Mercury: an efficient purely declarative logic programming language. JLP **29** (1996)
30. Tarau, P., De Bosschere, K., Demoen, B.: Partial Translation: Towards a Portable and Efficient Prolog Implementation Technology. Journal of Logic Programming **29** (1996) 65–83

A Generic Persistence Model for (C)LP Systems (and Two Useful Implementations)[*]

J. Correas[1], J.M. Gómez[1], M. Carro[1], D. Cabeza[1], and M. Hermenegildo[1,2]

[1] School of Computer Science, Technical University of Madrid (UPM)
[2] Depts. of Comp. Science and El. and Comp. Eng., U. of New Mexico (UNM)

Abstract. This paper describes a model of persistence in (C)LP languages and two different and practically very useful ways to implement this model in current systems. The fundamental idea is that persistence is a characteristic of certain dynamic predicates (i.e., those which encapsulate state). The main effect of declaring a predicate persistent is that the dynamic changes made to such predicates *persist* from one execution to the next one. After proposing a syntax for declaring persistent predicates, a simple, file-based implementation of the concept is presented and some examples shown. An additional implementation is presented which stores persistent predicates in an external database. The abstraction of the concept of persistence from its implementation allows developing applications which can store their persistent predicates alternatively in files or databases with only a few simple changes to a declaration stating the location and modality used for persistent storage. The paper presents the model, the implementation approach in both the cases of using files and relational databases, a number of optimizations of the process (using information obtained from static global analysis and goal clustering), and performance results from an implementation of these ideas.

Keywords: Prolog, Databases, Persistency, Query Optimization

1 Introduction

State is traditionally implemented in Prolog and other (C)LP systems through the built-in ability to modify predicate definitions dynamically at runtime.[1] Generally, fact-only dynamic predicates are used to store information in a way that

---

[*] This work has been supported in part by the European Union IST program under contract IST-2001-34717 "Amos" and IST-2001-38059 "ASAP" and by MCYT projects TIC 2002-0055 "CUBICO" and HI2000-0043 "ADELA." M. Hermenegildo is also supported by the Prince of Asturias Chair in Information Science and Technology at UNM. J. Correas is supported by a grant from Madrid Regional Government. The authors would like to thank I. Caballero, J.F. Morales, S. Genaim, and C. Taboch for their collaboration in some implementation aspects and for feedback and discussions on the system, and the anonymous reviewers for their suggestions.
[1] In the ISO standard these predicates have to be marked explicitly as *dynamic*.

B. Jayaraman (Ed.): PADL 2004, LNCS 3057, pp. 104–119, 2004.
© Springer-Verlag Berlin Heidelberg 2004

provides global visibility (within a module) and preserves information through backtracking. This internal rule database, albeit a non-declarative component of Prolog, has practical applications from the point of view of the needs of a programming language.[2]

However, Prolog internal rule database implementations associate the lifetime of the internal state with that of the process, i.e., they deal only with what happens when a given program is running and changes its private rule database. Indeed, the Prolog rule database lacks an important feature: data persistence. By data persistence we refer to rule database modifications surviving across program executions (and, as a later evolution, maybe being accessible to other programs –even concurrently). This feature, if needed, must be explicitly implemented by the programmer in traditional systems.

In this paper we present a conceptual model of persistence by proposing the concept of *persistent predicates*, and a number of implementations thereof. A persistent predicate is a special kind of dynamic, data predicate that "resides" in some persistent medium (such as a set of files, a database, etc.) and which is typically external to the program using such predicates. The main effect is that any changes made to a persistent predicate from a program "survive" across executions , i.e., if the program is halted and restarted the predicate that the new process sees is in precisely the same state as it was when the old process was halted (provided no change was made in the meantime to the storage by other processes or the user). Notably, persistent predicates appear to a program as ordinary dynamic predicates: calls to these predicates can appear in clause bodies in the usual way without any need to wrap or mark them as "external" or "database" calls and updates to persistent predicates can be made calling the standard `asserta/1`, `assertz/1`, `retract/1`, etc. predicates used for ordinary dynamic predicates, but suitably modified. Updates to persistent predicates are guaranteed to be atomic and transactional, in the sense that if an update terminates, then the external storage has definitely been modified. This model provides a high degree of conceptual compatibility with previously existing programs which access only the local rule database,[3] while bringing at the same time several practical advantages:

- The state of dynamic predicates is, at all times, reflected in the state of the external storage device. This provides security against possible data loss due to, for example, a system crash.
- Since accesses to persistent predicates are *viewed* as regular accesses to the Prolog rule database, analyzers (and related tools) for full Prolog can deal with them in the same way as with the standard dynamic predicates, resulting in a series of optimizations, some of which will be shown. Using explicit accesses to files or external databases through low-level library predicates would make this task much more difficult.

---

[2] Examples of recent proposals to extend its applicability include using it to model reasoning in a changing world [1], and as the basis for communication of concurrent processes [2] and objects [3].

[3] The "logical view" of updates [4] is not enforced in the case of using a relational database as storage, in the same way as with concurrent data predicates [2].

Finally, perhaps the most interesting advantage of the notion of persistent predicates is that it abstracts away how the predicate is actually stored. Thus, a program can use persistent predicates stored in files or in external relational databases interchangeably, and the type of storage used for a given predicate can be changed without having to modify the program except for replacing a single declaration in the whole program. The program always contains standard internal database access and aggregation predicates, independently of whether the storage medium is the internal Prolog rule database, file-based, or database-based. It also minimizes impact on the host language, as the semantics of the access to the rule database is compatible with that of Prolog.

Our approach builds heavily on the well known and close relationship between (Constraint) Logic Programming and relational databases [5]: for example, operations in the relational algebra can be easily modeled using Horn clauses (plus negation for some operations), where database tables are seen as fact-only predicates, and every record is seen as a fact. On the other hand, the embedding into Prolog allows combining full Prolog code (beyond DATALOG) with the accesses to the persistent predicates.

A number of current Prolog systems offer external database interfaces, but often with ad-hoc access builtins. In those cases in which some kind of transparency is provided (e.g. Quintus *ProDBI*, SICStus and LPA *Prodata*, ECLiPSe), the system just allows performing queries on tables as if they were Prolog predicates, but does not allow updating tables using the same transparent approach. We argue that none of these cases achieve the same level of flexibility and seamless integration with Prolog achieved in our proposal.

Implementations of this model have been used in real-world applications such as the Amos tool (see `http://www.amosproject.org`), part of a large, ongoing international project aimed at facilitating the reuse of Open Source code by means of a powerful, ontology-based search engine working on a large database of code information.

2   A Proposal for Persistent Predicates in Prolog

We will now define a syntax for the declaration of persistent predicates. We will also present briefly two different implementations of persistent predicates which differ on the storage medium (files of Prolog terms in one case, and an external relational database in the other). Both implementations aim at providing a semantics compatible with that of the Prolog internal rule database, but enhanced with persistence over program executions.

2.1   Declaring Persistent Predicates

The syntax that we propose for defining persistent predicates is based on the assertion language of Ciao Prolog [6], which allows expressing in a compact, uniform way, types, modes, and, in general, different (even arbitrary) properties of predicates.

In order to specify that a predicate is persistent we have to flag it as such, and also to define where the persistent data is to be stored. Thus, a minimum declaration is:

```
:- include(library(persdb)).

:- pred employee/3 + persistent(payroll).
:- pred category/2 + persistent(payroll).

:- persistent_db(payroll, file('/home/clip/accounting')).
```

The first declaration states that the persistent database library is to be used to process the source code file: the included code loads the persdb library support predicate definitions, and defines the local operators and syntactic transformations that implement the persdb package. The second and third line state that predicates employee/3 and salary/2 are persistent and that they live in the storage medium to be referred to as payroll, while the fourth one defines which type of storage medium the payroll identifier refers to.[4] It is the code in the persdb package that processes the persistent/1 and persistent_db/2 declarations, and which provides the code to access the external storage and keeps the information necessary to deal with it. In this particular case, the storage medium is a disk file in the directory specified in the directive. The predicates in Figure 2 use these declarations to compute the salary of some employee, and to increment the number of days worked:

`salary(Empl,Salary):-`
`    employee(Empl,Categ,Days),`
`    category(Categ,PerDay),`
`    Salary is Days * PerDay.`
	`one_more_day(Empl):-`
	`    retract(employee(Empl,Categ,Days)),`
	`    Days1 is Days + 1,`
	`    assert(employee(Empl,Categ,Days1)).`

Fig. 1. Accessing and updating a persistent predicate

If the external storage is to be kept in an SQL database, argument type information is required in order to create the table (if the database is empty) and also to check that the calls are made with compatible types. It is also necessary to establish a mapping (views) between the predicate functor and arguments and table name and columns. In this example, suitable declarations are:

```
:- include(library(persdb)).

:- pred employee/3 :: string * string * int +
        persistent(employee(ident, category, time), payroll).
:- pred category/2 :: string * int          +
        persistent(category(category, money), payroll).

:- persistent_db(payroll, db(paydb, admin, 'Pwd', 'db.comp.org')).
```

---

[4] The persistent_db/2 information can also be included in the argument of persistent, but using persistent_db/2 declarations allows factoring out information shared by several predicates.

The `db/4` structure indicates database name (`paydb`), database server (`db.comp.org`), database user (`admin`) and password (`Pwd`). This information is processed by the persdb package, and a number of additional formats can be used. For example, the port for the database server can be specified (as in `'db.comp.org':2020`), the precise database brand can be noted (as, for example `odbc/4` or `oracle/4` instead of the generic `db/4`), etc. This instructs the persdb package to use different connection types or to generate queries specialized for particular SQL dialects. In addition, values for the relevant fields can also be filled in at run time, which is useful for example to avoid storing sensitive information, such as password and user names, in program code. This can be done using hook facts or predicates, which can be included in the source code, or asserted by it, perhaps after consulting the user. These facts or predicates are then called when needed to provide values for the arguments whose value is not specified in the declaration. For example, a declaration such as:

```
:- persistent_db(payroll, db(paydb, puser/1, ppwd/1, 'db.comp.org')).
```

would call the hook predicates `puser/1` and `ppwd/1`, which are expected to be defined as `puser(User):- ...` and `ppwd(Password):- ...`.

Note also that, as mentioned before, the declarations corresponding to `employee/3` and `category/2` specify the name of the table in the database (which can be different from that of the predicate) and the name of each of its columns. It may also have a type signature. If a table is already created in the database, then this declaration of types is not strictly needed, since the system will retrieve the schema from the database. However, it may still be useful so that (compile-time or run-time) checking of calls to persistent predicates can be performed. Furthermore, types and modes can be read and inferred by a global analysis tool, such as, e.g., CiaoPP [6,7], and used to optimize the generation of SQL expressions and to remove superfluous runtime checks at compile time (see Section 2.3).

A dynamic version of the **persistent** declaration exists, which allows defining new persistent predicates on the fly, under program control. Also, in order to provide greater flexibility, lower-level operations (of the kind available in traditional Prolog-SQL interfaces) are also available, which allow establishing database connections manually. These are the lower-level library operations the above examples are compiled into. Finally, a persistent predicate can also be made to correspond to a complex view of several database tables. For further illustration, Figure 2 shows an example queue elements are kept as persistent data facts so that the program state can be recovered in subsequent executions.

2.2   File-Based Implementation

The file-based implementation of persistent predicates provides a light-weight, simple, and at the same time powerful form of persistence. It has the advantage of being standalone in the sense that it does not require any external support other than the file management capabilities provided by the operating system: these persistent predicates are stored in files under direct control of the persistent

Program	Execution
| ```
:- module(queue, [main/0]).
:- include(library(persdb)).

:- pred queue/1 +
   persistent(file('/tmp/queue')).

main:-
   write('Action:'),
   read(A),
   handle_action(A),
   main.

handle_action(halt) :-
   halt.
handle_action(in(Term)) :-
   assertz(queue(Term)).
handle_action(out) :-
   (  retract(queue(Term))
   -> write('Out '), write(Term)
   ;  write('EMPTY!') ), nl.
handle_action(list) :-
   findall(T,queue(T),Contents),
   write('Contents: '),write(Contents),nl.
``` | ```
$ ./queue
Action: in(first).
Action: in(second).
Action: list.
Contents: [first, second]
Action: halt.


$ ./queue
Action: out.
Out first
Action: list.
Contents: [second]
Action: out.
Out second
Action: out.
EMPTY!
Action: halt.
``` |

Fig. 2. Queue example and execution trace

library. This implementation is especially useful when building small to medium-sized standalone (C)LP applications which require persistent storage and which may have to run in an environment where the existence of an external database manager is not ensured. Also, it is very useful even while developing applications which will connect to databases, because it allows working with persistent predicates maintained in files when developing or modifying the code and then switching to using the external database for testing or "production" by simply changing a declaration.

The implementation pursues at the same time efficiency and security. Each predicate uses three files: the *data file*, which stores a *base state* for the predicate; the *operations file*, which stores the differential between the base state and the predicate state in the program (i.e., operations pending to be integrated into the data file); and the *backup file*, which stores a security copy of the data file. Such files, in plain ASCII format, can be edited by hand using any text editor, or even easily read and written by other applications.

When no program is accessing the persistent predicate (because, e.g., no program updating that particular predicate is running), the data file reflects exactly the facts in the Prolog internal rule database. When any insertion or deletion is performed, the corresponding change is made in the Prolog internal rule database, and a record of the operation is *appended* to the operations file. In this moment the data file does not reflect the state of the internal Prolog rule database, but it can be reconstructed by applying the changes in the operations file to the state in the data file. This strategy incurs only in a relatively small, constant overhead per update operation (the alternative of keeping the data file always up to date would lead to an overhead linear in the number of records in it).

When a program using a file-based persistent predicate starts up, the data file is first copied to a backup file (preventing data loss in case of system crash during this operation), and all the pending operations are performed on the data file by loading it into memory, re-executing the updates recorded in the operations file, and saving a new data file. The order in which the operations are performed and the concrete O.S. facilities (e.g., file locks) used ensure that even if the process aborts at any point in its execution, the data saved up to that point can be completely recovered upon a successful restart. The data file can also be explicitly brought up to date on demand at any point in the execution of the program.

2.3   External Database Implementation

We present another implementation of persistent predicates which keeps the storage in a relational database. This is clearly useful, for example, when the data already resides in such a database, the amount of data is very large, etc. A more extensive description of this interface can be found in [8,9].

One of the most attractive features of our approach is that this view of external relations as just another storage medium for persistent predicates provides a very natural and transparent way to perform simple accesses to relational databases from (C)LP programs. This implementation allows reflecting selected columns of a relational table as a persistent predicate. The implementation also provides facilities for reflecting complex views of the database relations as individual persistent predicates. Such views can be constructed as conjunctions, disjunctions or projections of database relations.

The architecture of the database interface (Figure 3), has been designed with two goals in mind: simplifying the communication between the Prolog side and the relational database server, and providing platform independence, allowing inter-operation when using different databases.

The interface is built on the Prolog side by stacking several abstraction levels over the socket and native code interfaces (Figure 3). Typically, database servers allow connections using TCP/IP sockets and a particular protocol, while in other cases, linking directly a shared object or a DLL may be needed. For the cases where remote connections are not provided (e.g., certain versions of ODBC), a special-purpose mediator which acts as a bridge between a socket and a native interface has been developed [8,9]. Thus, the low level layer is highly specific for each database implementation (e.g. MySQL, Postgres, ORACLE, etc.). The mid-level interface (which is similar in level of abstraction to that present in most current Prolog systems) abstracts away these details.

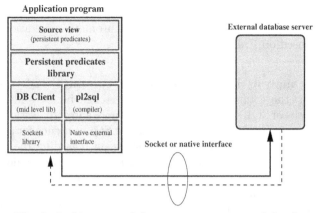

Fig. 3. Architecture of the access to an external database

The higher-level layer implements the concept of persistent predicates so that calls and database updates to persistent predicates actually act upon relations stored in the database by means of automatically generated mid-level code. In the base implementation, at compile-time, a "stub" definition is included in the program containing one clause whose head has the same predicate name and arity as the persistent predicates and whose body contains the appropriate mid-level code, which basically implies activating a connection to the database (logging on) if the connection is not active, compiling on the fly and sending the appropriate SQL code, retrieving the solutions (or the first solution and the DB handle for asking for more solutions, and then retrieving additional solutions on backtracking or eventually failing), and closing the connection (logging off the database), therefore freeing the programmer from having to pay attention to low-level details.

The SQL code in particular is generated using a Prolog to SQL translator based on the excellent work of Draxler [10]. Modifications were made to the code of [10] so that the compiler can deal with the different idioms used by different databases, the different types supported, etc. as well as blending with the high-level way of declaring persistence, types, modes, etc. that we have proposed (and which is in line with the program assertions used throughout in the Ciao system). Conversions of data types are automatically handled by the interface, using the type declarations provided by the user or inferred by the global analyzers.

In principle the SQL code corresponding to a given persistent predicate, literal, or group of literals needs to be generated dynamically at run-time for every call to a persistent predicate since the mode of use of the predicate affects the code to be generated and can change with each run-time call. Clearly, a number of optimizations are possible. In general, a way to improve performance is by reducing overhead in the run-time part of the Prolog interface by avoiding any task that can be accomplished at compile-time, or which can be done more efficiently by the SQL server itself. We study two different optimization techniques based on these ideas: the use of static analysis information to pre-compute the SQL expressions at compile time (which is related to adornment-based query optimization in deductive databases [11]), and the automatic generation of complex SQL queries based on Prolog query clustering.

Using static analysis information to pre-compute SQL expressions. As pointed out, the computation of SQL queries can be certainly sped up by creating skeletons of SQL sentences at compile-time, and fully instantiating them at run-time. In order to create the corresponding SQL sentence for a given call to a persistent predicate at compile-time, information regarding the instantiation status of the variables that appear in the goal is needed. This mode information can be provided by the user by means of the Ciao assertion language. More interestingly, this information can typically be obtained automatically by using program analysis, which in the Ciao system is accomplished by **CiaoPP**, a powerful program development tool which includes a static analyzer, based on Abstract Interpretation [6,7]. If the program is fed to CiaoPP, selecting the appropriate options, the output will contain, at every program point, the abstract substitution resulting from the analysis using a given domain. The essential information here is argument groundness (i.e., *modes*, which are computed using the sharing+freeness domain): we need to know which database columns must appear in the `WHERE` part of the SQL expression.

For example, assume that we have an database-based persistent predicate as in Section 2:

```
:- pred employee/3 :: string * string * int +
        persistent(employee(ident, category, time), payroll).
```

and consider also the program shown in the left side of Figure 2. The literal `employee/3` will be translated by the persistence library to a mid-level call which will at run-time call the `pl2sql` compiler to compute an SQL expression corresponding to `employee(Empl,Categ,Days)` based on the groundness state of `Empl`, `Categ` and `Days`. These expressions can be precomputed for a number of combinations of the groundness state of the arguments, with still some run-time overhead to select among these combinations. For example, if the static analyzer can infer that `Empl` is ground when calling `employee(Empl,Categ,Days)`, we will be able to build at compile-time the SQL query for this goal as:

```
SELECT ident, category, time FROM employee WHERE ident = '$Empl$';
```

The only task that remains to be performed at run-time, before actually querying the database, is to replace `$Empl$` with the actual value that `Empl` is instantiated to and send the expression to the database server.

A side effect of (SQL-)persistent predicates is that they provide useful information which can improve the analysis results for the rest of the program: the assertion that declares a predicate (SQL-)persistent also implies that on success all the arguments will be ground. This additional groundness information can be propagated to the rest of the program. For instance, in the definition of `salary/2` in Figure 2, `category/2` happens to be a persistent predicate living in an SQL database. Hence, we will surely be provided with groundness information for `category/2` so that the corresponding SQL expression will be generated at compile-time as well.

Query clustering. The second possible optimization on database queries is query clustering. A simple implementation approach would deal separately with each literal calling a persistent predicate, generating an individual SQL query for every such literal. Under some circumstances, mainly in the presence of intensive backtracking, the flow of tuples through the database connection generated by the Prolog backtracking mechanism will produce limited performance.

In the case of complex goals formed by consecutive calls to persistent predicates, it is possible to take advantage of the fact that database systems include a great number of well-developed techniques to improve the evaluation of complex SQL queries. The Prolog to SQL compiler is in fact able to translate such complex conjunctions of goals into efficient SQL code. The compile-time optimization that we propose requires identifying literals in clause bodies which call SQL-persistent predicates and are contiguous (or can be safely reordered to be contiguous) so that they can be clustered and, using mode information, the SQL expression corresponding to the entire complex goal compiled as a single unit. This is a very simple but powerful optimization, as will be shown.

For example, in predicate `salary/2` of Figure 2, assuming that we have analysis information which ensures that `salary/2` is always called with a ground term in its first argument, a single SQL query will be generated at compile-time for both calls to persistent predicates, such as:

```
SELECT ident, category, time, rel2.money
FROM employee, category rel2
WHERE ident = '$Empl$' AND rel2.category = category;
```

2.4   Concurrency and Transactional Behaviour

There are two main issues to address in these implementations of persistence related to transactional processing and concurrency. The first one is *consistency*: when there are several processes changing the same persistent predicate concurrently, the final state must be consistent w.r.t. the changes made by every process. The other issue is *visibility*: every process using a persistent predicate must be aware of the changes made by other processes which use that predicate. A further, related issue is what means exist in the source language to express that a certain persistent predicate may be accessed by several threads or processes, and how several accesses and modifications to a set of persistent predicates are grouped so that they are implemented as a single transaction.

Regarding the source language issue, the Ciao language already includes a way to mark dynamic data predicates as concurrent [2], stating that such predicates could be modified by several threads or processes. Also, a means has been recently developed for marking that a group of accesses and modifications to a set of dynamic predicates constitute a single atomic transaction [12]. Space limitations do not allow describing locking and transactional behaviour in the implementation of persistent predicates proposed. The current solutions are outlined in [13,12] and these issues are the subject of future work.

3   Empirical Results

We now study from a performance point of view the alternative implementations of persistence presented in previous sections. To this end, both implementations (file-based and SQL-based) of persistent predicates, as well as the compile-time optimizations previously described, have been integrated and tested in the Ciao Prolog development system [14].

3.1   Performance without Compile-Time Optimizations

The objective in this case is to check the relative performance of the various persistence mechanisms and contrast them with the internal Prolog rule database. The queries issued involve searching on the database (using both indexed and non-indexed queries) as well as updating it.

The results of a number of different tests using these benchmarks can be found in Table 1, where a four-column, 25,000 record database table is used to check the basic capabilities and to measure access speed. Each one of the four columns has a different measurement-related purpose: two of them check indexed accesses —using int and string basic data types—, and the other two check non-indexed accesses. The time spent by queries for the different combinations are given in the rows *non-indexed numeric query, non-indexed string query, indexed numeric query*, and *indexed string query* (time spent in 1,000 consecutive queries randomly selected). Row *assertz* gives the time for creating the 25,000 record table by adding the tuples one by one. Rows *non-indexed numeric retract, non-indexed string retract, indexed numeric retract*, and *indexed string retract* provide the timings for the deletion of 1,000 randomly selected records by deleting the tuples one by one.

The timings were taken on a medium-loaded Pentium IV Xeon 2.0Ghz with two processors, 1Gb of RAM memory, running Red Hat Linux 8.0, and averaging several runs and eliminating the best and worst values. Ciao version 1.9.78 and MySQL version 3.23.54 were used.

The meaning of the columns is as follows:

prologdb (data). Is the time spent when accessing directly the internal (assert/retract) state of Prolog.

prologdb (concurrent). In this case tables are marked as *concurrent*. This toggles the variant of the assert/retract database which allows concurrent access to the Prolog rule database. Atomicity in the updates is ensured and several threads can access concurrently the same table and synchronize through facts in the tables (see [2]). This measurement has been made in order to provide a fairer comparison with a database implementation, which has the added overhead of having to take into account concurrent searches/updates, user permissions, etc.[5]

---

[5] Note, however, that this is still quite different from a database, apart, obviously, from the lack of persistence. On one hand databases typically do not support structured data, and it is not possible for threads to synchronize on access to the database,

persdb. This is the implementation presented in Section 2.2, i.e., the file-based persistent version. The code is the same as above, but marking the predicates as persistent. Thus, in addition to keeping incore images of the rule database, changes are automatically flushed out to an external, file-based transaction record. This record provides persistence, but also introduces the additional cost of having to save updates. The implementation ensures atomicity and also basic transactional behavior.

persdb/sql. This is the implementation presented in Section 2.3, i.e., where all the persistent predicates-related operations are made directly on an external SQL database. The code is the same as above, but marking the predicates as SQL-persistent. No information is kept incore, so that every database access imposes an overhead on the execution.[6]

sql. Finally, this is a native implementation in SQL of the benchmark code, i.e., what a programmer would have written directly in SQL, with no host language overhead. To perform these tests the database client included in MySQL has been used. The SQL sentences have been obtained from the Ciao Prolog interface and executed using the MySQL client in batch mode.

Table 1. Speed in milliseconds of accessing and updating

	prologdb (data)	prologdb (concurrent)	persdb	persdb/sql	sql
assertz (25000 records)	590.5	605.5	5,326.4	16,718.3	3,935.0
non-indexed numeric query	7,807.6	13,584.8	7,883.5	17,721.0	17,832.5
non-indexed string query	8,045.5	12,613.3	9,457.9	24,188.0	23,052.5
indexed numeric query	1.1	3.0	1.1	1,082.4	181.3
indexed string query	1.1	3.0	1.5	1,107.9	198.8
non-indexed numeric retract	7,948.3	13,254.5	8,565.0	19,128.5	18,470.0
non-indexed string retract	7,648.0	13,097.6	11,265.0	24,764.5	23,808.8
indexed numeric retract	2.0	3.3	978.8	2,157.4	466.3
indexed string retract	2.0	3.1	1,738.1	2,191.9	472.5

Several conclusions can be drawn from Table 1:

Sensitivity to the amount of data to be transferred. Some tests made to show the effect of the size of the data transferred on the access speed (which can be consulted in [13]) indicate that the methods which access to

---

as is done with concurrent dynamic predicates. On the other hand, in concurrent dynamic predicates different processes cannot access the same data structures, which is possible in SQL databases. However, SQL databases usually use a server process to handle requests from several clients, and thus there are no low-level concurrent accesses to actual database files from different processes, but rather from several threads of a single server process.

[6] Clearly, it would be interesting to perform caching of read data, but note that this is not trivial since an invalidation protocol must be implemented, given there can be concurrent updates to the database. This is left as future work.

external processes (**persdb/sql** and **sql**) are specially sensitive to the data size, more than the file-based persistent database, whilst the internal Prolog rule database is affected to some extent only.

Incidence of indexing. The impact of indexing is readily noticeable in the tables, especially for the internal Prolog rule database but also for the file-based persistent database. The MySQL-based tests do present also an important speedup, but not as relevant as that in the Prolog-only tests. This behavior is probably caused by the overhead imposed by the SQL database requirements (communication with MySQL daemon, concurrency and transaction availability, much more complex index management, integrity constraint handling, etc). In addition to this, Prolog systems are usually highly optimized to take advantage of certain types of indexing, while database systems offer a wider class of indexing possibilities which might not be as efficient as possible in some determinate cases, due to their generality.

Impact of concurrency support. Comparing the Prolog tests, it is worth noting that concurrent predicates bring in a non-insignificant load in rule database management (up to 50% slower than simple data predicates in some cases), in exchange for the locking and synchronization features they provide. In fact, this slow-down makes the concurrent Prolog internal rule database show a somewhat lower performance than using the file-based persistent database, which has its own file locking mechanism to provide inter-process concurrent accesses (but not from different threads of the same process: in that case both concurrency and persistence of predicates needs to be used).

Incidence of the Prolog interface in SQL characteristics. Comparing direct SQL queries (i.e., typed directly at the database top-level interface) with using persistent predicates, we can see that only in the case of non-indexed queries times are similar, whereas indexed queries and database modifications show a significant difference. This is due to the fact that in the experiments the setting was used in which a different connection to the database server was open for every query requested, and closed when the query had finished (useful in practice to limit the number of open connections to the database, on which there is a limitation). We plan to perform additional tests turning on the more advanced setting in which the database connection is kept open.

3.2   Performance with Compile-Time Optimizations

We have also implemented the two optimizations described in Section 2.3 (using static analysis information and query clustering) and measured the improvements brought about by these optimizations. The tests have been performed on two SQL-persistent predicates (p/2 and q/2) with 1,000 facts each and indexed on the first column. There are no duplicate tuples nor duplicate values in any column (simply to avoid overloading due to unexpected backtracking). Both p/2 and q/2 contain exactly the same tuples.

Table 2 presents the time (in milliseconds) spent performing 1,000 repeated queries in a failure-driven loop. In order to get more stable measures average times were calculated for 10 consecutive tests, removing the highest and lowest values. The system used to run the tests was the same as in section 3.1.

The *single queries* part of the table corresponds to a simple call to p(X,Z). The first row represents the time spent in recovering on backtracking all the 1,000 solutions to this goal. The second and third rows present the time taken when performing 1,000 queries to p(X,Z) (with no backtracking, i.e., taking only the first solution), with, respectively, the indexing and non-indexing argument being instantiated. The two columns correspond to the non-optimized case in which the translation to SQL is performed on the fly, and to the optimized case in which the SQL expressions are pre-computed at compile-time, using information from static analysis.

The *'complex queries*:p(X,Z),q(Z,Y)' part of the table corresponds to calling this conjunction with the rows having the same meaning as before. Information about variable groundness (on the first argument of the first predicate in the second row and on the second argument of the first predicate in the third row) obtained from global analysis is used in both of these rows. The two columns allow comparing the cases where the queries for p(X,Z) and q(Z,Y) are processed separately (and the join is performed in Prolog via backtracking) and the case where the compiler performs the clustering optimization and pre-compiles p(X,Z),q(Z,Y) into a single SQL query.

Finally, the *'complex queries*:p(X,Z),r(Z,Y)' part of the table illustrates the special case in which the second goal calls a predicate which only has a few tuples (but matching the variable bindings of the first goal). More concretely, r/2 is a persistent predicate with 100 tuples (10% of the 1,000 tuples of p/2). All the tuples in r/2 have in the first column a value which appears in the second column of p/2. Thus, in the non-optimized test, the Prolog execution mechanism will backtrack over the 90% of the solutions produced by p/2 that will not succeed.

Table 2. Comparison of optimization techniques

Single queries: p(X,Y)		
	on-the-fly SQL generation	pre-computed SQL expressions
Traverse solutions	36.6	28.5
Indexed ground query	1,010.0	834.9
Non-indexed ground query	2,376.1	2,118.1
Complex queries: p(X,Z),q(Z,Y)		
	non-clustered	clustered
Traverse solutions	1,039.6	51.6
Indexed ground query	2,111.4	885.8
Non-indexed ground query	3,550.1	2,273.8
Complex queries: p(X,Z),r(Z,Y)		
	non-clustered	clustered
Asymmetric query	1146.1	25.1

Table 3. Comparison of optimization techniques (*Prolog time only*)

Single queries: p(X,Y)		
	on-the-fly SQL generation	pre-computed SQL expressions
Indexed ground query	197.5	27.6
Non-indexed ground query	195.4	27.3
Complex queries: p(X,Z),q(Z,Y)		
	non-clustered on-the-fly	pre-computed clustered queries
Indexed ground query	406.8	33.3
Non-indexed ground query	395.0	42.6

The results in Table 2 for single queries show that the improvement due to compile-time SQL expression generation is between 10 and 20 percent. These times include the complete process of a) translating (dynamically or statically) the literals into SQL and preparing the query (with our without optimizations), and b) sending the resulting SQL expression to the database and processing the query in the database. Since the optimization only affects the time involved in a), we measured also the effect of the optimizations when considering only a), i.e., only the time spent in Prolog. The results are shown in Table 3. In this case the run-time speed-up obtained when comparing dynamic generation of SQL at run time and static generation at compile time (i.e., being able to pre-compute the SQL expressions thanks to static analysis information) is quite significant. The difference is even greater if complex queries are clustered and translated as a single SQL expression: the time spent in generating the final SQL expression when clustering is pre-computed is only a bit greater than in the atomic goal case, while the non-clustered, on-the-fly SQL generation of two atomic goals needs twice the time of computing a single atomic goal. In summary, the optimization results in an important speedup on the Prolog side, but the overall weight of b) in the selected implementation (due to opening and closing DB connections) is more significant. We believe this overhead can be reduced considerably and this is the subject of ongoing work.

Returning to the results in Table 2, but looking now at the complex goals case, we observe that the speed-up obtained due to the clustering optimization is much more significant. Traversing solutions using non-optimized database queries has the drawback that the second goal is traversed twice for each solution of the first goal: first to provide a solution (as is explained above, p/2 and q/2 have exactly the same facts, and no failure happens in the second goal when the first goal provides a solution), and secondly to fail on backtracking. Both call and redo imply accessing the database. In contrast, if the clustering optimization is applied, this part of the job is performed inside the database, so there is only one database access for each solution (plus the last access when there are no more solutions). In the second and third rows, the combined effect of compile-time SQL expression generation and clustering optimization causes a speed-up of around 50% to 135%, depending on the cost of retrieving data from the database tables: as the cost of data retrieval increases (e.g., access based on a non-indexed column), the speed-up in grouping queries decreases.

Finally, the asymmetric complex query (in which the second goal succeeds for only a fraction of the solutions provided by the first goal) the elimination of useless backtracking yields the most important speed-up, as expected.

References

1. Kowalski, R.A.: Logic Programming with Integrity Constraints. In: Proceedings of JELIA. (1996) 301–302
2. Carro, M., Hermenegildo, M.: Concurrency in Prolog Using Threads and a Shared Database. In: 1999 International Conference on Logic Programming, MIT Press, Cambridge, MA, USA (1999) 320–334
3. Pineda, A., Bueno, F.: The O'Ciao Approach to Object Oriented Logic Programming. In: Colloquium on Implementation of Constraint and LOgic Programming Systems (ICLP associated workshop), Copenhagen (2002)
4. Lindholm, T.G., O'Keefe, R.A.: Efficient Implementation of a Defensible Semantics for Dynamic Prolog Code. In Lassez, J.L., ed.: Logic Programming: Proceedings of the Fourth Int'l. Conference and Symposium, The MIT Press (1987) 21–39
5. Ullman, J.D.: Database and Knowledge-Base Systems, Vol. 1 and 2. Computer Science Press, Maryland (1990)
6. Hermenegildo, M., Puebla, G., Bueno, F., López-García, P.: Program Development Using Abstract Interpretation (and The Ciao System Preprocessor). In: 10th International Static Analysis Symposium (SAS'03). Number 2694 in LNCS, Springer-Verlag (2003) 127–152
7. Hermenegildo, M., Bueno, F., Puebla, G., López-García, P.: Program Analysis, Debugging and Optimization Using the Ciao System Preprocessor. In: 1999 Int'l. Conference on Logic Programming, Cambridge, MA, MIT Press (1999) 52–66
8. Caballero, I., Cabeza, D., Genaim, S., Gomez, J., Hermenegildo, M.: persdb˙sql: SQL Persistent Database Interface. Technical Report CLIP10/98.0 (1998)
9. Cabeza, D., Hermenegildo, M., Genaim, S., Taboch, C.: Design of a Generic, Homogeneous Interface to Relational Databases. Technical Report D3.1.M1-A1, CLIP7/98.0 (1998)
10. Draxler, C.: Accessing Relational and Higher Databases through Database Set Predicates in Logic Programming Languages. PhD thesis, Zurich University, Department of Computer Science (1991)
11. Ramakrishnan, R., Ullman, J.D.: A survey of research on deductive database systems. Journal of Logic Programming **23** (1993) 125–149
12. Pattengale, N.D.: Transactional semantics. Technical Report CLIP3/04.0, Technical University of Madrid (UPM), Facultad de Informática, 28660 Boadilla del Monte, Madrid, Spain (2004)
13. Correas, J., Gomez, J.M., Carro, M., Cabeza, D., Hermenegildo, M.: A Generic Persistence Model for (C)LP Systems (and two useful implementations). Technical Report CLIP3/2003.1(2004), Technical University of Madrid, School of Computer Science, UPM (2004) `http://clip.dia.fi.upm.es/papers/persdb-tr1.pdf`.
14. Bueno, F., Cabeza, D., Carro, M., Hermenegildo, M., López-García, P., Puebla, G.: The Ciao Prolog System. Reference Manual (v1.8). The Ciao System Documentation Series–TR CLIP4/2002.1, School of Computer Science, Technical University of Madrid (UPM) (2002) System and on-line version of the manual available at `http://clip.dia.fi.upm.es/Software/Ciao/`.

Pruning in the Extended Andorra Model

Ricardo Lopes[1], Vítor Santos Costa[2], and Fernando Silva[1]

[1] DCC-FC & LIACC, University of Porto
Rua do Campo Alegre, 823, 4150-180 Porto, Portugal
Tel. +351 226078830, Fax. +351 226003654
{rslopes,fds}@ncc.up.pt
[2] COPPE/Sistemas, Universidade Federal do Rio de Janeiro, Brasil
vitor@cos.ufrj.br

Abstract. One of the major problems that actual logic programming systems have to address is whether and how to prune undesirable parts of the search space. A region of the search space would definitely be undesirable if it can only repeat previously found solutions, or if it is well-known that the whole computation will fail. Or it may be the case that we are interested in a subset of solutions. In this work we discuss how the BEAM addresses pruning issues. The BEAM is an implementation of David Warren's Extended Andorra Model. Because the BEAM relies on a very flexible execution mechanism, all cases of pruning discussed above should be considered. We show that all these different forms of pruning can be supported, and study their impact in applications.

Keywords: Logic Programming, Extended Andorra Model, Pruning, Language Implementation.

1 Introduction

Logic programs are sets of statements defining an intended model for a problem. Logic programming offers programmers a simple, yet powerful, first-order logic based language, for which efficient inference mechanisms exist and which has been used to program significant applications. Most work on logic programming relies the Prolog language, which uses an efficient selection function and search rule for inference. Prolog has well-known limitations, though, which have been recognised since the early days of logic programming [11]. Approaches that propose more flexible execution strategies, such as tabling [1] and co-routining [3, 2], have thus been proposed.

One of the major problems that actual logic programming systems have to address is whether and how to prune undesirable parts of the search space. A region of the search space would definitely be undesirable if it can only repeat previously found solutions, or if it is well-known that the whole computation will fail. Or it may be the case that we are interested in a single solution, and thus there is no point in performing extra computation. We may want any solution, but in many cases programmers have an implicit ordering over the quality of

B. Jayaraman (Ed.): PADL 2004, LNCS 3057, pp. 120–134, 2004.

solutions. Last, programmers often go a step further and explicitly want to do incomplete search. Programs that rely on ordering or that demand incomplete search, are only meaningful given a specified selection function and search rule, and can be extremely difficult to run with other execution mechanisms.

In this work we discuss how pruning issues are addressed in the BEAM [1], an implementation of the Extended Andorra Model. Because the BEAM relies on a very flexible execution mechanism, all cases of pruning discussed above should be considered. Our work presents several contributions. The BEAM supports early completion of successful or failed computations naturally in its execution rules. The BEAM supports explicit pruning through the pruning operators *cut* and *commit*, by using the notions of quiet and noisy pruning, as originally proposed by Warren [21] and Haridi [5]. Quiet pruning allows for full co-routing, and is the desirable solution. Noisy pruning allows for Prolog compatibility, but reduces the amount of co-routing.

The paper is organised as follows. First, we present the BEAM design. Next, we give an overview of the issues related with cut on an EAM implementation and how we address them in BEAM.

2   The BEAM

We briefly present the BEAM, an implementation of the main concepts in Warren's Extended Andorra Model with Implicit Control [15], with several refinements [13]. Our implementation owes to the experience in the design and implementation of Andorra-I, a predecessor of the BEAM, to Gupta's first EAM interpreter [4], and to the work in the AKL language [9]. The BEAM model has been implemented for the Herbrand domain [12], although the EAM does support other constraint domains [19,8].

2.1   BEAM Concepts

A BEAM *computation* is a series of rewriting operations, performed on And-Or Trees. And-Or Trees contain two kinds of nodes: *and-boxes* represent a conjunction of positive literals, and store goals $G_1, \ldots, G_n$, new local variables $X_1, \ldots, X_m$, and a set of constraints σ; or-boxes represent alternative clauses.

A *configuration* is an And-Or Tree, describing a state of the computation. A *computation* is a sequence of configurations obtained by successive applications of rewrite rules that define valid state transitions. The *initial configuration* is an and-box representing the query. The constraints over the top-and box on a final configuration are called an *answer*. We define an And-Or Tree as *compact* when all children of and-boxes are or-boxes and when all children of or-boxes are and-boxes.

A goal is said to be *deterministic* when there is at most one candidate that succeeds for the goal. Otherwise it is said to be *non-deterministic*.

---

[1] Not to be confused with the Erlang BEAM virtual machine [6].

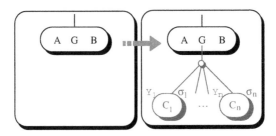

Fig. 1. BEAM reduction rule.

A variable is said to be *local* to an and-box Δ when first defined in Δ, and *external* to Δ otherwise. An and-box Δ is said to be *suspended* if the computation on Δ cannot progress deterministically, and if Δ is waiting for an event that will allow it to resume computation.

2.2   Rewrite Rules

Execution in the EAM proceeds as a sequence of rewrite operations on configurations. The BEAM's rewrite rules are based on the David Warren's rules. They are designed to be correct and complete, and to allow for efficient implementation. The BEAM rewrite rules are:

1. **Reduction** resolves the goal G against the heads of all clauses defining the procedure for G. Figure 1 shows how resolution expands the tree.

$$G \rightarrow \{[\exists Y_1 : \sigma_1 \ \& \ C_1] \vee \ldots \vee [\exists Y_n : \sigma_n \ \& \ C_n]\}$$

2. **Promotion** promoting the variables and constraints from an and-box Δ to the nearest and-box Δ' above. Δ must be a single alternative to the parent or-box, as shown in Fig. 2. In contrast the original EAM and in AKL, Promotion does not merge the two boxes; this is performed by a separate simplification rule. We explain the reason with more detail in Section 4.

$$[\exists X : \sigma \ \& \ A \ \& \ \{[\exists Y : \theta \ \& \ W]\} \ \& \ B]\} \rightarrow [\exists X, Y : \sigma\theta \ \& \ A \ \& \ \{[W]\} \ \& \ B]$$

As in the original EAM promotion rule, promotion propagates results from a local computation to the level above. However, promotion in the BEAM does not merge the two and-boxes because the structure of the computation may be required towards pruning: if we discard intermediate and-boxes we may have no detail on the scope of a cut. This contrasts to the original EAM and to AGENTS [10] which require choice-boxes for this purpose.

3. **Propagation**: this rule allows us to propagate constraints from an and-box to all subtrees below. This rule is thus symmetrical to the promotion rule.

$$[\exists X, Z : Z = \sigma(X) \ \& \ldots \& \ \{\ldots \vee [\exists Y : G] \vee \ldots\} \ \& \ldots] \rightarrow$$

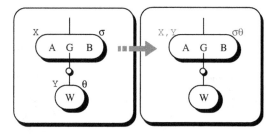

Fig. 2. BEAM promotion rule.

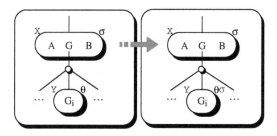

Fig. 3. BEAM propagation rule.

$$[\exists X, Z : Z = \sigma(X) \;\&\ldots\&\; \{\ldots \vee [\exists Y : Z = \sigma(X) \;\&\; G] \vee \ldots\} \;\&\ldots]$$

We call the and-box that propagates the constraint the *top and-box*. Figure 3 shows how the propagation rule makes the constraint available to the underlying and-boxes. The propagation rule is expensive. We thus only apply it on demand, that is, we only propagate constraints to the and-boxes that actually will consume the constraint.

4. **Splitting**, or non-determinate promotion distributes a conjunction across a disjunction, in a way similar to the forking rule of the original EAM. For the reasons discussed in Section 4 the BEAM does not merge the split and-box with the parent and-box.

$$[\exists X : \sigma \;\&\; A \;\&\; \{C_1 \vee \ldots \vee [\exists Y : \theta \;\&\; C_i] \vee \ldots \vee C_n\} \;\&\; B] \rightarrow$$

$$\{[\exists X : \sigma \;\&\; A \;\&\; \{[\exists Y : \theta \;\&\; C_i]\} \;\&\; B] \vee$$

$$[\exists X : \sigma \;\&\; A \;\&\; \{C_1 \vee \ldots \vee C_{i-1} \vee C_{i+1} \vee \ldots \vee C_n\} \;\&\; B]\}$$

The previous rules give the main principles for the EAM. The BEAM also includes several simplification rules, that allow one to propagate success and failure and to recover space by discarding unneeded boxes. The major rules allow discarding fully succeed boxes, propagate failure, and allow merging of and-boxes. We refer the reader to [12] for a more complete description.

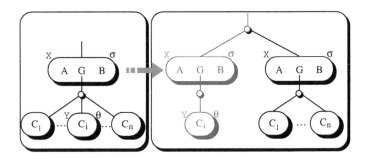

Fig. 4. BEAM splitting rule.

2.3   Control in the BEAM

A rewrite operation *matches* an And-Or Tree if the left-hand side matches a sub-tree in the configuration. If a number of rewrite-rules match, one must decide which one to choose. Arguably, one could choose the same rule as Prolog, and clone Prolog execution. The real power of the EAM is that we have the flexibility to use different strategies. In particular, we will try to use the one which, we believe, will lead to the least computation with maximum efficiency. The key ideas are:

1. Failure propagation rules have priority over all the other rules to allow propagation of failure as fast as possible.
2. Success propagation and and-compression should always be done next, because they simplify the tree.
3. Promotion and propagation should follow, because their combination may force some boxes to fail.
4. Splitting is the most expensive operation, and should be avoided. Therefore:
   a) Deterministic reductions, that is, reductions that do not create or-boxes and thus will never lead to splitting, or reductions which do not constrain external variables, should go ahead first;
   b) Non-deterministic reductions that constrain external variables should be avoided because they lead to splitting. The exception is if the user explicitly says that non-deterministic reduction will be eventually required [14].
   c) Splitting should be used when no deterministic reductions are available.

3   Implicit Pruning

The BEAM implements two major simplifications that improve the search space by pruning logically redundant branches. The two rules are symmetrical, but whilst one is concerned with failed boxes, the other is concerned with successful boxes:

1. **false-in-and-simplification:**

$$[\exists X : \theta \& A \& \ldots \& \texttt{false} \& \ldots \& B] \rightarrow \texttt{false}$$

If a failure occurs at any point of the and-box, the and-box can be removed and failure is propagated to the upper boxes. This rule can be considered a generalisation of the failure propagation rules used in Independent And-Parallel systems [7].

2. **true-in-or-simplification:**

$$\{\ldots \vee \ \texttt{true} \ \vee \ldots\} \rightarrow \texttt{true}$$

This form provides implicit pruning of redundant branches in the search tree, and it is somewhat similar to the XSB group's work on early completion of tabled computations [16,17].

These two rules can provide substantial pruning. In a pure logic environment, the presence of a true-box in a branch of an or-box should allow immediate pruning of all the other branches in the or-box. In an environment with side-effects, the user may still want the other branches to execute anyway. To guarantee Prolog compatibility, the BEAM allows the true-in-or simplification and the false-in-and simplification to be enabled for the leftmost goal only. We thus allow the user to explicitly disable these simplifications. A second possibility, in the style of Andorra-I, is to do compile-time analysis to automatically disable the true-in-or and false-in-and optimization for the boxes where some branches include builtins calls with side-effects, such as `write/1`

4   Explicit Pruning

The implicit pruning mechanisms we provide are not always sufficient for managing the search space. The BEAM therefore supports two explicit pruning operators. Cut (!) and commit (|) prune alternatives clauses for the current goal, plus alternatives for all goals created for the current clause. Cut only prunes alternatives for clause that appear first in the textual ordering, commit prunes every alternative. Both operators disallow goals to their right from exporting constraints to the goals to the left, prior to execution. After the execution of a cut or commit, all boxes to the left of the cut operator should be discarded and their constraints on external variables should be promoted to the current and-box.

Figure 5 gives an example of pruning. In this example the and-boxes for the sibling clause I and for the rightmost alternative G2 will be discarded. The constraints for G1 will be promoted to the and-box for G, ! , H.

The rule for cut can be written as follows:

$$\{[\exists Y : \theta_1 \& \{[W : \theta_2 \& \texttt{true}] \vee \ldots\} \& \ ! \ \& \ A] \vee B\} \rightarrow \{[\exists Y, X : \theta_1 \& \theta_2 \& A]\}$$

The conjunction of goals in the clause to the left of the cut or commit is known to be the *guard* of the cut. Note that our rule says that cut only applies when the goals in the guard have been unfolded into a configuration of the form:

$$\{[W : \theta_2 \& \texttt{true}] \vee \ldots\}$$

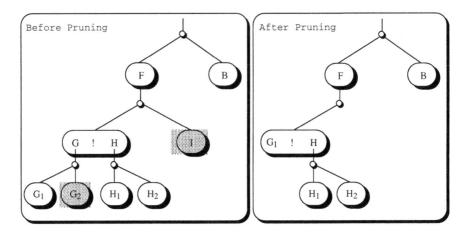

Fig. 5. Cut scope.

That is, when the leftmost branch of the guard has been completely resolved and all of its deterministic constraints exported. The cut rule can thus be applied to three situations:

1. If θ_2 is empty or entailed by the current environment (that is, if it can be simplified to empty). We say that the cut is *quiet* [18]. Or,
2. if the disjunction consists of a single alternative. In this case we say that the cut is *degenerate*.
3. Otherwise, the cut is said to be *noisy*. The BEAM allows noisy cuts to execute if:
   - only splitting rules are available, and,
   - the and-box with the cut is leftmost in the current scope.

   These conditions are necessary, but not sufficient, to support Prolog semantics for noisy cuts.

We next discuss in more detail the issues in the design of explicit pruning for the BEAM. In the following discussion we refer mainly to cut, but similar restrictions apply to the usage of the commit operator.

4.1   Control for Cut

Both splitting or Warren's forking should be used carefully when duplicating an and-box that contains a cut. Consider the example presented in Figure 6a. The lower-leftmost and-box contains a cut (X,!,Y). The and-box W is the only box within the cut scope. Suppose that all boxes are suspended and that the only available rule is fork/splitting. Both Warren's forking and the BEAM's splitting will transform the computational state presented in this example into an incorrect one. After applying the forking rule, the and-box C is in danger of being deleted by the execution of cut (see figure 6b). On the other hand, when applying splitting, the and-box W leaves the scope of the cut (see figure 6c).

This problem is solved in our BEAM by explicitly disallowing splitting to an and-box containing a cut. Therefore, the scheduler does allow clauses with a cut to continue execution even when head unification constrains external variables (note that these bindings may not be made visible to the parent boxes). In this regard the BEAM is close to the AGENTS. On the other hand, the BEAM differs from the AGENTS in that goals to the right of the cut may also execute first: the cut does not provide sequencing.

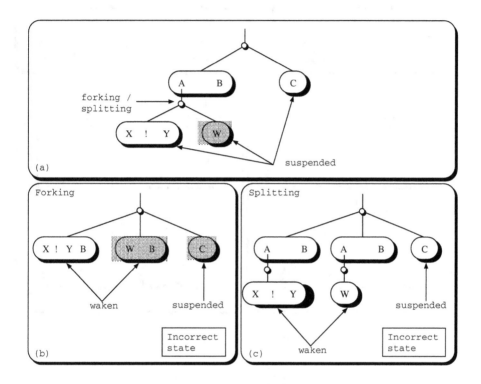

Fig. 6. Incorrect use of fork/splitting and cut.

As a results of this rule we have that:

- splitting can be applied freely to stable goals within the guard of the cut, as in this case splitting may not export constraints for variables external to the guard, or change the scope of the cut (see example on Figure 7).
- a cut can always execute immediately if it is the leftmost call in the and-box and if the and-box does not have external constraints.
  $$\{[\exists Y : \theta_1 \equiv \{\} \ \& \ \text{true} \ \& \ ! \ \& \ Y] \vee W\} \rightarrow \{[\exists Y : \theta_1 \equiv \{\} \& \ Y]\}$$
  Consider the example illustrated in figure 8a. Both alternatives to the goal a suspended trying to bind the external variable X. The first alternative to the goal b contains a *quiet* cut that will be allowed to execute since it respects the conditions described previously: the alternative does not impose

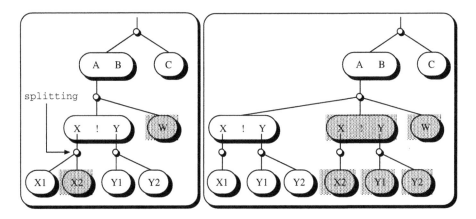

Fig. 7. Correct use of splitting and cut.

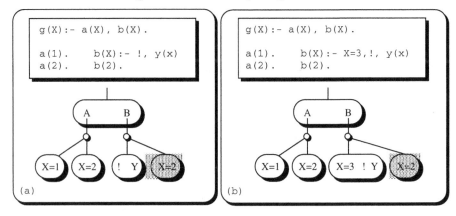

Fig. 8. Cut example.

external constraints, and the cut is the leftmost call in the and-box. Note that in normal Prolog execution, the second alternative to b would also never execute, since the cut always executes, independently of value generated in the a goal to X.

Figure 8b illustrates a different situation. In this case, the cut would not be allowed to execute since the alternative restricts the external variable X to the value 3. Thus, the computation in this example would only be allowed to continue with a splitting on a. After the splitting, the values 1 and 2 would be promoted to X and thus make the first alternative to b fail.

– if an and-box containing a cut becomes leftmost in the tree, the cut can execute immediately when all the calls before it succeed (even if there are external constraints).

$$[\exists X_1 : \theta_1 \ \& \ \textbf{true} \ \& \ \{\ldots\{[\exists X_n : \theta_n \ \& \ \textbf{true} \ \& \ ! \ \& \ Y] \lor W\}\ldots\}\& \ Z] \rightarrow$$
$$[\exists X_1 : \theta_1 \ \& \ \textbf{true} \ \& \ \{\ldots\{[\exists X_n : \theta_n \ \& \ Y]\}\ldots\}\& \ Z]$$

For example, on Figure 9 the cut is allowed to execute immediately when X succeeds even if there are external constraints.

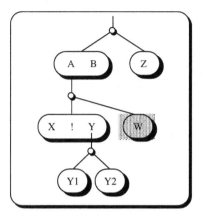

Fig. 9. Cut in the leftmost box in the tree.

Allowing early execution of cuts will in most cases prune alternatives early and thus reduce the search space.

One interesting problem occurs when the parent or-box for the and-box containing the cut degenerates to a single alternative. In this case, promotion and and-compression would allow us to merge the two resulting and-boxes. As a result, cut could prune goals in the original parent and-box. Figure 10 shows an example where promotion of an and-box containing a cut leads to an incorrect state as the and-box C is in danger of being removed by execution of cut.

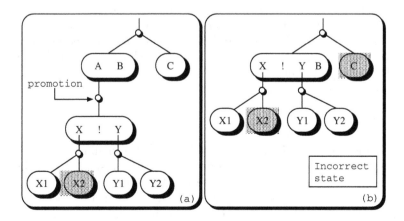

Fig. 10. Incorrect use of promotion and cut.

We address this problem by disallowing and-compression when the inner and-box has a cut. Note that promotion is still allowed. Thus deterministic constraints are still allowed to be exported.

$$[\exists Z_1, \ldots, Z_n : A \ \& \ \{[\exists W_1, \ldots, W_n : Z_i = \theta(W_j) \ \& \ X \ \& \ ! \ \& \ Y]\} \ \& \ B] \rightarrow$$
$$[\exists Z_1, \ldots, Z_n, W_1, \ldots, W_n : Z_i = \theta(W_j) \ \& \ A \ \& \ \{[X \ \& \ ! \ \& \ Y]\} \ \& \ B]$$

The and-boxes are kept separated, as shown on Fig. 10a, but any variable that is local to the parent and-box (A in the example) also becomes local to the and-box containing the cut (and vice versa). This is achieved in our implementation by changing the and-box parameter *level* [2] to be equal to the parent and-box. And-boxes with the same *level* value, share all variables.

Our restriction preserves cut scope, hence guaranteeing that the BEAM will never go into the incorrect state presented on Figure 10b.

4.2   Quiet Pruning

Note that our algorithm only allows non-leftmost execution of quiet guards: all constraints to exported variables must be either entailed by the current environment, or deterministic. We follow here the Andorra-I definition of quietness that allows deterministic non-entailed constraints [18]. Guards that execute quietly generate the same result independently of how external goals are executed.

To classify guards as quiet, BEAM uses for each and-box two fields: a pointer `externals` that maintains a list of bindings to external variables and, the field `side_effects`, that is used to mark when side-effects predicates are present in the goals or sub-goals of the and-box. The `external` variables generalize the Prolog's trail, allowing both unwinding and the rewinding of bindings performed in the current and-box. Our scheme for the external variables representation is very similar to the *forward trail* [22] used in the SLG-WAM [20,17]. The SLG-WAM's *forward trail* is also a list rather than a WAM stack trail. It contains, information about the value to which the variable was bound, the address of the bounded variable and a pointer to the previous trail frame.

In contrast to quiet guards, noisy guards can be used to implement meta-predicates. Their meaning depends on program execution order. In general, sequencing as performed in Andorra-I is the only form of guaranteeing correct execution for these programs [18]. We have allowed noisy pruning in the BEAM in order to support Prolog programming style.

5   Results

We next discuss the performance of the BEAM for a small group of well-known benchmarks that use cuts in their code. Table 1 gives a small description of the benchmarks used. The benchmarks are divided into two classes: deterministic and non-deterministic. The **send_money** and the **scanner** are benchmarks where the Andorra rule allows the search space to be reduced. The **merge** program

---

[2] depth counter that can be used to classify variables as local or external

uses the commit operator while all the other benchmarks use the cut operator to reduce the search space. Because commit is not supported on YAP, the merge uses the cut operator instead.

Table 1. The benchmarks.

	Name	Description
	kkqueens	smart finder of the solutions for the n-queens problem.
Det.	**serialise**	calculate serial numbers of a list.
	merge	merge two lists of 100 elements.
Non.	**crypt**	cryptomultiplication program.
Det.	**send_money**	the SEND+MORE=MONEY puzzle.
	scanner	a program to reveal the content of a box.

Table 2 show how the BEAM and YAP perform for the selected group of benchmarks. For each benchmark we present the timings with the original code (with cuts/commit), plus timings for a modified version of the benchmarks without cuts/commit. The runtimes are presented in milliseconds and are the best execution time obtained in a series of ten runs. Timings were measured an Intel Pentium IV 1.8Mhz (800Mhz FSB) with 512Kb *on chip* cache, equipped with 512MB RAMBUS and running Mandrake Linux 9.2. The BEAM was configured with 64Mb of *Heap* plus 32Mb of *Box Memory*. Just for reference, we also present the results for YAP 4.0 (also known as YAP 98). YAP 4.0 is the version of Yap we based our work on. For BEAM we also present the number of splits performed in each benchmark.

Table 2. Benchmarks results (time in milliseconds).

Benchs.	Mode	BEAM		YAP 4.0
		Splits	*Time*	*Time*
kkqeens	with Cuts	0	170	84
	no Cuts	0	380	85
serialise	with Cuts	0	0.19	0.06
	no Cuts	83	17	0.07
merge	with Commits	0	0.30	0.18
	no Commits	101	44	0.18
crypt	with Cuts	742	40	3.2
	no Cuts	742	50	3.2
send_money	with Cuts	277	12	23350
	no Cuts	1564	60	169630
scanner	with Cuts	31	60	>12h
	no Cuts	31	60	

The original version of the programs kkqueens, serialise and merge run in BEAM deterministically.

BEAM runs `kkqueens` without cuts about two times slower, although it still executes deterministically. The problem arises because the BEAM does not perform compilation analysis to classify the predicates as deterministic. The BEAM is therefore unable to pre-compile this program as deterministic. Introducing cuts, allows the BEAM to apply the deterministic reduce and promotion rules in a single step, thus avoid unnecessary and-boxes [13]. This is an useful application of cuts: they allow one to recognise determinacy easily.

The `serialise` and `merge` benchmarks strongly depend on cuts, otherwise, the BEAM is about a hundred times slower. This was a surprising result for the BEAM: YAP runs the two versions with about the same performance. To understand these results, consider the following code from the `serialize` program:

```
split([X|L],X,L1,L2)      :- !, split(L,X,L1,L2).
split([X|L],Y,[X|L1],L2) :- before(X,Y), !,
                            split(L,Y,L1,L2).
split([X|L],Y,L1,[X|L2]) :- before(Y,X), !,
                            split(L,Y,L1,L2).
split([],_,[],[]).
```

The BEAM runs this code deterministically because goals preceding the cut may be called even when the clause generates non-deterministic constraints to external variables. Without cuts, the BEAM stalls because it tries to constrain external variables non-deterministically. The same problem exists in the `merge` benchmark. A solution to this problem would be to explicitly declare the `before/2` built-in a *test*, that is, a predicate that could always go ahead if its arguments were fully bound.

Comparing the systems for non-deterministic benchmarks is harder, since the search spaces are quite different for YAP and the BEAM. `crypt` is one example where the Andorra Model does not provide improvements to the search space. Note that in general one would not be terribly interested in the BEAM for these applications because splitting is very expensive. Still, this example is interesting because BEAM runs crypt without cuts with a very a small penalty.

`send_money` and `scanner` are two examples where the Andorra rule reduces, very significantly, the search space.

The `send_money` is a good example where the user explicit notation is used in the top-level predicate to force the system to stop looking for other alternatives after finding the first solution. In this benchmark, the BEAM is able to perform very well when compared to standard Prolog Systems. Cut is helpful to inform the system that we are only interested in the first solution.

The `scanner` results were very surprising, as the BEAM performs as well with and without cuts. This results implies that the BEAM scheduler in this case is still able to, without any explicit control, find the best strategy to find the solution. Therefore, it confirms that the implicit pruning optimizations implemented are archiving also good results.

6   Conclusions

We have discussed how to address pruning in an implementation of the Extended Andorra Model with Implicit Control. Our approach contrasts with the AKL design [9], where pruning is embedded in the language itself through the notion of guards. In our case, pruning is an annotation that users can apply either to improve program performance, or to control the search space.

One advantage of the BEAM is that it offers natural support for implicit pruning. Explicit pruning is more complex than in Prolog. In a nutshell, it requires disabling some optimisations for boxes that provide scope information for pruning. We address the interaction between pruning and co-routining by using quiet cuts.

Our work in pruning has clearly benefited from the crisp separation that the EAM with Implicit Control provides between the rewrite rules and the control rules. Implicit pruning appears as simplification rules. The actual complexity of explicit pruning is explained by the necessary work in maintaining its context.

Our results show that both implicit and explicit pruning are required in actual logic programming systems. They also suggest future work on new control declarations that could harness some of the functionality of cut, without having to run the dangers. We plan to continue this work in our future goal of integrating the BEAM with the YAP Prolog, towards being able to experiment with further applications.

Acknowledgments. We would like to gratefully acknowledge the contributions we received from Salvador Abreu, Gopal Gupta and Enrico Pontelli. The work presented in this paper has been partially supported by project APRIL (Project POSI/SRI/40749/2001) and funds granted to *LIACC* through the *Programa de Financiamento Plurianual, Fundação para a Ciência e Tecnologia* and *Programa POSI.*

References

1. W. Chen and D. S. Warren. Tabled Evaluation with Delaying for General Logic Programs. *Journal of the ACM*, 43(1):20–74, January 1996.
2. K. L. Clark, F. G. McCabe, and S. Gregory. IC-PROLOG – language features. In K. L. Clark and S. A. Tärnlund, editors, *Logic Programming*, pages 253–266. Academic Press, London, 1982.
3. A. Colmerauer. Theoretical Model of Prolog II. In M. van Caneghen and D. H. D. Warren, editors, *Logic Programming and its Applications*, pages 3–31. Ablex Publishing Corporation, 1986.
4. G. Gupta and D. H. D. Warren. An Interpreter for the Extended Andorra Model. Technical report, Dep. of Computer Science, University of Bristol, November 1991.
5. S. Haridi and S. Jansson. Kernel Andorra Prolog and its Computational Model. In D. H. D. Warren and P. Szeredi, editors, *Proceedings of the Seventh International Conference on Logic Programming*, pages 31–46. MIT Press, 1990.

6. B. Hausman. Hybrid implementation techniques in Erlang BEAM. In L. Sterling, editor, *Proceedings of the 12th International Conference on Logic Programming*, pages 816–816, Cambridge, June 13–18 1995. MIT Press.

7. M. V. Hermenegildo and R. I. Nasr. Efficient Management of Backtracking in AND-parallelism. In *Third International Conference on Logic Programming*, number 225 in Lecture Notes in Computer Science, pages 40–54. Imperial College, Springer-Verlag, July 1986.

8. J. Jaffar and M. Maher. Constraint Logic Programming: a Survey. *The Journal of Logic Programming*, 19/20, May/July 1994.

9. S. Janson. *AKL - A Multiparadigm Programming Language*. PhD thesis, SICS Swedish Institute of Computer Science, Uppsala University, 1994.

10. S. Janson and J. Montelius. Design of a Sequential Prototype Implementation of the Andorra Kernel Language. Sics research report, Swedish Institute of Computer Science, 1992.

11. R. A. Kowalski. *Logic for Problem Solving*. Elsevier North-Holland Inc., 1979.

12. R. Lopes. *An Implementation of the Extended Andorra Model*. PhD thesis, Universidade do Porto, December 2001.

13. R. Lopes, V. S. Costa, and F. Silva. On deterministic computations in the extended andorra model. In C. Palamidessi, editor, *Ninettenth International Conference on Logic Programming, ICLP03*, volume 2916 of *Lecture Notes in Computer Science*, pages 407–421. Springer-Verlag, December 2003.

14. R. Lopes and V. Santos Costa. The BEAM: Towards a first EAM Implementation. In *ILPS97 Workshop on Parallelism and Implementation Technology for (Constraint) Logic Programming Languages, Port Jefferson*, October 1997.

15. V. S. C. Ricardo Lopes and F. Silva. On the beam implementation. In F. M. Pires and S. Abreu, editors, *11th Portuguese Conference on Artificial Intelligence, EPIA 2003*, volume 2902 of *Lecture Notes in Artificial Intelligence*, pages 131–135. Springer-Verlag, December 2003.

16. K. Sagonas. *The SLG-WAM: A Search-Efficient Engine for Well-Founded Evaluation of Normal Logic Programs*. PhD thesis, Department of Computer Science, State University of New York, Stony Brook, USA, August 1996.

17. K. Sagonas and T. Swift. An Abstract Machine for Tabled Execution of Fixed-Order Stratified Logic Programs. *ACM Transactions on Programming Languages and Systems*, 20(3):586–634, May 1998.

18. V. Santos Costa. *Compile-Time Analysis for the Parallel Execution of Logic Programs in Andorra-I*. PhD thesis, University of Bristol, August 1993.

19. E. Shapiro. The family of Concurrent Logic Programming Languages. *ACM computing surveys*, 21(3):412–510, 1989.

20. T. Swift. *Efficient Evaluation of Normal Logic Programs*. PhD thesis, Department of Computer Science, State University of New York, Stony Brook, USA, Dec. 1994.

21. D. H. D. Warren. The Extended Andorra Model with Implicit Control. Presented at ICLP'90 Workshop on Parallel Logic Programming, Eilat, Israel, June 1990.

22. D. S. Warren. Efficient Prolog Memory Management for Flexible Control Strategies. In *International Symposium on Logic Programming*, pages 198–203, Silver Spring, MD, February 1984. Atlantic City, IEEE Computer Society.

USA-Smart: Improving the Quality of Plans in Answer Set Planning

Marcello Balduccini

Computer Science Department
Texas Tech University
Lubbock, TX 79409 USA
phone: +1 806 742 1191
fax: +1 806 742 3519
marcello.balduccini@ttu.edu

Abstract. In this paper we show how CR-Prolog, a recent extension of A-Prolog, was used in the successor of USA-Advisor (USA-Smart) in order to improve the quality of the plans returned. The general problem that we address is that of improving the quality of plans by taking in consideration statements that describe "most desirable" plans. We believe that USA-Smart proves that CR-Prolog provides a simple, elegant, and flexible solution to this problem, and can be easily applied to any planning domain. We also discuss how alternative extensions of A-Prolog can be used to obtain similar results.

Keywords: Planning, answer set programming, preferences.

1 Introduction

In recent years, A-Prolog – the language of logic programs with the answer set semantics [11] – was shown to be a useful tool for knowledge representation and reasoning [10]. The language is expressive and has a well understood methodology of representing defaults, causal properties of actions and fluents, various types of incompleteness, etc. The development of efficient computational systems [15,6,14,18] has allowed the use of A-Prolog for a diverse collection of applications [12,17,19,16].

In previous papers [17,2], we have shown how A-Prolog was used to build a decision support system for the Space Shuttle (USA-Advisor). USA-Advisor is capable of checking the correctness of plans and of finding plans for the operation of the Reaction Control System (RCS) of the Space Shuttle. Plans consist of a sequence of operations to open and close the valves controlling the flow of propellant from the tanks to the jets of the RCS.

Under normal conditions, pre-scripted plans exist that tell the astronauts what should be done to achieve certain goals. However, failures in the system may render those plans useless, and the flight controllers have to come up with alternative sequences that allow the completion of the mission and ensure the safety of the crew. USA-Advisor is designed to help in this task by ensuring that plans meet both criteria. Moreover, its

B. Jayaraman (Ed.): PADL 2004, LNCS 3057, pp. 135–147, 2004.

ability to quickly generate plans allows the controllers to concentrate on higher-level tasks.

In this paper we show how CR-Prolog [1,3], a recent extension of A-Prolog, was used in the successor of USA-Advisor (USA-Smart) in order to improve the quality of the plans returned. The general problem that we address here is that of improving the quality of plans by taking in consideration statements that describe "most desirable" plans. We believe that USA-Smart proves that CR-Prolog provides a simple, elegant, and flexible solution to this problem, and can be easily applied to any planning domain.

The present work builds on the ability of CR-Prolog to return "most reasonable" solutions to a problem encoded by a CR-Prolog program. Besides regular A-Prolog rules, the programmer specifies a set of rules (cr-rules) that may possibly be applied – although that should happen as rarely as possible – as well as a set of preferences on the application of the cr-rules. The "most reasonable" solutions correspond to those models that best satisfy the preferences expressed, and minimize the applications of cr-rules.

The paper is structured as follows. We start with a brief, informal, presentation of CR-Prolog. Next, we describe the Reaction Control System and the design of USA-Smart. In the following two sections we present the planner used in USA-Smart. Finally, we discuss related work, summarize the paper, and draw conclusions.

2   CR-Prolog

CR-Prolog is an extension of A-Prolog that consists of the introduction of consistency-restoring rules (cr-rules) with preferences.

CR-Prolog programs consist of regular rules and cr-rules. A *regular rule* is a statement:

$$r : h_1 \text{ or } h_2 \text{ or } \ldots \text{ or } h_k : - l_1, \ldots, l_m, \atop \text{not } l_{m+1}, \ldots, \text{not } l_n \tag{1}$$

where r is the name of the rule, h_i's and l_i's are literals, h_1 or $\ldots$ or h_k is the head, and $l_1, \ldots, l_m, \text{not } l_{m+1}, \ldots, \text{not } l_n$ is the body. The intuitive reading of (1), in terms of the beliefs that a rational agent complying with the rule should have, is: "if the agent believes $l_1, \ldots, l_m$ and does not believe $l_{m+1}, \ldots, l_n$, then it must believe one element of the head of the rule."[1] In order to increase the readability of the programs, we allow regular rules with *choice atoms* in the head [15]:

$$r : L\{p(\bar{X}) : q(\bar{X})\}U : - l_1, \ldots, l_m, \atop \text{not } l_{m+1}, \ldots, \text{not } l_n \tag{2}$$

Intuitively, the head of this rule defines subset $p \subseteq q$, such that $L \leq |p| \leq U$. Although this form can be translated in rules of type (1), it allows for more concise programs, in particular when writing planners.

---

[1]   As usual with the semantics of epistemic disjunction, the rule forces the agent to believe only *one* literal, bu he may be forced to believe also other elements of the head by other rules in the program.

A *cr-rule* is a statement of the form:

$$r: \quad h_1 \text{ or } h_2 \text{ or } \ldots \text{ or } h_k \; +- \; l_1, \ldots, l_m,$$
$$\text{not } l_{m+1}, \ldots, \text{not } l_n \tag{3}$$

The cr-rule intuitively says that, if the agent believes $l_1, \ldots, l_m$ and does not believe $l_{m+1}, \ldots, l_n$, then it "may possibly" believe one element of the head. This possibility is used only if there is no way to obtain a consistent set of beliefs using regular rules only. (For the definition of the semantics of CR-Prolog, see [3].)

Let us see how cr-rules work in practice. Consider the following program:

$$r_1 : p \text{ or } q \; +- \text{ not } t.$$
$$r_2 : s.$$

Since the program containing only r_2 is consistent, r_1 need not be applied. Hence, there is only one answer set: $\{s\}$. On the other hand, program

$$r_1 : p \text{ or } q \; +- \text{ not } t.$$
$$r_2 : s.$$
$$r_3 : \; : -\text{not } p, \text{not } q.$$

has two answer sets: $\{s, p\}$ and $\{s, q\}$. (An empty head means that the body of the rule must never be satisfied.)

Preferences between cr-rules are encoded by atoms of the form $prefer(r_1, r_2)$, where r_1 and r_2 are names of cr-rules. The intuitive reading of the atom is "do not consider sets of beliefs obtained using r_2 unless you have excluded the existence of belief sets obtained using r_1." We call this type of preference *binding*.

To better understand the use of preferences, consider program Π_1:

$$r_1 : p \; +- \text{ not } t.$$
$$r_2 : q \; +- \text{ not } t.$$
$$r_3 : prefer(r_1, r_2).$$

Π_1 has one answer set: $\{prefer(r_1, r_2)\}$. Notice that cr-rules are not applied, and hence the preference atom has no effect. Now consider program $\Pi_2 = \Pi_1 \cup \{r_4 : \; : -\text{not } p, \text{not } q\}$. Now cr-rules must be used to restore consistency. Since r_1 is preferred to r_2, the answer set is: $\{p, prefer(r_1, r_2)\}$. Finally, consider $\Pi_3 = \Pi_2 \cup \{r_5 : \; : -p\}$. Its answer set is: $\{q, prefer(r_1, r_2)\}$.

In the rest of the discussion, we will omit rule names whenever possible. Now we describe in more detail the RCS and present the design of USA-Smart.

3   The RCS and the Design of USA-Smart

The RCS is the Shuttle's system that has primary responsibility for maneuvering the aircraft while it is in space. It consists of fuel and oxidizer tanks, valves and other plumbing needed to provide propellant to the maneuvering jets of the Shuttle. It also includes electronic circuitry: both to control the valves in the propellant lines and to prepare the jets to receive firing commands.

The RCS is divided in three subsystems: the forward RCS, the left RCS, and the right RCS. Each subsystem controls jets located in different parts of the craft. For most maneuvers, two or more subsystems have to be used concurrently. Each subsystem has its own propellant tanks, plumbing, circuitry, and jets. There is almost no connection between the subsystems, with the only important exception of the crossfeed, which connects the plumbing of the left and right subsystems. The crossfeed is valve-controlled, and is intended to be used when one of the two subsystems is affected by faults that prevent the use of its own propellant. It is NASA's policy to use the crossfeed as sparingly as possible, in order to keep the level of propellant in the two subsystems balanced.

The RCS is computer controlled during takeoff and landing. While in orbit, however, astronauts have the primary control. When an orbital maneuver is required, the astronauts must perform whatever actions are necessary to prepare the RCS. These actions generally require flipping switches, which are used to open or close valves, or to activate the proper circuitry. Acting on the valves will allow propellant to reach the jets that are involved in the maneuver. When the operation is complete, the jets are "ready for the maneuver." In emergency situations, such as when some switches are faulty, the astronauts communicate the problem to the ground flight controllers, who will come up with a sequence of computer commands to perform the desired task and will instruct the Shuttle's computer to execute them. At the same time, they will send to the astronauts a sequence of operations on the switches that must be combined with the computer commands. Instructing the computer to operate the valves is quite complex, since it requires modifying the computer's software and uploading it to the Shuttle. For this reason, flight controllers prefer the use of switches, when possible.

During normal Shuttle operations, there are pre-scripted plans that tell the astronauts which switches should be flipped to achieve certain goals. The situation changes when there are failures in the system. The number of possible sets of failures is too large to pre-plan for all of them. Continued correct operation of the RCS in such circumstances is necessary to allow for the completion of the mission and to help ensure the safety of the crew.

USA-Smart is designed to help achieve this goal by generating plans for emergency situations, and by verifying the correctness, and the safety, of the plans proposed by the flight controllers.

Like its predecessor, USA-Smart consists of a collection of largely independent modules, represented by lp-functions[2], and a graphical Java interface. The interface provides a simple way for the user to enter information about the history of the RCS, its faults, and the task to be performed. The two tasks possible are: checking if a sequence of occurrences of actions satisfies goal G, and finding a plan for G of a length not exceeding

---

[2] By lp-function we mean a CR-Prolog program Π with input and output signatures $\sigma_i(\Pi)$ and $\sigma_o(\Pi)$ and a set $dom(\Pi)$ of sets of literals from $\sigma_i(\Pi)$ such that, for any $X \in dom(\Pi)$, $\Pi \cup X$ is consistent, i.e. has an answer set.

some number of steps, N. Based on this information, the graphical interface verifies if the input is complete, selects an appropriate combination of modules, assembles them into a CR-Prolog program, Π, and passes Π as input to a reasoning system for computing answer sets (in USA-Smart this role is played by CRMODELS[3], which performs the underlying computations using SMODELS[4][15]). In this approach the task of checking a plan P is reduced to checking if there exists a model of the program $\Pi \cup P$.

Plan generation is performed by the planning module; the corresponding correctness theorem [16] guarantees that there is a one-to-one correspondence between the plans and the set of answer sets of the program. Finally, the Java interface extracts the appropriate answer from the CRMODELS output and displays it in a user-friendly format.

The modules used by USA-Smart are:

- the plumbing module;
- the valve control module;
- the circuit theory module;
- the planning module.

The first three modules describe the behavior of the RCS, and are examined in detail in [17,2]. The planning module establishes the search criteria used by the program to find a plan.

4 Planning in USA-Smart

The structure of the planning module follows the *generate, (define) and test* approach described in [7,13,9]. Since the RCS contains more than 200 actions, with rather complex effects, and may require very long plans, this standard approach needs to be substantially improved. This is done by adding various forms of heuristic, domain-dependent information[5]. In particular, the generation part takes advantage of the division of the RCS in three, largely independent, subsystems. A plan for the RCS can therefore be viewed as the composition of three separate plans that can operate in parallel.

Plan generation is implemented using the following rule, $AGEN$:

```
0{occurs(A,T): action_of(A,R)}1 :- subsystem(R),
                                    involved(R,T).
```

The intuitive reading of involved(R,T) is "subsystem R is involved at time T in the maneuver being performed", and action_of(A,R) means "A is an action that operates on subsystem R." Overall, $AGEN$ selects at each time step, T, at most one action, A, for each subsystem, R, that is involved in the maneuver. (To save space, we omit from the rules the specification of the domains of variables.)

The precise definition of involved(R,T) is given by the following two rules. The first rule says that subsystem R is involved in the maneuver at time T if the goal for that subsystem has not yet been achieved.

---

[3] http://www.krlab.cs.ttu.edu/Software

[4] http://www.tcs.hut.fi/Software/smodels

[5] Notice that the addition does not affect the generality of the algorithm.

```
involved(R,T) :- subsystem(R),
                 not goal(T,R).
```

The second rule says that subsystem $R1$ is involved in the maneuver at time T if the cross-feed must be used, and if $R1$ is connected through the crossfeed to another subsystem, $R2$, whose goal has not yet been achieved.

```
involved(R1,T) :- subsystem(R1), has_crossfeed(R1),
                  subsystem(R2), has_crossfeed(R2),
                  neq(R1,R2),
                  not goal(T,R2).
```

In our approach, the test phase of the search is the one that most directly controls the quality of plans. Tests are expressed by constraints, so that, when a sequence of actions is not a desirable solution according to some test, the body of the corresponding constraint is satisfied. This guarantees that only "desirable plans" are returned.

The first step is ensuring that the models of the program contain valid plans. This is obtained by the constraint:

```
:- not goal.
```

The definition of goal is:

```
goal :-
        goal(T1,left_rcs),
        goal(T2,right_rcs),
        goal(T3,fwd_rcs).
```

The rationale for this definition is that the goal of preparing the Shuttle for a maneuver is split into several subgoals, each setting some jets, from a particular subsystem, ready to fire. The overall goal is stated as a composition of the goals of the individual subsystems.

Several other constraints that are used to encode heuristic, domain-dependent information are described in [17,2].

In order to improve the quality of plans with respect to the results obtained with USA-Advisor, the planner of USA-Smart must be able to:

1. avoid the use of the crossfeed if at all possible;
2. avoid the use of computer commands if at all possible;
3. avoid the generation of irrelevant actions.

Notice that these requirements are in some sense defeasible. The planner is allowed to return a solution that does not satisfy some of the requirements, if no better solution exists.

The A-Prolog based planner used in USA-Advisor is unable to cope with requirements of this type. In fact, A-Prolog lacks the expressive power necessary to compute *best* or *preferred* solutions.

The adoption of CR-Prolog solves the problem. The key step in encoding a defeasible test is the introduction of a cr-rule that determines whether the corresponding constraints must be applied. Since cr-rules are used as rarely as possible, the test will be ignored only when strictly necessary. Moreover, preferences on cr-rules allow to specify which tests are more important.

Consider requirement 1 above. The corresponding test is encoded by:

```
r1(R,T): xfeed_allowed(R,T) +- subsystem(R).

:- subsystem(R), action_of(A,R),
   occurs(A,T),
   opens_xfeed_valve(A),
   not xfeed_allowed(R,T).
```

The cr-rule says that the use of the crossfeed may possibly be allowed at any time step T. The constraint says that it is impossible for action A of subsystem R to occur at T if A opens a crossfeed valve, and the use of the crossfeed is not allowed in R at time step T.

Requirement 2 is encoded in a similar way.

```
r2(R,T): ccs_allowed(R,T) +- subsystem(R).

:- subsystem(R), action_of(A,R),
   occur(A,T),
   sends_computer_command(A),
   not ccs_allowed(R,T).
```

The cr-rule says that computer commands may possibly be allowed at any time step T. The constraint says that it is impossible for action A of subsystem R to occur at T if A sends a computer command and computer commands are not allowed in R at time step T.

As we mentioned above, CR-Prolog also allows to express the relative importance of defeasible tests. For example, if the flight controllers decide that modifying the software of the Shuttle's computer is preferable to losing the balance of the propellant between the left and right subsystems, the following rule can be added to the planner:

```
prefer(r2(R2,T2),r1(R1,T1)).
```

Notice that preferences are not restricted to occur as facts. The rule

```
prefer(r2(R2,T2),r1(R1,T1)) :- computer_reliable.
```

says that the use of computer commands is preferred to the use of the crossfeed only if the on-board computer is reliable. In this case, if we want to make sure that computer commands are used only as a last resort, we can add:

```
prefer(r1(R1,T1),r2(R2,T2)) :- -computer_reliable.
```

(Here "-" is classical negation.)

Avoiding the generation of irrelevant actions (requirement 3 above) is obtained by a test that ensures that all non-empty time steps in the plan for a subsystem are strictly necessary. The test is encoded as:

```
r3(R,T): non_empty(R,T) +- subsystem(R).
```

```
:- subsystem(R), action_of(A,R),
   occurs(A,T),
   not non_empty(R,T).
```

The cr-rule says that any time step T of the plan for subsystem R may possibly be non-empty. The constraint says that it is impossible for action A of subsystem R to occur at time step T if T is empty in the plan for R.

Experimental results confirm that the plans generated by USA-Smart are of a significantly higher quality than the plans generated by USA-Advisor.

We have applied USA-Smart to 800 problem instances from [16], namely the instances with 3, 5, 8, and 10 mechanical faults, respectively, and no electrical faults. For these experiments, we did not include in the planner the preference statements previously discussed.[6]

The planning algorithm iteratively invokes the reasoning system with maximum plan length L, checks if a model is returned, and iterates after incrementing L if no model was found. If no plans are found that are 10 or less time steps long, the algorithm terminates and returns no solution. This approach guarantees that plans found by the algorithm are the shortest (in term of number of time steps between the first and the last action in the plan). Notice that the current implementation of CRMODELS returns the models ordered by the number of (ground) cr-rules used to obtain the model, with the model that uses the least cr-rules returned first. Hence, the plan returned by the algorithm is both the shortest and the one that uses the minimum number of cr-rules.

Overall, computer commands were used 27 times, as opposed to 1831 computer commands generated by USA-Advisor. The crossfeed was used 10 times by USA-Smart, and 187 times by USA-Advisor. Moreover, in 327 cases over 800, USA-Smart generated plans that contained less actions than the plans found by USA-Advisor (as expected, in no occasion they were longer). The total number of irrelevant actions avoided by USA-Smart was 577, which is about 12% of the total number of actions used by USA-Advisor (4601).

In spite of the improvement in the quality of plans, the time required by USA-Smart to compute a plan (or prove the absence of a solution) was still largely acceptable. Many plans were found in seconds; most were found in less than 2 minutes, and the program almost always returned an answer in less than 20 minutes (the maximum that

---

[6] This decision is due to the fact that the current version of CRMODELS handles preferences very inefficiently. Work is well under way in the implementation of a new, efficient algorithm that will be able to deal with preferences efficiently.

the Shuttle experts consider acceptable). The only exception consists of about 10 cases, when planning took a few hours. These outliers were most likely due to the fact that CRMODELS is still largely unoptimized.

5   Advanced Use of Preferences

The quality of plans is significantly influenced by the set of preferences included in the planner. We have shown in the previous section a simple example of preferences used in USA-Smart. Now we examine more complex preferences, the way they interact with each other, and the effect on the solution returned by the planner.

The first preference that we show deals with the source of the propellant that is delivered to the jets. In the Space Shuttle, the RCS can optionally be powered with fuel coming from the three main jets of the craft, that are controlled by the Orbital Maneuvering System (OMS). However, the propellant cannot be delivered back from the RCS to the OMS if later needed. Since the OMS jets are critical for safe re-entry, the use of the OMS propellant for the RCS is avoided unless there is no other choice. Summing up, either the crossfeed or the OMS-feed may possibly be used to deliver propellant to the jets, but *the OMS-feed should not be used unless no plan can be found, that uses the crossfeed.* This statement can be encoded by the following rules: (to simplify the presentation, we will make the decisions independent of time and of subsystem – e.g. if the use of the crossfeed is allowed, it may occur at any time step in any subsystem)

```
xfeed: xfeed_allowed +-.
oms:   omsfeed_allowed +-.

prefer(xfeed,oms).
```

A similar preference can be included in the planner if we model the capability of the crew to repair damaged switches in the control panels of the RCS. Since such repairs may take a very long time, and short-circuits may occur during the process, either computer commands or switch repairs may be possibly included in the plan, but switch repairs should be included only if no plans that use computer commands are found. The statement is encoded by:

```
ccs: ccs_allowed +-.
rep: repair_allowed +-.

prefer(ccs,rep).
```

It is interesting to examine the interaction between the two preferences above. Suppose that we are given an initial situation in which:

- jets in the left subsystem must be used;
- leaking valves prevent the use of the propellant in the tanks of the left subsystem;
- the wires connecting the on-board computer to the valves that control the crossfeed are damaged;
- the switches that enable the OMS-feed are stuck.

Clearly the only reasonable choices available to deliver propellant to the jets are:

1. via the OMS-feed using computer commands, or
2. via the crossfeed after repairing the switches.

Let us imagine the reasoning of a flight controller trying to decide between the two alternatives. Should the plan use the propellant in the OMS tanks ? Since it is quite risky, that is normally done only if the crossfeed cannot be used, and alternative 2 allows the use of the crossfeed. On the other hand, alternative 2 requires the repair of the switches. That, again, is dangerous, and is normally done only is there is no way to use computer commands. Hence, he is back to alternative 1. It is reasonable to expect that, after some thinking, the flight controller would discuss the problem with his colleagues in order to consider all the relevant aspects of the remaining part of the mission (notice that these data are *not* available to USA-Smart). Only after taking all these elements into account, he would finally be able to make a decision.

Given the above encoding of the preferences, and an appropriate encoding of the initial situation, USA-Smart would reason in a way that mimics the flight controller's thoughts. Alternative 1 uses the OMS-feed, and there is another alternative that uses the crossfeed, while rule `prefer(xfeed,oms)` says that the OMS-feed can be used only if there is no way to use the crossfeed. Hence, alternative 1 cannot be used to generate a plan. Similarly, alternative 2 cannot be used to generate a plan. Therefore, the problem has no solution, with the given information.[7]

The behavior of the planner is due to the use of binding preferences. According to the informal semantics described in Section 2, rule `prefer(xfeed,oms)` is best seen as an order that describes how reasoning must be performed. When conflicts arise on the specification of how reasoning should be performed, the reasoner does not return any of the conflicting belief sets, following the intuition that such conflicts must be considered carefully.

On the other hand, there are cases when it is desirable to specify weaker preferences, that can be violated if conflicts arise. This typically happens when the situation is not particularly dangerous. The example that follows describes the use of weaker preferences in the domain of the RCS.

In the RCS, it is possible in principle to allow the propellant to reach (lightly) damaged jets, as well as go through valves that are stuck open. None of the options is particularly dangerous: a specific command must be sent to turn on the jets, so propellant can be safely allowed to reach damaged jets[8]; stuck valves can be safely traversed by the propellant without any leaks (unless they are also leaking). Nonetheless, severe problems may occur in an (unlikely) emergency in which it is necessary to shut off quickly the flow of propellant, if the only valve that is in the path is stuck. For this reason, it seems reasonable to prefer the delivery of propellant to damaged jets over the use of stuck valves. This idea is formalized in CR-Prolog by:

---

[7] With the addition of a few other cr-rules, it is actually possible to allow USA-Smart to return a model whose literals give details on the problem encountered. We do not describe this technique here, because it is out of the scope of the paper.

[8] We are assuming that the firing command is working correctly.

```
d: dam_jets_allowed +-.
v: stuck_valves_allowed +-.

prefer(d,v) :- not -prefer(d,v).
p1: -prefer(d,v) +-.
```

The last two rules encode a weaker type of preference. The first is a default saying that, *normally*, cr-rule v cannot be considered unless there are no solutions that use cr-rule d. The second rule encodes a strong exception to the default, saying that the preference between d and v may be possibly violated.

To see how weak preferences work, let us consider the interaction of the previous rules with:

```
s: repair_switches_allowed +-.
c: repair_ccs_allowed +-.

prefer(s,c) :- not -prefer(s,c).
p2: -prefer(s,c) +-.
```

These rules express the fact that the crew can either repair the switches of the control panel, or repair the wires that give the on-board computer control of the valves of the RCS. The former repair is preferred to the latter (as working on the computer command wires requires shutting down the on-board computer).

Now let us consider a situation in which both switches and computer commands are damaged, and we cannot avoid delivering propellant either through a stuck valve or to a damaged jet (without firing it). The damages to the switches are such that, even after repairing them, the goal can be achieved only by delivering the propellant through the stuck valve. The two reasonable solutions are: repairing the computer commands and delivering the propellant to the damaged jet, or repairing the switches and delivering the propellant to the stuck valve. Intuitively, since there are no major risks involved, both solutions are viable. Because of the use of defaults, and of cr-rules p1 and p2, USA-Smart would consider both solutions equivalent, and return indiscriminately one plan associated with them. [9]

6   Related Work

The amount of literature on planning with preferences is huge. Because of space constraints, we will restrict the attention only to those logical approaches to planning in which the language allows the representation of *state contraints*[10]. This capability is crucial to model most of the RCS, e.g. the electrical circuits.

In its simplest form, the `minimize` statement of SMODELS [15] instructs the reasoning system to look for models that minimize the number of atoms, from a given set, that

---

[9] The conclusion can be formally proven from the semantics of CR-Prolog.

[10] Also called *static causal laws* in the context of action languages.

are present in the model. In its complete form, the statement allows to minimize the sum of the weights associated with the specified atoms. Encoding defeasible tests using minimize seems non-trivial because of the possibility to specify only one statement in the program. Moreover, it is not entirely clear how preferences on tests could be encoded. The *weak constraints* of DLV [6] provide an elegant way to encode defeasible tests. A weak constraint is a constraint that can be violated if necessary. A numerical weight can be specified to express the cost of violating the constraint. Unfortunately, examples show that the use of weak constraints to encode preferences for planning is affected by the same problems that we discussed in the context of diagnosis [1]. This is true also for the approaches that rely on a translation to the language of DLV, e.g. DLV$^\mathcal{K}$ [8]. Another alternative is the use of LPOD [4,5], which extends A-Prolog by allowing the specification of a list of alternatives in the head of rules. The alternatives are listed from the most preferred to the least preferred. If the body of the rule is satisfied, one alternative must be selected following the preference order. Moreover, preferences can be specified between rules, so that the reasoning system tries to pick the best alternatives possible for preferred rules. Preferences in LPOD are intended in the weaker meaning discussed in the previous section (in [5], the authors argue that *Pareto* preference is superior to the other types of preferences that they considered in the paper). Hence, it is definitely possible to encode in this language both defeasible tests and the weak preferences of Section 5. However, it is not clear if there is a way to encode binding preferences in LPOD. The ability to encode binding preferences is very important in USA-Smart, as it allows for a more cautious form of reasoning, which is essential in delicate situation such as the Shuttle's missions.

7   Conclusions

In this paper, we have shown how CR-Prolog was used in our decision support system for the Space Shuttle in order to improve significantly the quality of the plans returned. The general problem that we have addressed is that of improving the quality of plans by taking into consideration statements that describe "most desirable" plans. We believe that USA-Smart proves that CR-Prolog provides a simple, elegant, and flexible solution to this problem, and can be easily applied to any planning domain. We have also discussed how alternative extensions of A-Prolog can be used to obtain similar results.

The author is very thankful to Michael Gelfond for his suggestions. This work was partially supported by United Space Alliance under Research Grant 26-3502-21 and Contract COC6771311, and by NASA under grant NCC9-157.

References

1. Marcello Balduccini and Michael Gelfond. Logic programs with consistency-restoring rules. In Patrick Doherty, John McCarthy, and Mary-Anne Williams, editors, *International Symposium on Logical Formalization of Commonsense Reasoning*, AAAI 2003 Spring Symposium Series, Mar 2003.

2. Marcello Balduccini, Michael Gelfond, Monica Nogueira, and Richard Watson. The USA-Advisor: A Case Study in Answer Set Planning. In *Proceedings of the 6th International Conference on Logic Programming and Nonmonotonic Reasoning*, pages 439–442, Sep 2001.

3. Marcello Balduccini and Veena S. Mellarkod. CR-Prolog2: CR-Prolog with Ordered Disjunction. In *ASP03 Answer Set Programming: Advances in Theory and Implementation*, volume 78 of *CEUR Workshop proceedings*, Sep 2003.

4. Gerhard Brewka. Logic programming with ordered disjunction. In *Proceedings of AAAI-02*, 2002.

5. Gerhard Brewka, Ilkka Niemela, and Tommi Syrjanen. Implementing ordered disjunction using answer set solvers for normal programs. In Sergio Flesca and Giovanbattista Ianni, editors, *Proceedings of the 8th European Conference on Artificial Intelligence (JELIA 2002)*, Sep 2002.

6. Francesco Calimeri, Tina Dell'Armi, Thomas Eiter, Wolfgang Faber, Georg Gottlob, Giovanbattista Ianni, Giuseppe Ielpa, Christoph Koch, Nicola Leone, Simona Perri, Gerard Pfeifer, and Axel Polleres. The dlv system. In Sergio Flesca and Giovanbattista Ianni, editors, *Proceedings of the 8th European Conference on Artificial Intelligence (JELIA 2002)*, Sep 2002.

7. Yannis Dimopoulos, J. Koehler, and B. Nebel. Encoding planning problems in nonmonotonic logic programs. In *Proceedings of the 4th European Conference on Planning*, volume 1348 of *Lecture Notes in Artificial Intelligence (LNCS)*, pages 169–181, 1997.

8. Thomas Eiter, Wolfgang Faber, Nicola Leone, Gerard Pfeifer, and Axel Polleres. Answer set planning under action costs. *Journal of Artificial Intelligence Research*, 19:25–71, 2003.

9. Selim Erdogan and Vladimir Lifschitz. Definitions in answer set programming. In *Proceedings of LPNMR-7*, Jan 2004.

10. Michael Gelfond. Representing knowledge in A-Prolog. In Antonis C. Kakas and Fariba Sadri, editors, *Computational Logic: Logic Programming and Beyond, Essays in Honour of Robert A. Kowalski, Part II*, volume 2408, pages 413–451. Springer Verlag, Berlin, 2002.

11. Michael Gelfond and Vladimir Lifschitz. Classical negation in logic programs and disjunctive databases. *New Generation Computing*, pages 365–385, 1991.

12. K. Heljanko. Using logic programs with stable model semantics to solve deadlock and reachability problems for 1-safe Petri nets. *Fundamenta Informaticae*, 37(3):247–268, 1999.

13. Vladimir Lifschitz. *Action Languages, Answer Sets, and Planning*, pages 357–373. The Logic Programming Paradigm: a 25-Year Perspective. Springer Verlag, Berlin, 1999.

14. Fangzhen Lin and Yuting Zhao. Assat: Computing answer sets of a logic program by sat solvers. In *Proceedings of AAAI-02*, 2002.

15. Ilkka Niemela, Patrik Simons, and Timo Soininen. Extending and implementing the stable model semantics. *Artificial Intelligence*, 138(1–2):181–234, Jun 2002.

16. Monica Nogueira. *Building Knowledge Systems in A-Prolog*. PhD thesis, University of Texas at El Paso, May 2003.

17. Monica Nogueira, Marcello Balduccini, Michael Gelfond, Richard Watson, and Matthew Barry. An A-Prolog decision support system for the Space Shuttle. In *PADL 2001*, pages 169–183, 2001.

18. Enrico Pontelli, Marcello Balduccini, and F. Bermudez. Non-monotonic reasoning on beowulf platforms. In Veronica Dahl and Philip Wadler, editors, *PADL 2003*, volume 2562 of *Lecture Notes in Artificial Intelligence (LNCS)*, pages 37–57, Jan 2003.

19. Timo Soininen and Ilkka Niemela. Developing a declarative rule language for applications in product configuration. In *Proceedings of the First International Workshop on Practical Aspects of Declarative Languages*, May 1999.

ASP − PROLOG : A System for Reasoning about Answer Set Programs in Prolog

Omar Elkhatib, Enrico Pontelli, and Tran Cao Son

Department of Computer Science
New Mexico State University
{okhatib|epontell|tson}@cs.nmsu.edu

Abstract. We present a system (ASP − PROLOG) which provides a tight and well-defined integration of Prolog and Answer Set Programming (ASP). The combined system enhances the expressive power of ASP, allowing us to write programs that *reason* about *dynamic* ASP modules and about collections of stable models. These features are vital in a number of application domains (e.g., planning, scheduling, diagnosis). We describe the design of ASP − PROLOG along with its implementation, realized using CIAO Prolog and *Smodels*.

1   Introduction

Stable model semantics [4] is a widely accepted approach to provide semantics to logic programs with negation. Stable model semantics relies on the idea of accepting multiple minimal models as a description of the meaning of a program. In spite of its wide acceptance and its extensive mathematical foundations, stable models semantics have only recently found its way into "practical" logic programming. The recent successes have been sparked by the availability of efficient inference engines (such as *Smodels* [13], Cmodels [7], ASSAT [9], and DLV [3]) and a substantial effort towards *understanding* how to write programs under stable models semantics [12,11,8]. This has led to the development of a novel *programming paradigm*, commonly referred to as *Answer Set Programming (ASP)*. ASP is a computation paradigm in which logical theories (Horn clauses with negation) serve as problem specifications and solutions are represented by *collection of models*. ASP has been concretized in a number of related formalisms— e.g., disjunctive logic programming [3]. In comparison to other non-monotonic logics, ASP is syntactically simple and, at the same time, very expressive. ASP has been adopted in various domains (e.g., [8,5,14]).

Most existing ASP inference engines have been extended to provide frontends that are suitable to encode different types of knowledge. *Smodels* provides a rich set of built-in structures to express choices, weight-constraints, and restricted forms of optimizations. *DLV* provides different classes of constraint rules (e.g., weak constraints), aggregates, and alternative front-ends (e.g., diagnosis, planning), allowing the development of programs in specific applications domains using very high-level languages. In spite of these extensions, there are aspects of reasoning that cannot be conveniently expressed in ASP:

B. Jayaraman (Ed.): PADL 2004, LNCS 3057, pp. 148–162, 2004.

- The development of an ASP program is mostly viewed as a monolithic and batch process. Most existing ASP systems offer only a batch approach to execution of programs—programs are completely developed, they go through a "compilation" process, executed and finally stable models are proposed to the user. The process lacks of any level of interaction with the user. In particular, it does not directly support an interactive development of programs (as it is possible in the case of Prolog), where one can immediately explore the results of simply adding/removing rules.
- ASP programmers can control the computation of stable models through the rules that they include in the logic program. Nevertheless, ASP systems offer very limited capabilities for reasoning on the *whole class* of stable models associated to a program—e.g., to perform selection of models according to user-defined criteria or to compare across models. These activities are very important in many application domains—e.g., to express soft constraints on models, to support preferences when using ASP to perform planning.
- ASP systems are independent systems; interaction with other languages can be performed only through low level and complex APIs; this prevents programmers from writing programs that manipulate ASP programs and stable models as first-class citizens. We would like to be able to write programs in a high-level language (Prolog in this case), which are capable to access ASP programs, modify their structure (by adding or removing rules and facts), and access and reason with stable models. This type of features is essential in many ASP applications. For example, ASP planners require to pre-specify the maximum length of the plan; the ability to access and modify ASP programs would allow us to write programs that automatically modify the length of the plan until a plan with the desired property is found.

In this project we propose a system, called ASP − PROLOG. The system represents a tight and semantically well-defined integration of ASP in Prolog. The language is developed using the module and class capabilities of CIAO Prolog. ASP − PROLOG allows programmers to assemble a variety of different modules to create a program; along with the traditional types of modules supported by CIAO Prolog, it allows the presence of an arbitrary number of *ASP modules*, each a collection of ASP rules and facts. Each Prolog module can access any ASP module (using the traditional module qualification of Prolog), read its content, access its models, and modify it (using the traditional **assert** and **retract**).

We are not aware of any system with the same capabilities as ASP − PROLOG. Relatively limited work has been presented exploring effective ways of integrating ASP in the context of other programming languages. *Smodels* provides a very low level API [17] which allows C++ programs to use *Smodels* as a library. DLV does not document any external API, although a Java wrapper has been recently announced [1]. XASP [2] proposes an interface from XSB to the API of *Smodels*. It provides a subset of the functionalities of ASP − PROLOG, with a deeper integration with the capabilities of XSB of handling normal logic programs.

2   Brief Semantic Foundations

In this section, we discuss the semantic foundation of $\mathsf{ASP} - \mathsf{PROLOG}$ and motivate the basic constructions of the language. For simplicity, we will assume a pure Prolog system, though in the real systems, full-blown Prolog will be allowed.

2.1   Language Formalization

Let us consider a language signature $\langle \mathcal{F}, \mathcal{V}, \Pi \rangle$, where
- $\mathcal{V}$ is a denumerable set of variables;
- $\mathcal{F}$ is a set of function symbols; in particular, $\mathcal{F} = \mathcal{F}_P \cup \mathcal{F}_A \cup \mathcal{F}_C$, where $\mathcal{F}_P$ are called *user* functions, $\mathcal{F}_A$ are called *ASP* functions, and $\mathcal{F}_C$ are called *interface* functions. We assume that $\mathcal{F}_A \subseteq \mathcal{F}_P$ and $\mathcal{F}_A$ is finite.
- Π is a set of predicate symbols; in particular, $\Pi = \Pi_P \cup \Pi_A \cup \Pi_C$, where $\mathtt{true}, \mathtt{false} \in \Pi_P \cap \Pi_A$ and
  - Π_P are called *user-defined* predicates;
  - Π_A are called *ASP-defined* predicates;
  - Π_C are called *Interface* predicates. In this presentation we will limit our attention to $\Pi_C = \{\mathtt{assert}, \mathtt{retract}, \mathtt{models}\}$.
- $\mathcal{F}_A \cup \Pi_A \subseteq \mathcal{F}_C$.

The function ar determines the arity of the various symbols. We assume that $\forall f \in \mathcal{F}_A : ar(f) = 0$, and $\mathtt{assert}$, $\mathtt{retract}$, and $\mathtt{models}$ are all unary predicates.

The language adopted is multi-sorted, and it is based on the two sorts P (i.e., *Prolog*) and A (i.e., *ASP*). The language should meet the following requirements:
- each function (predicate) symbol f in $\mathcal{F}_P$ (Π_P) has sort $\mathsf{P}^{ar(f)} \to \mathsf{P}$ ($\mathsf{P}^{ar(f)}$);
- each function (predicate) symbol f in $\mathcal{F}_A$ (Π_A) has sort $\mathsf{A}^{ar(f)} \to \mathsf{A}$ ($\mathsf{A}^{ar(f)}$);
- the symbols in $\mathcal{F}_A$ and Π_A are of sort A and P at the same time.

Intuitively, the sort A is used to identify terms and atoms that belong to ASP modules, while P is used for the construction of Prolog modules. We assume that terms and atoms are well-formed w.r.t. sorts. An atom built using symbols from Π_A and $\mathcal{F}_A \cup \mathcal{V}$ is called an *ASP-atom*; an atom built using symbols from $\mathcal{F}_P \cup \mathcal{V}$ and Π_P is called a *Prolog-atom*; an atom built using symbols from $\mathcal{F}_P \cup \mathcal{V}$ and Π_C is called an *Interface-atom*.

Definition 1. *An* ASP-literal *is either an ASP-atom or a formula of the type* not A, *where A is an ASP-atom. An* ASP clause *is a rule of the form*

$$A :- L_1 \wedge \ldots \wedge L_n \tag{1}$$

$$:- L_1 \wedge \ldots \wedge L_n \tag{2}$$

where A is a ground ASP-atom, and $L_1, \ldots, L_n$ are ground ASP-literals. Rules of type (2) are known as constraint *rules.*

Definition 2 (ASP constraint). *An* ASP constraint *is a formula of the type* $L_1 \wedge \ldots \wedge L_k$, *where $k \geq 0$ and each L_i is*

- *an ASP-literal (A or not A); or*
- *a formula of the type $\alpha : L$ where α is a P-term and L is an ASP-literal.*

Definition 3 (Interface Constraints). *An* Interface constraint *is a conjunction $L_1 \wedge \ldots \wedge L_k$ ($k \geq 0$) of interface atoms of the type*

$$\texttt{assert}(A :- B_1, \ldots, B_n) \quad \texttt{retract}(A :- B_1, \ldots, B_n) \quad \texttt{models}(t)$$

where $A :- B_1, \ldots, B_n$ is an ASP clause and t is a P-term.

Definition 4 (ASP – PROLOG rule). *A* ASP – PROLOG *rule is a formula of the form*

$$H :- C_1, C_2 \, [] \, B_1, \ldots, B_k$$

where H, C_1, C_2, and $B_1, \ldots, B_k$ are a Prolog-atom, an ASP-constraint, an Interface constraint, and Prolog-atoms, respectively.

A static ASP – PROLOG *rule (or, simply, a static rule) is a* ASP – PROLOG *rule that does not contain any interface constraint based on* assert *or* retract.

Definition 5 (ASP – PROLOG program). *A* ASP – PROLOG *program[1] is a pair $\langle Pr, As \rangle$ where Pr is a set of* ASP – PROLOG *rules and As is a set of ASP rules. A static* ASP – PROLOG *program is a* ASP – PROLOG *program $\langle Pr, As \rangle$ such that all the rules in Pr are static.*

For example, the following is an ASP clause: $p(a) :- q(a) \wedge r(b)$ where p, q, r are in Π_A and a, b are in $\mathcal{F}_A$.

2.2   Operational Semantics

Let us denote with $\mathcal{H}_A$ ($\mathcal{H}_P$) the Herbrand universe built using the symbols in $\mathcal{F}_A$ ($\mathcal{F}_P$). The notation $\mathcal{H}$ will represent the complete Herbrand universe. We will also use the notation $\mathcal{B}_A$ (resp. $\mathcal{B}_P$, $\mathcal{B}$) to denote the Herbrand base obtained from the symbols of $\mathcal{F}_A \cup \Pi_A$ (resp. $\mathcal{F}_P \cup \Pi_P$, $\mathcal{F} \cup \Pi$).

Let us start by focusing on static programs. The absence of assert and retract operations in the interface constraints guarantees that the content of the As part of the program will remain unchanged throughout the execution.

Let $P = \langle Pr, As \rangle$ be a static ASP – PROLOG program. The component As is a standard answer-set program [12]; let us denote with

$$\mathcal{M}(As) = \{M \subseteq \mathcal{B}_A \mid M \text{ is a stable model of } As\}$$

The semantics for P can be derived as a natural extension of the semantics of pure logic programming; the notion of model should simply be extended to accommodate for the meaning of ASP-constraints and interface constraints. The only additional element we require is a map used to *name* the models of the

---

[1] For the sake of simplicity we focus on a single ASP module; the presentation can be easily generalized to accommodate multiple ASP modules.

As part of the program; let $\nu : \mathcal{M}(As) \to \mathcal{H}_P$ be an injective function, called the *model-naming function*. Then, a pair $\langle M, \nu \rangle$ is a model of the program if $M \subseteq \mathcal{B}_P$ and it satisfies all the Pr rules; in particular, the model will satisfy a ground ASP-constraint and interface constraint if:

- A is an ASP-literal, then $\langle M, \nu \rangle \models A$ iff $\forall S \in \mathcal{M}(As).S \models A$
- A is an ASP-constraint of the form $t : B$, then $\langle M, \nu \rangle \models A$ iff $\exists S \in \mathcal{M}(As).(\nu(S){=}t \wedge S {\models} B)$
- A is an interface constraint of the type $\mathtt{models}(t)$, then $\langle M, \nu \rangle \models A$ iff $\exists S \in \mathcal{M}(As).\nu(S){=}t$

It is straightforward to extend these definitions to deal with entailment of an arbitrary goal and to define when clauses are satisfied by the model. Observe that, given a program $P = \langle Pr, As \rangle$ and a fixed model naming function ν, we have that there exists a unique minimal model $\langle M, \nu \rangle$ of P, according to the ordering $\sqsubseteq$ defined as: $\langle M_1, \nu \rangle \sqsubseteq \langle M_2, \nu \rangle$ iff $M_1 \subseteq M_2$.

Let us now proceed in extending the semantics structure when updates to the ASP theory are allowed through the $\mathtt{assert}$ and $\mathtt{retract}$ interface constraints. We will focus on a top-down operational semantics.

Definition 6 (Update). *Given a program $P = \langle Pr, As \rangle$ and an interface constraints p, we define the* update *of P w.r.t. p (i.e., $\mathcal{U}(P, p)$) as follows:*

$$\mathcal{U}(P, p) = \begin{cases} \langle Pr, As \cup \{r\} \rangle & \text{if } p = \mathtt{assert}(r) \\ \langle Pr, As \setminus \{r\} \rangle & \text{if } p = \mathtt{retract}(r) \end{cases}$$

Let R be a *computation rule* [10]—i.e., a function $R : \mathcal{B}^* \to \mathcal{B}$ which is used to select a subgoal; in particular we will denote with R_{Prolog} the computation rule that selects always the leftmost subgoal.

Definition 7 (State). *A state is a tuple $\langle G, \sigma, \tau, As \rangle$ where*

- $G \in \mathcal{B}^*$ *is called the* goal list
- σ *is a substitution (i.e., a function from $\mathcal{V}$ to $\mathcal{H}$)*
- τ *is a function $\tau : \mathcal{H}_P \to 2^{\mathcal{B}_A}$ called* model retrieval function.
- As *is an ASP-program.*

Given a program $P = \langle Pr, As \rangle$, the initial state *is the tuple $\langle G_0, \epsilon, \tau_0, As \rangle$, where G_0 is the initial goal, ϵ is the empty substitution (i.e., the function such that for all $X \in \mathcal{V}.\epsilon(X) = X$), and τ_0 is the function that is undefined for every input.*

The notion of entailment is defined through a transition relation between states.

Definition 8 (Derivation Step). *Let $\langle G, \sigma, \tau, As \rangle$ be a state. The relation*
$$\langle G, \sigma, \tau, As \rangle \vdash_R \langle G', \sigma', \tau', As' \rangle$$
holds if:

- $R(G) = A$
- *if A is a P-atom, then there exist a rule $H :- \bar{B} \in Pr$, such that $\theta = mgu(A, H)$, $\sigma' = \sigma \circ \theta$, $\tau = \tau'$, $As = As'$, and $G' = ([A/\bar{B}]G)\theta$.*
- *if A is an ASP-literal, then there exists a ground substitution θ for A such that $\forall S \in \mathcal{M}(As).S \models A\theta$, $G' = (G \setminus \{A\})\theta$, $\sigma' = \sigma \circ \theta$, $\tau' = \tau$, $As' = As$.*

- *if A is of the form $t : H$, then there exists a grounding substitution θ for $t :$ H such that $\tau(t\theta)$ is defined, $\tau(t\theta) \in \mathcal{M}(As)$, $\tau(t\theta) \models H\theta$, $G' = (G \setminus \{A\})\theta$, $\sigma' = \sigma \circ \theta$, $\tau = \tau'$, $As = As'$.*
- *if A is of the form* models(t)*, then there exists a grounding substitution θ for t such that $\tau(t\theta)$ is defined, $\tau(t\theta) \in \mathcal{M}(As)$, $G' = (G \setminus \{A\})\theta$, $\sigma' = \sigma \circ \theta$, $\tau' = \tau$, and $As' = As$.*
- *if A is of the form* assert(r)*, then $G' = G \setminus \{A\}$, $\sigma' = \sigma$, $As' = As \cup \{r\}$, K is a set of terms from $\mathcal{H}_P$ (model names) such that*
  - *$|K| = |\mathcal{M}(As')|$*
  - *for each $t \in K$ we have that $\tau(t)$ is undefined*
  - *$s_1, \ldots, s_r$ is an enumeration of K*
  - *$S_1, \ldots, S_r$ is an enumeration of $\mathcal{M}(As)$*
  - *$\tau' = \tau \circ \{s_1 \mapsto S_1, \ldots, s_r \mapsto S_r\}$*
- *if A is of the form* retract(r)*, θ is a grounding substitution such that $r\theta \in As$, then $G' = (G \setminus \{A\})\theta$, $\sigma' = \sigma \circ \theta$, $As' = As \setminus \{r\theta\}$, K is a set of terms from $\mathcal{H}_P$ (model names) such that*
  - *$|K| = |\mathcal{M}(As')|$*
  - *for each $t \in K$ we have that $\tau(t)$ is undefined*
  - *$s_1, \ldots, s_r$ is an enumeration of K*
  - *$S_1, \ldots, S_r$ is an enumeration of $\mathcal{M}(As)$*
  - *$\tau' = \tau \circ \{s_1 \mapsto S_1, \ldots, s_r \mapsto S_r\}$*

Definition 9 (Entailment). *Given a program $P = \langle Pr, As \rangle$ and a goal G, we say that $P \models G\sigma$ iff $\langle G, \epsilon, \tau_0, As \rangle \vdash_R^* \langle \emptyset, \sigma, \tau, As' \rangle$.*

3   The ASP – PROLOG System

The ASP – PROLOG system has been developed as an extension of the CIAO Prolog system [6]. The choice of CIAO was fairly natural, being a flexible Prolog system, with a rich set of features aimed at facilitating the extension of the language (e.g., module system and object oriented capabilities). The handling of the ASP modules is left to the *Smodels* system [13].

3.1   Concrete Syntax

The abstract syntax presented in the previous section has been refined in the ASP – PROLOG system to better match the characteristics of Prolog. Each ASP – PROLOG program is composed of a collection of *modules*. We recognize two types of modules: *Prolog* modules—which contain standard CIAO Prolog code—and *ASP* modules—each contains an ASP program. We will use an ASP program—called plan.pl—that solves planning problems in the block world domain, as a running example to illustrate the most important syntactically features of our system. For our purpose, it is enough to know that plan.pl consists of rules specifying the initial configuration (left side of Fig 1), the goal configuration (right side of Fig 1), and the effects of the actions (e.g., *move(a, b)* will make a on b if nothing is on top of b, a) in this domain. The program has an input parameter called *steps* that determines the (maximal) length of the plan. A call to this program looks like

```
lparse -c steps=5 plan.pl | smodels 0
```

which will return all stable models of `plan.pl`, each corresponds to a plan of length 5. We will now detail the syntax of ASP – PROLOG.

Fig. 1. A planning problem in the block world domain with 5 blocks a, b, c, d, and e.

Module Interface. Prolog modules are required to declare their intention to access any ASP modules; this is accomplished through the declarations

$$:- \textbf{use\_asp}(module\_name, file\_name)$$
$$:- \textbf{use\_asp}(module\_name, file\_name, parameters)$$

where the *module_name* is the name used to address the ASP module, *file_name* is the file containing the ASP code, and *parameters* is a list of parameters with their values, to be passed from the Prolog module to the ASP module.

Example 1. A CIAO module might refer to the ASP module `plan` as follows:

```
:- module(program1, [blocks_solve/0]).
:- use_asp(plan, 'plan.lp', [(steps, 0)]).
```

The first line defines the CIAO module named `blocks_solve`. The second line declares that `blocks_solve` will access the ASP module `plan` with parameter *steps* whose value is initiated with 0.

Interface Constraints. We have provided a number of predicates that allow Prolog modules to query and manage ASP modules:

- `model/2`: in ASP – PROLOG models of an ASP module can be retrieved using indices; the `model` predicate relates an index number to the term representing the corresponding model. The `model` predicate has to be qualified with the ASP module on which it is meant to be applied. E.g., the goal

```
plan:model(1, Q)
```

will allow a Prolog module to access the first model of the module `plan.pl`. More precisely, variable Q will be instantiated with the first model of plan.pl. The goal will fail if the program plan.pl does not have a stable model.[2]

- total_stable_model/1: the predicate is satisfied if the argument is the number of models of the ASP module. For example,

plan:total_stable_model(X), X>0

will succeed if plan.pl has at least one stable model and fails otherwise.

- assert/1 and retract/1: the argument of these predicates is a list of ASP rules. The effect of assert is to add all the rules in the list to the ASP module, while retract will remove the rules from the ASP module. For example, if we are interested only in plans that do not move block a on the table during their execution, we can add a ASP-constraint that prevents the occurrence of the action $move(a, table)$. From a Prolog module, we can issue

assert(plan:[(:-move(a, table, T), time(T))])

which will add the constraint ":-move(a, table, T), time(T)." to plan.pl.

- assert_nb/1 and retract_nb/1: the ASP – PROLOG system provides also an alternative version of the assert and retract predicates. The main difference is that the modifications derived from assert and retract, as illustrated in the semantics description in Section 2, will be undone during backtracking, while the modifications to an ASP module performed using assert_nb and retract_nb will remain unaffected by backtracking.

- change_parm/1: most ASP inference engines allow the user to specify (typically as command-line arguments) various parameters that affect the ASP computation (e.g., initial value for constants); the predicate change_parm allows the user to read and modify the value of such parameters dynamically. The following Prolog fragment allows us to change the *steps* parameter of plan.pl:

```
blocks_solve :- plan:total_stable_models(X), X>0,
                chk_condition(1, X, Q), print_solution(Q, 0).
blocks_solve :- plan:change_parm([(steps,V)]), V1 is V+1,
                plan:change_parm([(steps,V1)]), blocks_solve.
```

Here, the predicate chk_condition will check whether a plan satisfies certain condition or not (see below) and print_solution will print the solution to the screen. The first call to change_parm will instantiate V to the current value of steps, while the second will modify the value of the constant.

- compute/2: this predicate has been introduced to specifically match another control feature provided by *Smodels*—it allows the presence of a compute statement, used to establish bounds on the number of models and to specify elements that have to be present in all the models. The compute predicate allows the Prolog module to dynamically affect these properties. For example, if we want to limit the maximum number of models to 3 in the ASP module plan, then we can issue the goal plan : compute(3,_).

---

[2] model is a simplified version of models/1 described earlier.

- `clause/2`: this predicate is used to allow a Prolog module to access the rules of an ASP module—in the same spirit as the `clause` predicate is employed in Prolog to access the Prolog rules present in the program. The two arguments represent respectively the head and the body of the rule.

Example 2. Let us assume that the ASP module `plan` contains the following rules defining the predicate `p`:

$$p(a) :- q(a), r(a). \qquad p(b) :- r(b).$$

Then the Prolog goal `plan:clause(p(X), Y)` has two solutions:

$$\{X \mapsto a, Y \mapsto (q(a), r(a))\} \qquad \{X \mapsto b, Y \mapsto r(b)\}$$

Observe that, due to the fact that the syntax of *Smodels* is not ISO-compliant, certain *Smodels* constructs (e.g., cardinality and weight constraints) have a slightly different syntactic representation when used within Prolog modules. For example, if an ASP module (e.g., module plan) contains the rule
$$p :- 1\{r, s, t\}2.$$
then the execution of the goal `plan:clause(p,X)` will produce the substitution $\{X \mapsto' \{\}'(1, (r, s, t), 2)\}$.

ASP Constraints. The syntax used to express ASP constraints is the same one described in the abstract syntax. E.g., if we would like to find plans that do not move block a to the *table* (represented by the atom $move(a, table, t)$ where t is some number between 0 and *steps*), we can use the following rules:

```
chk_condition(Y, _, Q) :- plan:model(Y, Q), chk_cond(Q), !.
chk_condition(Y, X, Q) :- Y=<X, Y1 is Y+1, chk_condition(Y1, X, Q).
chk_cond(Q) :- Q: move(a, table, _), !, fail.
chk_cond(_).
```

The next group of rules extract a plan from a stable model and display it on the screen:

```
print_solution(Q, T) :- Q:move(_, _, T), !, print_sol(Q, T),
                        T1 is T+1, print_solution(Q, T1).
print_solution(_, _).
print_sol(Q, T) :- Q:move(X, Y, T), display('move '), display(X),
                   display(' on '), display(Y), display(' at time '),
                   display(T), nl, fail.
print_sol(_, _).
```

3.2 System Implementation

The overall structure of the implementation is depicted in Figure 2. The system is composed of two parts, a *preprocessor* and the actual CIAO Prolog system.

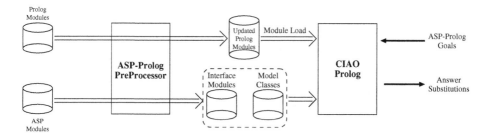

Fig. 2. Overall Structure of ASP − PROLOG Implementation

Preprocessing. The input to the preprocessor is composed of *(i)* the main Prolog module (Pr); *(ii)* a collection of CIAO Prolog modules $(m_1, m_2, \ldots, m_n)$; *(iii)* a collection of ASP modules $(e_1, e_2, \ldots, e_m)$. The output of the preprocessor is: a modified version of the main Prolog module (NP), a modified version of the other Prolog modules $(nm_1, nm_2, \ldots, nm_n)$, and for each ASP module e_i the preprocessor creates a CIAO module (im_i) and a class definition (c_i).[3]

The transformation of the Prolog modules consists of a simple rewriting process, used to adapt the syntax of the interface constraints and make it compatible with CIAO Prolog's syntax. For example, the rules passed as arguments to `assert` and `retracts` have to be quoted to allow the peculiarities of ASP syntax (e.g., the use of braces for choice rules) to be accepted.

The transformation of each ASP module leads to the creation of two entities that will be employed during the actual program execution: an *interface module* and a *model class*. These are described in the following subsections.

The preprocessor will also automatically invoke the CIAO Prolog toplevel and load all the appropriate modules for execution. The interaction with the user is the same as that of the standard CIAO Prolog toplevel.

Interface Modules. The preprocessor generates one interface module for each ASP module present in the original input program. The interface module is implemented as a standard CIAO Prolog module and it provides the client Prolog modules with the predicates used to access and manage the ASP module. The interface module is created for each ASP module by instantiating a generic module skeleton to the content of the specific ASP module considered.

The overall structure of the interface module is illustrated in Figure 3. The module has an export list which includes all the predicates used to manipulate ASP modules (e.g., `assert`, `retract`, `model`) as well as all the predicates that are defined within the ASP module.[4] The typical module declaration generated for an interface module will look like:

---

[3] CIAO provides the ability to define classes and create class instances [15].

[4] Due to a limitation in the current implementation of CIAO's module system, we cannot dynamically add new predicates to an existing ASP module—as CIAO does not support, yet, dynamic redefinition of a module.

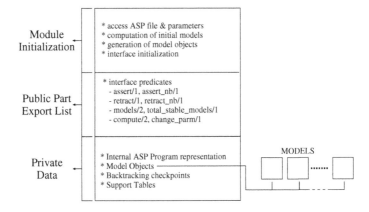

Fig. 3. Structure of the Interface Module

```
:— module('t23.xxx', [ assert/1, retract/1,
                       assert_nb/1, retract_nb/1,
                       model/2, change_parm/1, compute/2,
                       total_stable_model/1,
                       p/0, q/0, r/0 ]).
```

The definition of the various exported predicates (except for the predicates defined in the ASP module) is derived by instantiating a generic definition of each predicate. Each module has an initialization part, which is in charge of setting up the internal data structures (e.g., the internal representation of the ASP module, tables to store parameters and stable models), and invoke the answer set solvers for the first time on the ASP module—in the current prototype we are using *Smodels* as answer set solver. The result of the computation of the models will be encoded as a collection of *Model Objects* (see the description of the Model Classes in the next subsection). The module will maintain a number of internal data structures, including a representation of the ASP code, a representation of the parameters to be used for the computation of the stable models (e.g., values of constants), a list containing the objects representing the models of the ASP module, a counter of the number of stable models currently present, etc.

Model Classes. The preprocessor generates a CIAO class definition for each ASP module. The objects obtained from the instantiation of such class will be used to represent the individual models of the ASP module. Prolog modules can obtain reference to these objects (e.g., using the **model** predicate supplied by the interface module) and use them to directly query the content of one model. The definition of the class is obtained through a straightforward parsing of the ASP module, to collect the names of the predicates defined in it; the class will provide a public method for each of the predicates present in the ASP module. In addition, the class defines also a public method **add/1** which is employed by the interface module to initialize the content of the model.

Each model is stored in one instance of the class; the actual atoms representing the model are stored internally in the objects as facts of the form $s(\langle \texttt{fact} \rangle)$.

For instance, if we have a simple ASP module containing the rules:

$$p :- q. \qquad q :- r. \qquad r.$$

then the preprocessor will generate a class definition of the type:

```
:- class(t23_class).
:- dynamic s/1.        %% used to store the facts of the model
%% export declarations for the ASP predicates
:- export(p/0).
:- export(q/0).
:- export(r/0).
%% utility method for building the model
:- export(add/1).
%% definition of the methods
p :- s(p).
q :- s(q).
r :- s(r).
%% add a new element to the model
add(X) :- assertz_fact(s(X)).
```

3.3 Implementation Details

Interface Predicates: The various interface predicates are implemented in CIAO Prolog in a fairly straightforward way. Some general observations:

- The implementation of **assert** proceeds by adding the new rules to the module and recomputing the models; the structure of the main clause implementing it is

```
assert(L) :- assert1(L),
         module_concat('t23.xxx', assert2(L), M), und(M).
assert2(L) :- \+ empty_list(L), retract_nbf(L).
```

The **module_concat** and **und** are internal predicates of CIAO Prolog that allows us to specify what action to take upon backtracking through the clause; in this case, **assert2** will be called upon backtracking, which will undo the modifications and restore the previous set of models. **assert_nb** will avoid the final step—since changes will not be undone during backtracking.

- The implementation of **retract** follows a similar structure; rules are removed (if they are present) from the module and the models are recomputed accordingly. The modifications are cached to ensure undoing upon backtracking. The main clauses implementing it are:

```
retract(L) :- \+ empty_list(L), !, retract1(L),
         store_list_rr(L1),
         module_concat('t23.xxx', retract2(L1), M), und(M).
retract2(L) :- \+ empty_list(L), assert_nb(L).
```

The **retract1** performs the modification of the module and the recomputation of the models; **store_list_rr** places the modifications in the trail structure; the final declarations in the `retract` rule indicate what predicate should be call upon backtracking—`retract2`. As we can see, `retract2` simply restores the rules that have been previously removed (using `assert_nb`), and restores the original set of models.

- the same structure can be found in the implementation of `compute`; if called with arguments unbound, then the predicate will access the current `compute` configuration (i.e., it will indicate how many models have been requested and whether there is a core of literals that have to be true in every model); if called with bound arguments, having a value different then the current `compute` configuration, then the models will be recomputed with the new configuration. As for `assert` and `retract`, the `compute` will set up a hook to allow for undoing effect of the changes during backtracking.

Internal Data Structures: A number of tables are maintained by each interface module to support the execution of ASP modules. Some of the relevant internal structures include:

- *fn:* used to maintain a (Prolog-based) representation of the rules composing the ASP module;
- *uf:* a temporary table aimed at supporting the process of rules unification during execution of `assert` and `retract`;
- *stable_ref:* a table (implemented as Prolog facts) that maintain references to the current models of the ASP module (as pairs *model number/object reference* that maps name of models to objects representing the models);
- *retract_rule:* a trail structure that caches the modifications performed by `assert` and `retract`; this is required to allow undoing of the chances;
- *prm:* a table (encoded as Prolog facts) that stores the parameters to be used during the computation of the models of the ASP module.

4   Examples

Let us continue with the example of the planning problem. The planner is aimed at computing the movements of blocks from initial state to a goal state. We have three blocks `a`, `b` and `c`. Initially, block `a` is on block `b`, block `b` is on the table and block `c` is on the table. The goal state is: block `b` is on `c`, block `c` is on `a` and finally block `a` is on the table. The objective is to determine what block moves (represented by facts of the type `move(source,destination,time)`) are required to achieve the goal state—assuming that we can move only one block at a time, and we can move only blocks that are not covered by other blocks. The Prolog module allows the user to

- use the Prolog program to explore the space of possible plans—e.g., if we do not want to accept plans that move block `a` to block `b`, then we can add the goal

    ```
    setof(T, (plan:model(Y,Q),Q:move(a,b,T)), [] )
    ```

which will determine a model (if any) that does not contain any fact of the form move(a,b,T).

- we can perform selection of models according to some quantitative criteria. For example, if we assume that each moveop action has a *cost*—i.e., the facts generated during planning have the form

$$move(source, destination, time, cost)$$

then we can select the plan with the lowest cost by writing

```
    ...
    setof([X,Y], plan:model(X,Y), List),   %% collect all models
    find_smallest_plan(List,P,Cost).
find_smallest_plan([[Index,Model]], Model, Cost) :-
    findall(C, Model:move(_,_,_,C), Costs),
    sum_list(Costs,Cost).
find_smallest_plan([ [Index,Model] | Rest], MinModel, MinCost) :-
    find_smallest_plan(Rest,M1,C1),
    findall(C,Model:move(_,_,_,C),Costs),
    sum_list(Costs, Cost),
    ( Cost < C1 -> MinModel = Model, MinCost=Cost;
                   MinModel = M1, MinCost=C1 ).
```

5   Conclusion and Future Work

In this paper we presented ASP – PROLOG, a system which provides a tight and semantically well-founded integration between Prolog (in the form of CIAO Prolog) and answer set programming (in the form of *Smodels*). The system allows to create programs which are composed of Prolog modules and ASP modules. ASP modules contain either complete or fragments of ASP programs, expressed using the *lparse* input language [18]. Prolog modules are capable of accessing ASP modules, to read and/or modify their content—through the traditional Prolog assert and retract predicates. Prolog modules are also capable of accessing the stable models of each ASP module, and use them during the execution—e.g., to solve goal against them. At the syntax level, ASP – PROLOG guarantees the same style of programming and syntax as traditional Prolog programming, integrating ASP modules and stable models as first-class citizens of the languages. ASP – PROLOG allows to extend the expressive power of ASP, allowing to write Prolog programs that can dynamically modify ASP modules, reason about stable model, and promotes incremental and 'what-if' approaches to the construction of ASP programs.

The prototype implementation of ASP – PROLOG, built using CIAO Prolog and *Smodels*, is available at www.cs.nmsu.edu/~okhatib/asp_prolog.html. We will continue the development of ASP – PROLOG by:

- using ASP – PROLOG in the development of various ASP applications where an interactive environment is more appropriate; and
- investigating the possibility of a reverse communication process, where the ASP modules are capable of proactively requesting information from the

Prolog modules—an investigation in this direction is in progress to allow ASP modules to make use of CLP capabilities [16].

Acknowledgments. This work is partially supported by NSF grants CCR9875279, CCR9900320, CDA9729848, EIA0130887, EIA9810732, and HRD9906130.

References

1. The DLV Wrapper Project. `160.97.47.246:8080/wrapper`, 2003.
2. L. Castro, T. Swift, and D.S. Warren. *XASP: Answer Set Programming with XSB and Smodels.* SUNY Stony Brook, 2002. `xsb.sourceforge.net/packages/xasp.pdf`.
3. T. Eiter, N. Leone, C. Mateis, G. Pfeifer, and F. Scarcello. The KR System `dlv`: Progress Report, Comparisons, and Benchmarks. In *KR-98*, pages 406–417, 1998.
4. M. Gelfond and V. Lifschitz. The Stable Model Semantics for Logic Programs. In *ICLPS-88*, pages 1070–1080. MIT Press, 1988.
5. K. Heljanko and I. Niemela. Answer Set Programming and Bounded Model Checking. In *TPLP*, 3(4):519–550, 2003.
6. M. Hermenegildo, F. Bueno, D. Cabeza, M. Carro, M.J. García de la Banda, P. López-García, and G. Puebla. The CIAO Multi-Dialect Compiler and System: An Experimentation Workbench for Future (C)LP Systems. In *Parallelism and Implementation of Logic and Constraint Logic Programming*, pages 65–85. Nova Science, Commack, NY, USA, April 1999.
7. Y. Lierler and M. Maratea. Cmodels-2: SAT-based Answer Set Solver Enhanced to Non-tight Programs. In *LPNMR'04*, pages 346–350, 2004.
8. V. Lifschitz. Action Languages, Answer Sets, and Planning. In *The Logic Programming Paradigm*. Springer Verlag, 1999.
9. F. Lin and Y. Zhao. ASSAT: Computing Answer Sets of A Logic Program By SAT Solvers. In *AAAI*, pages 112–117, 2002.
10. J.W. Lloyd. *Foundations of Logic Programming.* Springer-Verlag, Heidelberg, 1987.
11. V.W. Marek and M. Truszczyński. Stable Models and an Alternative Logic Programming Paradigm. In K.R. Apt, V.W. Marek, M. Truszcziński, and D. S. Warren, editors, *The Logic Programming Paradigm*. Springer Verlag, 1999.
12. I. Niemela. Logic Programs with Stable Model Semantics as a Constraint Programming Paradigm. *Annals of Mathematics and AI*, 25(3/4):241–273, 1999.
13. I. Niemela and P. Simons. Smodels - An Implementation of the Stable Model and Well-Founded Semantics for Normal LP. In *LPNMR-97*, pages 421–430, 1997.
14. M. Nogueira, M. Balduccini, M. Gelfond, R. Watson, and M. Barry. An A-Prolog Descision Support System for the Space Shuttle. In *PADL-01*, pages 169–183, 2001.
15. M. Pineda and F. Bueno. The O'Ciao Approach to Object Oriented Logic Programming. In *Colloquium on Implementation of Constraint Logic Programming Systems*, 2002.
16. T.C. Son and E. Pontelli. Planning with preferences using logic programming. In *LPNMR'04*, pages 247–260, 2004.
17. T. Syrjänen. Lparse User's Manual. `http://www.tcs.hut.fi/Software/smodels/`.
18. T. Syrjänen. Implementation of Local Grounding for Logic Programs with Stable Model Semantics. Technical Report B-18, Helsinki University of Technology, 1998.

Simplifying Dynamic Programming via Tabling*

Hai-Feng Guo[1] and Gopal Gupta[2]

[1] Department of Computer Science
University of Nebraska at Omaha, Omaha, NE 68182-0500, USA
haifengguo@mail.unomaha.edu
[2] Department of Computer Science
University of Texas at Dallas, Richardson, TX 75083-0688 USA
gupta@utdallas.edu

Abstract. In the dynamic programming paradigm the value of an optimal solution is recursively defined in terms of optimal solutions to subproblems. Such dynamic programming definitions can be very tricky and error-prone to specify. This paper presents a novel, elegant method based on tabled logic programming that simplifies the specification of such dynamic programming solutions. Our method introduces a new mode declaration for tabled predicates. The arguments of each tabled predicate are divided into indexed and non-indexed ones so that tabled predicates can be regarded as functions: indexed arguments represent input values and non-indexed arguments represent output values. The non-indexed arguments in a tabled predicate can be further declared to be *aggregate*, e.g., the minimum, so that while generating answers, the global *table* will dynamically maintain the smallest value for that argument. This mode declaration scheme, coupled with recursion, provides a considerably easy-to-use method for dynamic programming: there is no need to define the value of an optimal solution recursively, instead, defining a general solution suffices. The optimal value as well as its corresponding concrete solution can be derived implicitly and automatically using tabled logic programming systems. Experimental results are shown to indicate that the mode declaration improves both time and space performances in solving dynamic programming problems on tabled LP systems. Additionally, our mode declaration scheme provides an alternative implementation vehicle for preference logic programming.

1 Introduction

Tabled logic programming (TLP) systems [15,17,7,11] have been put to many innovative uses, such as model checking [10] and non-monotonic reasoning [14], due to their highly declarative nature and efficiency. A tabled logic programming system can be thought of as an engine for efficiently computing fixed points, which is critical for many practical applications. A TLP system is essential for extending traditional LP system (e.g., Prolog) with tabled resolutions. The main advantages of tabled resolution are that a TLP system terminates more often

---

* This research is supported by NSF Nebraska EPSCoR grant.

B. Jayaraman (Ed.): PADL 2004, LNCS 3057, pp. 163–177, 2004.
© Springer-Verlag Berlin Heidelberg 2004

by computing fixed points, avoids redundant computation by memoing the computed answers, and keeps the declarative and procedural semantics consistent for pure logic programs.

The main idea of tabled resolution is never to compute the same call twice. Answers to certain calls are recorded in a global *memo table* (heretofore referred to as a *table*), so that whenever the same call is encountered later, the tabled answers are retrieved and used instead of being recomputed. This avoidance of recomputation not only gains better efficiency, more importantly, it also gets rid of many infinite loops, which often occur due to static computation strategies (e.g., SLD resolution [8]) adopted in traditional logic programming systems.

Dynamic programming algorithms are particularly appropriate for implementation with tabled logic programming [16]. Dynamic programming is typically used for solving optimization problems. It is a general recursive strategy in which optimal solution to a problem is defined in terms of optimal solutions to its subproblems. Dynamic programming, thus, recursively reduces the solution to a problem to repetitively solving its subproblems. Therefore, for computational efficiency it is essential that a given subproblem is solved only once instead of multiple times. From this standpoint, tabled logic programming *dynamically* incorporates the dynamic programming strategy [16] in the logic programming paradigm. TLP systems provide implicit tabulation scheme for dynamic programming, ensuring that subproblems are evaluated only once.

In spite of the assistance of tabled resolution, solving practical problems with dynamic programming is still not a trivial task. The main step in the dynamic programming paradigm is to define the value of an optimal solution recursively in terms of the optimal solutions to subproblems. This definition could be very tricky and error-prone. As the most widely used TLP system, XSB provides table aggregate predicates [15,14], such as bagMin/2 and bagMax/2, to find the minimal or maximal value from tabled answers respectively. Those predicates are helpful in finding the optimal solutions, and therefore in implementing dynamic programming algorithms. However, users still have to define optimal solutions explicitly, that is, specify how the optimal value of a problem is recursively defined in terms of the optimal values of its subproblems. Furthermore, the aggregate predicates require the TLP system to collect all possible values, whether optimal or non-optimal, into the memo table, which could dramatically increase the table space needed.

Another important issue in dynamic programming is that once the optimal value is found for a problem, the concrete solution leading to that optimal value needs to be constructed. This requires that each computed value be associated with some evidence (or explanation [13]) for solution construction. In the tabled logic programming formulation, an extra argument is added to the tabled predicates in which a representation of the explanation is conveniently built. Unfortunately, to put explanation as an extra tabled predicate argument results in recording of the explanation as part of the answers to tabled calls. This can dramatically increase the size of the global table space because there can be many explanations for a single answer in the original program. Similar issues are raised in [16] on generating parse-trees: determining whether there is a parse-tree can be done in time cubic on the length of the string (worst case) whereas the number of parse trees may be exponential. Therefore, from a complexity standpoint, use of TLP for dynamic programming has certain negative aspects.

This paper presents a novel declarative method based on the tabled logic programming paradigm for simplifying dynamic programming solutions to problems. The method introduces a new mode declaration for tabled predicates. The mode declaration classifies arguments of a tabled predicate as indexed or non-indexed. Each non-indexed argument can be thought of as a function value uniquely determined by indexed arguments. The tabled logic programming system is optimized to perform variant checking based only on the indexed arguments. This new declaration for tabled predicates and modified procedure for variant checking makes it easier to collect a single associated explanation for a tabled answer, e.g., a concrete solution for an optimal value in the dynamic programming paradigm, even though, in principle, multiple explanations may exist for the same tabled answer. The collected explanation can be shown very concisely without involving any self-dependency among tabled subgoals.

The mode declaration can further extend one of the non-indexed arguments to be an aggregated value, e.g., the minimum function, so that the global *table* will record answers with the value of that argument appropriately aggregated. Thus, in the case of the minimum function, a tabled answer can be dynamically replaced by a new one with a smaller value during the computation. This mode declaration is essential for obtaining the optimal solution from a general specification of the dynamic programming solution.

Our mode declaration scheme can be further extended to provide an elegant and easy way of specifying and executing preference logic programs [6]. Preference logic programs selectively choose the "best" solutions based on preferences.

The rest of the paper is organized as follows: Section 2 introduces tabled logic programming (TLP), followed by the typical TLP-based approach for dynamic programming in subsection 2.1. Section 3 presents our new annotation for declaring tabled goals, followed by a detailed demonstration of how dynamic programming can benefit from this new scheme. Section 4 addresses the implementation issues of the mode declaration scheme and Section 5 presents the running performance on some dynamic programming benchmarks. Section 6 discusses the potential extension to preference logic programming. Finally, section 7 gives our conclusions.

2   Tabled Logic Programming (TLP)

Traditional logic programming systems (e.g., Prolog) use SLD resolution [8] with the following *computation strategy*: subgoals of a resolvent are solved from left to right and clauses that match a subgoal are applied in the textual order they appear in the program. It is well known that SLD resolution may lead to non-termination for certain programs, even though an answer may exist via the declarative semantics. That is, given any static computation strategy, one can always produce a program in which no answers can be found due to non-termination even though some answers may logically follow from the program. In case of Prolog, programs containing certain types of left-recursive clauses are examples of such programs.

Tabled logic programming eliminates such infinite loops by extending logic programming with tabled resolution. The main idea is to memorize the answers to some calls and use the memorized answers to resolve subsequent variant calls. Tabled resolution adopts a dynamic computation strategy while resolving subgoals in the current resolvent against matched program clauses or tabled answers. It keeps track of the nature and type of the subgoals; if the subgoal in the current resolvent is a variant of a former tabled call, tabled answers are used to resolve the subgoal; otherwise, program clauses are used following SLD resolution.

In a tabled logic programming system, only tabled predicates are resolved using tabled resolution. Tabled predicates are explicitly declared as

:- table p/n.

where p is a predicate name and n is its arity. A global data structure *table* is introduced to memorize the answers of any subgoals to tabled predicates, and to avoid any recomputation.

2.1   Dynamic Programming with TLP

We use the *matrix-chain multiplication* problem [4] as an example to illustrate how tabled logic programming can be adopted for solving dynamic programming problems. A product of matrices is *fully parenthesized* if it is either a single matrix or the product of two fully parenthesized matrix products, surrounded by parentheses. Thus, the matrix-chain multiplication problem can be stated as follows (detailed description of this problem can be found in any major algorithm textbook covering dynamic programming):

Problem 1 *Given a chain* $\langle A_1, A_2, ..., A_n \rangle$ *of* n *matrices, where for* $i = 1, 2, ..., n$, *matrix* A_i *has dimension* $p_{i-1} \times p_i$, *fully parenthesize the product* $A_1 A_2 ... A_n$ *in a way that minimizes the number of scalar multiplications.*

To solve this problem by dynamic programming, we need to define the cost of an optimal solution recursively in terms of the optimal solutions to subproblems. Let $m[i, j]$ be the minimum number of scalar multiplications needed to compute the matrix $A_{i..j}$, which denotes a sub-chain of matrices $A_i A_{i+1} ... A_j$ for $1 \leq i \leq j \leq n$. Thus, our recursive definition for the minimum cost of parenthesizing the product $A_{i..j}$ becomes

$$m[i, j] = \begin{cases} 0 & \text{if } i = j, \\ \min_{i \leq k < j} \{m[i, k] + m[k + 1, j] + p_{i-1} p_k p_j\} & \text{if } i < j. \end{cases}$$

A tabled Prolog coding is given in Program 1 to solve the matrix-chain multiplication problem. The predicate scalar_cost(PL, V, P0, Pn) is tabled, where PL, P0 and Pn are given by the user to represent the dimension sequence $[p_0, p_1, ..., p_n]$, the first dimension p_0 and the last dimension p_n, respectively, and V is the minimum cost of scalar multiplications to multiply $A_{1..n}$; the built-in predicate findall(X,G,L) is used to find all the instances of X as a list L such that each instance satisfies the goal G; the predicate break(PL, PL1, PL2, Pk) is used to split the dimension sequence at the point of Pk into two parts to simulate the parenthesization; and the predicate list_min(L, V) finds a minimum number V from a given list L.

Program 1 *A tabled logic program for matrix-chain multiplication problems:*

```
:- table scalar_cost/4.
scalar_cost([P1, P2], 0, P1, P2).
scalar_cost([P1, P2, P3 | Pr], V, P1, Pn) :-
    findall(V, ( break([P1, P2, P3 | Pr], PL1, PL2, Pk),
                 scalar_cost(PL1, V1, P1, Pk),
                 scalar_cost(PL2, V2, Pk, Pn),
                 V is V1 + V2 + P1 * Pk * Pn ), VL),
    list_min(VL, V).
break([P1, P2, P3], [P1, P2], [P2, P3], P2).
break([P1, P2, P3, P4 | Pr], [P1, P2], [P2, P3, P4 | Pr], P2).
break([P1, P2, P3, P4 | Pr], [P1 | L1], L2, Pk) :-
    break([P2, P3, P4 | Pr], L1, L2, Pk).
```

Consider the problem for a chain $\langle A_1, A_2, A_3 \rangle$ of three matrices. Suppose that the dimensions of the matrices are 10×100, 100×5, and 5×50, respectively. We can give a query :- scalar_cost([10, 100, 5, 50], V, 10, 50) to find the minimum value of its scalar multiplications. As a result, V is instantiated to 7500, corresponding to the optimal parenthesization $((A_1A_2)A_3)$.

Program 1 shows that the programmer has to find the optimal value by comparing all possible multiplication costs explicitly. In fact, for a general optimization problem, the definition of an optimal solution could be quite complicated due to heterogeneous solution construction. Then, comparing all possible solutions explicitly to find the optimal one can be tricky and error-prone. In this paper we present a simple method to separate the task of finding the optimal solution from the task of specifying the general dynamic programming formulation. Using our method, the programmer is only required to define *what* a general solution is, while searching for the optimal solution is left to the TLP system.

The next issue we are interested in is finding the actual parenthesization (explanation) that leads to the optimal answer. Of course, the above program is of no help, since it only finds the optimal value for the number of scalar multiplications. A standard method [13] to construct explanation in logic programming is to add an extra argument to tabled predicates for the explanation. However, this extra argument results in recording explanation as part of the answers to tabled calls, which can dramatically increase the size of global table space. Consider a program for computing reachability, we can introduce a tabled predicate reach/3 as shown in Program 2, where the third argument E is used to generate the path from X to Y, and app/3 is a standard predicate to append a list to another. Obviously, there are infinite number of paths from a to any node due to the cycle between **a** and **b**, thus making the fixed point infinite. Therefore, from this standpoint of computational complexity, tabling predicates has certain drawbacks. In this paper we show how this drawback can be removed.

Program 2 *A tabled logic program defining a reachability relation predicate with path information as an extra argument:*

```
:- table reach/3.
reach(X, Y, E) :- reach(X, Z, E1), arc(Z, Y, E2), app(E1, E2, E).
reach(X, Y, E) :- arc(X, Y, E).
arc(a, b, [(a,b)]).    arc(a, c, [(a,c)]).    arc(b, a, [(b,a)]).
:- reach(a, Y, E).
```

Similar problems have been studied on justification in [12,9]. One reasonable solution is presented in [9] by asserting the first evidence into a dynamic database for each tabled answer. However, the evidence has to be organized as segments indexed by each tabled answer. That is, an extra procedure is required to construct the full evidence.

3   A Declarative Method

In this section, we present a new method that considerably simplifies the development of dynamic programming applications. Our method introduces a special mode declaration for tabled predicates. The mode declaration is used to classify arguments as indexed or non-indexed for each tabled predicate. *Only indexed arguments in a tabled predicate are used for variant checking.*

Variant checking is a crucial operation for tabled resolution as it leads to avoidance of non-termination. It is used to differentiate both tabled goals and their answers. While computing the answers to a tabled goal p with tabled resolution, if another tabled subgoal q is encountered, the decision regarding whether to consume tabled answers or to try program clauses depends on the result of variant checking. If q is a variant of p, the variant subgoal q will be resolved by unifying it with tabled answers, otherwise, traditional Prolog resolution is adopted for q. Additionally, when an answer to a tabled goal is generated, variant checking is used to check whether the generated answer is variant of an answer that is already recorded in the table. If so, the table is not changed; this step is crucial in ensuring that a fixed point is reached.

We use *dynamic reordering of alternatives* (DRA) resolution [7] in the rest of the paper as an example of tabled resolution. However, the new mode declaration method can also be applied to other tabled resolutions, such as SLG [3] and SLDT [17], since essentially only the variant checking operation is modified.

3.1   Mode Declaration for Evidence Construction

The new mode declaration for tabled predicates can be described in the form of
$$:-\ \texttt{table\_mode}\ p(a_1, ..., a_n).$$
where p is a tabled predicate name, $n \geq 0$, and each a_i has one of the following forms:

+ denotes that this is an indexed argument;
− denotes that this is a non-indexed argument.

Only indexed arguments are used for variant checking; for each tabled call, any answer generated later for the same value of the indexed arguments is discarded because it is a variant (w.r.t. the indexed arguments) of a previously tabled answer.

Consider the reachability example again. Suppose we declare the mode as ":- table_mode $reach(+, +, -)$"; this means that the first two arguments of the predicate reach/3 are used for variant checking. The new computation of the query reach(a,Y,E) is shown in Figure 1. Since only the first two arguments of reach/3 are used for variant checking, the last two answers "Y=b, E=[(a,b),(b,a),(a,b)]" and "Y=c, E=[(a,b),(b,a),(a,c)]", shown on the rightmost two sub-branches, are variant answers to "Y=b, E=[(a,b)]" and "Y=c, E=[(a,c)]" respectively. Therefore, no new answers are added into the table at those points. The computation is then terminated properly with three answers. As a result, each reachable node from a has a simple path.

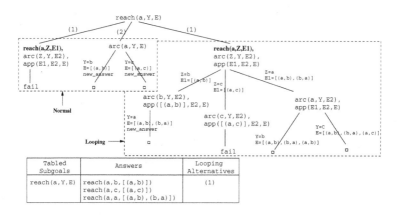

Fig. 1. DRA Resolution with Mode Declaration

The mode directive table_mode makes it very easy and efficient to extract explanation for tabled predicates. In fact, our strategy of ignoring the explanation argument during variant checking results in only the first explanation for each tabled answer being recorded. Subsequent explanations are filtered by our modified variant checking scheme. This feature ensures that those generated explanations are concise and that cyclic explanations are guaranteed to be absent. For the reachability instance shown in Figure 1, each returned path is simple such that all arcs are distinct.

Essentially, if we regard a tabled predicate as a function, then all the non-indexed arguments are uniquely defined by the instances of indexed arguments. For the previous example, the third argument of reach/3 returns a single path depending on the first two arguments. Therefore, variant checking should be done w.r.t. only indexed arguments during tabled resolution. From this viewpoint, the mode declaration makes tabled resolution more efficient and flexible.

3.2   Declaration of Aggregates

The mode directive `table_mode` can be further extended to associate a non-indexed argument of a tabled predicate with some optimum constraint. Currently, a non-indexed argument for each tabled answer only records the very first instance. This "very first" property can actually be generalized to any optimum, e.g., the minimum value, in which case the global table will record answers with the value of that argument as small as possible. That is, a tabled answer can be dynamically replaced by a new one with a smaller value during the computation. In general, given a tabled call $p(I_1, I_2, \ldots, I_n, NI)$ where the I_i for $1 \leq i \leq n$ are indexed arguments and NI is a single non-indexed argument, let $p(i_1, i_2, \ldots, i_n, u)$ be the entry for predicate p (with arity $n+1$) in the table. Suppose, a new solution is found during tabled execution represented by $p(i_1, i_2, \ldots, i_n, v)$, then, in general, the user can define an aggregation predicate f such that the new value of the non-indexed argument is updated to w such that $f(u,v,w)$ holds. By default, f is defined as $f(X,\_,X)$ (the value of the non-indexed argument is set to the first one found). For dynamic programming applications, f can be set to the `min` predicate as follows:

$$f(X,Y,Z) \;:\!\!-\; min(X,Y,Z).$$

This can easily be generalized to the case where multiple non-indexed arguments are present.

Currently, we allow `min`, `max` and `last` as the only aggregation predicates. These are specified via special mode declarations.

min denotes that this argument is a minimum;
max denotes that this argument is a maximum;
last denotes that this argument records the last answer.

These three new modes are included in the directive `table_mode` to declare the aggregation operation for tabled predicates; all modes also imply that the arguments are non-indexed. The mode `last` is useful for preference logic programming, which will be discussed in Section 6. In absence of any aggregation directive, only the first solution is maintained for each set of distinct input values.

The aggregation declaration can be used to make control of execution implicit during dynamic programming, making the specification of dynamic programming problems more declarative and elegant. For the matrix-chain multiplication, instead of defining the cost of an optimal solution, we only need to specify what the cost for a general solution is. Let $m[i,j]$ be the number of scalar multiplications needed to compute the matrix $A_{i..j}$ for $1 \leq i \leq j \leq n$, where n is the total number of matrices. The recursive definition for the cost of parenthesizing $A_{i..j}$ becomes

$$m[i,j] = \begin{cases} 0 & \text{if } i = j, \\ m[i,k] + m[k+1,j] + p_{i-1}p_kp_j & \text{where } i \leq k < j, \text{ if } i < j. \end{cases}$$

Program 3 *A tabled logic program with optimum mode declaration for matrix-chain multiplication problems:*

```
:- table scalar_cost/4.
:- table_mode scalar_cost(+, min, -, -).
scalar_cost([P1, P2], 0, P1, P2).
scalar_cost([P1, P2, P3 | Pr], V, P1, Pn) :-
    break([P1, P2, P3 | Pr], PL1, PL2, Pk),
    scalar_cost(PL1, V1, P1, Pk),
    scalar_cost(PL2, V2, Pk, Pn),
    V is V1 + V2 + P1 * Pk * Pn.
```

The mode declaration `scalar_cost(+,min,-,-)` means that only the first argument (the list of matrix dimensions) is used for variant checking when an answer is generated, and a minimum value is expected for the second argument (the cost of scalar multiplication). Arguments with different modes are tested in the following order during variant checking of a recently generated answer: (1) the indexed argument with '+' mode has the highest priority to be checked to identify whether it is a new answer. If that is the case, a new tabled entry is required to record the answer; otherwise a tabled answer with the same indexed argument is found. (2) This tabled answer is then compared with the recently generated one w.r.t the argument with the optimum mode 'min'; if the new answer has a smaller value on the optimum argument, then a replacement of the tabled answer is required such that the tabled answer keeps the minimum value as expected for this argument.

Figure 2 shows the recursion tree produced by the query
`:- scalar_cost([10,100,5,50],V,10,50).`
Consider the tabled call `scalar_cost([10,100,5,50],V,10,50)`. Its first tabled answer has V=75000. However, when the second answer V=7500 is computed, it will automatically replace the previous answer following the declared optimum mode. Thus, there is at most one instance of `scalar_cost([10,100,5,50],V,10,50)` that exists in the table at any point in time, and it represents the optimal value computed up to that point.

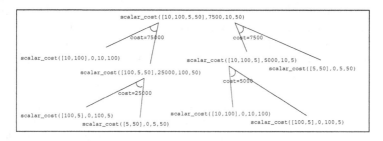

Fig. 2. Recursion tree for computing `scalar_cost([10,100,5,50],V,10,50)`

As long as the tabled Prolog engine is set to compute the fixed point semantics for logic programs with bounded term depth, the optimal value for the dynamic programming problem under consideration will always be found. Intuitively, given a tabled call C, the DRA resolution first finds all the answers for C using clauses not containing variant calls. Once this set of answers is computed and tabled, it is treated as a set of facts, and used for computing rest of the answers from the clauses leading to variant calls (looping alternatives). Whenever an answer to C is generated, it will be selectively added to the table either as a new entry or as a replacement based on the defined mode of the corresponding predicate. The process stops when no new answers can be computed via the looping alternatives, i.e., a fixed point is reached. In this regard, with the assistance of mode declaration and tabled resolution, the computation of program clauses only defining general solutions will still produce the optimal solution.

3.3   Dynamic Programming with Evidence Construction

To make the matrix-chain multiplication problem complete, we need to construct an optimal parenthesization solution corresponding to the minimal cost of scalar multiplication. This construction can be achieved with the strategy described in Section 3.1, by introducing an extra non-indexed argument whose instantiation becomes the solution. The complete tabled logic program is shown below:

Program 4 *A tabled logic program for the complete matrix-chain multiplication problem:*

```
:- table scalar_cost_evid/5.
:- table_mode scalar_cost_evid(+, min, -, -, -).
scalar_cost_evid([P1, P2], 0, P1, P2, (P1,P2)).
scalar_cost_evid([P1, P2, P3 | Pr], V, P1, Pn, (E1*E2)) :-
    break([P1, P2, P3 | Pr], PL1, PL2, Pk),
    scalar_cost_evid(PL1, V1, P1, Pk, E1),
    scalar_cost_evid(PL2, V2, Pk, Pn, E2),
    V is V1 + V2 + P1 * Pk * Pn.
```

4   Implementation

The mode declaration scheme has been implemented in the authors' TALS [7] system, a tabled Prolog system implemented on the top of the WAM engine of the commercial ALS Prolog engine [1]. No change is required to the DRA resolution mechanism; therefore, the same idea can also be applied to other tabled Prolog systems.

Two major changes to the global data structure *table* are needed to support mode declarations. First, each table predicate is associated with a new item *mode*, which is represented as a bit string. The default mode for each argument in a table predicate is '-'. Second, the answers to a tabled call are selectively recorded depending on its mode declaration. The declared modes essentially specify the user preferences or selection constraints among the answers. When a new answer to a tabled goal is generated, variant checking on indexed arguments is invoked to determine whether the answer is variant to a previously tabled one. If that is the case, declared modes on non-indexed arguments are used to select a better answer to table; otherwise, a new table entry is added to record the answer. In fact, if an indexed argument is instantiated in advance before a tabled goal is called, variant checking on this indexed argument can be avoided since its value is same for all the answers; furthermore, it is not necessary to record the pre-instantiated value with each tabled answer because the same value has already been stored in the tabled call entry. This optimization leads to improvements on both time and space system performance.

Another important implementation issue is the replacement of tabled answers. In the current TALS system, if the tabled subgoal only involves numerals as arguments, then the tabled answer will be completely replaced if necessary. If the arguments involve structures, however, then the answer will be updated by a link to the new answer. Space taken up by the old answer has to be recovered by garbage collection (the ALS Prolog's garbage collector has not yet been extended by us to include table space garbage recovery). As a result, if arguments of tabled predicates are bound to structures, more table space is used up.

5   Experimental Results

Our experimental benchmarks include five typical dynamic programming examples. matrix is the matrix-chain multiplication problem; lcs is longest common subsequence problem; obst finds an optimal binary search tree; apsp finds the shortest paths for all pairs of nodes; and knap is the knapsack problem. All tests were performed on an Intel Pentium 4 Mobile CPU 1.8GHz machine with 512M RAM running RedHat Linux 9.0.

Table 1. Running time performance comparison: Seconds/(Ratio)

Benchmark	without evidence construction					with evidence construction				
	matrix	lcs	obst	apsp	knap	matrix	lcs	obst	apsp	knap
without mode	2.18	0.94	0.90	4.17	54.59	3.09	5.93	11.69	6.70	140.46
	(1.0)	(1.0)	(1.0)	(1.0)	(1.0)	(1.0)	(1.0)	(1.0)	(1.0)	(1.0)
with mode	1.14	0.43	0.32	2.90	40.64	2.27	0.67	0.73	3.10	41.77
	(0.52)	(0.46)	(0.36)	(0.70)	(0.74)	(0.73)	(0.11)	(0.06)	(0.46)	(0.30)

Table 1 compares the running time performance between the programs with and without mode declaration. The first group of benchmarks are programs only seeking the optimal values without evidence construction, while the second group are programs for the same dynamic programming problems with evidence construction. The experimental data indicates, based on the ratios in Table 1, that the programs with mode declaration consume only 11% to 74% time that the corresponding programs without mode declaration do.

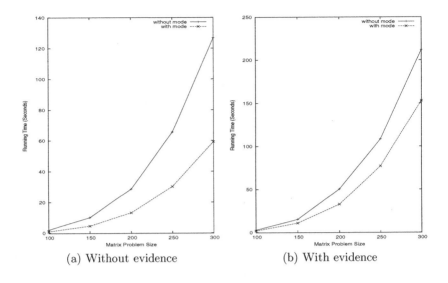

(a) Without evidence   (b) With evidence

Fig. 3. Time Performance of Matrix-chain Multiplication

Figure 3 shows the timing information against different input sizes for matrix-chain multiplication problems. Notice that the numbers on the X-axis represent the total number of matrices to be multiplied, and the numbers on the Y-axis represent the running time in seconds. Whether without evidence construction (Figure 3(a)) or with evidence construction (Figure 3(b)), the graphs indicate that the running timings of the programs with mode declaration are consistently better than those without mode declaration.

Additionally, we compare the running space performance between the programs with and without mode declaration in Table 2. For benchmarks without evidence construction, our experiments indicate that with mode declaration, programs consume only 7% to 72% space compared to those without mode declaration. With evidence construction included, space performance can either be better or worse depending on the problem. For the `matrix` and `obst` problems that try to find the optimal binary tree structure, the programs without mode declaration generate all possible answers and then only table the optimal one, while the programs with mode declaration and implicit aggregation generate all possible answers and selectively table the better answers until the optimal one is found. In the latter case, some non-optimal answers may be replaced in the table during the computation, however, the space taken by those old answers, including tree structures, cannot be recovered immediately; if the optimal answer happens to be the first tabled answer, then no other un-optimal answers will be recorded. This is the reason why the benchmarks `matrix` and `obst` (with evidence construction) with mode declaration take more space than those without mode, as shown in Table 2.

Table 2. Running space comparison: Megabytes/(Ratio)

Benchmark	without evidence construction					with evidence construction				
	matrix	lcs	obst	apsp	knap	matrix	lcs	obst	apsp	knap
without mode	4.98	78.75	2.65	20.17	222.65	9.22	92.99	4.44	29.90	399.95
	(1.0)	(1.0)	(1.0)	(1.0)	(1.0)	(1.0)	(1.0)	(1.0)	(1.0)	(1.0)
with mode	0.57	23.44	0.25	14.60	14.86	11.64	44.24	17.46	21.39	305.19
	(0.11)	(0.30)	(0.09)	(0.72)	(0.07)	(1.26)	(0.48)	(3.93)	(0.72)	(0.76)

6   Preference Declaration with Modes

Preference logic programming (PLP) [6] is an extension of constraint logic programming for declaratively specifying problems requiring optimization or comparison and selection among alternative solutions to a query. PLP essentially separates the definition of a problem itself from the criteria specification of its solution selection or optimization; PLP has been shown useful by practical applications such as in artificial intelligence [2] and data mining [5].

The mode declaration scheme is essential for associating arguments in tabled predicates with some optimum or selection constraints, which are solved implicitly during tabled resolution. Tabling systems can selectively choose "better" answers for a given tabled predicate call guided by the declared mode. This is indeed the intent of PLP. For the optimization instance, in the program solving matrix-chain multiplication problems (see Program 3), the table mode `scalar_cost(+,min,_,_)` implies the following preference:

scalar_cost(M,C1,A,B) $\preceq$ scalar_cost(M,C2,A,B) $\leftarrow$ C2 < C1.

where the symbol $\preceq$ and $\leftarrow$ are to be read as "is less preferred than" and "if", respectively.

Program 5 *Consider the following logic program solving "dangling else" ambiguity in parsing if-then-else constructs:*

```
:- table ifstmt/3.
:- table_mode ifstmt(+,+,last).
ifstmt(L1,L2,false).                                        (1)
ifstmt(L1,L2,New) :- ifstmt1(New,L1,L2),ifstmt(L1,L2,Old),
                     prefer(ifstmt,New,Old).                (2)
ifstmt1(if(C,T)) --> [if], cond(C), [then], stmtseq(T).     (3)
ifstmt1(if(C,T,E)) --> [if], cond(C), [then], stmtseq(T),
                       [else], stmtseq(E).                  (4)
prefer(ifstmt, _, false).                                   (5)
prefer(ifstmt, if(C,if(C1,T,E)), if(C,if(C1,T),E)).         (6)
```

The predicate `ifstmt1/3` uses two DCG rules to define the ambiguous grammar for `if-then-else` constructs; the predicate `ifstmt(L1,L2,T)` returns a preferred parse tree T given a list difference between L1 and L2, where the preferences are defined by the predicate `prefer/3`. Clause (6) implies the following unconditional preference rule:

```
ifstmt(L1,L2,if(C,if(C1,T),E)) ⪯ ifstmt(L1,L2,if(C,if(C1,T,E)));
```
a dummy preference rule is defined by clause (5) to indicate that
$$\texttt{ifstmt(L1,L2,false)} \preceq \texttt{ifstmt(L1,L2,\_)}.$$
Clause (1) is a dummy clause to put an initial answer `false` into the table for any call to `ifstmt`; clause (2) performs as follows: whenever the first subgoal `ifstmt1(New,L1,L2)` generates a new answer, `ifstmt(L1,L2,Old)` retrieves the last answer from the global `table` (note that this subgoal always succeeds due to the dummy answer `false`); the parse tree `New` will be tabled only if it is preferred over the `Old` answer. Therefore, the declared mode `ifstmt(+,+,last)` is used to catch the *last* parse tree, which is actually the best one based on preferences.

Program 5 shows how to use the mode declaration scheme to solve selection or optimization problems with general preference rules. It is worthy to mention that program 5 can be automatically transformed once the problem is specified (such as the DCG rules) and the preference rules are given (such as clause (6)). Other parts of the program can be generated based on the declared modes.

7   Conclusion

A new mode declaration for tabled predicates is introduced in TLP systems to aggregate information dynamically recorded in the table. The mode declaration classifies arguments of tabled predicates as either indexed or non-indexed. As a result, (i) a tabled predicate can be regarded as a function in which non-indexed arguments (outputs) are uniquely defined by the indexed arguments (inputs); (ii) concise explanation for tabled answers can be easily constructed in non-indexed (output) arguments; (iii) the efficiency of tabled resolution may be improved since only indexed arguments are involved in variant checking; and (iv) the non-indexed arguments of a tabled predicate can be further qualified with an aggregate mode such that an optimal value can be sought without explicit coding of the comparison.

This new mode declaration scheme, coupled with recursion, provides an elegant method for specifying dynamic programming problems: there is no need to define the value of an optimal solution recursively, instead, defining the value of a general solution is enough. The optimal value, as well as its associated solution, is obtained automatically by the TLP systems. Additionally, the mode declaration scheme provides an elegant way for specifying and implementing preference logic programming. This new scheme has been implemented in the authors' TALS system with very encouraging results.

Acknowledgments. We are grateful to David S. Warren, C. R. Ramakrishnan, Bart Demoen and Kostis Sagonas for general discussions about tabled logic programming and to Peter Stuckey for discussion on work presented in this paper.

References

1. Applied Logic Systems, Inc. http://www.als.com
2. A. Brown, S. Mantha, and T. Wakayama: Preference Logics: Towards a Unified Approach to Non-Monotonicity in Deductive Reasoning. *Annals of Mathematics and Artificial Intelligence*, 10:233–280, 1994.
3. Weidong Chen and David S. Warren: Query Evaluation under the Well Founded Semantics. *ACM Symposium on Principles of Database Systems*, pp. 168–179, 1993.
4. T.H. Cormen, C.E. Leiserson, and R.L. Rivest: Introduction to Algorithms. The MIT Press, 2001.
5. Baoqiu Cui, Terrance Swift: Preference Logic Grammars: Fixed Point Semantics and Application to Data Standardization. *Artificial Intelligence*, 138(1-2): 117–147, 2002.
6. K. Govindarajan, B. Jayaraman, and S. Mantha: Preference Logic Programming. In Proceedings of *International Conference on Logic Programming (ICLP)*, pages 731–745, 1995.
7. Hai-Feng Guo and Gopal Gupta: A Simple Scheme for Implementing Tabled Logic Programming Systems Based on Dynamic Reordering of Alternatives. In Proceedings of *International Conference on Logic Programming (ICLP)*, pages 181–196, 2001.
8. J.W. Lloyd. Foundations of Logic Programming. Springer-Verlag, 1987.
9. G. Pemmasani, H-F. Guo, Y. Dong, C.R. Ramakrishnan, and I.V. Ramakrishnan: Online Justification for Tabled Logic Programs. To appear in Proceedings of *International Symposium of Functional and Logic Programming*, Apr. 2004.
10. Y.S. Ramakrishnan, C.R. Ramakrishnan, I.V. Ramakrishnan, S.A. Smolka, T. Swift, D.S. Warren: Efficient Model Checking using Tabled Resolution. In Proceedings of *Computer Aided Verification (CAV'97)*, pages 143–154 1997.
11. R. Rocha, F. Silva, and V. S. Costa: On a Tabling Engine That Can Exploit Or-Parallelism. In *ICLP* Proceedings, pages 43–58, 2001.
12. A. Roychoudhury, C.R. Ramakrishnan, and I.V. Ramakrishnan: Justifying proofs using memo tables. *Second International ACM SIGPLAN conference on Principles and Practice of Declarative Programming (PPDP)*, pp. 178–189, 2000.
13. Günther Specht: Generating Explanation Trees even for Negations in Deductive Database Systems. Proc. of *the 5th Workshop of Logic Programming Environments*, 1992.
14. Terrance Swift: Tabling for Non-Monotonic Programming. *Annals of Mathematics and Artificial Intelligence*, 25(3-4): 201-240, 1999.
15. XSB system. http://xsb.sourceforge.net
16. David S. Warren: Programming in Tabled Prolog (Draft Book). www.cs.sunysb.edu/~warren.
17. Neng-Fa Zhou, Y. Shen, L. Yuan, and J. You: Implementation of a Linear Tabling Mechanism. In Proceedings of *Practical Aspects of Declarative Languages (PADL)*, 2000.

Symbolic Execution of Behavioral Requirements

Tao Wang, Abhik Roychoudhury, Roland H.C. Yap, and S.C. Choudhary

School of Computing, National University of Singapore, Singapore 117543.
{wangtao,abhik,ryap,shishirc}@comp.nus.edu.sg

Abstract. Message Sequence Charts (MSC) have traditionally been used as a weak form of behavioral requirements in software design; they denote scenarios which may happen. Live Sequence Charts (LSC) extend Message Sequence Charts by also allowing the designer to specify scenarios which must happen. Live Sequence Chart specifications are executable; their simulation allows the designer to play out potentially aberrant scenarios prior to software construction. In this paper, we propose the use of Constraint Logic Programming (CLP) for symbolic execution of requirements described as Live Sequence Charts. The utility of CLP stems from its ability to execute in the presence of uninstantiated variables. This allows us to simulate multiple scenarios at one go. For example, several scenarios which only differ from each other in the value of a variable may be executed as a single scenario where the variable is left uninstantiated. Similarly, we can simulate scenarios with an unbounded number of processes. We use the power of CLP to also simulate charts with non-trivial timing constraints. Current works on MSC/LSCs use data/control variables mainly for ease of specification; they are instantiated to concrete values during simulation. Thus, our work advances the state-of-the-art in simulation and checking of MSC based software requirements.

1 Introduction

Message Sequence Charts (MSCs) [16] have traditionally played an important role in software development. MSCs describe scenarios of system behaviors. These scenarios are constructed prior to the development of the system, as part of the requirements specification phase. MSCs can be used to depict the interaction between different components (objects) of a system, as well as the interaction of the system to the external environment (if the system is reactive). Syntactically, a MSC consists of a set of vertical lines, each vertical line denoting a process (or a system component). Computations within a process are shown via internal events, while any communication between processes is denoted by a uni-directional arrow (typically labeled by a message name). Figure 1(a) shows a simple MSC with two processes; $m1$ and $m2$ are messages sent from p to q and a is an internal action.

The main limitation of MSCs is that they only denote a scenario which *may* occur. In other words, an MSC only captures an existential requirement: some execution trace (behavior) of the system contains a linearization of the events in

B. Jayaraman (Ed.): PADL 2004, LNCS 3057, pp. 178–192, 2004.

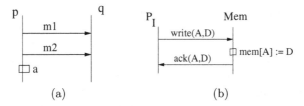

Fig. 1. (a) A simple MSC, and (b) MSC with variables

the MSC. They do not capture universal requirements, that is, temporal properties which *must* hold in all behaviors of the system. To fill this gap, Damm and Harel recently proposed an important extension of MSCs called Live Sequence Charts (LSCs) [5]. In the LSC formalism, a chart may be marked as existential or universal. Each chart consists of a pre-chart and a body chart. An existential chart is similar to a conventional MSC. It denotes the property: the pre-chart followed by the body chart may execute in some run of the system. A universal chart denotes the following property: *if the pre-chart is satisfied in any execution trace of the system, then the body chart must be executed.*

The LSC formalism serves as an important extension of MSCs; it allows us to describe the set of all allowed behaviors of a reactive system. A collection of universal charts can serve as a complete behavioral specification: any trace (over a pre-defined alphabet) which does not violate any of the universal charts is an allowed behavior. Furthermore, LSC based behavioral specifications are *executable*. The advantage of simulating LSC specifications via a play engine is obvious: it allows the user to visualize/navigate/detect *unintended behaviors which were mistakenly allowed in the requirements*. These unintended behaviors are called " violations" since they denote an inconsistency in the overall requirements specification (*i.e.* one requirement "violates" another). A full description of the LSC language and the accompanying execution engine (called the play engine) appears in the recent book [10].

Executing behavioral requirements prior to system development however needs to consider the fact that the requirements are often at a higher level than the implementation. Concretely, this may boil down to the behavioral requirements not specifying: (a) data values exchanged between objects, or (b) the number of objects of a process class. Figure 1(b) shows a chart with variables. In this chart, processor I requests main memory to write value D in address A. The main memory performs this task and sends an acknowledgment. This chart uses two kinds of variables: A and D are variables appearing in events; I is a variable representing a process instance (the instance of the processor in question). In fact, if we want the requirements to contain the values of these variables, this leads to an arbitrarily large (potentially unbounded) number of scenarios. Furthermore, these scenarios are structurally "similar" and can be specified together. To avoid this problem, the authors of the LSC formalism extend the LSC specification language [13]. Each vertical line in a chart now denotes a group of objects rather than a concrete object. Furthermore, data exchanged between objects can be depicted by variables (rather than concrete values), thereby enabling value-passing. This allows us to specify several similar scenarios using a single chart, as shown in [13]. However, [13] uses the formal variables mostly for concise specification; they are instantiated to concrete values during simulation. This does *not* allow symbolic execution, that is, executing several similar scenarios together.

In this paper, we propose the use of Constraint Logic Programming (CLP) for symbolic simulation of LSC based behavioral requirements. We leverage on the constraint processing capabilities of a CLP engine in several ways. Unification in the CLP engine captures value passing, and is used as a solver for equality constraints. More general constraints (such as inequalities are used to symbolically represent values of data variables, groups of objects, and timing. Also note that the search strategy of LSC simulation involves resolving non-determinism, since several events may be enabled at a given point during simulation. Thus, a LSC simulator may have to make "choices" among enabled events. These choices need to be *searched* to detect "violations" (*i.e.* inconsistencies) in the specification. A logic programming engine provides natural support for such search via backtracking (this is not fully supported in the existing LSC play engine [8]).

We note that CLP has been shown to be useful for symbolic representation of sets of system states [6]. Use of CLP for symbolic simulation of event based systems has been investigated in [14]. There have also been recent uses of CLP for animation/simulation of formal specifications (*e.g.* [4]).

Contributions. We now summarize the main contributions of the paper.

- We develop a methodology and toolkit for symbolic execution of Live Sequence Charts, a visual language for describing behavioral requirements. We exploit three different features of LSCs for symbolic execution. First, data variables (such as D in Figure 1(b)) can remain partially instantiated. Secondly, control variables (such as the instance I in Figure 1(b)) can also remain partially instantiated during simulation. This allows us to directly simulate a process with unboundedly many instances. Thirdly, time is maintained as a collection of constraints instead of a fixed value (for the simulation of charts with timing constraints). By keeping the variables symbolic, we achieve the simulation of many different concrete runs in a single run.
- We do not realize concrete objects which are behaviorally indistinguishable. This approach contrasts with the work of [13] which blows up a class of objects in the specification to finitely many concrete objects during execution.
- The search strategy of our tool is derived from a logic programming based search engine; hence it can naturally backtrack over choices. This allows us to search for violations (*i.e.* inconsistencies) in behavioral requirements. Since requirements are specified at a high-level, they are likely to have non-determinism even if the implementation is deterministic.

Our simulation engine for LSCs is implemented on top of the ECL^iPS^e constraint logic programming system [7].

Section Organization. The rest of the paper is organized as follows. Section 2 provides an overview of LSCs. Section 3 describes how a CLP engine is suitable for executing LSCs with data variables (of potentially unbounded domain). Section 4 describes the use of our engine for simulating LSCs with unbounded number of process instances. Section 5 explains the simulation of charts involving timing constraints. Section 6 describes the implementation of our engine and experimental results. Finally, section 7 concludes the paper with discussion and future work.

2   Live Sequence Charts

Live Sequence Charts (LSCs) [5] is a powerful visual formalism which serves as an enriched requirements specification language. Descriptions in the LSC language are executable, and the execution engine which supports it is called the *Play Engine* [10]. In this section we summarize the existing work on LSCs. We start with MSCs, show how they are extended to LSCs, and then briefly describe existing work on play engine.

2.1   Message Sequence Charts

Message Sequence Charts (MSCs) [1,16] are written in a visual notation as shown in Figure 1(a). Each vertical line denotes a process which executes events. Semantically, a MSC denotes a set of events (message send, message receive and internal events corresponding to computation) and prescribes a partial order over these events. This partial order is the transitive closure of (a) the total order of the events in each process (time flows from top to bottom in each process) and (b) the ordering imposed by the send-receive of each message (the send event of a message must happen before its receive event). The events are described using the following notation. A send of message M from process P to process Q is denoted as $\langle P!Q, M \rangle$. A receive event by process Q to a message M sent by process P is denoted as $\langle Q?P, M \rangle$. An internal event A executed by process P is denoted as $\langle P, A \rangle$. As mentioned earlier, the message M as well as the processes P, Q can contain variables. Variables transmitted via messages can appear in internal events as well.

Consider the chart in Figure 1(a). Using the above notation, the total order for process p is $\langle p!q, m1 \rangle \leq \langle p!q, m2 \rangle \leq \langle p, a \rangle$ where $e1 \leq e2$ denotes that event $e1$ "happens-before" event $e2$. Similarly for process q we have $\langle q?p, m1 \rangle \leq \langle q?p, m2 \rangle$ For the messages we have $\langle p!q, m1 \rangle \leq \langle q?p, m1 \rangle$ and $\langle p!q, m2 \rangle \leq \langle q?p, m2 \rangle$. The transitive closure of these four ordering relations defines the partial order of the chart. Note that it is *not* a total order since from the transitive closure we cannot infer that $\langle p!q, m2 \rangle \leq \langle q?p, m1 \rangle$ or $\langle q?p, m1 \rangle \leq \langle p!q, m2 \rangle$.

2.2   Universal and Existential Charts

In the Live Sequence Chart (LSC) terminology, each chart is a concatenation of a pre-chart followed by a body chart. The notion of concatenation requires some explanation. Consider a chart $Pre \circ Body$ where $\circ$ denotes concatenation. This means that all processes first execute the chart Pre and then they execute the chart $Body$; no event of chart $Body$ takes place before any event of chart Pre. In the terminology of Message Sequence Charts, a LSC is a *synchronous* concatenation of its pre-chart and body-chart [2]. Following the notational convention of LSCs, we always show the pre-chart inside a *dashed hexagon*. The body chart of a universal chart is shown inside a rectangular box. *All examples shown in this paper are universal charts.* Now let us consider the chart in Figure 3. The process r cannot send the message $m1(X)$ before the pre-chart is finished. Note that this is required even though r does not take part in the pre-chart. This restriction is imposed so that the body chart is executed only when the pre-chart is successfully completed.

In the LSC language, charts are classified as existential or universal. A system model M satisfies an existential chart $Pre \circ Body$ if there exists a reachable state of M from which an outgoing trace executes (a linearization of) Pre followed by (a linearization of) $Body$. On the other hand, a system model M satisfies a universal chart $Pre \circ Body$ if : from every reachable state of M if a (linearization of) the pre-chart Pre is executed, then it must be followed by (a linearization of) the body chart $Body$. Thus, for any execution trace of M, whenever Pre is executed, $Body$ *must* be executed.

Along with universal/existential charts, LSCs also allow locations or events in a chart to be universal or existential in a similar fashion. Indeed our CLP based simulation engine works for the whole LSC language with existential/universal charts as well as existential/universal chart elements (such as location, condition etc). For details on syntax of the LSC visual language, the reader is referred to [5]. Automata based semantics of the language appear in [12].

2.3   The Play Engine

A LSC based system description can serve as a behavioral requirements specification. It specifies the desired inter-object relationships in a reactive system before the system (or even an abstract model of it) is actually constructed. It is beneficial to simulate the LSC based behavioral requirements since it detects inconsistencies and under-specification. LSC based descriptions of reactive systems can be executed by providing an event performed by the user. The LSC simulation engine then computes a "maximal response" to this user-provided event, which is a maximal sequence of events performed by different components of the reactive system (as a result of the user-provided event). This maximal response to the user-provided event is called a ***super-step*** (see [10], Chapter 5). Simulation then continues with the user providing another event. In the course of simulation, pre-charts of given universal charts are monitored. If the pre-chart of a universal chart is successfully completed, then we generate a "live copy" – a copy of the body chart. During simulation, there may be several live copies of the same chart active at the same time. Such copies may be "violated" during simulation; this happens when the partial order of the events appearing in the body chart is violated, or any condition which must be satisfied is evaluated to be false.

To see how this happens, consider the example in Figure 2 consisting of two universal charts. When the user turns on the host, a live copy of both the charts are created. Subsequently the temporal order of events in one of these copies is bound to be violated during simulation. In other words, simulation detects an inconsistency in the temporal properties denoted by the two universal charts of Figure 2. This is called a **violation** in the LSC literature [10]. In the rest of the paper, we discuss how to support symbolic execution of LSCs with variables and/or constraints for the purposes of simulation (finding one violation-free behavior).

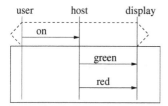 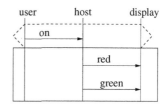

Fig. 2. A LSC specification with "violations"

3   Data Variables

In this section, we describe how the symbolic execution engine of a Constraint Logic Programming (CLP) system (such as ECL^iPS^e [7]) can be used to execute Live Sequence Charts. We start with the handling of data variables (*i.e.* variables appearing in chart events). When dealing with such variables, a distinction needs to be made between the LSC specification and the execution of LSC specifications. Even though variables can appear in the LSC specification, it is possible to develop an execution mechanism which avoids all variables. This can be achieved by requiring all variables to be bound during execution. Thus, the variables are used for ease of specification. On the other hand, if we use a CLP engine as the LSC execution engine this can lead to a symbolic execution mechanism for LSCs. We have pursued this avenue.

Data variables correspond to variables appearing in (and transmitted via) messages. Typically, a data variable appearing in a chart will appear at least twice ; this allows for propagation of data values. For example, in Figure 1(b) the data variables A and D appear multiple times. If the underlying engine of these chart specifications cannot execute with uninstantiated variables, then the first occurrence of each variable needs to be distinguished. This is the occurrence which binds the variable to a value. This can be problematic since no unique "first occurrence" of a variable may exist in a chart (the events of a chart are only guaranteed to satisfy a partial order). For example, consider the chart in Figure 3 with three processes p, q and r. The two send events $\langle p!q, m(X)\rangle$ and $\langle r!q, m1(X)\rangle$ are incomparable according to the partial order of the chart. If we chose one of them to be the first occurrence then the execution engine can demand that this first occurrence binds X; other occurrences of X simply propagate this binding. To solve this problem, [13] suggests fixing one of the events as the first based on the geometry of the chart.

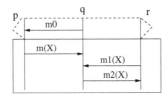

Fig. 3. Non-unique first occurrence of a data variable

For any data variable, fixing any particular occurrence as the first occurrence constrains the partial order of the chart. In other words, it lets the simulation engine play out only certain behaviors allowed by the chart. A CLP based execution engine will naturally avoid this problem. In our engine, value passing between variables is supported by CLP's unification. Given a LSC specification, its simulation involves identifying enabled events, executing them and checking for violations of chart specifications. In Figure 3, both $\langle p!q, m(X)\rangle$ and $\langle r!q, m1(X)\rangle$ are initially enabled and our simulation engine can choose to execute either of them. More importantly, if it chooses to execute $\langle p!q, m(X)\rangle$, it does not require X to be bound at all. This constitutes a truly symbolic simulation, where many charts (which only differ in the value of variable X) are simulated together.

4   Control Variables

LSCs have been extended to use symbolic process instances [13]. A symbolic process in a chart represents a parameterized process class which at run-time produces several instances or objects. In other words, these classes always produce finitely many instances at run-time; but there is no a-priori bound on the number of instances. The identification number (or the parameter) of the instances is a control variable. As per the LSC language, we allow such control variables (denoting the instance number) to be existential or universal. Existentially quantified control variables are handled like data variables; they may be bound to a particular instance via execution. Universally quantified control variables however represent many possible process instances, and need to be handled differently.

Consider a process $p(X)$ where the instance number X is universally quantified. Since $p(X)$ in general represents unboundedly many instances, we need to disambiguate messages to and from $p(X)$. We use constraints on X for this purpose. Consider a message from process $p(X)$ to process $q(Y)$ where both X and Y are universally quantified. We require such messages to be of the form $c(X), M, c'(Y)$ where M is the message content and c, c' are constraints on X, Y respectively. The domain of the constraints c and c' depends on the type of X and Y. The variables representing instance numbers are integers, and we will consider only unary inequality and equality constraints (*i.e.,* interval constraints).[1]

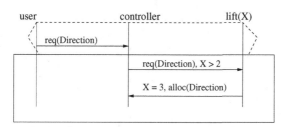

Fig. 4. A chart with universally quantified control variable (X in this case)

An Example. We consider the universal chart shown in Figure 4. In this chart, $lift(X)$ represents a class of instances with X being a universally quantified control variable. The pre-chart consists of the *user* process requesting movement in a specific direction (up or down). This is captured by the variable *Direction*. During execution, the user will give a concrete request, say $req(up)$. Hence *Direction* will be unified to *up*. Now, the user's request is conveyed to the *controller* process which forwards this request to only some of the lifts. In this chart, it forwards the request to all lifts whose instance number is greater than 2. One of these lifts responds to the controller; which lift responds is captured by the constraint $X = 3$. In Figure 5, we illustrate a symbolic simulation strategy applicable to parameterized process classes by simulating the example of Figure 4. To notationally distinguish the progress in simulation from the specification of a body chart, we use bold boxes in Figure 5. Initially there is only one copy of the lift process denoted as $lift(X)$; this represents *all* lifts. Since the pre-chart does not involve the $lift$ process, there is only one copy of the chart after the execution of the pre-chart. Now, when the controller forwards the message $req(Direction)$ it forwards it to only lifts with instance number greater than 2. Thus, the existing live copy is destroyed and two separate copies are created: one with $lift(X)$ s.t. $X \leq 2$, and the other with $lift(X)$ s.t. $X > 2$. In other words, the two separate copies of *lift(X)* are created in a demand-driven fashion, based on the chart execution. Finally, when the message *alloc(Direction)* is sent, the live copy corresponding to $lift(X)$ s.t. $X > 2$ is discarded to create two fresh live copies. The

---

[1] Bigger classes of general constraints can be handled using the underlying CLP engine's constraint solver but even this unary restriction is already quite expressive.

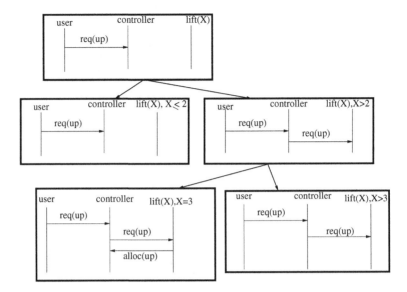

Fig. 5. Simulation of a Chart with Control and Data Variables

simulation strategy sketched above is truly symbolic. Separate copies of process instances are not created unless required by the messages in the chart.

Formal description of our approach. In general, our simulation strategy works as follows. At any time in execution for a parameterized process $p(X)$, let the domain of X be divided into $k \geq 1$ mutually exclusive partitions so far. Each of the partitions is associated with a constraint on X, which is in fact an interval constraint; let the intervals corresponding to the k partitions be $I_1, \ldots, I_k$ where for all $1 \leq j \leq k$ we have $I_j = [l_j, u_j]$ (the lower and upper bounds of the interval). Now, consider a message send from $p(X)$ or a message receive into $p(X)$, with associated interval constraint $c(X)$. Let $I^c = [l^c, u^c]$ be the interval corresponding to $c(X)$. Any live copy I_j (where $1 \leq j \leq k$) satisfies one of the following four cases.

- Case 1 : If $l_j \leq u_j < l^c \leq u^c$ or $l^c \leq u^c < l_j \leq u_j$ (I_j and I^c are disjoint intervals), then the copy for I_j is not progressed with the new message send/receive.
- Case 2: If $l^c \leq l_j \leq u_j \leq u^c$ (I^c contains I_j) then the copy for I_j is progressed with the new message send/receive.
- Case 3: If $l_j \leq l^c \leq u^c \leq u_j$ (I_j contains I^c) we discard the live copy for I_j and replicate it to create three live copies $[l_j, l^c - 1]$, $[l^c, u^c]$ and $[u^c + 1, u_j]$. The live copy $[l^c, u^c]$ is progressed with the new message send/receive, while the other two are not progressed.
- Case 4: Otherwise, either $l_j < l^c \leq u_j < u^c$ or $l^c < l_j \leq u^c < u_j$ (but not both). We discard the live copy corresponding to I_j and replicate it to

create two new live copies: (a) for the portion of I_j common to I^c, which is progressed with the message send/receive and (b) the portion of I_j not common to I^c, which is not progressed. Thus, if $l_j < l^c \leq u_j < u^c$, we create live copies for $[l^c, u_j]$ (common to I^c) and $[l_j, l^c - 1]$. If $l^c < l_j \leq u^c < u_j$ we create live copies for $[l_j, u^c]$ (common to I^c) and $[u^c + 1, u_j]$.

In case 3, the behaviors of the live copies for $[l_j, l^c - 1]$ and $[u^c + 1, u_j]$ are identical; we could maintain a single live copy for them. Indeed we do so in our implementation by maintaining a set of intervals for each live copy, instead of a single interval. This is a straightforward extension of the above simulation strategy and we omit the details.

Key idea in our approach. Our simulation strategy can handle LSC descriptions containing parameterized process classes. The key idea of our approach is to *not* maintain all of the concrete instances of a process class explicitly (as is done in the play engine of Harel and Marelly [10,13]). In other words, their play engine [10] uses universal control variables only for concise specification; these variables are instantiated into all possible values during simulation. Instead, we maintain the values of a control variable symbolically via constraints. In particular, a process class gets split into subclasses during simulation based on *behaviors*. Each subclass is annotated with a constraint, which in general can represent unboundedly many instances (corresponding to unboundedly many control variable values). Instances which are behaviorally indistinguishable are grouped into a subclass. As a simple example, consider the instances $lift(1)$ and $lift(2)$ in Figure 4. Their behaviors are *indistinguishable* from each other; hence it is not necessary to maintain such instances separately during simulation.

5   Timing Constraints

LSCs are used as a full-fledged requirements specification language for reactive systems. Reactive systems often involve real-time response to external stimulus; thus a requirements specification of such systems may contain timing constraints. Consequently, the LSC specification language also allows timing constraints to appear in charts. Primarily this involves the addition of a global variable $Time$ (representing a global clock) which is visible to all processes. Several other global variables T_i may appear in the chart which capture the time value at a certain snapshot of the chart's execution. For example consider the universal chart in Figure 6(a) obtained from [9,10]. This chart specifies that the light must turn on between 1 and 2 time units after the switch is turned on. Note that even though $T1 := Time$ is an internal computation it manipulates global variables.

The existing play engine of Harel and Marelly [9] simulates LSCs with timing constraints as follows. The simulator starts with $Time = 0$ and waits for external stimulus. Once the stimulus arrives, the simulator freezes time and computes a "maximal response" of the system as before (that is, a maximal sequence of events which get enabled after the external stimulus arrives). These events are

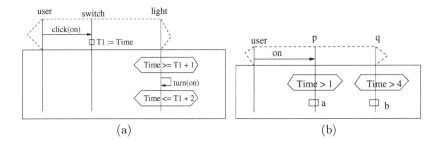

Fig. 6. (a) LSC with timing constraints (b) Choice in evaluating timing constraints

assumed to take zero time. After the system response, the simulator again allows time to progress. Note that in the presence of timing constraints, certain events in the chart may be stuck which would have otherwise been enabled. For example, in Figure 6(a), after the pre-chart is completed, the light has to wait for time to progress by at least one time unit.

The above simulation strategy is not symbolic in the sense that all constraints on *Time* are reduced to *tests* when they are evaluated. Furthermore, time is explicitly progressed (by the simulator's own clock or by user specified ticks) so that these tests can be evaluated to true. We now describe our approach for simulating LSCs with timing constraints.

Our Approach. We take a different approach in our CLP based simulation engine; we do not force progress of time. Instead, each occurrence of the *Time* variable (encountered during simulation) is captured as a different variable $Time_i$ in our simulation engine. Thus initially, we have $Time_0 = 0$; the next occurrence of *Time* during the simulation is denoted as the variable $Time_1$ where $Time_1 \geq Time_0$. Since our variables are assign-once variables, therefore the flow of time in *Time* is captured by a sequence of variables

$$Time_0, Time_1, Time_2 \ldots$$

Suppose that we have introduced timing variables $Time_0, \ldots, Time_i$ at any point during simulation. Any event/condition containing the global variable *Time* introduces a new variable $Time_{i+1}$. We introduce the constraints

- $Time_{i+1} \geq Time_j$ where $j \leq i$ is any index such that the event/condition involving $Time_j$ "happens-before" the event/condition involving $Time_{i+1}$ in the partial order of the chart. In practice, we only introduce a transitive reduction of such constraints (*e.g.* while introducing the variable $Time_2$, if we introduce $Time_2 \geq Time_1$ and we already have $Time_1 \geq Time_0$, the constraint $Time_2 \geq Time_0$ is redundant).
- a constraint from the event/condition involving $Time_{i+1}$ by replacing *Time* with $Time_{i+1}$ in the event/condition.

Timing constraints appearing in LSCs translate to constraints (not tests) on the $Time_i$ variables during simulation.

Examples. Let us revisit the universal LSC of Figure 6(a). Initially, we set $Time_0 = 0$. The user provides the stimulus $\langle user!switch, click(on)\rangle$. The simulator then executes $\langle switch?user, click(on)\rangle$. The internal action involving the update of $T1$ is now executed. Since this is the first occurrence of $Time$ after $Time_0$, we introduce the constraint $T1 = Time_1 \wedge Time_1 \geq Time_0$. Now, we encounter the "hot condition" `Time >= T1 + 1`. In LSC terminology [5], a ***hot condition*** is a condition whose falsehood leads to the violation of the chart; it is analogous to an assertion at a program point. Instead of explicitly progressing time, we introduce another $Time_i$ variable which will be able to satisfy this condition and let the simulation proceed. Thus, we introduce the constraint $Time_2 \geq T1 + 1 \wedge Time_2 \geq Time_1$. We then execute the events $\langle light!light, turn(on)\rangle$ and $\langle light?light, turn(on)\rangle$. Finally, we need to evaluate the hot condition `Time <= T1 + 2`. The time at which this hot condition is evaluated refers to a potentially new time, since time might have increased since $Time_2$. So, we introduce a constraint $Time_3 \leq T1 + 2 \wedge Time_3 \geq Time_2$.

Note that when several hot conditions involving $Time$ are blocking simulation, we do not affix any order on the times at which they are evaluated. As a trivial example, consider the universal chart in Figure 6(b). In this chart we will accumulate the following constraints during simulation.

$$Time_0 = 0 \ \wedge \ Time_1 \geq Time_0 \ \wedge Time_1 > 1 \ \wedge Time_2 \geq Time_0 \ \wedge Time_2 > 4$$

$Time_1$ and $Time_2$ correspond to the time of evaluation of the hot conditions in processes p and q. Note that $Time_1$ and $Time_2$ are incomparable. This is because the chart's partial order does not specify any ordering on the evaluation of these conditions.

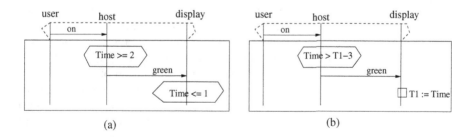

(a)   (b)

Fig. 7. (a) A LSC with inconsistent timing constraints (b) A LSC requiring symbolic representation of time

Clearly, for LSCs with timing constraints, additional violations are possible during simulation if the timing constraints are inconsistent with the monotonically increasing flow of time. Our simulation engine will detect and report such violations. For example consider the universal chart of Figure 7(a). Initially, we start with $Time_0 = 0$ and execute the pre-chart of the LSC. A live copy of the chart is now created, and we need to satisfy the hot condition `Time >= 2`. This is achieved by adding the constraint $Time_1 \geq 2 \wedge Time_1 \geq Time_0$. The simulator then sends and receives the *green* message and tries to satisfy the hot condition `Time <= 1`. This again introduces a new variable $Time_2$ and constraints on this variable. At this point the constraint store becomes:

$$Time_0 = 0 \ \wedge Time_1 \geq Time_0 \wedge Time_1 \geq 2 \ \wedge Time_2 \geq Time_1 \ \wedge Time_2 \leq 1$$

The constraint store is now inconsistent (since it implies $Time_2 \geq 2 \wedge Time_2 \leq 1$), giving a violation.

Additional power of our approach. The symbolic representation of time flow in our simulator allows us to simulate more LSC descriptions. Let us consider the universal chart in Figure 7(b). It says that after the host is turned on by the user, the host should send a *green* message to the display; furthermore, the *green* message should be received within 3 time units of being sent. This example LSC description cannot be simulated in the play engine of [9] simply because the hot condition `Time > T1 - 3` refers to a variable `T1` which is uninstantiated. So, the play engine of [9] will get blocked waiting for `T1` to get instantiated. However, `T1` cannot get instantiated unless the *green* message is sent and received; thus the play engine of [9] will be deadlocked forever. On the other hand, our play engine will evaluate the hot condition `Time > T1-3` by adding the constraint $Time_1 > T1 - 3 \wedge Time_1 \geq Time_0$. This will allow the simulation to proceed and constraints on $T1$ will be accumulated subsequently.

6   Implementation

We have used the ECL^iPS^e constraint logic programming system to develop a symbolic simulation engine for LSC descriptions. Our engine supports data variables in processes, control variables (to support many instances of a process) as well as timing constraints. The natural support for backtracking in a ECL^iPS^e engine makes it convenient to perform automated simulation of various allowed behaviors in a LSC description. Whenever a violation is detected, the simulator reports the trace of the illegal path, and backtracks to find a violation free path. Our current implementation supports simulation of both existential and universal charts. Existential charts are simulated in a manner somewhat similar to pre-charts. In other words, they are monitored and progressed in each super-step but their violation is not reported.

Examples simulated using our tool. We have used our tool for automated simulation of some LSC examples (*including the examples given in this paper and in [5,13]*). Three of them are non-trivial and are described below. In [5], the authors presented LSC description of an automated rail-car system with several cars operating on a cyclic path with several terminals. We simulate the LSC for the rail-car system using our ECL^iPS^e implementation. This LSC involves 7 classes, 19 messages, 11 conditions, 1 assignment and other control structures like subchart and if-then-else structures. We also simulate portions of a netphone example which has appeared in literature. In particular, [13] describes a model of a telephone network system with LSCs. We have simulated two use cases of this system; these are the only two use cases whose full description is publicly available [10,13]. One use case specifies the protocol for initial set-up of the identification number of various phones in a telephone network. It contains 4 LSCs, with 4 classes, 7 messages, 3 conditions and other operations. The other user case describes part of the conversation establishment protocol. It consists of 3 LSCs, with 5 classes, 11 messages, 6 conditions and other operations.

Timings and Web-site. For all our examples, detection and simulation of one violation free path takes less than 0.1 second. The timings are obtained by running ECL^iPS^e on top of SUN OS 5.8 in a SunFire 4800 machine with 750 MHz Ultra Sparc III CPU (only one processor was used in the experiments).

Existing works on LSCs/play engine present the rail-car and netphone examples, but do not report timings for their simulation. Hence, a performance comparison is problematic. However more important than a performance comparison is to check whether our simulator provides tolerable levels of efficiency to the user. Our timing of less than 0.1 second for simulating non-trivial LSC examples (like the rail-car example of [5]) seems to indicate that our simulator is reasonably efficient. In other words, the symbolic execution mechanism does not compromise efficiency in a significant way. Our prototype simulator toolkit is available from the following web-site (along with description of our examples) http://www.comp.nus.edu.sg/~wangtao/symbolic_simulator_engine.htm

Possible Improvements. So far, our focus has been in building a constraint based engine for symbolic simulation of LSCs. We have concentrated less on the user-interface issues, such as how a LSC is provided as input to the simulator. Currently, our simulator takes in textual input (describing a LSC), and we lack a full-fledged Graphical User Interface (GUI) to input LSC descriptions. In contrast, the play engine of Harel et. al employs a sophisticated play-in approach [10] which allows the user to input LSCs without fully drawing them. In future we will work on integrating the play-in approach as a front end to our simulator.

7   Discussion

Message Sequence Charts (MSCs) are widely used as a requirements specification of inter-object interactions prior to software development; they constitute one of the behavioral diagram types in the Unified Modeling Language (UML) framework [3]. We note that the recent years have seen a spurt of research activity in developing/analyzing complete system specifications based on MSCs – [2,5,11,15] to name a few. LSC is one such visual language with an execution engine. LSC based executable specifications are useful since they allow simulation/analysis of requirements early in the software design cycle. Our work in this paper is geared towards using CLP technology for symbolic execution of such behavioral requirements. In future, we plan to apply our ideas for simulating descriptions written in other executable specification languages based on MSCs (*e.g.* the Communicating Transaction Processes (CTP) modeling language [15]).

Acknowledgments. This work was partially supported by a research grant from A*STAR (Singapore) under the Embedded and Hybrid Systems program.

References

1. R. Alur, G.J. Holzmann, and D.A. Peled. An analyzer for message sequence charts. In *Intl. Conf. on Tools and Algorithms for Construction and Analysis of Systems (TACAS), LNCS 1055*, 1996.
2. R. Alur and M. Yannakakis. Model checking of message sequence charts. In *International Conference on Concurrency Theory (CONCUR), LNCS 1664*, 1999.
3. G. Booch, I. Jacobsen, and J. Rumbaugh. *Unified Modeling Language for Object-oriented development.* Rational Software Corporation, 1996.
4. M. Butler and M. Leuschel. ProB: A model checker for B. In *Formal Methods in Europe (FME), LNCS 2805*, 2003.
5. W. Damm and D. Harel. LSCs: Breathing life into message sequence charts. *Formal Methods in System Design*, 19(1), 2001.
6. G. Delzanno and A. Podelski. Model checking in CLP. In *International Conference on Tools and Algorithms for Construction and Analysis of Systems (TACAS)*, 1999.
7. ECL^iPS^e. The ECL^iPS^e Constraint Logic Programming System, 2003. Available from http://www-icparc.doc.ic.ac.uk/eclipse/.
8. D. Harel, H. Kugler, R. Marelly, and A. Pnueli. Smart play-out of behavioral requirements. In *Intl. Conf. on Formal Methods in Computer Aided Design (FM-CAD)*, 2002.
9. D. Harel and R. Marelly. Playing with time: On the specification and execution of time-enriched LSCs. In *IEEE/ACM Intl. Symp. on Modeling, Analysis and Simulation of Computer and Telecommunication Systems (MASCOTS)*, 2002.
10. D. Harel and R. Marelly. *Come, Let's Play: Scenario-Based Programming Using LSCs and the Play-Engine.* Springer-Verlag, 2003.
11. J.G. Hendriksen, M. Mukund, K.N. Kumar, and P.S. Thiagarajan. Message sequence graphs and finitely generated regular MSC languages. In *International Colloquium on Automata, Languages and Programming (ICALP)*, 2000.
12. J. Klose and H. Wittke. An automata based interpretation of Live Sequence Charts. In *Intl. Conf. on Tools and Algorithms for Construction and Analysis of Systems (TACAS)*, 2001.
13. R. Marelly, D. Harel, and H. Kugler. Multiple instances and symbolic variables in executable sequence charts. In *Intl. Conf. on Object Oriented Programming, Systems, Languages and Applications (OOPSLA)*, 2002.
14. S. Narain and R. Chadha. Symbolic discrete event simulation. In *Discrete Event Systems, Manufacturing Systems and Communication Networks*, 1994.
15. A. Roychoudhury and P.S. Thiagarajan. Communicating transaction processes. In *IEEE Intl. Conf. on Appl. of Concurrency in System Design (ACSD)*, 2003.
16. Z.120. Message Sequence Charts (MSC'96), 1996.

Observing Functional Logic Computations*

Bernd Braßel[1], Olaf Chitil[2], Michael Hanus[1], and Frank Huch[1]

[1] Institut für Informatik, CAU Kiel, Olshausenstr. 40, D-24098 Kiel, Germany
{bbr,mh,fhu}@informatik.uni-kiel.de
[2] Computing Laboratory, University of Kent, Canterbury, Kent CT2 7NF, UK
O.Chitil@kent.ac.uk

Abstract. A lightweight approach to debugging functional logic programs by observations is presented, implemented for the language Curry. The Curry Object Observation System (COOSy) comprises a portable library plus a viewing tool. A programmer can observe data structures and functions by annotating expressions in his program. The possibly partial values of observed expressions that are computed during program execution are recorded in a trace file, including information on non-deterministic choices and logical variables. A separate viewing tool displays the trace content. COOSy covers all aspects of modern functional logic multiparadigm languages such as lazy evaluation, higher order functions, non-deterministic search, logical variables, concurrency and constraints. Both use and implementation of COOSy are described.

1 Introduction

With improvements in the implementation of declarative languages and computer architecture, applications written in declarative languages have become larger. Because of this increase in application size, the need for debugging tools has become crucial. The step-by-step style of imperative debugging is not sufficient for declarative programs (first detailed discussion in [16]). This is especially true for the complex operational behaviour of lazy evaluation [11]. The programmer needs a debugging model that matches the high-level programming model of the declarative language.

Gill introduced a method for observing the values that expressions evaluate to during the execution of a lazy functional program [5]. These values give insight into how a program works and thus help the programmer locating bugs. Not only data structures but also functions can be observed. Observing does not change the normal behaviour of a program. If an expression is only partially evaluated, then exactly this partial value is observed. The most distinguishing feature of the method is that it can be implemented for a full lazy functional language by a small portable library. The programmer just imports the library and annotates expressions of interest with an observation function. Gill's Haskell

---

* This work has been partially supported by the DFG under grant Ha 2457/1-2.

B. Jayaraman (Ed.): PADL 2004, LNCS 3057, pp. 193–208, 2004.
© Springer-Verlag Berlin Heidelberg 2004

Object Observation Debugger (HOOD)[1] has become a valuable tool for Haskell [13] programmers and was integrated into the popular Haskell system Hugs[2].

In this paper we extend the observation method to the more demanding setting of functional logic programming in the language Curry [7,10]. The implementation as a library of observation combinators proves to be flexible in that it is not necessary to deal specially with some language features such as concurrency and constraints. However, two logical language features, namely non-determinism and logical variables, do require fundamental extensions of the implementation. In return for these complications we are able to observe more than just values. We observe additional information about non-determinism and the binding of logical variables that proves to be helpful for locating bugs in functional logic programs. In this paper we describe both the use and the implementation of the Curry Object Observation System (COOSy).

The next section gives a short demonstration of observations in purely functional Curry programs. In Section 3 we look at a number of Curry programs using non-determinism and logical variables; we see which information can be obtained by observations and how this information can be used to locate bugs. Sections 4 and 5 present the implementation of COOSy in Curry. In Section 6 we relate our work to others'. Section 7 concludes. We assume familiarity with Haskell [13] and Curry [7,10] or the basic ideas of functional logic programming (see [6] for a survey).

2   Observations in Functional Programs

We review the idea of debugging by observation at the hand of a tiny program written in the purely functional subset of Curry:

Example 1 (A first observation).

```
max x y | x > y = x              maxList = foldl max 0
        | x < y = y              main = maxList [1,7,3,7,8]
```

Instead of the expected value 8, we get the message "No more solutions" from the run-time system when evaluating main. Why has the computation failed?

First we may want to know what happened to the argument list of the function maxList. Using COOSy (i.e., importing the COOSy library), we can obtain this information by putting an observe expression around the list. The first argument of observe is an expression built from combinators provided by COOSy that describes the type of the observed expression. The second argument is a label to help matching observed values with observed expressions. The third argument is the expression to be observed.

```
import COOSy
...
main = maxList (observe (oList oInt) "ArgList" [1,7,3,7,8])
```

---

[1] http://www.haskell.org/hood
[2] http://www.haskell.org/hugs

We execute the program. The function `observe` behaves like an identity on its third argument and thus does not change the program behaviour, *except* that the value of the third argument is also recorded in a trace file. We then view the information contained in the trace file with a separate COOSy tool shown in Figure 1.

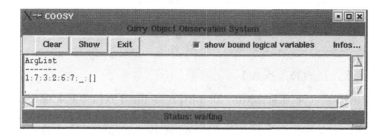

Fig. 1. Screenshot of the COOSy GUI

When we press the "Show" button, the GUI shows the human-readable representation, called *protocol*, of our first example observation. Note that observations are recorded even though the program execution fails. This is crucial for debugging purposes. In Figure 1 we can see that the argument list was evaluated to `1:7:3:7:_:[]`. The underscore means that the last number in the list has not been evaluated. Why is that? Trusting good old `foldl`, we turn to examine the call to `max`:

```
maxList = foldl (observe (oInt ~> oInt ~> oInt) "max" max) 0
```

The symbol `~>` denotes the observation of functions, here of type `Int->Int->Int`.

```
{ \ ! _  -> !
, \ 7 7  -> !
, \ 7 3  -> 7
, \ 1 7  -> 7
, \ 0 1  -> 1}
```

The result of the observation is presented on the left. The observable value of a function is a set of mappings from arguments to results. Each single mapping is written as a pseudo-lambda expression. The symbol `!` denotes a failed computation.

Now the error can be clearly located: Whereas many calls to `max` give satisfactorily results, the call "`max 7 7`" fails. Our definition of `max` does not handle equal arguments! Note that the first mapping, "`\ ! _ -> !`", is perfectly sensible: with a fail in the first argument `max` fails as well without evaluating the second argument.

We can use the type descriptor `oOpaque` in the first argument of `observe` to blend out (large) data structure components:

Example 2 (oOpaque — blending out information).

```
main = map maxList (observe (oList oOpaque) "xs" [[1..n] | n <-[1..10]])
```

The corresponding observation is

```
#:#:#:#:#:#:#:#:#:#:[]
```

The type descriptor oOpaque becomes vital when we observe polymorphic values so that the types of components are statically unknown at the observation point:

Example 3 (oOpaque — observing polymorphic values).

```
myLength = observe (oList oOpaque ~> oInt) "length" length
main     = myLength [1..10] + myLength "Hello"
```

We still observe the structure of the argument lists:

```
{ \ (_:_:_:_:_:_:_:_:_:_:[]) -> 10 }
```

```
{ \ (_:_:_:_:_:[]) -> 5 }
```

Curry provides type descriptors for all pre-defined types. For new data types or for the purpose of displaying values in our own way we can define our own type descriptors; see Section 4.2. Alternatively, we can use the `derive` function provided by COOSy that takes a Curry program and adds type descriptors for all user-defined algebraic data types.

3 Observations in Functional Logic Programs

In addition to the functional features of Haskell, Curry provides also features for logic programming. In particular, a function can be non-deterministic, i.e., have more than one result for a given argument, because it can be defined by a set of non-confluent rules. Furthermore, Curry expressions can contain logical (existentially quantified) variables. Both features give rise to new observations.

3.1 Observing Non-deterministic Functions

Consider the following program which uses a non-deterministic function to compute all permutations of a given list:

Example 4 (Observing non-determinism).

```
perm []     = []                    insert x []     = [x]
perm (x:xs) = insert x (perm xs)    insert x (y:ys) = y:insert x ys
main = perm [1,2,3]                 insert x xs     = x:xs
```

Naturally, we implanted a little bug you will have spotted already. The effect of this bug is not a wrong result but too many of the right ones. Correctly the program computes the lists [1,2,3], [1,3,2], [2,1,3], [2,3,1], [3,1,2], and [3,2,1], but these lists are computed twice, thrice, twice, thrice, four, and eight times, respectively. To isolate the bug, we set an observation point at the call of the non-deterministic function of our program:

```
perm (x:xs) = observe oInsert "insert" insert x (perm xs)
        where oInsert = oInt ~> oList oInt ~> oList oInt
```

Now, we can make use of another nice feature of COOSy: observations can be viewed before the end of the whole computation. To debug Example 4, we view the observation only when a few solutions are computed. For the first result [3,2,1] we get the following protocol for the label `insert`:

```
{\ 3 [] -> 3:[]}

{\ 2 (3:[]) -> 3:2:[]}

{\ 1 (3:2:[]) -> 3:2:1:[]}
```

The blank lines show that all three entries belong to different observations (one for each recursive call to `perm`). Of course, this protocol yields no hint to the bug, as we have only seen a single solution so far. We prompt the system for the next solution, which is again [3,2,1]. This could give us a hint towards the error.

The resulting protocol is:

```
{\ 3 []   -> 3:[]}

{\ 2 (3:[]) -> 3:2:[]}
{\ 2 (3:[]) -> 3:2:[]}

{\ 1 (3:2:[]) -> 3:2:1:[]}
{\ 1 (3:2:[]) -> 3:2:1:[]}
```

The observations of `insert` are ordered in three packages of calls belonging together. The lines within one package are non-deterministic alternatives of a single call to `insert`. The colouring provides the information about what was already computed for the previous solution and what is newly constructed. For instance, in the second package the alternative solution only constructed a new end of the list. This is a very good hint towards finding the error, but it can get even more obvious if we look at the protocol for the first three solutions. The third solution is again [3,2,1] and the protocol starts like this:

```
{\ 3 [] -> 3:[]}
{\ 3 [] -> 3:[]}
```

Now in these first two lines it is clear that `insert` yields two results for the very same arguments 3 and []. The source of this is easy to spot in the program and we conclude that the two rules "insert x xs = x:xs" and "insert x [] = [x]" overlap more than they should. Deleting the latter yields the correct program which computes all and only the desired solutions.

3.2 Observing Logical Variables

Curry features another extension of functional programming: the use of logical variables. We first demonstrate how COOSy represents logical variables.

Example 5 (Representation of logical variables).

```
main = observe oInt "Logical Variable" x where x free
```

The clause "where x free" declares the variable x as a logical (existentially quantified, free) variable. Running the program, we obtain the observation on the left in which we can see that COOSy represents unbound logical variables as "?".

```
Logical Variable
----------------
?
```

Let us observe a logical variable which is bound in the course of the computation:

```
f 1 = 1
main = f (observe oInt "Variable + Binding" x) where x free
```

Now the result is (?/1). Changing f in this example to f 1 = 1 and f 2 = 2 we get the result on the left (after computing all possible solutions). Note that the colouring indicates that the same logical variable was bound to different values.

```
(?/1)
(?/2)
```

The next example includes a new little bug:

Example 6 (Searching a bug in a function defined with logical features).

```
last xs | append ys [y] =:= xs = y        append []     ys = ys
         where y,ys free                  append (x:xs) ys = x:append xs xs
```

The function `last` is intended to compute the last element of a list by solving the equation `append ys [y] =:= xs`. When considering the call `last [1,2,3]`, this equation is (or rather *should be*) only solvable if ys is bound to [1,2] and y is bound to 3, as "`append [1,2] [3]`" should equal [1,2,3].

However, testing our little program, the result of `last [1,2,3]` is not the expected 3 but rather a logical variable. Where should we begin to find the bug? Let us be cautious about this error and start at the top, slowly advancing down the program. First we shall look at the whole list computed in the guard of `last`:

```
last xs | observe oInts "as" (append ys [y]) =:= xs = y where y,ys free
```

```
?/1:[]
?/1:[]
?/1:?/2:[]
?/1:?/2:?/3:[]
?/1:?/2:?/3:_:_
```

With oInts = oList oInt. The result of the observation is on the left. This result is peculiar. Knowing how the program should work, it is okay that there are three states of evaluation where the system guesses that 1, 2 and 3 might be the last element of the list. But why are there two versions of "`?/1:[]`"? We should find out more about the arguments of `append`:

```
last xs | append (observe oInts "ys" ys) [y] =:= xs = y where y,ys free
```

This yields the observation:

```
(?/[])
(?/(?/1:(?/[])))
(?/(?/1:(?/(?/2:(?/[])))))
(?/(?/1:(?/(?/2:(?/(?/3:(?/[])))))))
(?/(?/1:(?/(?/2:(?/(?/3:(?/(?:?))))))))
```

We see immediately why COOSy has the option to turn off the representation of bound variables as the result after selecting it is so much more readable.

```
[]
1:[]
1:2:[]
1:2:3:[]
1:2:3:?:?
```

This looks quite correct, with the small exception that ys should not be bound to the whole list [1,2,3] but maximally to [1,2]. A similar observation of the second argument y resulting in (?/1) is also wrong of course, but we already know that y is not bound correctly, or the final result could never be a logical variable.

Seeing all this, we cannot help but search for our error in `append`:

```
last xs | observe oApp "App" append ys [y] =:= xs = y where y,ys free
```

where oApp = oList oInt ~> oList oInt ~> oList oInt. The observation yields (with representation of bound logical variables turned off again):

```
{\[]        (1:[]) -> 1:[]}
{\(1:[])       _   -> 1:[]}
{\(1:2:[])     _   -> 1:2:[]}
{\(1:2:3:[])   _   -> 1:2:3:[]}
{\(1:2:3:?:?)  _   -> 1:2:3:_:_}
```

We can clearly see that whenever the first argument of append is a non-empty list, the second argument is not evaluated. Looking into the rule append (x:xs) ys = x:append xs xs, we now easily spot the bug where our eyes were clouded only seconds ago.

For the purpose of this paper, we have only presented very small buggy programs. Similarly to other language implementations, Curry implementations [9] provide warnings for some of these bugs (e.g., single occurrences of a variable in a defining rule), but it should be clear that there are also many larger wrong programs where such compiler warnings are not produced.

4   Implementation for Functional Programs

Now we delve into the depths of our first implementation for purely functional Curry programs, before we consider non-determinism and logical variables in the next section. Our implementation roughly follows Gill's HOOD implementation, outlined in [5]. We start with the format of our protocol files and then describe how these files are written.

4.1   Format of the Trace Files

Each time the computation makes progress with the evaluation of an observed expression an event is recorded in the trace file. To distinguish unevaluated expressions from failed or non-terminating computations, we need to trace two types of events:

Demand. The incident that a value is needed for a computation and consequently its evaluation is started is called a *Demand Event*.

Value. The incident that the computation of a value (to head normal form) has succeeded is called a *Value Event*.

From the nature of evaluation in Curry we can conclude:

- No Value without Demand: If a value was computed, there must have been a corresponding Demand Event for the data.
- A Demand Event without a corresponding Value Event indicates a failed or non-terminated computation.
- The correspondence between Value and Demand Events has to be recorded in the protocol.

Keeping these facts in mind, we can now turn to the format of the trace files. A *trace* is a list of events, each of which is either a Demand or a Value Event. To model the correspondence between Demands and Values, we construct an identification of the events by numbering them: `type EventID = Int`. For each Value one of its arguments has to be its own ID and another one is the ID of the corresponding Demand, which we will call its *parent*. There are two more important things we have to know about a Value Event: (1) Because a value is built from constructor symbols, we need the arity of the constructor. (2) We need a string indicating what the value should be printed like in the GUI.

Recording the arity of a value is important for another task of the COOSy system: The traced data structures have to be reconstructed correctly. In order to achieve this, more than the arity has to be recorded. A Demand has to be tagged with the information which argument of which value it demands. This

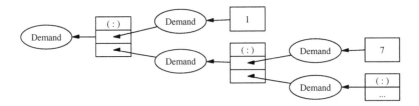

Fig. 2. Graphical representation of COOSy trace of Example 7

means that two numbers have to be added: (1) the `EventID` of the Value Event, which is the parent of the Demand and (2) a number between 1 and the arity of that Value. The first Demand of an observation is tagged with a parent ID of -1 and argument number of 0 to indicate that it has no parent and denotes the root of the data structure. Putting it all together we have:

```
data Event = Value   Int     String                 EventID   EventID
             --       arity   value representation   own ID    parent ID
           | Demand Int                              EventID   EventID
             --       number of argument             own ID    parent ID
```

Example 7 (Trace representation). The trace of Example 1 begins like this:

```
[Demand 0 0 -1, Value 2 "(:)" 1   0,Demand 2   2 1, Value 2 "(:)" 3   2,
 Demand 2 4   3, Value 2 "(:)" 5   4,...
 Demand 1 16 1, Value 0 "1"   17 16,Demand 1 18 3, Value 0 "7"   19 18,...]
```

Note that the pattern of alternating Demands and Values is not necessary in general.

To make traces more comprehensible, we use a graphical representation, where ellipses denote Demands and Values are denoted by rectangular records which contain a field for each argument. The parent and structural information is visualised by arrows, see Figure 2.

Functions are treated in the same way as data structures: A functional value is built like any binary constructor, connecting its argument with its result. To represent a function with more than one argument, the result is a functional value as well (curryfied representation of functions). The only special treatment of functions is in the pretty printer.

4.2   Writing the Trace

When the function `observe` is initially called, it

1. gets a new `EventID` from a global state (to make sure that the ID is unambiguous),
2. writes a Demand Event into the trace file as a side effect (by `unsafePerformIO`),
3. evaluates the observed value to head normal form,

4. deconstructs the result, if it is not a constant (constructor with arity 0),
5. constructs a new term with the same head symbol where observe is called for each argument of the result constructor together with the information which of the arguments it observes.

Example 8 (Observing user-defined data structures). We want to formulate an observer for the data type data Nat = 0 | S Nat for which an observation might be "main = observe oNat "Nat" (S (S 0))".

The function observe calls the actual observing function observer with the initial values for parent and argument number -1 and 0, respectively. Both functions are independent of the observed type.

```
observe oType label x = observer oType label x (-1) 0
```

```
observer oType label x parent argNr = unsafePerformIO $
    do eventID <- recordEvent label (Demand argNr) parent
       return (seq x (oType x label eventID))
```

The function seq evaluates x to head normal form and then returns its second argument. When this evaluation of x succeeds, the function oType is responsible for recording the value in the trace file. The function recordEvent first obtains a new EventID and then writes the Event to a trace file. There is a separate trace file for each user-defined label, to simplify filtering events from different observations directly when they occur.

```
recordEvent label event parent =
    do eventID <- getNewID
       writeToTraceFile label (event eventID parent)
       return eventID
```

As an example for a function oType, observing the type Nat could be implemented as follows:

```
oNat 0 label parent = unsafePerformIO $
    do recordEvent label (Value 0 "0") parent
       return 0
```

This is the code for the constant 0. For the unary constructor S we need to call the function observer again, recursively starting the observation of the arguments by means of the observer oNat:

```
oNat (S x) label parent = unsafePerformIO $
    do eventID <- recordEvent label (Value 1 "S") parent
       return (S (observer x oNat eventID 1))
```

These functions are fairly schematic for each type, depending only on the arity of the constructors. Therefore, COOSy provides functions o0, o1, o2... for constructors of arity 0,1,2... Using these, the definition of oNat simply looks like this:

```
oNat 0     = o0 "0" 0
oNat (S x) = o1 oNat "S" S x
```

The function oNat is the *standard observer* for the type Nat. Standard observers are automatically derivable as mentioned at the end of Section 2.

5   Extending COOSy for Logical Language Features

To handle the full language Curry, we have to extend our implementation

- to put together information from observations of non-deterministic computations correctly
- and to observe logical variables.

5.1   Non-deterministic Functions

In the extended setting, the number of values corresponding to a single Demand Event is not limited. The problem is that we need some kind of separation; which values belong to which part of the computation? The following program demonstrates the problem:

Example 9 (Showing the need of predecessors).

```
coin = 0            plus 0      x = x                          main = plus 0 coin
coin = S 0          plus (S x) y = S (plus x y)
```

Observing `plus` in `main` using `observe (oNat ~> oNat ~> oNat) " + " plus`,

```
{\ 0 0      -> 0}
{\ 0 (S 0) -> S 0}
```

we would like to obtain the observation on the left. However, looking at the trace of Example 9 (Figure 3), we spot a problem. The function `plus` has two arguments and therefore is represented as argument1 -> (argument2 -> result). We see in Figure 3 that the first argument of `plus` was simply evaluated to 0. Because the second argument is the non-deterministic function `coin`, its demand yields two values! In consequence, there are two results. The problem is: *Which argument belongs to which result?* There is simply not enough information in the trace of

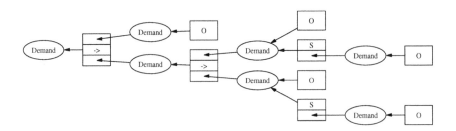

Fig. 3. COOSy trace of Example 9

Figure 3 to answer this question. So we have to store more information in the COOSy trace. In addition to the reference chain denoting the structural information (the *parents*), we also have to trace a reference chain denoting which event belongs to which branch of the computation. Therefore, each Demand and each Value Event is extended by a further `EventID`: the ID of the event which occurred just before in the same branch of the computation, called the *predecessor*. We have extended Figure 3 with this new reference chain, denoted by dotted arrows, and the result is shown in Figure 4. The extended output can be separated correctly into the non-deterministic computations by following the predecessor chain starting at each result. The predecessor chain comprises exactly the parts of the trace that correspond to the computation yielding the result.

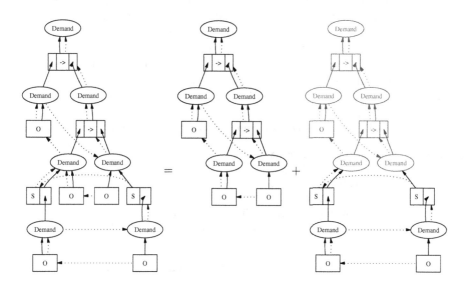

Fig. 4. Separating the extended COOSy trace of Example 9

5.2 Writing the Predecessor Chain

The predecessor in a given computation is a matter of the rewrite or narrowing strategy. Consequently, it is clear that we can only obtain this information by exploiting non-declarative features.

It is also clear that the observer functions introduced in Section 4.2 have to be extended by a further argument providing the information about the predecessors:

```
observer oType l x parent argNr preds = unsafePerformIO $
        do eventID <- recordEvent l (Demand argNr) parent preds
           return (seq x (oType x l eventID preds))
```

The functions oType for observing the different types of data have to be extended analogously. Still unclear is the type of this new argument preds. As it is impossible to know beforehand which part of a given term will be evaluated next without implementing the whole search strategy, we need some means of propagating information across the term structure. Fortunately, logical variables provide such a tool. If the new argument of the function `observer` is a logical variable, its binding will be visible throughout the whole observation. Thus, whenever a new event is written to the trace file, the variable can be bound to the corresponding `EventID`. However, because the order of evaluation is unknown, we need instead of a single `EventID` a list of IDs terminated by a logical variable to be bound to the next event in line.

This is where we have to use a non-declarative feature. Whenever we want to write a new event to the trace file, we need to go through the list of predecessors until we find the logical variable which marks its end. This variable is then bound to the new `EventID` followed by a new logical variable. In order to find the variable marking the end of the list, we need a test function `isVar` which returns `True` whenever its argument is a logical variable and `False` otherwise. While this function can easily be implemented in any Curry implementation, this test is clearly non-declarative.[3]

The extended function `recordEvent` can now be defined as

```
recordEvent label event parent preds
  = do eventID <- getNewID
       let (pred,logVar) = getPred parent preds
           newLogVar free
       doSolve (logVar =:= (eventID:newLogVar))
       writeToTraceFile label (event eventID parent pred)
       return eventID
```

where `doSolve` solves the given constraint and `getPred` is defined as

```
getPred p xs = if isVar xs then (p,xs) else getPred (head xs) (tail xs)
```

5.3 Information Concerning Logical Variables

As Section 3.2 demonstrated, COOSy also allows observation of logical variables. This task is more complex than it sounds.

Whenever a value is computed, we have to test if it is a logical variable. Otherwise, we would get into the unfortunate situation that the observing functions would either begin to guess solutions for the variable or suspend until it is bound. Influencing the computation in this way would of course be disastrous for COOSy as a debugging tool. Hence the function `observer` has to test the observed expression with `isVar` (Section 5.2) before proceeding. However, what to do if this test yields true? First of all, we need to write an event of a new kind to the trace file and, consequently, we have to extend the type of events:

```
data Event = Demand ... | Value ... | LogVar EventID EventID EventID
                --              ownID   parent  predecessor
```

---

[3] Consider the definition `rightFirst | x=:=0 & y=:=isVar x = y where x,y free`
The function `rightFirst` returns `True` whenever the right constraint `y=:=isVar x` was evaluated before the left one. This should not be possible because `&` denotes the concurrent conjunction of constraints, i.e., the combined constraint c_1 & c_2 is solved by solving the constraints c_1 and c_2 *in any order*.

Thus, for each logical variable we store its own ID as well as the ones of its parent and its predecessor. There is one serious problem left, though. What we would like to observe is not only the fact that a logical variable has been computed but also the values it will be bound to, see Examples 5 and 6. How are we going to do this? The values to which the variable will be bound are guessed by the search strategy or directly in the code of other parts of the program. Therefore we introduce one last unsafe feature: a special kind of constraint which suspends on the observed logical variable, while the rest of the computation continues unchanged. As soon as the variable is bound, the constraint is woken up and the new value can be recorded in the trace file. The "as soon as" is crucial because otherwise information about the binding might not be written at all in the case of a failed computation. The complete code is:

```
observer x oType parent argNr preds = unsafePerformIO $ do
  eventID <- recordEvent (Demand argNr) parent preds
  if isVar x
    then do idLogVar <- recordEvent LogVar eventID preds
            spawnConstraint (seq x (x =:= oType x label idLogVar preds))
                            (return x)
    else return (oType x label eventID preds)
```

Note that `isVar` already evaluates `x` to head normal form, so we do not need `seq` in the `else`-branch. However, we need `seq` to make sure that the spawned constraint suspends as long as `x` is not bound to a value. `spawnConstraint` is the last non-standard feature of the PAKCS [9] implementation of Curry we have to explain. It can be thought of as a normal guarded rule like `isZero x | x=:=0 = x` which could be written using `spawnConstraint` as

```
isZero x = spawnConstraint (x=:=0) x.
```

However, there are two important differences: (1) the right-hand side is evaluated even if the evaluation of the guard suspends and (2) the spawned constraint gets a higher priority than any normal constraint.

The Curry environment PAKCS prints a warning when suspended constraints are left at the end of an evaluation. This warning will occur in COOSy whenever an observed logical variable is never bound to a value. However, as the constraints spawned by COOSy are essentially identities (with the side effect of writing into the trace file), this warning does not restrict the soundness of the evaluation.

6   Related Work

COOSy extends Gill's idea of observing values in lazy functional languages to functional logic languages. COOSy also differs in that the function `observe` takes a type description as first argument whereas in HOOD there is no such argument because the function `observe` is overloaded, using the Haskell class system which is not yet provided by Curry. While overloading is convenient for simple examples, a type descriptor is more flexible as Example 3 demonstrates. It is a serious limitation of HOOD that it cannot observe polymorphic expressions.

The version of HOOD integrated in Hugs overcomes this problem through a polymorphic `observe`. Its implementation, however, requires reflective features from the runtime system, which would be hard to provide for most compilers.

The most influential approach to debugging declarative programs is *declarative (or algorithmic) debugging*. It was originally introduced by Shapiro for logic programming languages [16]. The system asks questions about part of the computation such as "Should `factorial 3` yield `17`?" which the user has to answer with "yes" or "no". After a series of questions and answers, the system can give the location of the bug in the program. There exist numerous implementations and the approach has been extended to constraint logic programming [18], assertions [4], functional programming [11,12,14] and functional logic programming [2]. Declarative debugging relies on a simple big-step semantics for the programming language. Hence the approach is less suited for imperative languages, side effects in general and even the search strategies of logic languages.

A large number of methods for debugging lazy functional languages have been proposed [12, Chapter 11]. Most of these rely on following the sequence of actual reductions of the computation. However, for a human user the evaluation order of a lazy functional program is confusing. It is far easier—and also goal-oriented for debugging—to navigate *backwards* through a computation trace from an erroneous result to the cause of the bug [1,17].

Each approach to debugging has its strengths and weaknesses, as already a comparison of three systems shows [3]. Hence later versions of the Haskell tracing system Hat[4] enable the generation of a single trace from a computation which can be viewed in several different ways. Hat includes viewing tools for redex trailing, declarative debugging and observations [19].

Like HOOD, COOSy differs in a number of ways from most other debugging tools for declarative languages. First of all it is implemented by a small portable library, whereas most other tools are either implemented as full program transformations or even modifications of several phases of a compiler. In return, observations are limited to values and information about demand and logical variables. Further information via a library would require extensive reflective features in the programming language. Like most debugging tools, COOSy records a trace as a separate data structure. In this trace only information about expressions under observation are recorded. In contrast, most tools record information about the full computation. While full recording enables the user to inspect the full computation after a single run, it poses serious space problems. Observation with COOSy does slow down computation considerably but only proportionally to the size of the observed data and not to the length of the full computation. COOSy requires the user to annotate his program with applications of `observe`. While any program modification poses the danger of introducing additional bugs and substantial modifications would be tiresome, this does provide a simple and intuitive interface to using the system.

---

[4] `http://www.haskell.org/hat`

7   Conclusion

We presented a new lightweight method for detecting bugs in functional logic programs. The user of the Curry Object Observation System (COOSy) annotates expressions of interest in his program. During program execution information about the values of observed expressions are recorded in a trace file. A separate viewing tool displays this information in the form of mostly familiar expressions.

In this paper we extended the debugging-by-observation method as introduced and implemented by HOOD [5] for functional languages to functional logic languages. The challenge was the support of non-deterministic computations and logical variables. The implementation method of HOOD would record confusing information on values obtained in non-deterministic computations and no information on any parts of values whose computation involved logical variables. Our implementation even records additional information in the trace on non-determinism and logical variables which are displayed by the viewing tool in an easy-to-read way and which give the user vital clues for debugging.

It is essential for debugging that observations do not change the semantics of the program and work for computations that fail with run-time errors or have to be interrupted because of non-termination. The separation of faulty program and viewing tool, afforded by the trace files, enables debugging of programs that create dynamic web pages and which are run on a web server in batch mode [8].

A number of examples demonstrated how COOSy helps locating bugs in faulty programs. Through gaining more experience in using COOSy—especially on larger programs with real bugs—we hope to distill general strategies for debugging with COOSy. Furthermore, we intend to extend the viewing tool in the future. Currently, it gives only a static snapshot of the observed values. Instead, observed values could be shown and constantly updated concurrently to the computation. We could also take advantage of the sequential recording of events in the trace. The viewing tool could allow the user to step forwards and backwards through an animation, similar to GHood [15]. Animations would give the programmer further insights into the workings of his program and might be particularly useful for educational purposes.

COOSy is written in Curry, requiring only a few non-declarative extensions that are easy to implement. COOSy is freely available for the Curry system PAKCS [9][5] and will be distributed with future versions of PAKCS.

References

1. Simon P. Booth and Simon B. Jones. Walk backwards to happiness - debugging by time travel. In *Automated and Algorithmic Debugging*, pages 171–183, 1997.
2. R. Caballero, F.J. López-Fraguas, and M. Rodríguez-Artalejo. Theoretical foundations for the declarative debugging of lazy functional logic programs. In *FLOPS 2001*, pages 170–184. Springer LNCS 2024, 2001.

---

[5] `http://www.informatik.uni-kiel.de/~pakcs/COOSy`

3. O. Chitil, C. Runciman, and M. Wallace. Freja, Hat and Hood – a comparative evaluation of three systems for tracing and debugging lazy functional programs. In *IFL 2000*, pp. 176–193. Springer LNCS 2011, 2001.
4. W. Drabent, S. Nadjm-Tehrani, and J. Maluszynski. The use of assertions in algorithmic debugging. In *Proc. FGCS'88*, pages 573–581, 1988.
5. Andy Gill. Debugging Haskell by observing intermediate data structures. In Graham Hutton, editor, *ENTCS*, volume 41. Elsevier, 2001.
6. M. Hanus. The integration of functions into logic programming: From theory to practice. *Journal of Logic Programming*, 19&20:583–628, 1994.
7. M. Hanus. A unified computation model for functional and logic programming. In POPL '97, pages 80–93, 1997.
8. M. Hanus. High-level server side web scripting in Curry. In *PADL'01*, pages 76–92. Springer LNCS 1990, 2001.
9. M. Hanus, S. Antoy, M. Engelke, K. Höppner, J. Koj, P. Niederau, R. Sadre, and F. Steiner. PAKCS: The Portland Aachen Kiel Curry System. Available at http://www.informatik.uni-kiel.de/~pakcs/, 2003.
10. M. Hanus (ed.). Curry: An integrated functional logic language (vers. 0.7.2). Available at http://www.informatik.uni-kiel.de/~curry, 2002.
11. H. Nilsson and P. Fritzson. Algorithmic debugging for lazy functional languages. *Journal of Functional Programming*, 4(3):337–370, 1994.
12. Henrik Nilsson. *Declarative Debugging for Lazy Functional Languages*. PhD thesis, Linköping, Sweden, 1998.
13. Simon Peyton Jones et al. Haskell 98 language and libraries: the revised report. *Journal of Functional Programming*, 13(1), 2003.
14. B. Pope and Lee Naish. Practical aspects of declarative debugging in Haskell-98. In *ACM PPDP '03*, pages 230–240, 2003.
15. Claus Reinke. GHood – graphical visualisation and animation of Haskell object observations. In *Proceedings of the 2001 ACM SIGPLAN Haskell Workshop*, 2001.
16. E. Shapiro. *Algorithmic Program Debugging*. MIT Press, 1983.
17. J. Sparud and C. Runciman. Tracing lazy functional computations using redex trails. *LNCS*, 1292:291–308, 1997.
18. A. Tessier. Declarative debugging in constraint logic programming. *LNCS*, 1179:64–73, 1996.
19. M. Wallace, O. Chitil, T. Brehm, and C. Runciman. Multiple-view tracing for Haskell. In *Proceedings of the 2001 ACM SIGPLAN Haskell Workshop*, 2001.

Parametric Fortran – A Program Generator for Customized Generic Fortran Extensions[*]

Martin Erwig and Zhe Fu

School of EECS
Oregon State University
{erwig|fuzh}@cs.orst.edu

Abstract. We describe the design and implementation of a program generator that can produce extensions of Fortran that are specialized to support the programming of particular applications. Extensions are specified through parameter structures that can be referred to in Fortran programs to specify the dependency of program parts on these parameters. By providing parameter values, a parameterized Fortran program can be translated into a regular Fortran program.
We describe as a real-world application of this program generator the implementation of a generic inverse ocean modeling tool. The program generator is implemented in Haskell and makes use of sophisticated features, such as multi-parameter type classes, existential types, and generic programming extensions and thus represents the application of an advanced applicative language to a real-world problem.

Keywords: Fortran, Generic Programming, Program Generation, Haskell

1 Introduction

Fortran is widely used in scientific computing. For example, scientific models to predict the behavior of ecological systems are routinely transformed by scientists from a mathematical description into simulation programs. Since these simulation programs have to deal with huge data sets (up to terabytes of data), they are often implemented in a way that exploits the given computing resources as efficiently as possible. In particular, the representation of the data in the simulation programs is highly specialized for each model. Alas, this high degree of specialization causes significant software engineering problems that impact the advance of scientists in evaluating and comparing their models. One particular problem is that simulation programs currently have to be rewritten for each individual forecasting model, even though the underlying algorithms are principally the same for all models. Since Fortran lacks the flexibility to apply the same subroutine on different data structures, scientists have to rewrite programs for every model.

---

[*] This work was supported by the National Science Foundation under the grant ITR/AP-0121542.

B. Jayaraman (Ed.): PADL 2004, LNCS 3057, pp. 209–223, 2004.

We provide a solution to this problem by an extension of Fortran, called *Parametric Fortran*, which is essentially a framework that allows the creation of domain-specific Fortran extensions. A Parametric Fortran program is a Fortran program in which parts, such as statements, expressions, or subroutines, are parameterized by special variables. Every syntactic element of Fortran can be parameterized. When the values of these parameters are given, a program generator can create a Fortran program from the parameterized program, guided by these values. Scientists can implement their algorithm in Parameterized Fortran by using parameters to represent the model-dependent information. When the information about a specific model is given in the form of values for the parameters, a specialized Fortran program can be generated for this model. Therefore, scientists only need to write their programs once and can generate different instances for different models automatically.

The program generator, which is implemented in Haskell [15], takes a Parametric Fortran program and parameter definitions and their values as inputs and produces a Fortran program, see Figure 1.

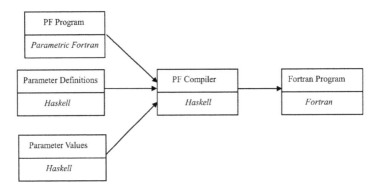

Fig. 1. System architecture

Two different groups of people are concerned with Parametric Fortran. First, scientists who write programs in Fortran want to *use* the genericity provided by Parametric Fortran. Second, computer scientists who *provide* programming support in the form of new Fortran dialects for scientists by extending Parametric Fortran with new parameter types. Rather than defining one particular extension of Fortran, our approach is to provide a framework for extending Fortran on a demand basis and in a domain-specific way.

In the remainder of this Introduction we outline the approach by two simple examples. In Section 2 we illustrate the use of Parametric Fortran in a real-world application. In Section 3 we describe the implementation of Parametric Fortran. We discuss related work in Section 4 and present some conclusions in Section 5.

1.1   Array Addition for Arbitrary Dimensions

The following example shows how to write a Parametric Fortran subroutine to add two arrays of arbitrary dimensions.[1] For simplicity, we suppose that the size of each dimension is 100.

```
{ dim: subroutine arrayAdd(a, b, c)
      real :: a, b, c
      c = a + b
  end subroutine arrayAdd }
```

The program is parameterized by an integer dim. The value of dim will guide the generation of the Fortran subroutine. The brackets { and } delimit the scope of the dim parameter, that is, every Fortran syntactic object in the scope is parameterized by dim. For dim = 2, the following Fortran program will be generated.

```
subroutine arrayAdd(a, b, c)
      integer :: i1, i2
      real, dimension (1:100, 1:100) :: a, b, c
      do i1 = 1, 100
        do i2 = 1, 100
          c(i1, i2) = a(i1, i2) + b(i1, i2)
        end do
      end do
  end subroutine arrayAdd
```

We can observe that in the generated program, a, b, and c are all 2-dimensional arrays. When a variable declaration statement is parameterized by an integer dim, the variable will be declared as a dim-dimensional array in the generated program. The assignment statement that assigns the sum of a and b is wrapped by 2 loops over both dimensions, and index variables are added to each array expression. The declarations for these index variables are also generated. This particular behavior of the program generator is determined by the definition of the parameter type for dim.

1.2   Dimension-Independent Array Slicing

We can also define an array slicing subroutine, which slices an n-dimensional array on the dth dimension. In the subroutine slice, a is the input n-dimensional array, b is the result $(n-1)$-dimensional array, and k is the index on the dth dimension of the input array. This program is parameterized by two parameters. The parameter dim is an integer representing the number of dimensions of a. It only parameterizes the declaration of a. The parameter slice is a pair of integers of the form (n,d), representing that the generated code slices the dth dimension

---

[1] This example is meant for illustration. Dimension-independent array addition is already supported in Fortran by array syntax.

of an n-dimensional array. The parameter `slice` is not a Fortran variable, but a variable of Parametric Fortran. Therefore, it causes no conflict with the name of the subroutine.

```
subroutine slice(a, k, b)
    {dim:   real :: a}
    {slice: real :: b}
    integer :: k
    {slice: b = a(k)}
end subroutine slice
```

For example, when `dim` is 3 and `slice` is (3,2), the generated Fortran subroutine will be able to compute the kth slice of the second dimension of a 3-dimensional array. As in the first example, we assume for simplicity that the size of each dimension is 100.

```
subroutine slice(a, k, b)
    integer :: i1, i2
    real, dimension (1:100, 1:100, 1:100) :: a
    real, dimension (1:100, 1:100) :: b
    integer :: k
    do i1 = 1, 100
      do i2 = 1, 100
        b(i1, i2) = a(i1, k, i2)
      end do
    end do
end subroutine slice
```

The declaration of `a` is parameterized by an integer, which has the same meaning as in the first example. The declaration of `b` is parameterized by the parameter `slice`, which is a pair of integers (n,d). This parameterization means that in the generated program `b` has (n-1) dimensions and that array indices are added such that the already existing index expression (in the example: k) will appear at the dth dimension. How the different types of parameters guide the program generation has to be defined as part of the parameter definition, which specifies the program generator. Since n represents the number of the dimensions and d represents one of the n dimensions, d must be in the range 1 to n. The program generator can report an error if the value of `slice` is, for example, (2,3). We also have to ensure that n must be equal to `dim`. Otherwise, the generated Fortran program will contain a type error.

2 An Application in Scientific Computing

We consider as a real-world application the generation of inversion tools in the domain of ocean modeling. The Inverse Ocean Modeling (IOM) system [3,9] is a data assimilation system, which enables the developers of ocean models to combine their models with real observations of the ocean. The output of the

IOM is a weighted least-squared best-fit to the equations of motion and to the data. The IOM consists of tools that are used for solving the equations of best fit.

Since every ocean model uses its own data structure to describe the ocean, it is impossible to write a system in Fortran that works with different ocean models, although the algorithm for inverse ocean modeling is the same for all models. The genericity that is inherent in the problem cannot be expressed by Fortran.

With Parametric Fortran the IOM tools can be written in a generic way so that different Fortran programs can be generated automatically as needed. Using an extension of Fortran supports the idea of "gentle slope" [14] and allows the developers of the IOM, who are familiar with Fortran, to start writing the tools without first having to learn a completely new language. Moreover, most of their current programs can be modified to Parametric Fortran programs with reasonable effort. The main task is to identify the parameters for representing the model-dependent information.

2.1   An Example Tool: Markovian Convolution in Time

The IOM tool described here is an example of a convolution tool used for averaging over weighted values. The basic idea is to compute the value of one point by averaging over the weighted values of its neighbors. The weights of its neighbors depend on the distances from the point. The *Markovian Convolution in Time* is formally defined by the following continuous equation.

$$b(t) = \int_0^T \exp(-|t - t'|/\tau)a(t')dt'$$

The weighting function is $\exp(-|t - t'|/\tau)$, and the variables t and t' range over time, which means that the convolution is in time. The coefficient τ is the correlation time scale, which is provided by the ocean modelers when they use the tool. The smaller τ is, the more quickly the values of the old points will be forgotten.

The above formula is a continuous equation. Computer simulations are based on the following corresponding discrete equations that can be derived from the continuous one through techniques developed in [3].

$$
\begin{aligned}
h_L &= 0 & \frac{h_n - h_{n-1}}{\Delta t} + \tau^{-1} h_{n-1} &= -2\tau^{-1} a_n \\
b_U &= -(\tau/2)h_U & \frac{b_{n+1} - b_n}{\Delta t} - \tau^{-1} b_{n+1} &= h_n
\end{aligned}
$$

In the above equations, h represents a temporary array, and L (U) is the lower (upper) boundary of the arrays. The arrays are over time and space where different models may use different array dimensions for space. The number of time dimension is always one. However, different models may have different numbers of space dimensions. Therefore, the IOM has to provide different subroutines for all the possible data structures used in all the models. Moreover, the IOM should also be able to provide tools for any new model that uses data structures in a completely new way.

2.2 Expressing Markovian Convolution in Parametric Fortran

For parameterizing Markovian Convolution, we first have to find the parameters representing the model-dependent information. In this example, the model-dependent information is the number of space dimensions of the arrays, and the size (lower bound and upper bound) of each dimension. We suppose that the time dimension is always the first dimension of the arrays in all the models. In the convolution tool that is actually implemented for the IOM system we also parameterize the position of the time dimension, but for simplicity we do not do that in this example. We can define a Haskell data type Dim to represent the model-dependent information as follows.

```
data Space = Space Int [(IExpr, IExpr)]
data IExpr = ICon Int | IVar VName | ...
```

For example, the parameter value Dim 2 [(IVar "X", IVar "Y"), (ICon 1, ICon 100)] specifies that the number of dimensions of the arrays in the model is 2, that the first dimension is bounded by variables X and Y, (where X is the lower bound and Y is the upper bound), and that the second dimension is bounded by 1 and 100.

Since the only dependent information is given by the space dimensions of the arrays, including the number of dimensions and the boundaries of each dimension, we only need one parameter type Space. Every array has the same type, which means that the array variable declarations can be parameterized by the same parameter. However, one parameter is not sufficient to parameterize the body of the subroutine because we want to be able to group assignment statements in the same loop, instead of getting a separate loop for each assignment. This distinction of different "loop groups" requires additional information to indicate if a loop over space dimensions needs to be generated, which is captured by two tags.

```
data Pos a = Loop a | Inside a
```

We use Pos Space to parameterize both declarations and assignments. If an assignment is parameterized by Loop s, a loop over the space dimensions is generated. However, if an assignment is parameterized by Inside s, no loop will be generated, the program generator just adds index variables to each array expression. The Parametric Fortran code for the Markovian Convolution is shown below.

```
subroutine timeConv {d: (L, U, a, b)}
  real :: dt, tau
  {d: real, dimension (!L:!U) :: a, b, h}
  integer :: n
  {d:
    {x: h(!L) = 0.0}
    {x(a,b,h):
      do n = L, U
         h(n) = h(n-1) - dt*(h(n-1)/tau + 2.0*a(n)/tau)
      end do
      b(U) = -0.5*h(U)/tau
      do n = L, U
         b(n) = b(n+1) - dt*(h(n) + b(n+1)/tau)
      end do
    }
  }
end subroutine timeConv
```

The value of parameter d is Loop s, where s represents the space dimensions of the arrays. The parameter d is used to parameterize 3 parts of the subroutine.

- The parameter list of the generated Fortran subroutine to add the new variables used in s's value as dimension boundaries
- The declarations of the array variables to append the space dimensions to the current time dimension of these arrays
- The body of the subroutine to create loops.

The symbol ! is used to stop the downward propagation of a parameter for a particular part of the syntax tree. For example, since L is a non-array variable, we do not want to parameterize it by x in the first assignment.[2] The parameter x has the value of Inside s since the assignments parameterized by x do not need their own loops to be generated. However, all the array expressions in the assignment statements parameterized by x will be filled by index variables of the space dimensions. We also provide a form of applicability constraint for parameters by allowing a list of variables to be added after the parameter. For instance, the syntax {x(a,b,h):...} expresses that the parameter x only parameterizes the variables a, b, and h, or array expressions using these names, such as h(n). When we generate the Fortran subroutine timeConv for the model in which the arrays have 1 space dimension and the boundaries of that dimension is (X:Y), we can assign d and x the following values.

```
d, x :: Pos Space
s    :: Space
s = Space 1 [(IVar "X", IVar "Y")]
d = Loop s
x = Inside s
```

---

[2] Since every node in the syntax tree can be annotated only by one parameter, we could not use d and x to annotate the whole body. Therefore, we have parameterized the first assignment and the remaining sequence of assignments separately.

With these parameter values the program generator creates the following sub-routine.

```
subroutine timeConv (X, Y, L, U, a, b)
  integer :: i1
  real    :: dt, tau
  real, dimension (L:U, X:Y) :: a, b, h
  integer :: n
  do i1 = X, Y
    h(L,i1) = 0.0
    do n = L, U
      h(n,i1) = h(n-1,i1) - dt*(h(n-1,i1)/tau + 2.0*a(n,i1)/tau)
    end do
    b(U,i1) = -0.5*h(U,i1)/tau
    do n = L, U
      b(n,i1) = b(n+1,i1) - dt*(h(n,i1) + b(n+1,i1)/tau)
    end do
  end do
end subroutine timeConv
```

The program generator had the following effects. (1) X and Y are added to the parameter list of the generated subroutine. (2) The arrays a, b, and h are declared as 2-dimensional arrays. (3) The body of the subroutine is wrapped by a loop over the space dimension. (4) Every array expression is extended by an additional index variable i1. (5) i1's declaration is generated.

3   Implementation of the Parametric Fortran Compiler

3.1   The Parametric Fortran Parser

For the implementation of the front end of Parametric Fortran we have used the Haskell scanner generator Alex [5] and the parser generator Happy [13]. The parser deals with a subset of Fortran language and ignores some esoteric "features". For example, we do not allow spaces inside identifiers. Figure 2 shows part of the syntax of Parametric Fortran. It illustrates for the syntactic categories *Stmt* and *Expr* how every syntactic category of Fortran is extended by two forms of parameterization.

We use {p:e} to represent that the syntactic object e is parameterized by the parameter p. The semantics of such a parameter annotation is that e itself is parameterized by p and also that p is propagated downward to all (parameteri-zable) descendants in the syntax tree. We use !e to stop the effect of a possibly propagated parameter on e, which means e and all of its subexpressions are not parameterized at all. A parameter can be extended by a list of variables that restrict the downward propagation to just this set of variables. For example, in {p(v):e} only variable occurrences of v and array expressions v(...) inside e will be parameterized by p. This form of parameter applicability constraints is currently limited to variables, a language for allowing the specification of tree patterns to be parameterized is part of future work.

$$
\begin{array}{lll}
StmtP & ::= & !\{Stmt\} \mid \{Param\!:\!Stmt\} \mid Stmt \\
ExprP & ::= & !\,Expr \mid \{Param\!:\!Expr\} \mid Expr \\
Param & ::= & PName \mid PName(VName,\dots,VName) \\
Stmt & ::= & Assg \mid DoStmt \mid StmtP\ StmtP \\
Assg & ::= & VName{=}ExprP \mid Array{=}ExprP \\
DoStmt & ::= & \mathbf{do}\ VName{=}ExprP,ExprP\ StmtP \\
Expr & ::= & PName \mid VName \mid Array \mid Const \mid UOp\ ExprP \\
 & & \mid\ ExprP\ BOp\ ExprP \mid (Expr) \\
Array & ::= & VName(ExprP,\dots,ExprP) \\
UOp & ::= & \text{-} \\
BOp & ::= & {+} \mid {-} \mid {*} \mid {/}
\end{array}
$$

Fig. 2. Syntax of Parameterized Fortran.

3.2 Abstract Syntax

For lack of space, we only show an excerpt of the abstract Fortran syntax. For example, Stmt only contains assignment, loop, and sequential statements. The Haskell definitions of the data types for Fortran statements and expressions are shown below.

```
data Stmt = Assg VarName [ExprP] ExprP
          | For  VarName ExprP ExprP StmtP
          | Sequ StmtP StmtP
            deriving (Typeable,Data)

data Expr = IntCon Int
          | RealCon Float
          | Var VarName [ExprP]
          | Bin BinOp ExprP ExprP
            deriving (Typeable,Data)
```

The data types StmtP and ExprP represent parameterized Fortran statements and expression. A syntactic object may contain parameterized sub-objects, for example, a Fortran assignment statement, which is of type Stmt, may contain parameterized Fortran expressions, which are of type ExprP. These data types must be instances of type classes Typeable and Data, because we have to apply the functions cast and everywhere (described below) to elements of these types.

Since every Fortran syntactic category can be parameterized, we need a data type for each parameterized Fortran syntactic category. The following code shows the data type definitions for parameterized Fortran statements and expressions.

```
data StmtP = forall p . Param p Stmt => F p Stmt
data ExprP = forall p . Param p Expr => E p Expr
```

We use existential types to facilitate the use of parameters of different types at different nodes in the syntax tree.

3.3   A Type Class for Program Generation

We define a multiple parameter type class `Param` to represent the relation between a parameter type and the data type of a syntactic category. Again, the context `Data p` is needed because we want to use the function `everywhere` to implement traversals of the syntax tree together with a type-based selective application of a generator function.

```
class (Show p,Data p,Show e) => Param p e where
  showP  :: p -> e -> String
  gen    :: p -> e -> e
  check  :: p -> e -> Bool
  -- default implementations
  gen   _   = id
  check _ _ = True
```

In the above definition, `p` represents the parameter type and `e` represents the syntactic category. The member function `showP` is used for pretty-printing the parameterized program. The program generator `gen` takes a parameter value and a Fortran syntactic object as input and generates a non-parameterized syntactic object. The member function `check` can be used to implement validity checks for parameterized program. For lack of space we cannot describe the details of this part of the program generator.

The data type `Void` is a parameter type used in those cases in which no parameter is needed. `Void` can be used to parameterize any syntactic category. In Section 3.5 we will demonstrate how parameterized programs are transformed to programs parameterized by `Void`. Programs that are parameterized by `Void` are pretty-printed as plain Fortran programs by `showP`. The `Void` parameter uses the default definition for `gen` and `check`.

```
data Void = Void deriving (Eq,Typeable,Data)

instance Show Void where
   show Void = ""

instance Show a => Param Void a where
```

Since parameters in Parametric Fortran programs are variables, we define the type of variable names `VarName` as an instance of the type class `Param`. Similar to `Void`, `VarName` can be used to parameterize any syntactic category and its `gen` function does nothing. The Parametric Fortran parser is a function of type `String->FortranP`. In the parsing result, all parameters are of type `VarName`. For generating the Fortran programs, we have to supply values for the parameters so that every parameter name in the abstract syntax tree can be replaced by the parameter's value. We have defined a derived type class `Par p` to be able to succinctly express that `p` is a valid parameter type of Parametric Fortran.

```
class (Param p Expr, Param p Stmt, ...) => Par p where
```

In other words, only if the type p can be used to parameterize all the Fortran syntactic categories, it is an instance of the type class `Par`. We use a heterogeneous list `param` of type `PList` to store parameters of different types.

```
data ParV  = forall p . Par p => ParV p
type PList =  [(VarName, ParV)]
```

Parameter names are replaced by parameter values through a collection of functions that look up the values of parameters in the list `param`. For example, the function `substE` maps expressions parameterized by parameter names to expressions parameterized by the parameters' values.

```
substE :: ExprP -> ExprP
substE (E p e) = case lookup (getName p) param of
                      Nothing        -> E Void e
                      Just (ParV p') -> E p' e


getName :: forall p . Par p => p -> VarName
getName = (\p->(VarName "")) `extQ` id
```

We have similar functions for all other other syntactic categories. The function `getName` in the above definition is a generic function that works on any parameter type, but only gets a valid value for the type `VarName`. This genericity is realized by the function `extQ`, which was introduced in [12] to extend generic queries of type `Typeable a => a->r` by a new type-specific case.

3.4   Defining Parameter Types as Instances of `Param`

In the array slicing example, we have two parameter types, `Dim` and `Slice`. The type `Dim` specifies the number of dimensions of an array. The type `Slice` is used for parameterizing the dimension to be sliced.

```
data Dim   = Dim Int
data Slice = Slice Int Int
```

To use these types to parameterize Fortran programs, we have to make them instances of the `Param` type class for all Fortran syntactic categories. Figure 3 shows how to define the `gen` function for the parameter type `Dim` for every Fortran syntactic category. Most instance declarations use the default definition of `gen`. We only have to consider the cases of extending a type by dimensions, adding loops around a statement, and filling an expression with index variables.

The index variables used for extending array expressions and generating loops are generated by the function `newVar::Int->VName`. The names of these generated index variables are illegal Fortran names. The program generator just marks the places where a new variable is needed. After a program is generated, the function `freshNames` traverses the complete program and renames every marked place with an unused variable name and add declarations for these variables to the program. Although we could have implemented the generation of fresh variables with a state monad directly, we decided not to do so, because that would have complicated the interface for implementing new parameters.

```
instance Param Dim Type  where
  gen (Dim d) (BaseType bt)  = ArrayT (indx d) bt
  gen (Dim d) (ArrayT rs bt) = ArrayT (rs++indx d) bt
  gen p       t              = t
      where indx d = replicate d [(a,b)]

instance Param Dim Stmt  where
  gen (Dim d) s | d>0 = gen (Dim (d-1)) (For (newVar d) a b (F Void s))
  gen p       s       = s

instance Param Dim Expr where
  gen (Dim d) (Var v es) = Var v (es++map (var . newVar) [1..d])
  gen p       e          = e

a = E Void (IntCon 1)
b = E Void (IntCon 100)

var :: VName -> ExprP
var v = E Void (Var v [])
```

Fig. 3. Example Parameter Implementation

3.5   Transformation Functions

For every Fortran syntactic category, a transformation function is defined.
Whereas **gen** has to be implemented for every new parameter type, the transformation functions are defined once and for all. They transform a parameterized
syntactic object into a Fortran object parameterized by **Void**. The following code
shows how these transformation functions are defined for Fortran statements and
Fortran expressions. The approach is to extract the parameter **p** from the node
in the syntax tree and apply the function **gen** with this parameter to the syntax
constructor under consideration. Other Fortran syntactic categories are dealt
with similarly.

```
transF :: StmtP -> StmtP
transF (F p f) = F Void (gen p f)

transE :: ExprP -> ExprP
transE (E p e) = E Void (gen p e)
```

We can observe that every transformation function has the type a->a. That
enables us to apply the function **everywhere** [12] to build a generic transformation function **genF**, which is basically the program generator. The function
everywhere is a generic traversal combinator that applies its argument function to every node in a tree. The argument function is a generic transformation function of type forall b. Data b => b->b. We can lift a non-generic
transformation function **f**, which has the type Data t => t->t, into a generic
transformation function **g** by the function **extT** as follows.

```
g = id 'extT' f
```

Therefore, `extT` allows the composition of different behaviors on different types into one generic function. In the definition of `genF`, we use `extT` to compose different transformation functions for different syntactic categories. By applying the function `everywhere` to a generic transformation function `g`, we obtain another generic transformation function, which applies `g` to every node in a tree. Therefore, `genF` can be defined in the following way.

```
genF :: Data g => g -> g
genF = everywhere (id     'extT'
                   transF 'extT'
                   transE 'extT' ...)
```

The function `genF` takes a parameterized Fortran program as input and outputs a Fortran program in which every syntactic object is parameterized by `Void`. The source code of the generated Fortran program can be obtained by calling the `showP` function.

4   Related Work

The Earth System Modeling Framework (ESMF) defines an architecture that allows the composition of applications using a component-based approach [6, 4]. The focus of the ESMF is to define standardized programming interfaces and to collect and provide data structures and utilities for developing model components.

Parametric Fortran was developed for the use in scientific computing. Most scientific computing applications deal with huge data sets. Usually, these data sets are represented by arrays. The data structures of these arrays, such as the number of dimensions, are often changed in different models to which the same algorithm will be applied. The programming languages APL [10] and J [11] have built-in mechanisms for computing with variable-dimensional arrays. However, since APL and J only provide efficient operations for array processing, they have not been widely used in scientific computing area, which also requires efficient numerical computations. Although Matlab [2] is popular for testing simulations on small examples, it is too inefficient for large data sets.

Parametric Fortran is essentially a metaprogramming tool. For a comprehensive overview over the field, see [16]. Existing Fortran metaprogramming tools include Foresys [18], whose focus is on the refactoring of existing Fortran code, for example, transforming a Fortran77 program into Fortran90 program. Sage++ [1] is a tool for building Fortran/C metaprogramming tools. However, to express applications as the ones shown here a user has to write metaprograms in Sage++ for transforming Fortran, which is quite difficult and error prone and probably beyond the capabilities of scientists who otherwise just use Fortran. In contrast, Parametric Fortran allows the users to work mostly in Fortran and express generic parts by parameters; most of the metaprogramming issues are hidden inside the compiler and parameter definitions. Macrofort [8] can generate Fortran code from Maple programs and does not provide the mechanism to deal with generic, model-dependent code. In metaprogramming systems like MetaML [19] or Template Haskell [17] the metaprogramming language is an extension of the object language. In Parametric Fortran, metaprogramming happens in two different languages: (i) parameters are defined in Haskell and (ii) parameter-dependencies in object programs is expressed in Parametric Fortran syntax.

There has also been a lot of work on the generation of Fortran code for simulations in all areas of science. All this work is concerned with the generation of efficient code for *one particular* scientific model. For example, CTADEL [20] is a Fortran code-generation tool, which is applied to weather forecasting; its focus is on solving weather-forecast models, especially, solving partial differential equations. This and other similar tools do not address the problem of the modularization of scientific models to facilitate generic specifications.

The work reported in [7] is similar to ours in the sense that scientific computations are described in functional way and are then translated into lower-level efficient code. But again, the approach does not take into account model-dependent specifications.

5   Conclusions

Parametric Fortran provides a framework for defining Fortran program generators through the definition of parameter structures. The system offers a two-level architecture to Fortran program parameterization and generation. On the first level, the definition of parameter structures creates a Fortran dialect for a particular class of applications. On the second level, programs for different problems can be implemented within one Fortran dialect employing parameters in similar or different ways. Any such Parametric Fortran program can be translated into different ordinary Fortran programs by providing different sets of parameter values.

We have successfully applied Parameteric Fortran in the area of scientific computing to enable the generic specification of inverse ocean modeling tools. The general, two-level framework promises opportunities for applications in many other areas as well. In one tool (space convolution) we had to employ a parameter that allows the parameterization by Fortran subroutines and provides limited support for higher-order subroutines. This extension turned out to be a straightforward task. From the experience we have gained so far and from the feedback from ocean scientists we conclude that Parameteric Fortran is a flexible and expressive language that provides customized genericity for Fortran through a pragmatic approach. The use of advanced Haskell features was essential in this approach.

References

1. F. Bodin, P. Beckman, D. Gannon, J. Gotwals, and S. Srinivas. Sage++: A Class Library for Building Fortran 90 and C++ Restructuring Tools. In *Second Object-Oriented Numerics Conference (OON-SKI'94)*, pages 122–138, 1994.

2. S. J. Chapman. *MATLAB Programming for Engineers*. Brooks Cole, 2001.
3. B. Chua and A. F. Bennett. An Inverse Ocean Modeling System. *Ocean Modelling*, 3:137–165, 2001.
4. R. E. Dickenson, S. E. Zebiak, J. L. Anderson, M. L. Blackmon, C. DeLuca, T. F. Hogan, M. Iredell, M. Ji, R. Rood, M. J. Suarez, and K. E. Taylor. How Can We Advance Our Weather and Climate Models as a Community? *Bulletin of the American Meteorological Society*, 83(3), 2002.
5. C. Dornan. Alex: A Lex for Haskell Programmers, 1997. `http://haskell.org/libraries/alextar.gz`.
6. R. Ferraro, T. Sato, G. Brasseur, C. DeLuca, and E. Guilyardi. Modeling The Earth System. In *Int. Symp. on Geoscience and Remote Sensing*, 2003.
7. S. Fitzpatrick, T. J. Harmer, A. Stewart, M. Clint, and J. M. Boyle. The Automated Transformation of Abstract Specifications of Numerical Algorithms into Efficient Array Processor Implementations. *Science of Computer Programming*, 28(1):1–41, 1997.
8. C. Gomez and P. Capolsini. Macroc and Macrofort, C and Fortran Code Generation Within Maple. *Maple Technical Newsletter*, 3(1), 1996.
9. IOM. `http://iom.asu.edu/`.
10. K. E. Iverson. *Introduction to APL*. APL Press, 1984.
11. K. E. Iverson. *J Introduction and Dictionary*. Iverson Software Inc., Toronto, Canada, 1995.
12. R. Lämmel and S. Peyton Jones. Scrap Your Boilerplate: A Practical Design Pattern for Generic Programming. In *ACM SIGPLAN Workshop on Types in Language Design and Implementation*, pages 26–37, 2003.
13. S. Marlow and A. Gill. Happy User Guide, 2000. `http://www.haskell.org/happy/doc/html/happy.html`.
14. B. Myers, S. Hudson, and R. Pausch. Past, Present, and Future of User Interface Software Tools. *ACM Transactions on Computer-Human Interaction*, 7(1):3–28, 2000.
15. S. L. Peyton Jones. *Haskell 98 Language and Libraries: The Revised Report*. Cambridge University Press, Cambridge, UK, 2003.
16. T. Sheard. Accomplishments and Research Challenges in Meta-Programming. In *2nd Int. Workshop on Semantics, Applications, and Implementation of Program Generation*, LNCS 2196, pages 2–44, 2001.
17. T. Sheard and S. L. Peyton Jones. Template Metaprogramming for Haskell. In *Haskell Workshop*, 2002.
18. Simulog, SA, Guyancourt, France. *FORESYS, FORtran Engineering SYStem, Reference Manual v1.5*, 1996.
19. W. Taha and T. Sheard. MetaML and Multi-Stage Programming with Explicit Annotations. *Theoretical Computer Science*, 248(1–2):211–242, 2000.
20. R. van Engelen, L. Wolters, and G. Cats. The CTADEL Application Driver for Numerical Weather Forecast Systems. In *15th IMACS World Congress*, volume 4, pages 571–576, 1997.

Typing XHTML Web Applications in ML

Martin Elsman and Ken Friis Larsen

IT University of Copenhagen.
Glentevej 67, DK-2400 Copenhagen NV, Denmark
mael@itu.dk, ken@friislarsen.net

Abstract. In this paper, we present a type system for typing Web applications in SMLserver, an efficient multi-threaded Web server platform for Standard ML scriptlets. The type system guarantees that only conforming XHTML documents are sent to clients and that forms are used consistently and in a type-safe way. The type system is encoded in the type system of Standard ML using so-called phantom types.

1   Introduction

Traditionally, frameworks for developing Web applications give little guarantees about the conformity of generated HTML or XHTML documents, and, most often, no static mechanism guarantees that the particular use of form data is consistent with the construction of a corresponding form.

We present a static type system for SMLserver [5] that guarantees generated XHTML documents to conform to the XHTML 1.0 specification [21]. The conformity requirements are enforced by requiring the Web programmer to construct XHTML documents using a combinator library for which the different requirements are encoded in the types of element combinators using phantom types [1,7,8,13,18,19,20]. The type system also guarantees that forms in generated documents are consistent with actual form data submitted by clients.

A scriptlet in SMLserver is represented as a functor with the argument representing form data to be received from a client and the body representing program code to be executed when the scriptlet is requested by a client. In this sense, scriptlet functors are instantiated dynamically by SMLserver upon client requests, which may result in new documents being sent to clients. Because it is not possible to encode the recursive nature of scriptlets directly using Standard ML modules, an *abstract scriptlet interface*, containing typing information about accessible scriptlets and their form arguments, is generated prior to compilation, based on preprocessing of scriptlet functor arguments. The generated abstract scriptlet interface takes the form of an abstract Standard ML structure, which can be referred to by scriptlets and library code to construct XHTML forms and hyper-link anchors in a type safe way.

The type safe encoding is complete in the sense that it does not restrict what conforming XHTML documents it is possible to write. There are two exceptions to this completeness guarantee. First, a form must relate to its target scriptlet in the sense that form data submitted by a form is consistent with the scriptlet's

B. Jayaraman (Ed.): PADL 2004, LNCS 3057, pp. 224–238, 2004.

expectations of form data. Second, form variable arguments appearing in hyperlink anchors to scriptlets must be consistent with the scriptlet's expectations of form variable arguments.

1.1   Contributions

The paper contains two main contributions. First, in Sect. 2 and 3, we present a novel approach to enforce conformity of generated XHTML 1.0 documents [21], based on a typed combinator library that makes use of phantom types. Although others have suggested type systems for guaranteeing conformity of generated XHTML documents [17,18,19,20], no other approaches can be used for embedding XHTML documents in ML-like languages without support for type classes [12]. To the best of our knowledge, our encoding of linearity constraints using phantom types is novel.

Second, in Sect. 4, we present a type based technique for enforcing consistency between a scriptlet's use of form variables and the construction of forms that target that scriptlet. For this technique, we introduce the concept of *type lists* (i.e., lists at the type level), also encoded using phantom types. Moreover, we contribute with a type-indexed function [9,14,22] for swapping arbitrary elements in type lists.

The contributions are formally justified and the techniques are implemented in SMLserver and have been used for building various Web applications, including a form extensive quiz for employees at the IT University of Copenhagen. It is our experience that the approach scales well to large Web applications and that the type system catches many critical programming mistakes early in the application development. It is also our experience that type errors caused by erroneous use of XHTML combinators are understandable and pinpoint problems directly.

A formalization of scriptlets, in the style of [10], that captures the basic Web application model used by SMLserver is given in a companion technical report [6]. Related work is described in Sect. 5. Finally, in Sect. 6, we conclude.

2   Conformity of XHTML Documents

In essence, for a document to *conform* to the XHTML 1.0 specification [21], the document must be well-formed, valid according to a particular DTD, and obey certain element prohibitions.

Well-formedness: For a document to be well-formed, all start-tags must have a corresponding closing-tag, all elements must be properly nested, and no attribute name may appear more than once in the same start-tag.

Validity: A valid XHTML document must be derivable from the grammar described by the XHTML DTD.

Element prohibitions: The XHTML 1.0 specification describes a set of prohibitions that are not specified by the XHTML DTD [21, App. B], but which must be satisfied for an XHTML document to be conforming. For example, an element prohibition specifies that, to all depth of nesting, an anchor element `<a ...>` ... `</a>` must not be contained in other anchor elements.

2.1 Motivating Example

The program code in Fig. 1 shows an abbreviated interface to a typical library of combinators for generating XHTML (the signature `MICRO_XHTML`). Fig. 1 also shows some sample utility code for generating an XHTML table from a list of `string` lists (the function `toTable`).

```
signature MICRO_XHTML = sig          open MicroXHtml
  type elt                           fun concat es =
  val $ : string -> elt                foldr & ($"") es
  val & : elt * elt -> elt           fun toCols xs =
  val td    : elt -> elt               concat (map (td o $) xs)
  val tr    : elt -> elt             fun toRows xs =
  val table : elt -> elt               concat (map (tr o toCols) xs)
end                                  fun toTable strings =
structure MicroXHtml = ...             table(toRows strings)
```

Fig. 1. An unsafe XHTML combinator library and application code.

Although the `MicroXHtml` library ensures that well-formed XHTML code is generated [18] (ignoring the linearity condition for attributes), the library does not ensure that the generated XHTML code is valid. In particular, if the empty list is given as argument to the function `toTable`, a `table` element is generated containing no `tr` elements, which is not valid XHTML code according to the XHTML DTD. Similarly, if one of the lists in the argument to the function `toRows` is the empty list, a `tr` element is constructed containing no `td` elements.

An alternative interface could allow the programmer to construct XHTML documents directly through a set of datatype constructors. It turns out, however, that, due to XHTML 1.0 element prohibitions and the linearity well-formedness condition on attributes, such an approach cannot be made type safe in ML. Moreover, the approach would burden the programmer with the need for an excessive amount of tagging and datatype coercions.

2.2 Mini XHTML

To demonstrate the phantom type approach for a small subset of XHTML 1.0, consider the language Mini XHTML defined by the following DTD:

```
<!ENTITY  %block  "p|table|pre">      <!ELEMENT p      (%inline)*>
<!ENTITY  %inline "%inpre|big">       <!ELEMENT em     (%inline)*>
<!ENTITY  %flow   "%block|%inline">   <!ELEMENT big    (%inline)*>
<!ENTITY  %inpre  "#PCDATA|em">       <!ELEMENT pre    (%inpre)*>
<!ENTITY  %td     "td">               <!ELEMENT td     (%flow)*>
<!ENTITY  %tr     "tr">               <!ELEMENT tr     (%td)+>
                                      <!ELEMENT table  (%tr)+>
```

The DTD defines a context free grammar for Mini XHTML, which captures an essential subset of XHTML, namely the distinction between inline, block, flow, td, and tr entities, the notion of sequencing, and a weakened form of element prohibitions easily expressible in a DTD. We postpone the discussion of attributes to Sect. 3.

For constructing documents, we use the following grammar, where t ranges over a finite set of *tags* and c ranges over finite sequences of character data:

$$d ::= c \mid t(d) \mid d_1\, d_2 \mid \varepsilon$$

The construct $d_1\, d_2$ denotes a sequence of documents d_1 and d_2 and ε denotes the empty document.

To formally define whether a document d is valid according to the Mini XHTML DTD, we introduce the relation $\models d : \kappa$, where κ ranges over entity names (i.e., inline, inpre, block, flow, tr, and td) defined in the DTD. The relation $\models d : \kappa$ expresses that d is a valid document of entity κ. The relation is defined inductively by a straightforward translation of the DTD into inference rules, which allow inference of sentences of the form $\models d : \kappa$.

Valid Documents $\boxed{\models d : \kappa}$

$$\frac{\models d : \mathtt{inpre}}{\models d : \mathtt{inline}} \qquad \frac{\models d : \mathtt{inline}}{\models \mathtt{em}(d) : \mathtt{inpre}} \qquad \frac{\models d : \mathtt{inline}}{\models \mathtt{p}(d) : \mathtt{block}} \qquad \frac{\models d : \mathtt{inline}}{\models \mathtt{big}(d) : \mathtt{inline}}$$

$$\frac{\models d : \mathtt{inpre}}{\models \mathtt{pre}(d) : \mathtt{block}} \qquad \frac{\models d : \mathtt{flow}}{\models \mathtt{td}(d) : \mathtt{td}} \qquad \frac{\models d : \mathtt{td}}{\models \mathtt{tr}(d) : \mathtt{tr}} \qquad \frac{\models d : \mathtt{tr}}{\models \mathtt{table}(d) : \mathtt{block}}$$

$$\frac{}{\models c : \mathtt{inpre}} \qquad \frac{\models d : \mathtt{inline}}{\models d : \mathtt{flow}} \qquad \frac{\models d : \mathtt{block}}{\models d : \mathtt{flow}}$$

$$\frac{\models d_1 : \kappa \quad \models d_2 : \kappa}{\models d_1\, d_2 : \kappa} \qquad \frac{\kappa \in \{\mathtt{block}, \mathtt{inline}, \mathtt{inpre}, \mathtt{flow}\}}{\models \varepsilon : \kappa}$$

A signature for a combinator library for Mini XHTML is given in Fig. 2 together with a concrete implementation. The signature specifies a type constructor ('ent,'pre)elt for element sequences, which takes two *phantom type* parameters. The first phantom type parameter is used for specifying the entity

```
signature MINI_XHTML = sig              structure MiniXHtml :> MINI_XHTML =
 type ('blk,'inl)flw and tr and td      struct infix &
 type blk and inl and NOT and inpre      datatype e = Elt of string*e
 type ('ent,'pre)elt and preclosed        | Emp | Seq of e*e | S of string
 val $ : string->(('b,inl)flw,'p)elt     type ('ent,'pre)elt = e
 val p : ((NOT,inl)flw,'p)elt            type blk = unit and inl = unit
       -> ((blk,'i)flw,'p)elt             and NOT = unit
 val em : ((NOT,inl)flw,'p)elt           type ('b,'i)flw = unit
       -> (('b,inl)flw,'p)elt             and tr = unit and td = unit
 val pre : ((NOT,inl)flw,inpre)elt       type inpre = unit
       -> ((blk,'i)flw,'p)elt            type preclosed = unit
 val big : ((NOT,inl)flw,'p)elt          fun $ s = S s
       -> (('b,inl)flw,preclosed)elt     fun em e = Elt("em",e)
 val table : (tr,'p)elt                  fun p e = Elt("p",e)
       -> ((blk,'i)flw,'p)elt            fun big e = Elt("big",e)
 val tr : (td,'p)elt -> (tr,'p)elt       fun pre e = Elt("pre",e)
 val td : ((blk,inl)flw,'p)elt           fun td e = Elt("td",e)
       -> (td,'p)elt                     fun tr e = Elt("tr",e)
 val & : ('e,'p)elt * ('e,'p)elt         fun table e = Elt("table",e)
       -> ('e,'p)elt                     fun emp() = Emp
 val emp : unit -> (('b,'i)flw,'p)elt    fun e & e' = Seq(e,e')
end                                     end
```

Fig. 2. Mini XHTML combinator library.

of the element in terms of *entity types*, which are types formed with the NOT, blk, inl, flw, tr, and td type constructors (all implemented as type unit). For instance, the p combinator requires its argument to be an inline entity, expressed with the entity type (NOT,inl)flw, which classifies sequences of flow entities that do not contain block entities. The result type of the p combinator expresses that the result is a block entity, which may be regarded either as a pure block entity of type (blk,NOT)flw or as a flow entity with type (blk,inl)flw.

Using the infix sequence combinator &, it is impossible to combine a block entity with an inline entity and use the result as an argument to the p combinator, for example. The result of combining block entities and inline entities can be used only in contexts requiring a flow entity (e.g., as argument to the td combinator).

The 'pre type parameter of the elt type constructor is used for implementing the element prohibition of XHTML 1.0 that, to all depth of nesting, prohibits big elements from appearing inside pre elements. This element prohibition implies the satisfaction of the weaker DTD requirement that prohibits a big element to appear immediately within a pre element.

Specialized elaboration rules for constructing documents in Standard ML with the combinators presented in Fig. 2 follow. The rules allow inference of sentences of the form $\vdash e : (\tau_e, \tau_p)$elt, where e ranges over expressions, τ_e over entity types, and τ_p over nullary type constructors inpre and preclosed. We shall also use τ_b to range over the type constructors blk and NOT, and τ_i to range over the type constructors inl and NOT.

Expressions $\qquad\qquad\qquad\qquad\qquad\qquad\boxed{\vdash e : (\tau_e, \tau_p)\texttt{elt}}$

$$\frac{}{\vdash \$\,c : ((\tau_b, \texttt{inl})\texttt{flw}, \tau_p)\texttt{elt}} \qquad \frac{\vdash e : ((\texttt{NOT}, \texttt{inl})\texttt{flw}, \tau_p)\texttt{elt}}{\vdash \texttt{p}\ e : ((\texttt{blk}, \tau_i)\texttt{flw}, \tau_p)\texttt{elt}}$$

$$\frac{\vdash e : ((\texttt{NOT}, \texttt{inl})\texttt{flw}, \tau_p)\texttt{elt}}{\vdash \texttt{em}\ e : ((\tau_b, \texttt{inl})\texttt{flw}, \tau_p)\texttt{elt}} \qquad \frac{\vdash e : ((\texttt{NOT}, \texttt{inl})\texttt{flw}, \texttt{inpre})\texttt{elt}}{\vdash \texttt{pre}\ e : ((\texttt{blk}, \tau_i)\texttt{flw}, \tau_p)\texttt{elt}}$$

$$\frac{\tau_p = \texttt{preclosed} \quad \vdash e : ((\texttt{NOT}, \texttt{inl})\texttt{flw}, \tau_p)\texttt{elt}}{\vdash \texttt{big}\ e : ((\tau_b, \texttt{inl})\texttt{flw}, \tau_p)\texttt{elt}} \qquad \frac{\vdash e_1 : (\tau_e, \tau_p)\texttt{elt} \quad \vdash e_2 : (\tau_e, \tau_p)\texttt{elt}}{\vdash e_1\ \&\ e_2 : (\tau_e, \tau_p)\texttt{elt}}$$

$$\frac{\vdash e : (\texttt{tr}, \tau_p)\texttt{elt}}{\vdash \texttt{table}\ e : ((\texttt{blk}, \tau_i)\texttt{flw}, \tau_p)\texttt{elt}} \qquad \frac{\vdash e : (\texttt{td}, \tau_p)\texttt{elt}}{\vdash \texttt{tr}\ e : (\texttt{tr}, \tau_p)\texttt{elt}}$$

$$\frac{\vdash e : ((\texttt{blk}, \texttt{inl})\texttt{flw}, \tau_p)\texttt{elt}}{\vdash \texttt{td}\ e : (\texttt{td}, \tau_p)\texttt{elt}} \qquad \frac{}{\vdash \texttt{emp}() : ((\tau_b, \tau_i)\texttt{flw}, \tau_p)\texttt{elt}}$$

The implementation of the MINI_XHTML signature is defined in terms of documents by the function *doc*:

$$\begin{aligned}
doc(\$\ c) &= c & doc(\texttt{table}\ e) &= \textbf{table}(doc(e)) \\
doc(\texttt{p}\ e) &= \textbf{p}(doc(e)) & doc(\texttt{tr}\ e) &= \textbf{tr}(doc(e)) \\
doc(\texttt{em}\ e) &= \textbf{em}(doc(e)) & doc(\texttt{td}\ e) &= \textbf{td}(doc(e)) \\
doc(\texttt{pre}\ e) &= \textbf{pre}(doc(e)) & doc(e_1\ \&\ e_2) &= doc(e_1)\ doc(e_2) \\
doc(\texttt{big}\ e) &= \textbf{big}(doc(e)) & doc(\texttt{emp}()) &= \varepsilon
\end{aligned}$$

Before we state a soundness property for the combinator library, we define a binary relation $\tau \sim \kappa$, relating element types τ and DTD entities κ. As before, τ_p ranges over the type constructors $\{\texttt{inpre}, \texttt{preclosed}\}$.

$$\begin{aligned}
((\texttt{blk}, \texttt{NOT})\texttt{flw}, \tau_p)\texttt{elt} &\sim \texttt{block} & ((\texttt{NOT}, \texttt{NOT})\texttt{flw}, \tau_p)\texttt{elt} &\sim \texttt{inpre} \\
((\texttt{NOT}, \texttt{NOT})\texttt{flw}, \tau_p)\texttt{elt} &\sim \texttt{inline} & ((\texttt{blk}, \texttt{inl})\texttt{flw}, \tau_p)\texttt{elt} &\sim \texttt{flow} \\
((\texttt{NOT}, \texttt{NOT})\texttt{flw}, \tau_p)\texttt{elt} &\sim \texttt{block} & (\texttt{td}, \tau_p)\texttt{elt} &\sim \texttt{td} \\
((\texttt{NOT}, \texttt{inl})\texttt{flw}, \texttt{inpre})\texttt{elt} &\sim \texttt{inpre} & (\texttt{tr}, \tau_p)\texttt{elt} &\sim \texttt{tr} \\
\end{aligned}$$
$$((\texttt{NOT}, \texttt{inl})\texttt{flw}, \texttt{preclosed})\texttt{elt} \sim \texttt{inline}$$

The soundness lemma states that well-typed expressions are valid according to the Mini XHTML DTD. The lemma is easily demonstrated by structural induction on the derivation $\vdash e : \tau$.

Lemma 1 (Soundness). *If $\vdash e : \tau$ and $\tau \sim \kappa$ then $\models doc(e) : \kappa$.*

The soundness lemma is supported by the property that if $\vdash e : \tau$ then there exists an entity κ such that $\tau \sim \kappa$.

The library is not complete. It turns out that because of the element prohibitions encoded in the combinator library and because element prohibitions are not enforced by the DTD, there are documents that are valid according to the DTD, but cannot be constructed using the combinator library. It is possible, to weaken the types for the combinators so that the element prohibitions are enforced only to the extend that the prohibitions are encoded in the DTD.

The orthogonal five element prohibitions of XHTML 1.0 [21, Appendix B] can be composed using separate type parameters.

2.3   Motivating Example Continued

If the utility code from Fig. 1 (the function `toTable` and friends) is used with the `MiniXHtml` library from Fig. 2, two type errors occur. The type errors are caused by the use of the `concat` function for composing lists of `td` and `tr` elements. The problem with the `concat` function from Fig. 1 is that it may return the empty element, which cannot be used for the `tr` and `table` elements.

To resolve the type error (and avoid that invalid XHTML is sent to a browser), the `concat` function can be replaced with the following function `concat1`, which fails in case its argument is the empty list:

```
fun concat1 []        = raise List.Empty
  | concat1 [x]       = x
  | concat1 (x::xs) = x & concat1 xs
```

The remainder of the utility code in Fig. 1 can be left unchanged (except that all calls to `concat` must be replaced with calls to `concat1`).

3   Linearity of Attributes

An *attribute* is a pair of an attribute name and an attribute value. In general, we refer to an attribute by referring to its name. Each kind of element in an XHTML document supports a set of attributes, specified by the XHTML DTD. All elements do not support the same set of attributes, although some attributes are supported by more than one element. For instance, all elements support the `id` attribute, but only some elements (e.g., the `img` and `table` elements) support the `width` attribute. In this section we show how the linearity well-formedness constraint on attribute lists can be enforced statically using phantom types.

3.1   Attributes in Mini XHTML

The signature `MINI_XHTML_ATTR` in Fig. 3 specifies operations for constructing linear lists of attributes, that is, lists of attributes for which an attribute with

```
signature MINI_XHTML_ATTR = sig
  type ('a0,'a,'b0,'b,'c0,'c) attr
  type na and align and width and height
  val left  : align
  val right : align
  val align : align -> (na,align,'b,'b,'c,'c) attr
  val width  : int -> ('a,'a,na,width,'c,'c) attr
  val height : int -> ('a,'a,'b,'b,na,height) attr
  val % : ('a0,'a,'b0,'b,'c0,'c)attr * ('a,'a1,'b,'b1,'c,'c1)attr
        -> ('a0,'a1,'b0,'b1,'c0,'c1)attr
end
```

Fig. 3. Mini XHTML attribute library.

a given name appears at most once in a list. For simplicity, the Mini XHTML attribute interface provides support for only three different attribute names (i.e., `align`, `width`, and `height`). Singleton attribute lists are constructed using the functions `align`, `width`, and `height`. Moreover, the function `%` is used for appending two attribute lists. The interface specifies a nullary type constructor `na` (read: no attribute), which is used to denote the absence of an attribute. The type constructor `attr` is parameterized over six type variables, which are used to track linearity information for the three possible attribute names. Two type variables are used for each possible attribute name. The first type variable represents "incoming" linearity information for the attribute list, whereas the second type variable represents "outgoing" linearity information. The type of `%` connects outgoing linearity information of its left argument with incoming linearity information of its right argument. The result type provides incoming and outgoing linearity information for the attribute list resulting from appending the two argument attribute lists. In this respect, for each attribute name, the two corresponding type variables in the attribute type for an attribute list expression represent the decrease in linearity imposed by the attribute list.

As an example, consider the expression

`width 50 % height 100 % width 100`

This expression does not type because the `width` combinator requires the incoming linearity to be `na`, which for the second use of the combinator contradicts the outgoing linearity information from the first use of the `width` combinator. Notice also that the type of a well-typed attribute list expression is independent of the order attributes appear in the expression.

Specialized elaboration rules for constructing attribute lists in Standard ML with the combinators presented in Fig. 3 are given below. The rules allow inference of sentences of the form $\vdash e : (\tau_a, \tau_a, \tau_b, \tau_b, \tau_c, \tau_c)\,\mathtt{attr}$, where e ranges over Standard ML expressions, and where τ_n, $n \in \{a, b, c\}$ ranges over the types `na`, `align`, `width`, and `height`.

Attribute Typing Rules

$$\boxed{\vdash e : \tau}$$

$$\frac{\tau = (\mathtt{na}, \mathtt{align}, \tau_b, \tau_b, \tau_c, \tau_c)\mathtt{attr}}{\vdash \mathtt{align\ left} : \tau} \qquad \frac{\tau = (\mathtt{na}, \mathtt{align}, \tau_b, \tau_b, \tau_c, \tau_c)\mathtt{attr}}{\vdash \mathtt{align\ right} : \tau}$$

$$\frac{\tau = (\tau_a, \tau_a, \mathtt{na}, \mathtt{width}, \tau_c, \tau_c)\mathtt{attr}}{\vdash \mathtt{width}\ n : \tau} \qquad \frac{\tau = (\tau_a, \tau_a, \tau_b, \tau_b, \mathtt{na}, \mathtt{height})\mathtt{attr}}{\vdash \mathtt{height}\ n : \tau}$$

$$\frac{\vdash e_1 : (\tau_a^0, \tau_a, \tau_b^0, \tau_b, \tau_c^0, \tau_c)\mathtt{attr} \qquad \vdash e_2 : (\tau_a, \tau_a^1, \tau_b, \tau_b^1, \tau_c, \tau_c^1)\mathtt{attr}}{\vdash e_1\ \%\ e_2 : (\tau_a^0, \tau_a^1, \tau_b^0, \tau_b^1, \tau_c^0, \tau_c^1)\mathtt{attr}}$$

To state a soundness lemma for the attribute typing rules, we first define a partial binary function $\div$ according to the following equations:

$$\mathtt{align} \div \mathtt{na} = 1 \qquad\qquad \mathtt{height} \div \mathtt{na} = 1$$
$$\mathtt{width} \div \mathtt{na} = 1 \qquad\qquad \tau \div \tau = 0$$

The following lemma expresses that there is a correlation between the number of attributes with a particular name in an attribute list expression and the type of the expression; a proof appears in the companion technical report [6].

Lemma 2 (Attribute linearity). *If* $\vdash e : (\tau_a^0, \tau_a^1, \tau_b^0, \tau_b^1, \tau_c^0, \tau_c^1)\mathtt{attr}$ *then (1) the number of* align *attributes in* e *is* $\tau_a^1 \div \tau_a^0$, *(2) the number of* width *attributes in* e *is* $\tau_b^1 \div \tau_b^0$, *and (3) the number of* height *attributes in* e *is* $\tau_c^1 \div \tau_c^0$.

It turns out that no element supports more than a dozen attributes. As a consequence, to decrease the number of type variable parameters for the attr type constructor, we refine the strategy such that each attribute makes use of a triple of type variable parameters for each attribute, where the first type variable parameter denotes the particular attribute that the triple is used for and the two other type variable parameters are used to encode the linearity information as before. Given a DTD, it is possible to construct an *attribute interference graph,* which can be colored using a simple graph coloring algorithm and used to construct an attribute interface with the desired properties; see the companion technical report for details [6]. We have used this approach to generate an attribute combinator library for a large part of the XHTML 1.0-Strict DTD. As a result, 18 different attributes are supported using 21 type variable parameters in the attr type constructor.

3.2   Adding Attributes to Elements

To add attributes to elements in a type safe way, for each element name, we introduce a new attribute-accepting combinator, which takes as its first argument an attribute list. The attribute argument-type of the combinator specifies which attributes are supported by the element.

4 Form Consistency

Form consistency guarantees that form data submitted by clients, either as form variable arguments in a GET request or as posted data in a POST request, is consistent with the scriptlet's expectations of form data.

The programmer writes a Web application as a set of ordinary Standard ML library modules and a set of scriptlets. An example scriptlet looks as follows:

```
functor bmi (F : sig val h : int Form.var
                      val w : int Form.var
                  end) : SCRIPTLET =
   struct
     infix &
     val h = Form.getOrFail Page.page "Height" F.h
     val w = Form.getOrFail Page.page "Weight" F.w
     val bmi = Int.div(w * 10000, h * h)
     val txt = if bmi > 25 then "too high!"
               else if bmi < 20 then "too low!"
               else "normal"
     val response =
       Page.page "Body Mass Index"
       (p ($ ("Your BMI is " ^ txt)))
   end
```

The signature SCRIPTLET specifies a value response with type Http.response, which represents server responses.

SMLserver cannot guarantee that a user indeed enters an integer. In the bmi example, both the h and w form arguments are specified with the type int Form.var, which suggests that the user is supposed to provide integers for these form arguments. Using the function Form.getOrFail, the bmi scriptlet converts the form arguments into integers and responds with an error page in case one of the form arguments is not present in the form or is not an integer. The structure Form provided by SMLserver contains a library of combinators for checking form variables of different types.

If both form arguments h and w are integers, the bmi scriptlet computes the body mass index and constructs a message depending on the index. Finally, an XHTML page containing the message is bound to the variable response, using the user provided function Page.page, which takes a string title and a block element (a page body) as arguments and constructs a conforming XHTML document.

4.1 Static Tracking of Form Variables

The following simplified SIMPLE_XHTML signature specifies operations that propagate information about form input elements in a type safe way:

```
signature SIMPLE_XHTML = sig
  type ('a,'b)elt and nil and ('n,'t)name
  val inputtext : ('n,'t)name -> ('n->'a,'a)elt
  val inputsubmit : string -> ('n->'a,'a)elt
  val $ : string -> ('a,'a)elt
  val & : ('a,'b)elt * ('b,'c)elt -> ('a,'c)elt
end
```

As before, the type (’a,’b)elt denotes an XHTML element, but the type variables ’a and ’b are here used to propagate information about form variable names at the type level, where form variable names are represented as abstract nullary type constructors. For readability, we reuse the function type constructor -> as a list constructor for variable names at the type level. For representing the empty list of names, the nullary type constructor nil is used. We use the term *type list* to refer to lists at the type level constructed with -> and nil.

Consider the value inputtext with type (’n,’t)name -> (’n->’a,’a)elt. In this type, the type variable ’n represents a form variable name and ’t represents the ML type (e.g., int) of that variable. In the resulting element type, the name ’n is added to the list ’a of form variables used later in the form.

Whereas inputtext provides one way of constructing a leaf node in an elt tree, the operator $ provides a way of embedding string data within XHTML documents. The type for $ suggests that elements constructed with this operator do not contribute with new form variable names. The binary operator & constructs a new element on the basis of two child elements. The type of & defines the contributions of form variable names used in the constructed element as the contributions of form variable names in the two child elements.

To continue the Body Mass Index example, consider the scriptlet functor bmiform, which creates a form to be filled out by a user:

```
functor bmiform () : SCRIPTLET =
  struct open Scriptlets infix &
    val response = Page.page "Body Mass Index Form" (bmi.form
      (p( $"Enter your height (in cm)" & inputtext bmi.h & br()
        & $"Enter your weight (in kg)" & inputtext bmi.w
        & inputsubmit "Compute Index")))
  end
```

The bmiform scriptlet references the generated abstract scriptlet interface to construct a form element containing input elements for the height and weight of the user. The use of the functions inputtext and inputsubmit construct input elements of type text and submit, respectively.

SMLserver also provides a series of type safe combinators for constructing radio buttons, check boxes, selection boxes, and input controls of type hidden; see the companion technical report for details [6].

4.2   Abstract Scriptlet Interfaces

In the case for the `bmiform` and `bmi` scriptlets, the generated abstract scriptlet interface `Scriptlets` includes the following structure specifications:[1]

```
structure bmiform : sig
  val form : (nil,nil)elt -> (nil,nil)elt
  val link : ('x,'y)elt -> ('x,'y)elt
end
structure bmi : sig
  type h and w
  val h : (h,int) XHtml.name
  val w : (w,int) XHtml.name
  val form : (h->w->nil,nil)elt -> (nil,nil)elt
  val link : {h:int, w:int} -> ('x,'y)elt -> ('x,'y)elt
end
```

The abstract scriptlet interface `bmi` specifies a function `link` for constructing an XHTML hyper-link anchor to the `bmi` scriptlet. The function takes as argument a record with integer components for the form variables h and w. Because the `bmiform` scriptlet takes no form arguments (i.e., the functor argument is empty), creating a link to this scriptlet using the function `bmiform.link` takes no explicit form arguments.

The abstract scriptlet interface `bmi` specifies two abstract types h and w, which represent the form variables h and w, respectively. The variables h and w specified by the `bmi` abstract scriptlet interface are used as witnesses for the respective form variables when forms are constructed using the function `XHtml.inputtext` or other functions for constructing form input elements. The Standard ML type associated with the form variables h and w, here `int`, is embedded in the type for the two form variable names. This type embedding makes it possible to pass hidden form variable to forms in a type safe and generic way.

Central to the abstract scriptlet interface `bmi` is the function `bmi.form`, which makes it possible to construct a `form` element with the `bmi` scriptlet as the target action. The type list `h->w->nil` in the type of the `bmi.form` function specifies that form input elements for the form variables h and w must appear within the constructed `form` element. Notice that the types h and w within the type list `h->w->nil` are abstract type constructors and that the type lists in type parameters to the `elt` type can be constructed only through uses of the function `XHtml.inputtext` and other functions for constructing form input elements.

Notice also the importance of the order in which abstract type constructors appear within type lists.[2] For generating the abstract scriptlet interface, SMLserver induces the order of abstract type constructors from the order form variables are specified in the scriptlet functor argument.

---

[1] The abstract scriptlet interface has been simplified to include only `elt` type parameters that are used to track form variables.

[2] The Standard ML type system, does not—or so it seems—allow us to provide a type construction for sets if the maximum number of elements in the sets is not fixed.

4.3   Type-Indexed Type List Reordering

In some cases it is desirable to reorder the components of a type list appearing in a type parameter to the `elt` type. Such a reordering is necessary if two forms entailing different orderings of form variable names use the same target scriptlet.

To allow for arbitrary reorderings, we now present a function `swapn`, which allows, within an element type, the head component of a type list to be swapped with any other component of the type list. The function provides the programmer with a type safe mechanism for converting an element of type $(l,\mathtt{nil})\mathtt{elt}$ to an element of type $(l',\mathtt{nil})\mathtt{elt}$ where l and l' are type lists representing different permutations of the same set of elements. The function `swapn`, which is implemented as a type-indexed function [9,14,22], takes as its first argument a value with a type that represents the index for the component of the type list to be swapped with the head component. The specifications for the `swapn` function and the functions for constructing type list indexes are the following:

```
type ('old,'new)idx
val One   : unit -> ('a->'b->'x,'b->'a->'x)idx
val Succ  : ('a->'x,'b->'y)idx -> ('a->'c->'x,'b->'c->'y)idx
val swapn : ('x,'xx)idx -> ('x,'y)elt -> ('xx,'y)elt
```

As an example, the application `swapn(Succ(One()))` has type

```
('a->'b->'c->'x,'y)elt -> ('c->'b->'a->'x,'y)elt
```

which makes it possible to swap the head component (i.e., the component with index zero) in the enclosed type list with the second component of the type list. Safety of this functionality relies on the following lemma, which is easily proven by induction on the structure of $(\tau,\tau')\mathtt{idx}$:

Lemma 3 (Type indexed swapping). *For any value of type $(\tau,\tau')\mathtt{idx}$, constructed using `One` and `Succ`, the type lists τ and τ' are identical when interpreted as sets.*

5   Related Work

The Haskell WASH/CGI library [18,19,20] provides a type safe interface for constructing Web services in Haskell. The library uses a combination of type classes and phantom types to encode the state machine defined by the XHTML DTD and to enforce constructed documents to satisfy this DTD. Because Standard ML has no support for type classes, another approach was called for in SMLserver.

The JWIG project [4] (previously the `<bigwig>` project [2,3,17]) provides another model for writing Web applications for which generated XHTML documents are guaranteed to be well-formed and valid and for which submitted form data is guaranteed to be consistent with the reading of the form data. JWIG is based on a suite of program analyses that at compile time verifies that no runtime errors can occur while building documents or receiving form input.

For constructing XHTML documents, JWIG provides a template system with a tailor-made plugging operation, which in SMLserver and WASH/CGI amounts to function composition.

Both WASH/CGI and JWIG, allow state to be maintained on the Web server in so-called sessions. SMLserver does not support sessions explicitly, but does provide support for type safe caching of certain kinds of values [5]. The possibility of maintaining state on the Web server (other than in a database or in a cache) introduces a series of problems, which are related to how the Web server claims resources and how it behaves in the presence of memory leaks and system failures.

Other branches of work related to this paper include the work on using phantom types to restrict the composition of values and operators in domain specific languages embedded in Haskell and ML [8,13,18,19,20] and the work on using phantom types to provide type safe interaction with foreign languages from within Haskell and ML [1,7]. We are aware of no other work that uses phantom types to express linear requirements.

Phantom types have also been used in Haskell and ML to encode dependent types in the form of type indexed functions [9,14,22]. In the present work we also make use of a type indexed function to allow form fields to appear in a form in an order that is different than the order the corresponding form variables are declared in scriptlet functor arguments.

Finally, there is a large body of related work on using functional languages for Web programming. Preceding Thiemann's work, Meijer introduced a library for writing CGI scripts in Haskell [15], which provided low-level functionality for accessing CGI parameters and sending responses to clients. Peter Sestoft's ML Server Pages implementation and SMLserver [5] provide good support for programming Web applications in ML, although these approaches give no guarantees about the well-formedness and validity of generated documents.

Queinnec [16] suggests using continuations to implement the interaction between clients and Web servers. Graunke et al. [11] demonstrate how Web programs can be written in a traditional direct style and transformed into CGI scripts using CPS conversion and lambda lifting. It would be interesting to investigate if this approach can be made to work for statically typed languages.

6   Conclusion

Based on our experience with the construction and maintenance of community sites and enterprise Web applications—in SMLserver and other frameworks—we have contributed with two technical solutions to improve reliability and the quality of such applications. Our first contribution is a novel approach to enforce conformity of generated XHTML 1.0 documents, based entirely on the use of a typed combinator library in Standard ML. Our second technical contribution is a technique for enforcing consistency between a scriptlet's use of form variables and the construction of forms that target that scriptlet.

References

1. M. Blume. No-longer-foreign: Teaching an ML compiler to speak C "natively". In *Workshop on Multi-language Infrastructure and Interoperability*, September 2001.
2. C. Brabrand, A. Møller, and M. Schwartzbach. Static validation of dynamically generated HTML. In *Workshop on Program Analysis for Software Tools and Engineering*, June 2001.
3. C. Brabrand, A. Møller, and M. Schwartzbach. The <bigwig> project. *Transactions on Internet Technology*, 2(2):79–114, 2002.
4. A. Christensen, A. Møller, and M. Schwartzbach. Extending Java for high-level Web service construction. *Transactions on Programming Languages and Systems*, 25(6), November 2003.
5. M. Elsman and N. Hallenberg. Web programming with SMLserver. In *Int. Symposium on Practical Aspects of Declarative Languages*, January 2003.
6. M. Elsman and K. F. Larsen. Typing XHTML web applications in SMLserver. Technical Report ITU-TR-2003-34, IT University of Copenhagen, Denmark, 2003.
7. S. Finne, D. Leijen, E. Meijer, and S. Peyton Jones. Calling hell from heaven and heaven from hell. In *Int. Conference on Functional programming*, 1999.
8. M. Fluet and R. Pucella. Phantom types and subtyping. In *Int. Conference on Theoretical Computer Science*, August 2002.
9. D. Fridlender and M. Indrika. Functional pearl: Do we need dependent types? *Journal of Functional Programming*, 10(4):409–415, July 2000.
10. P. Graunke, R. Findler, S. Krishnamurthi, and M. Felleisen. Modeling web interactions. In *European Symposium On Programming*, April 2003.
11. P. Graunke, S. Krishnamurthi, R. Findler, and M. Felleisen. Automatically restructuring programs for the Web. In *Int. Conference on Automated Software Engineering*, September 2001.
12. C. V. Hall, K. Hammond, S. Peyton Jones, and P. Wadler. Type classes in Haskell. *Transactions on Programming Languages and Systems*, 18(2):109–138, 1996.
13. D. Leijen and E. Meijer. Domain specific embedded compilers. In *Conference on Domain-specific languages*, 2000.
14. C. McBride. Faking it: Simulating dependent types in Haskell. *Journal of Functional Programming*, 12(4&5):375–392, July 2002.
15. E. Meijer. Server side Web scripting in Haskell. *Journal of Functional Programming*, 10(1):1–18, January 2000.
16. C. Queinnec. The influence of browsers on evaluators or, continuations to program Web servers. In *Int. Conference on Functional Programming*, September 2000.
17. A. Sandholm and M. Schwartzbach. A type system for dynamic Web documents. In *Symposium on Principles of Programming Languages*, January 2000.
18. P. Thiemann. Programmable type systems for domain specific languages. In *Workshop on Functional and Logic Programming*, June 2002.
19. P. Thiemann. A typed representation for HTML and XML documents in Haskell. *Journal of Functional Programming*, 12(4&5):435–468, July 2002.
20. P. Thiemann. Wash/CGI: Server-side Web scripting with sessions and typed, compositional forms. In *Conference on Practical Aspects of Declarative Languages*, January 2002.
21. W3C. XHTML^{TM} 1.0: The extensible hypertext markup language, January 2000. Second Edition. Revised August 2002. http://www.w3.org/TR/xhtml1.
22. Z. Yang. Encoding types in ML-like languages. In *Int. Conference on Functional Programming*, September 1998.

Implementing Cut Elimination: A Case Study of Simulating Dependent Types in Haskell*

Chiyan Chen, Dengping Zhu, and Hongwei Xi

Computer Science Department
Boston University
{chiyan,zhudp,hwxi}@cs.bu.edu

Abstract. Gentzen's Hauptsatz – *cut elimination theorem* – in sequent calculi reveals a fundamental property on logic connectives in various logics such as classical logic and intuitionistic logic. In this paper, we implement a procedure in Haskell to perform cut elimination for intuitionistic sequent calculus, where we use types to guarantee that the procedure can only return a cut-free proof of the same sequent when given a proof of a sequent that may contain cuts. The contribution of the paper is two-fold. On the one hand, we present an interesting (and somewhat unexpected) application of the current type system of Haskell, illustrating through a concrete example how some typical use of dependent types can be simulated in Haskell. On the other hand, we identify several problematic issues with such a simulation technique and then suggest some approaches to addressing these issues in Haskell.

1 Introduction

The type system of Haskell, which was originally based on the Hindley-Milner type system [13], has since evolved significantly. With various additions (e.g., type classes [8], functional dependencies [11], higher-rank polymorphism, existential types), the type system of Haskell has become increasingly more expressive as well as more complex. In particular, type-checking in Haskell is now greatly involved. Though there is so far no direct support for dependent types in Haskell, many examples have appeared in the literature that make interesting use of types in Haskell in capturing the kind of program invariants that are usually caught by making use of dependent types.

Gentzen's sequent calculi [7] LJ (for intuitionistic logic) and LK (for classical logic) have played an essential rôle in various studies such as logic programming and theorem proving that are of proof-theoretical nature. The main theorem of Gentzen, *Hauptsatz*, implies that these sequent calculi enjoy the famous subformula property and are thus consistent. Let us use $\Gamma \vdash A$ for a sequent in the sequent calculus for LJ, where Γ and A represent a sequence of formulas and a formula, respectively. Then Gentzen's Hauptsatz for LJ essentially states that the following rule (**Cut**):

---

* Partially supported by the NSF Grants No. CCR-0224244 and No. CCR-0229480

B. Jayaraman (Ed.): PADL 2004, LNCS 3057, pp. 239–254, 2004.
© Springer-Verlag Berlin Heidelberg 2004

$$\frac{\Gamma \vdash A_1 \quad \Gamma, A_1 \vdash A_2}{\Gamma \vdash A_2} \quad \textbf{(Cut)}$$

is admissible or can be eliminated (from a logical derivation that makes use of it). Thus Gentzen's Hauptsatz is also known as *cut elimination theorem*.

While there exist various proofs of cut elimination in the literature, few of them are amenable to mechanization (in formal systems). In [17], three proofs of cut elimination (for intuitionistic, classical and linear sequent calculi, respectively) are encoded in the Elf system [16], which supports logical programming based on the LF Logical Framework [9]. There, logical derivations are represented through the use of higher-order abstract syntax [15], and totality (termination and exhaustive coverage) checks are performed to insure that the encodings indeed correspond to some valid proofs of cut elimination. However, we emphasize that it is out of the scope of the paper to compare functional programming with theorem proving. The cut elimination theorem is merely chosen as an interesting example. We could have, for instance, chosen a different example such as implementing a continuation-passing style (CPS) transformation in a typeful manner [2].

In Haskell, it is difficult to adopt a representation for logic derivations that is based on higher-order abstract syntax as the function space is simply too vast. When compared to Elf, which does not support general recursion, the function space in Haskell is far richer. Therefore, if higher-order abstract syntax is chosen to represent logical derivations, there are to be many representations that do not actually correspond to any logical derivations. Instead, we choose a first-order representation for logical derivations. We are to implement a function *cutDER* such that the type of *cutDER* guarantees that if d_1 and d_2 represent logical derivations of the sequents $\Gamma \vdash A_1$ and $\Gamma, A_1 \vdash A_2$, respectively, then the evaluation of *cutDER* d_1 d_2 always returns a logical derivation of $\Gamma \vdash A_2$ if it terminates. However, there is currently no facility in Haskell allowing us to guarantee that *cutDER* is a total function.

The primary contribution of the paper is two-fold. On the one hand, we present an interesting (and somewhat unexpected) application of the current type system of Haskell, illustrating through a concrete example how some typical use of dependent types can be simulated in Haskell. While it is certainly possible to present a general account for simulating dependent types in Haskell, we feel that such a presentation is not only less interesting but also difficult to follow. The example we present already contains all the nuts and bolts that a programmer needs to use this kind of programming style in general. On the other hand, we identify some problematic issues with such a simulation technique and then make some suggestions to address these issues in Haskell. Overall, we feel that though simulating dependent types in Haskell can occasionally lead to elegant (and often small) examples (which are often called *pearls* in the functional programming community), this programming style seems to have some serious difficulties in handling larger and more realistic examples that require some genuine use of dependent types, and we are to substantiate this feeling by pointing out such difficulties in some concrete Haskell programs.

```
data EQ a b = EQcon (a -> b) (b -> a)

idEQ :: EQ a a
idEQ = EQcon (\x -> x) (\x -> x)

symEQ :: EQ a b -> EQ b a
symEQ (EQcon to from) = EQcon from to

transEQ :: EQ a b -> EQ b c -> EQ a c
transEQ (EQcon to1 from1) (EQcon to2 from2) =
  EQcon (to2 . to1) (from1 . from2)

pairEQ :: EQ a1 b1 -> EQ a2 b2 -> EQ (a1, a2) (b1, b2)
pairEQ (EQcon to1 from1) (EQcon to2 from2) =
  EQcon (\(x1, x2) -> (to1 x1, to2 x2))
        (\(x1, x2) -> (from1 x1, from2 x2))

fstEQ :: EQ (a1, a2) (b1, b2) -> EQ a1 b1
fstEQ (EQcon to from) = -- bot = let x = x in x
  EQcon (\x -> fst (to (x, bot))) (\x -> fst (from (x, bot)))

sndEQ :: EQ (a1, a2) (b1, b2) -> EQ a2 b2
sndEQ (EQcon to from) = -- bot = let x = x in x
  EQcon (\x -> snd (to (bot, x))) (\x -> snd (from (bot, x)))
```

Fig. 1. Constructing Proofs Terms for Type Equality

The rest of the paper is organized as follows. In Section 2, we present some basic techniques developed for simulating dependent types in Haskell. We then give a detailed proof of cut elimination (for the implication fragment of the intuitionistic propositional logic) in Section 3 and relate it to an implementation in Haskell. We mention some closely related work and then conclude in Section 4.

2   Techniques for Simulating Dependent Types

We present in this section some basic techniques developed for simulating dependent types in Haskell. A gentle introduction to dependent types can be found, for instance, in [15]. Also, an interesting use of dependent types in encoding cut-elimination proofs can be found in [18].

2.1   Proof Terms for Type Equality

In the approach to simulating dependent types that we will present shortly, a key step is the use of terms in encoding equality on certain types (the purpose of such encoding will soon be made clear in the following presentation). In Figure 1, we first declare a binary type constructor EQ. Given two types τ_1 and τ_2, if there is a term $EQcon$ $\underline{to}$ $\underline{from}$ of the type EQ τ_1 τ_2, then we can use $\underline{to}$ and $\underline{from}$ to coerce terms of the types τ_1 and τ_2 into terms of the types τ_2 and τ_1, respectively. In fact, we only *intend* to use EQ to form a closed type $EQ\ \tau_1\ \tau_2$ if τ_1 and τ_2 are equal, and $EQcon$ to form a closed term $EQcon\ \underline{to}\ \underline{from}$ if $\underline{to}$ and $\underline{from}$ are (equivalent to) identity functions. However, this cannot be formally enforced. In [1], this issue is addressed by defining $EQ\ \tau_1\ \tau_2$ as $\forall f.f\ \tau_1 \rightarrow f\ \tau_2$. Unfortunately, this definition is not suitable for our purpose as there seems no way of defining functions such as $fstEQ$ and $sndEQ$ in Figure 1 if this definition is adopted. For instance, suppose that a function F is given of the type $\forall f.f\ (\tau_1, \tau_2) \rightarrow f\ (\tau_1', \tau_2')$; in order to use F to construct a function of the type $\forall f.f\ \tau_1 \rightarrow f\ \tau_1'$, we need to know that the pairing type constructor $(\cdot, \cdot)$ is 1-1 on its first argument; however, it is unclear as to how this information can be expressed in the type system of Haskell.

Conceptually, a term of type $EQ\ \tau_1\ \tau_2$ is intended to show that the types τ_1 and τ_2 are equal. Therefore, we use the name *proof term for type equality* or simply *proof term* for such a term. In Figure 1, we present a proof term $idEQ$ and various functions for constructing proof terms. For instance, if pf_1 and pf_2 are proof terms of types $EQ\ \tau_1\ \tau_1'$ and $EQ\ \tau_2\ \tau_2'$, respectively, then $pairEQ\ pf_1\ pf_2$ is a proof term of the type $EQ\ (\tau_1, \tau_2)\ (\tau_1', \tau_2')$; if pf is a term of the type $EQ\ (\tau_1, \tau_2)\ (\tau_1', \tau_2')$, then $fstEQ\ pf$ and $sndEQ\ pf$ are proof terms of the types $EQ\ \tau_1\ \tau_1'$ and $EQ\ \tau_2\ \tau_2'$, respectively; if pf_1 and pf_2 are proof terms of types $EQ\ \tau_1\ \tau_2$ and $EQ\ \tau_2\ \tau_3$, respectively, then $transEQ\ pf_1\ pf_2$ is a proof term of the type $EQ\ \tau_1\ \tau_3$.

Let $\underline{TC}$ be a type constructor that takes n types $\tau_1, \ldots, \tau_n$ to form a type $\underline{TC}\ \tau_1\ \cdots\ \tau_n$. Then the following rule derives $\underline{TC}\ \tau_1\ \cdots\ \tau_n \equiv \underline{TC}\ \tau_1'\ \cdots\ \tau_n'$ from $\tau_1 \equiv \tau_1', \ldots, \tau_n \equiv \tau_n'$,

$$\frac{\tau_1 \equiv \tau_1' \quad \cdots \quad \tau_n\ equiv \tau_n'}{\underline{TC}\ \tau_1\ \cdots\ \tau_n \equiv \underline{TC}\ \tau_1'\ \cdots\ \tau_n'} \quad \textbf{(\underline{tci}EQ)}$$

where $\equiv$ stands for equality on types, and for each $1 \leq k \leq n$, the following rule derives $\tau_i \equiv \tau_i'$ from $\underline{TC}\ \tau_1\ \cdots\ \tau_n \equiv \underline{TC}\ \tau_1'\ \cdots\ \tau_n'$:

$$\frac{\underline{TC}\ \tau_1\ \cdots\ \tau_n \equiv \underline{TC}\ \tau_1'\ \cdots\ \tau_n'}{\tau_k \equiv \tau_k'} \quad \textbf{(\underline{tce}k\textbf{EQ})}$$

We often need a function $\underline{tci}EQ$ of the following type:

$$EQ\ a_1\ a_1' \rightarrow \ldots \rightarrow EQ\ a_n\ a_n' \rightarrow EQ\ (\underline{TC}\ a_1 \ldots\ a_n)\ (\underline{TC}\ a_1' \ldots\ a_n')$$

and functions $\underline{tce}k EQ$ of the following types,

$$EQ\ (\underline{TC}\ a_1 \ldots\ a_n)\ (\underline{TC}\ a_1' \ldots\ a_n') \rightarrow EQ\ a_k\ a_k'$$

where k ranges from 1 to n. We say that $\underline{tci}EQ$ is the type equality introduction function associated with $\underline{TC}$ and $\underline{tce}k EQ$ $(1 \leq k \leq n)$ are type equality elimination functions associated with $\underline{TC}$. Note that if the binary type constructor EQ is defined as $\lambda a.\lambda a'.\forall f.f\ a \rightarrow f\ a'$, then it becomes rather difficult, if not impossible, to define type equality elimination functions.

When presenting some programs in Haskell later, we also need the following functions $toEQ$ and $fromEQ$:

```
toEQ :: EQ a b -> (a -> b)
toEQ (EQcon to from) = to

fromEQ :: EQ a b -> (b -> a)
fromEQ (EQcon to from) = from
```

If a proof term *pf* of type $EQ\ \tau_1\ \tau_2$ is given, then *toEQ pf* and *fromEQ pf* act like coercion functions between type τ_1 and type τ_2. We will later point out some actual uses of *toEQ* and *fromEQ*.

2.2   Representing Formulas and Sequences of Formulas

We use P for primitive propositions and $\bot$ for falsehood. The syntax for logic formulas is given as follows,

$$\text{formulas } A ::= P \mid \bot \mid A_1 \wedge A_2 \mid A_1 \vee A_2 \mid A_1 \supset A_2$$

where the logic connectives are standard. We use $|A|$ for the size of formula A, which is the number of logic connectives in A. We are to use types to encode formulas, so we introduce the following type constructors in Haskell.

```
data BOT = BOT -- encoding falsehood
data LAND a b = LAND a b -- encoding conjunction
data LOR a b = LOR a b -- encoding disjunction
data LIMP a b = LIMP a b -- encoding implication
```

For instance, the type *LIMP BOT (LAND BOT BOT)* represents the formula $\bot \supset (\bot \wedge \bot)$. We do not indicate how primitive propositions are encoded at this moment as this is not important for our purpose. Also, in the following presentation, we only deal with the implication connective $\supset$. It should be clear that the other connectives ($\wedge$ and $\vee$) can be treated in a similar (and likely simpler) manner. We need the following functions (the type equality introduction function and type equality elimination functions associated with the type constructor *LIMP*) for handling proof terms for type equality:

```
limpiEQ :: EQ a1 a2 -> EQ b1 b2 -> EQ (LIMP a1 b1) (LIMP a2 b2)
limpe1EQ :: EQ (LIMP a1 b1) (LIMP a2 b2) -> EQ a1 a2
limpe2EQ :: EQ (LIMP a1 b1) (LIMP a2 b2) -> EQ b1 b2
```

We omit the actual implementations of these functions, which are similar to the implementations of *pairEQ*, *fstEQ* and *sndEQ*.

We use Γ for a sequence of formulas defined as follows,

$$\text{formula sequences } \Gamma ::= \emptyset \mid \Gamma, A$$

where $\emptyset$ for the empty sequence. We use the unit type () to represent $\emptyset$, and the type (g, a) to represent Γ, A if g and a represent Γ and A, respectively. A judgment of the form $\Gamma \ni A$ means that the formula A occurs in the sequence

Γ, we use $\mathcal{I}$ for derivations of such judgments, which can be constructed from applying the following rules:

$$\frac{}{\Gamma, A \ni A} \text{ (one)} \qquad \frac{\Gamma \ni A}{\Gamma, A' \ni A} \text{ (shift)}$$

To represent derivations $\mathcal{I}$ of judgments of the form $\Gamma \ni A$, we would like to declare a datatype constructor IN and associate with it two term constructors $INone$ and $INshi$ of the following types,

$$INone : \forall a.\forall g'.IN\ a\ (g',a) \qquad INshi : \forall a.\forall g'.\forall a'.IN\ a\ g' \rightarrow IN\ a\ (g',a')$$

which correspond to the rules **(one)** and **(shift)**, respectively. Such a datatype constructor is called a recursive datatype constructor [19] and is not available in Haskell. Instead, we declare IN as follows for representing derivations $\mathcal{I}$:

```
data IN a g =
    forall g'. INone (EQ g (g',a))
  | forall g' a'. INshi (EQ g (g',a')) (IN a g')
```

Essentially, the declaration introduces a binary type constructor IN and assigns the two (term) constructors $INone$ and $INshi$ the following types:

$$\begin{aligned} INone\ &:\ \forall g.\forall a.\forall g'.EQ\ g\ (g',a) \rightarrow IN\ a\ g \\ INshi\ &:\ \forall g.\forall a.\forall g'.\forall a'.EQ\ g\ (g',a') \rightarrow IN\ a\ g' \rightarrow IN\ a\ g \end{aligned}$$

Assume that types g and a represent Γ and A, respectively. Then a term of the type $IN\ a\ g$ represents a derivation of $\Gamma \ni A$. This probably becomes more clear if the rules **(one)** and **(shift)** are presented in the following manner:

$$\frac{\Gamma = \Gamma', A}{\Gamma \ni A} \text{ (one)} \qquad \frac{\Gamma = \Gamma', A' \quad \Gamma' \ni A}{\Gamma \ni A} \text{ (shift)}$$

For instance, a derivation of $\Gamma, A_1, A_2, A_3 \ni A_1$ can be represented by the following term:

$$INshi(idEQ)(INshi(idEQ)(INone(idEQ)))$$

We are also in need of the type equality introduction function associated with IN, which returns a proof term of type $EQ\ (IN\ \tau_1\ \tau_2)\ (IN\ \tau_1'\ \tau_2')$ when given two proof terms of the types $EQ\ \tau_1\ \tau_1'$ and $EQ\ \tau_2\ \tau_2'$. We define the following function $iniEQ$ in Haskell to serve this purpose:

```
iniEQ :: EQ a1 a2 -> EQ g1 g2 -> EQ (IN a1 g1) (IN a2 g2)
iniEQ pf1 pf2 = EQcon to from
  where
    to (INone pf) =
      INone (transEQ (transEQ (symEQ pf2) pf) (pairEQ idEQ pf1))
    to (INshi pf i) =
      INshi (transEQ (symEQ pf2) pf) (toEQ (iniEQ pf1 idEQ) i)

    from (INone pf) =
      INone (transEQ (transEQ pf2 pf) (pairEQ idEQ (symEQ pf1)))
    from (INshi pf i) =
      INshi (transEQ pf2 pf) (toEQ (iniEQ (symEQ pf1) idEQ) i)
```

Please notice some heavy use of proof terms in the implementation of *iniEQ*. We now briefly explain why the first clause in the function *to* is well-typed: *to* needs to be assigned the type $IN\ a_1\ g_1 \to IN\ a_2\ g_2$; assume that *INone pf* is given the type $IN\ a_1\ g_1$; then *pf* has the type $EQ\ g_1\ (G, a_1)$ for some type G; and it can be verified that *transEQ* (*transEQ* (*symEQ pf₂*) *pf*) (*pairEQ idEQ pf₁*) can be assigned the type $EQ\ g_2\ (G, a_2)$ (assuming pf_1 and pf_2 have the types $EQ\ a_1\ a_2$ and $EQ\ g_1\ g_2$, respectively); so the following term

$$INone\ (transEQ\ (transEQ\ (symEQ\ pf_2)\ pf)\ (pairEQ\ idEQ\ pf_1))$$

can be assigned the type $IN\ a_2\ g_2$.

We point out that we seem unable to define the type equality elimination functions associated with *IN*. Fortunately, we do not need these functions when implementing cut elimination.

Definition 1. *Given two sequences Γ and Γ' of formulas, we write $\Gamma \supset \Gamma'$ if $\Gamma' \ni A$ implies $\Gamma \ni A$ for every formula A.*

This definition corresponds to the following type definition or type synonym in Haskell:

```
type SUP g g' = forall a. IN a g' -> IN a g
```

Assume g and g' represent Γ and Γ', respectively. Then a term of the type $SUP\ g\ g'$ essentially represents a proof of $\Gamma \supset \Gamma'$.

2.3   Representing Derivations

To simplify the presentation, we focus on a fragment of intuitionistic propositional logic that only supports the following three logical derivation rules:

$$\frac{\Gamma \ni A}{\Gamma \vdash A}\ \textbf{(AXI)} \qquad \frac{\Gamma \ni A_1 \supset A_2 \quad \Gamma \vdash A_1 \quad \Gamma, A_2 \vdash A}{\Gamma \vdash A}\ (\supset\textbf{L}) \qquad \frac{\Gamma, A_1 \vdash A_2}{\Gamma \vdash A_1 \supset A_2}(\supset\textbf{R})$$

We use $h(\mathcal{D})$ for the height of derivation $\mathcal{D}$, which is defined as usual. In order to represent logical derivations constructed from applying the above three logic derivation rules, we declare a binary datatype *DER* as follows:

```
data DER g a =
    DERaxi (IN a g)
  | forall a1 a2. DERimpl (IN (LIMP a1 a2) g) (DER g a1) (DER (g, a2) a)
  | forall a1 a2. DERimpr (EQ a (LIMP a1 a2)) (DER (g, a1) a2)
```

Clearly, the term constructors *DERaxi*, *DERimpl* and *DERimpr* correspond to the rules **(AXI)**, $(\supset\textbf{L})$ and $(\supset\textbf{R})$, respectively. If we can now prove that there is a total function of the following type,

$$\forall g. \forall a_1. \forall a_2. DER\ g\ a_1 \to DER\ (g, a_1)\ a_2 \to DER\ g\ a_2$$

then the rule **(Cut)** is admissible in sequent calculus for the implication fragment of intuitionistic propositional logic.

```
deriEQ :: EQ g1 g2 -> EQ a1 a2 -> EQ (DER g1 a1) (DER g2 a2)
deriEQ pf1 pf2 = EQcon to from
  where
    to (DERaxi i) = DERaxi (toEQ (iniEQ pf2 pf1) i)
    to (DERimpl i d1 d2) = DERimpl i' d1' d2'
      where
        i' = toEQ (iniEQ idEQ pf1) i
        d1' = toEQ (deriEQ pf1 idEQ) d1
        d2' = toEQ (deriEQ (pairEQ pf1 idEQ) pf2) d2
    to (DERimpr pf d') = DERimpr (transEQ (symEQ pf2) pf) d''
      where d'' = toEQ (deriEQ (pairEQ pf1 idEQ) idEQ) d'

    from (DERaxi i) = DERaxi (fromEQ (iniEQ pf2 pf1) i)
    from (DERimpl i d1 d2) = DERimpl i' d1' d2'
      where
        i' = fromEQ (iniEQ idEQ pf1) i
        d1' = fromEQ (deriEQ pf1 idEQ) d1
        d2' = fromEQ (deriEQ (pairEQ pf1 idEQ) pf2) d2
    from (DERimpr pf d') = DERimpr (transEQ pf2 pf) d''
      where d'' = fromEQ (deriEQ (pairEQ pf1 idEQ) idEQ) d'
```

Fig. 2. The type equality introduction function associated with *DER*

Also, we are to be in need of the type equality introduction function associated with *DER*, which is implemented in Figure 2. We are not able to implement the type equality elimination functions associated with *DER*, and fortunately we will not need them, either.

2.4   Implementing Some Lemmas

We now show that the following structural rules are all admissible:

$$\frac{\Gamma \vdash A}{\Gamma, A' \vdash A} \qquad \frac{\Gamma, A_1, A_2 \vdash A}{\Gamma, A_2, A_1 \vdash A} \qquad \frac{\Gamma \ni A \quad \Gamma, A \vdash A'}{\Gamma \vdash A'}$$

This should make it clear that the formulation of logic derivation rules presented here is equivalent to, for instance, the one in [18].

Lemma 1. *Assume* $\Gamma \supset \Gamma'$. *Then* $\Gamma, A \supset \Gamma', A$ *holds for every formula* A.

Proof. The straightforward proof of the lemma corresponds to the following implementation of *shiSUP* in Haskell:

```
shiSUP :: SUP g g' -> SUP (g, a) (g', a)
shiSUP f = \i -> case i of
  INone pf -> INone (pairEQ idEQ (sndEQ pf))
  INshi pf i -> INshi idEQ (f (toEQ (iniEQ idEQ (symEQ (fstEQ pf))) i))
```

We briefly explain why the first clause in the definition of *shiSUP* is well-typed. Assume that *INone pf* is assigned the type *IN b* (g', a), where b is a type variable, and we need to show that $INone\,(pairEQ\,idEQ\,(sndEQ\,pf))$ can be assigned the type $IN\,b\,(g,a)$: Note that pf is assigned the type $EQ\,(g',a)\,(G,b)$ for some type G, and thus $pairEQ\,idEQ\,(sndEQ\,pf)$ can be assigned the type $EQ\,(g,a)\,(g,b)$. Therefore, $INone\,(pairEQ\,idEQ\,(sndEQ\,pf))$ can be assigned the type $IN\,b\,(g,a)$. We encourage the reader to figure out the reasoning behind the well-typedness of the second clause in the implementation of $shiSUP$, which is considerably more "twisted".

Lemma 2. *Assume $\Gamma \supset \Gamma'$ and $\mathcal{D} :: \Gamma' \vdash A$. Then we can construct $\mathcal{D}' :: \Gamma \vdash A$ such that $h(\mathcal{D}') = h(\mathcal{D})$.*

Proof. Note that the lemma implies the admissibility of the following derivation rule:

$$\frac{\Gamma \supset \Gamma' \quad \Gamma' \vdash A}{\Gamma \vdash A} \quad \textbf{(Super)}$$

The proof is by structural induction on $\mathcal{D}$, which corresponds to the following implementation of the function $supDER$ in Haskell:

```
supDER :: SUP g g' -> DER g' a -> DER g a
supDER f = \d -> case d of
  DERaxi i -> DERaxi (f i)
  DERimpl i d1 d2 ->
    DERimpl (f i) (supDER f d1) (supDER (shiSUP f) d2)
  DERimpr pf d -> DERimpr pf (supDER (shiSUP f) d)
```

Of course, it needs to be verified that the height of the derivation returned by $shiSUP$ is the same as that of the one taken as an argument of $shiSUP$.

Lemma 3 (Weakening). *Assume $\mathcal{D} :: \Gamma \vdash A$. Then for each formula A', there exists a derivation $\mathcal{D}' :: \Gamma, A' \vdash A$ such that $h(\mathcal{D}') = h(\mathcal{D})$.*

Proof. Note that the lemma implies the admissibility of the rule **(Weakening)**. The proof is by showing $\Gamma, A' \supset \Gamma$ and then applying Lemma 2, which corresponds to the following implementation of the function $weakDER$ in Haskell:

```
weakSUP :: SUP (g, a) g -- the type = forall a'. IN a' g -> IN a' (g, a)
weakSUP i = INshi idEQ i

weakDER :: DER g a -> DER (g, a') a
weakDER = supDER weakSUP
```

Lemma 4 (Exchange). *Assume $\mathcal{D} :: \Gamma, A_1, A_2 \vdash A$. Then there exists a derivation $\mathcal{D}' :: \Gamma, A_2, A_1 \vdash A$ such that $h(\mathcal{D}') = h(\mathcal{D})$.*

Proof. Note that the lemma implies the admissibility of the rule **(Exchange)**. The proof is by showing $\Gamma, A, A' \supset \Gamma, A', A$ and then applying Lemma 2, which corresponds to the following implementation of the function $exchDER$ in Haskell:

```
exchSUP :: SUP ((g, a2), a1) ((g, a1), a2)
exchSUP (INone pf) = INshi idEQ (INone (pairEQ idEQ (sndEQ pf)))
exchSUP (INshi pf1 (INone pf2)) =
   INone (pairEQ idEQ (sndEQ (transEQ (fstEQ pf1) pf2)))
exchSUP (INshi pf1 (INshi pf2 i)) = INshi idEQ (INshi idEQ (fromEQ pf' i))
  where pf' = iniEQ idEQ (fstEQ (transEQ (fstEQ pf1) pf2))

exchDER :: DER ((g, a1), a2) a -> DER ((g, a2), a1) a
exchDER = supDER exchSUP
```

Again, some considerably complicated proof terms are used in the implementation of *exchDER*.

Lemma 5 (Contraction). *Assume* $\mathcal{D} :: \Gamma, A \vdash A'$. *If* $\Gamma \ni A$ *is derivable, then there exists a derivation* $\mathcal{D}' :: \Gamma \vdash A'$ *such that* $h(\mathcal{D}') = h(\mathcal{D})$.

Proof. Note that the lemma implies the admissibility of the rule **(Contraction)**. The proof is by showing that $\Gamma \ni A$ implies $\Gamma \supset \Gamma, A$ and then applying Lemma 2, which corresponds to the following implementation of the function *contractDER* in Haskell:

```
contractSUP :: IN a g -> SUP g (g, a)
contractSUP i = \j -> case j of
  INone pf ->  toEQ (iniEQ (sndEQ pf) idEQ) i
  INshi pf j' -> fromEQ (iniEQ idEQ (fstEQ pf)) j'

contractDER :: IN a g -> DER (g, a) a' -> DER g a'
contractDER i = supDER (contractSUP i)
```

We are now ready to establish that the rule **(Cut)** is admissible.

3   Implementing Cut Elimination

In this section, we prove the admissibility of the rule **(Cut)** in the sequent calculus for the implication fragment of the intuitionistic propositional logic. Meanwhile, we also implement a procedure in Haskell to perform cut elimination, which tightly corresponds to this proof.

Theorem 1 (Admissibility of Cut). *Assume that* $\mathcal{D}_1 :: \Gamma \vdash A_1$ *and* $\mathcal{D}_2 :: \Gamma, A_1 \vdash A_2$. *Then there exists a derivation of* $\Gamma \vdash A_2$.

Proof. The proof is by induction on the triple $\langle |A|, h(\mathcal{D}_2), h(\mathcal{D}_1) \rangle$, lexicographically ordered. We proceed by analyzing the structure of $\mathcal{D}_2$.

– $\mathcal{D}_2$ is of the following form:

$$\frac{\mathcal{I} :: \Gamma, A_1 \ni A_2}{\Gamma, A_1 \vdash A_2} \quad \textbf{(AXI)}$$

In this case, we analyze the structure of $\mathcal{I}$.

```
cutDER :: DER g a1 -> DER (g, a1) a2 -> DER g a2
cutDER d1 d2 = case d2 of
  DERaxi i -> case i of
    INone pf -> toEQ (deriEQ idEQ (sndEQ pf)) d1
    INshi pf i' -> DERaxi (fromEQ (iniEQ idEQ (fstEQ pf)) i')
  DERimpl i d21 d22 -> case i of
    INone pf -> case d1 of
      DERaxi i' -> contractDER i' d2
      DERimpl i' d11 d12 ->
        DERimpl i' d11 (cutDER d12 (exchDER (weakDER d2)))
      DERimpr pf' d1' ->
        cutDER (toEQ (deriEQ idEQ pf1)
                     (cutDER (toEQ (deriEQ idEQ pf0) d') d1'))
              d''
          where
            pf0 = limpe1EQ (transEQ (symEQ (sndEQ pf)) pf')
            pf1 = limpe2EQ (transEQ (symEQ pf') (sndEQ pf))
            d' = cutDER d1 d21
            d'' = cutDER (weakDER d1) (exchDER d22)
    INshi pf i' -> DERimpl i'' d' d''
      where
        i'' = fromEQ (iniEQ idEQ (fstEQ pf)) i'
        d' = cutDER d1 d21
        d'' = cutDER (weakDER d1) (exchDER d22)
  DERimpr pf d2' -> DERimpr pf (cutDER (weakDER d1) (exchDER d2'))
```

Fig. 3. Implementing Cut Elimination

- $\mathcal{I}$ is of the following form,

$$\frac{}{\Gamma, A \ni A}\text{(one)}$$

where $A = A_1 = A_2$. Then $\mathcal{D}_1$ is a derivation of $\Gamma \vdash A_2$.
- $\mathcal{I}$ is of the following form

$$\frac{\mathcal{I}_1 :: \Gamma \ni A_2}{\Gamma, A_1 \ni A_2}\quad\text{(shift)}$$

Then a derivation of $\Gamma \vdash A_2$ can be constructed as follows:

$$\frac{\mathcal{I}_1 :: \Gamma \ni A_2}{\Gamma \vdash A_2}\quad\text{(AXI)}$$

- $\mathcal{D}_2$ is of the following form:

$$\frac{\mathcal{I} :: \Gamma, A_1 \ni A_{11} \supset A_{12} \quad \mathcal{D}_{21} :: \Gamma, A_1 \vdash A_{11} \quad \mathcal{D}_{22} :: \Gamma, A_1, A_{12} \vdash A_2}{\Gamma, A_1 \vdash A_2}\quad(\supset\mathbf{L})$$

We now analyze the structure of $\mathcal{I}$.

- $\mathcal{I}$ is of the following form,

$$\frac{}{\Gamma, A_1 \ni A_{11} \supset A_{12}} \quad \textbf{(one)}$$

where $A_1 = A_{11} \supset A_{12}$. In this case, we need to analyze the structure of $\mathcal{D}_1$.

  * $\mathcal{D}_1$ is of the following form:

$$\frac{\mathcal{I}' :: \Gamma \ni A_1}{\Gamma \vdash A_1} \quad \textbf{(AXI)}$$

  Then applying Lemma 5 to $\mathcal{I}'$ and $\mathcal{D}_2$, we obtain a derivation of $\Gamma \vdash A_2$.

  * $\mathcal{D}_1$ is of the following form:

$$\frac{\mathcal{I}' :: \Gamma \ni A' \supset A'' \quad \mathcal{D}_{11} :: \Gamma \vdash A' \quad \mathcal{D}_{12} :: \Gamma, A'' \vdash A_1}{\Gamma \vdash A_1} \quad \textbf{($\supset$L)}$$

  Applying Lemma 3 to $\mathcal{D}_2$, we obtain a derivation $\mathcal{D}_{2w}$ of $\Gamma, A_1, A'' \vdash A_2$. Applying Lemma 4 to $\mathcal{D}_{2w}$, we obtain a derivation $\mathcal{D}_{2we}$ of $\Gamma, A'', A_1 \vdash A_2$. Note that $h(\mathcal{D}_{2we}) = h(\mathcal{D}_{2w}) = h(\mathcal{D}_2)$. By induction hypothesis on $\mathcal{D}_{12}$ and $\mathcal{D}_{2we}$, we have a derivation $\mathcal{D}'$ of $\Gamma, A'' \vdash A_2$. Therefore, we can derive $\Gamma \vdash A_2$ as follows:

$$\frac{\mathcal{I}' :: \Gamma \ni A' \supset A'' \quad \mathcal{D}_{11} :: \Gamma \vdash A' \quad \mathcal{D}' :: \Gamma, A'' \vdash A_2}{\Gamma \vdash A_2} \quad \textbf{($\supset$L)}$$

  * $\mathcal{D}_1$ is of the following form:

$$\frac{\mathcal{D}'_1 :: \Gamma, A_{11} \vdash A_{12}}{\Gamma \vdash A_{11} \supset A_{12}} \quad \textbf{($\supset$R)}$$

  This is the most interesting case in this proof. By induction hypothesis on $\mathcal{D}_1$ and $\mathcal{D}_{21}$, we have a derivation $\mathcal{D}'$ of $\Gamma \vdash A_{11}$. Applying Lemma 3 to $\mathcal{D}_1$, we obtain a derivation $\mathcal{D}_{1w}$ of $\Gamma, A_{12} \vdash A_1$. Applying Lemma 4 to $\mathcal{D}_{22}$, we obtain a derivation of $\mathcal{D}_{22e}$ of $\Gamma, A_{12}, A_1 \vdash A_2$. Note that $h(\mathcal{D}_{1w}) = h(\mathcal{D}_1)$ and $h(\mathcal{D}_{22e}) = h(\mathcal{D}_{22})$. By induction hypothesis in $\mathcal{D}_{1w}$ and $\mathcal{D}_{22e}$, we have a derivation $\mathcal{D}''$ of $\Gamma, A_{12} \vdash A_2$. By induction hypothesis on $\mathcal{D}'$ and $\mathcal{D}'_1$, we have a derivation $\mathcal{D}'''$ of $\Gamma \vdash A_{12}$, and then by induction hypothesis on $\mathcal{D}'''$ and $\mathcal{D}''$, we have a derivation of $\Gamma \vdash A_2$.

- $\mathcal{I}$ is of the following form:

$$\frac{\mathcal{I}' :: \Gamma \ni A_{11} \supset A_{12}}{\Gamma, A_1 \ni A_{11} \supset A_{12}} \quad \textbf{(shift)}$$

Then by induction hypothesis on $\mathcal{D}_1$ and $\mathcal{D}_{21}$, we have a $\mathcal{D}'$ derivation of $\Gamma \vdash A_{11}$. Applying Lemma 3 to $\mathcal{D}_1$, we obtain a derivation $\mathcal{D}_{1w}$ of $\Gamma, A_{12} \vdash A_1$. Applying Lemma 4 to $\mathcal{D}_{22}$, we obtain a derivation $\mathcal{D}_{22e}$

of $\Gamma, A_{12}, A_1 \vdash A_2$. Note that $h(\mathcal{D}_{1w}) = h(\mathcal{D}_1)$ and $h(\mathcal{D}_{22e}) = h(\mathcal{D}_{22})$. By induction hypothesis on $\mathcal{D}_{1w}$ and $\mathcal{D}_{22e}$, we have a derivation $\mathcal{D}''$ of $\Gamma, A_{12} \vdash A_2$. Therefore, a derivation of $\Gamma \vdash A_2$ can be constructed as follows:

$$\frac{\mathcal{I}' :: \Gamma \ni A_{11} \supset A_{12} \quad \mathcal{D}' :: \Gamma \vdash A_{11} \quad \mathcal{D}'' :: \Gamma, A_{12} \vdash A_2}{\Gamma \vdash A_2} \ (\supset \mathbf{L})$$

– $\mathcal{D}_2$ is of the following form,

$$\frac{\mathcal{D}_2' :: \Gamma, A_1, A_{21} \vdash A_{22}}{\Gamma, A_1 \vdash A_{21} \supset A_{22}} \ (\supset \mathbf{R})$$

where $A_2 = A_{21} \supset A_{22}$. Applying Lemma 3 to $\mathcal{D}_1$, we obtain a derivation $\mathcal{D}_{1w}$ of $\Gamma, A_{21} \vdash A_1$ such that $h(\mathcal{D}_{1w}) = h(\mathcal{D}_1)$. Applying Lemma 4 to $\mathcal{D}_2'$, we obtain a derivation $\mathcal{D}_{2e}'$ of $\Gamma, A_{21}, A_1 \vdash A_{22}$ such that $h(\mathcal{D}_{2e}') = h(\mathcal{D}_2')$. By induction hypothesis on $\mathcal{D}_{1w}$ and $\mathcal{D}_{2e}'$, we have a derivation $\mathcal{D}'$ of $\Gamma, A_{21} \vdash A_{22}$. Therefore, a derivation of $\Gamma \vdash A_2$ can be constructed as follows:

$$\frac{\mathcal{D}' :: \Gamma, A_{21} \vdash A_{22}}{\Gamma \vdash A_{21} \supset A_{22}} \ (\supset \mathbf{R})$$

We have covered all the cases in this implication fragment of intuitionistic propositional logic. The presented proof corresponds tightly to the actual Haskell implementation in Figure 3.

We would like to point out that an implementation of cut elimination for the entire intuitionistic propositional logic can be found at [3].

4   Related Work and Conclusion

We have recently seen various interesting examples in which the type system of Haskell is used to capture certain rather sophisticated programming invariants (e.g., some of such examples can be found in [1,4,6,10,12,14]). In many of such examples, the underlying theme seems, more or less, to be simulating or approximating some typical use of dependent types through the use of some advanced features in the type system of Haskell. However, we have presented an example that identifies in greater clarity some problematic issues with such a seemingly cute programming style.

In [12], an approach to simulating dependent types is presented that relies on the type class mechanism in Haskell. In particular, it makes heavy use of multiparameter type classes with functional dependencies [11]. This is an approach that seems entirely different from ours. With this approach, there is no need to manually construct proof terms, which are instead handled automatically through the type class mechanism in Haskell. However, this approach is greatly limited in its ability to simulate dependent types. For instance, it does not even seem possible to handle a simple type constructor like *IN*. On the other hand, we feel that our approach to simulating dependent types is both more intuitive and more general and it can handle the examples in [12] with ease.

The way we use proof terms for type equality clearly bears a great deal of resemblance to the one described in [1], where an approach to typing dynamic typing is proposed. There, the binary type constructor *EQ* is defined as follows,

```
type EQ a b = forall f. f a -> f b
```

taking the view of Leibniz on equality. With this definition, functions such as *idEQ*, *symEQ* and *transEQ* can be elegantly constructed. However, it is impossible to implement type equality elimination functions such as *fstEQ* and *sndEQ* in Haskell. To see the reason, let us assume that x is a variable of the type $\forall f.f(a_1, a_2) \rightarrow f(b_1, b_2)$; in order to construct a term of the type $\forall f.f(a_1) \rightarrow f(b_1)$, we need a function π_1 on types such that $\pi_1(a_1, a_2) = a_1$; but there is no such function on types in Haskell.[1] This is a rather serious limitation when the issue of simulating dependent types is concerned.

Certain use of proof terms for type equality can also be found in [4], where some examples are presented to promote programming with type representations. However, these examples, which are relatively simple, do not involve extensive use of proof terms for type equality. In particular, no examples there involve any use of type equality elimination functions. As a consequence, the difficulty in constructing proof terms is never clearly mentioned. Only recently is the need for type equality elimination functions identified [5].

Our approach to simulating dependent types seems not amenable to certain changes. For instance, we may declare the type constructor *IN* as follows, interchanging the positions of the two arguments of *IN*:

```
data IN g a =
    forall g'. INone (EQ g (g',a))
  | forall g' a'. INshi (EQ g (g',a')) (IN g' a)
```

However, such a minor change mandates that many proof terms in the implementation of cut elimination be completely reconstructed, which, already a rather time-consuming task, is further exacerbated by the fact that type error reporting in neither (current version of) GHC nor (current version of) Hugs offers much help in fixing wrongly constructed proof terms (except for identifying the approximate location of such terms).

We have pointed out that for some type constructors it is difficult or even impossible to implement the associated type equality elimination functions. A simple and direct approach to address the issue is to treat *EQ* as a *primitive* type constructor. In addition, *idEQ*, *symEQ* and *transEQ* as well as *toEQ* and *fromEQ* can be supplied as primitive functions, and for each type constructor <u>TC</u>, the type equality introduction function and type equality elimination functions associated with <u>TC</u> can also be assumed to be primitive. In this way, we not only obviate the need for implementing type equality introduction/elimination

---

[1] It would actually be problematic to add such a function into Haskell: What would then be something like $\pi_1(int)$? Should it be defined or undefined?

functions but can also guarantee that if there is a closed term *pf* of type $EQ \, \tau_1 \, \tau_2$, then τ_1 equals τ_2 and the terms *toEQ pf* and *fromEQ pf* are both equivalent to the identity function of the type $\tau_1 \to \tau_1$ (as long as the previously mentioned primitive functions are correctly provided). Of course, this simple approach does not address at all the difficulty in constructing proof terms, for which we may need to introduce guarded datatypes [19] or phantom types [5] into Haskell. However, such an introduction is likely to significantly complicate the (already rather involved) type inference in Haskell, and its interaction with the type class mechanism in Haskell, which is largely unclear at this moment, needs to be carefully investigated. As an comparison, we also include in [3] an implementation of cut elimination theorem written in a language that essentially extends ML with guarded recursive datatypes [19]. Clearly, this is a much cleaner implementation when compared with the one in Haskell.

In summary, we have presented an interesting example to show how certain typical use of dependent types can be simulated through the use of some advanced features of Haskell. When compared to various closely related work, we have identified in clearer terms some problematic issues with such a simulation technique, which we hope can be of help for the further development of Haskell or other similar programming languages.

References

1. BAARS, A. I., AND SWIERSTRA, S. D. Typing Dynamic Typing. In *Proceedings of the 7th ACM SIGPLAN International Conference on Functional Programming (ICFP '02)* (Pittsburgh, PA, October 2002).

2. CHEN, C., AND XI, H. Implementing Typeful Program Transformations. In *Proceedings of ACM SIGPLAN Workshop on Partial Evaluation and Semantics Based Program Manipulation* (San Diego, CA, June 2003), pp. 20–28.

3. CHEN, C., ZHU, D., AND XI, H. Implementing Cut Elimination: A Case Study of Simulating Dependent Types in Haskell, October 2003. Available at:
   `http://www.cs.bu.edu/~hwxi/academic/papers/CutElim`.

4. CHENEY, J., AND HINZE, R. A Lightweight Implementation of Generics and Dynamics. In *Proceedings of Haskell Workshop* (Pittsburgh, PA, October 2002), ACM Press, pp. 90–104.

5. CHENEY, J., AND HINZE, R. Phantom Types. Technical Report CUCIS-TR2003-1901, Cornell University, 2003. Available as
   `http://techreports.library.cornell.edu:8081/ Dienst/UI/1.0/Display/ cul.cis/TR2003-1901`.

6. FRIDLENDER, D., AND INDRIKA, M. Do we need dependent types? *Functional Pearl in the Journal of Functional Programming 10*, 4 (July 2000), 409–415.

7. GENTZEN, G. Untersuchungen über das logische Schließen. *Mathematische Zeitschrift 39* (1935), 176–210, 405–431.

8. HALL, C. V., HAMMOND, K., JONES, S. L. P., AND WADLER, P. L. Type Classes in Haskell. *ACM Transactions on Programming Languages and Systems 18*, 2 (March 1996), 109–138.

9. HARPER, R. W., HONSELL, F., AND PLOTKIN, G. D. A framework for defining logics. *Journal of the ACM 40*, 1 (January 1993), 143–184.

10. HINZE, R. Manufacturing Datatypes. *Journal of Functional Programming 11*, 5 (September 2001), 493–524. Also available as Technical Report IAI-TR-99-5, Institut für Informatik III, Universität Bonn.
11. JONES, M. P. Type Classes with Functional Dependencies. In *Proceedings of the 9th European Symposium on Programming* (Berlin, Germany, 1999), vol. 1782 of *Lecture Notes in Computer Science*, Springer-Verlag, pp. 230–244.
12. MCBRIDE, C. Faking It. *Journal of Functional Programming 12*, 4 & 5 (July 2002), 375–392.
13. MILNER, R. A theory of type polymorphism in programming. *Journal of Computer and System Sciences 17*, 3 (December 1978), 348–375.
14. OKASAKI, C. From Fast Exponentiation to Square Matrices: An Adventure in Types. In *Proceedings of the 4th ACM SIGPLAN International Conference on Functional Programming* (September 1999).
15. PFENNING, F. *Computation and Deduction.* Cambridge University Press. (to appear).
16. PFENNING, F. Logic programming in the LF logical framework. In *Logical Frameworks*, I. G. Huet and G. Plotkin, Eds. Cambridge University Press, 1991, pp. 149–181.
17. PFENNING, F. Structural Cut Elimination. In *Proceedings of the Tenth Annual IEEE Symposium on Logic in Computer Science* (San Diego, CA, June 1995), pp. 156–166.
18. PFENNING, F. Structural Cut Elimination I: intuitionistic and classical logic. *Information and Computation 157*, 1/2 (March 2000), 84–141.
19. XI, H., CHEN, C., AND CHEN, G. Guarded Recursive Datatype Constructors. In *Proceedings of the 30th ACM SIGPLAN Symposium on Principles of Programming Languages* (New Orleans, LA, January 2003), pp. 224–235.

Author Index

Lecture Notes in Computer Science

For information about Vols. 1–2994

please contact your bookseller or Springer-Verlag